Debating Dissent
Canada and the Sixties

Although the 1960s are overwhelmingly associated with student radicalism and the New Left, most Canadians witnessed the decade's political, economic, and cultural turmoil from a different perspective. *Debating Dissent* dispels the myths and stereotypes associated with the 1960s by examining what this era's transformations meant to diverse groups of Canadians – and not only to protestors, youth, or the white middle class.

With critical contributions from new and senior scholars, *Debating Dissent* integrates traditional conceptions of the 1960s as a 'time apart' within the broader framework of the 'long sixties' and post-1945 Canada, and places Canada within a local, national, and international context. Cutting-edge essays in social, intellectual, and political history reflect a range of historical interpretation and explore such diverse topics as narcotics, the environment, education, workers, Aboriginal and Black activism, nationalism, Quebec, women, and bilingualism. Touching on the decade's biggest issues, from changing cultural norms to the role of the state, *Debating Dissent* critically examines ideas of generational change and the sixties.

LARA CAMPBELL is an associate professor in the Department of Gender, Sexuality, and Women's Studies at Simon Fraser University.

DOMINIQUE CLÉMENT is an assistant professor in the Department of Sociology at the University of Alberta.

GREGORY S. KEALEY is the vice-president (research) and provost of the University of New Brunswick and a professor in the Department of History.

Debating Dissent

Canada and the Sixties

Edited by
Lara Campbell, Dominique
Clément, and Gregory S. Kealey

MARY M. STRIBLING LIBRARY

UNIVERSITY OF TORONTO PRESS
Toronto Buffalo London

© University of Toronto Press 2012
Toronto Buffalo London
www.utppublishing.com
Printed in Canada

ISBN 978-1-4426-4164-8 (cloth)
ISBN 978-1-4426-1078-1 (paper)

Printed on acid-free 100% post-consumer recycled
paper with vegetable-based inks

Library and Archives Canada Cataloguing in Publication

Debating dissent : Canada and the sixties / edited by Lara Campbell,
Dominique Clément, and Gregory S. Kealey.

(Canadian social history series)
Includes bibliographical references and index.
ISBN 978-1-4426-4164-8 (bound)
ISBN 978-1-4426-1078-1 (pbk.)

1. Canada – History – 1945–1963.   2. Canada – History – 1963–.
3. Canada – Social conditions – 1945–1971.   4. Nineteen sixties.
I. Campbell, Lara, 1970– II. Clément, Dominique, 1975–
III. Kealey, Gregory S., 1948–   IV. Series: Canadian social history series

FC625.D42 2012   971.064'3   C2012-901842-2

University of Toronto Press acknowledges the financial assistance to its
publishing program of the Canada Council for the Arts and the Ontario
Arts Council.

University of Toronto Press acknowledges the financial support of the
Government of Canada through the Canada Book Fund for its publishing
activities.

This book has been published with the help of a grant from the Canadian
Federation for the Humanities and Social Sciences, through the Awards
to Scholarly Publications Program, using funds provided by the Social
Sciences and Humanities Research Council of Canada.

FC
625
.D4
2012

Contents

Preface

For many years we (the editors) have been conscious of the dearth of literature on this topic, and yet, many of our colleagues across Canada were already developing histories of the 1960s. So we invited a dozen authors, each specializing in a different thematic area, to contribute to this project. The contributors participated in a workshop in Fredericton, New Brunswick, to debate and shape their submissions.[1] This collection is the result of our collective deliberations and constitutes, among other things, a statement about how we should approach studies of the 1960s in Canada.

The authors represent a diverse disciplinary mix. Among the contributors are established scholars, many of whom lived the 1960s, and several scholars early in their careers who were interested in challenging our preconceptions of the 'sixties.' The collection's strength is in its diversity: from French- and English-Canadian experiences to a broad regional sample. Our goal was to offer an accessible and engaging collection of essays. For this reason, each chapter includes an initial overview of the topic to introduce non-specialists to it and a list of suggested readings for further study.

This book challenges the decadal approach to the 1960s. Instead, we have embraced the notion of a 'long sixties' wherein the sixties becomes a set of ideas associated with a moment in time that goes beyond the decade of the 1960s. The terms '1960s' and 'sixties,' thus,

---

1 Thank you to Van Gosse and Joan Sangster, who participated in the workshop and offered helpful critiques.

appear throughout the text. This inconsistency is partly a reflection of the conflicts within the existing literature about how to conceive of the 1960s. It also serves a useful purpose in this volume: we use '1960s' when referring to events specific to that decade, but refer to the 'sixties' when explaining larger themes and implications for this moment in history.

Our ambition was to provide a major contribution to modern Canadian history and develop a basis for future transnational comparative research on the sixties. This book is a powerful reminder of the extent to which Canada was integrated and attuned to developments in the Western world. These studies are also highly topical. Concerns about health care and mass retirements, for instance, have stimulated vigorous public debates about the nature of generational change and the legacy of the sixties. And as the contributors gathered in Fredericton, the world marked the fortieth anniversary of the riots in Paris in 1968 and the protests across the globe. A sustained scholarly analysis of the 1960s is now possible, as sufficient distance since the 1960s permits us to identify those qualities that define it as a self-contained historical period. We hope that this book will encourage historians around the world to consider the Canadian experience, and provide scholars with the methodological tools for historicizing generational change and the sixties. A cohort of young scholars has recently entered the academic profession and initiated a critical reflection of this era. *Debating Dissent* offers an opportunity for different generations of scholars to begin this dialogue.

The editors would like to thank the Social Sciences and Humanities Research Council, the University of Alberta, the University of New Brunswick, and Simon Fraser University for their financial support.

Debating Dissent
Canada and the Sixties

Introduction: Time, Age, Myth: Towards a History of the Sixties

Lara Campbell and Dominique Clément

The 1960s are overwhelmingly associated with youth and social protest in the popular imagination. This is considered the formative period for the baby boom generation. And yet, our understanding of the 1960s is largely based on myths, stereotypes, and misconceptions. Our book challenges readers to conceptualize the '1960s,' not as a decade in Canadian history, but as a social, political, cultural, and economic *phenomenon*. Rather than oversimplify it as a decade of protest, we present the 'sixties' as a transformative *era* for Canadian society that was diffuse and widespread. Many of the authors in this collection link developments in the 1960s to trends in the years preceding or succeeding the decade itself. We therefore apply the term '1960s,' or 'sixties,' not solely as a temporal reference point on an historical map, but as a way of conceiving and identifying historical trends. In other words, we associate the sixties or 1960s with ideas and developments that transcend the decade but are nonetheless associated with a particular moment in time.

Americans are obsessed with this period. In the past ten years alone more than one hundred books (and innumerable articles) have been published on the 1960s.[1] The 1960s continue to haunt America today. As the editor of a recent American collection suggests, 'we live in a world that the Sixties made. We are still fighting over that legacy in ways that matter deeply, no matter how mindlessly partisan and trivialized those struggles sometimes appear. It behooves us, therefore, to examine those huge changes.'[2]

No similar obsession with this period has been manifest in Canada. In fact, Canada is strangely absent in the literature on the 1960s. Arthur Marwick's seminal 903-page book *The Sixties: Cultural Revolution in Britain, France, Italy and the United States, c. 1958– c. 1974,* for instance, makes almost no reference to Canada.[3] Until recently, historians in Canada have failed to develop a historiography of the 1960s. Doug Owram's *Born at the Right Time* (1996) and François Ricard's *La génération lyrique* (1994) were among the first substantial studies of the boomer generation.[4] There are many studies on students and youth protest, such as Marcel Martel's *Not This Time: Canadians, Public Policy, and the Marijuana Question, 1961–1975,* and Jean-Philippe Warren's edited volume *Les mouvements étudiants des années 1960.*[5] Unfortunately, none of these accounts integrate the experience of French and English Canadians, and they focus almost exclusively on youth and social protest. Obviously, these themes are critical in any study of the 1960s, but a focus on activism denies the experience and voice of the masses of people who did not participate in social movements. The diversity of topics within this collection indicates that Canadian historians have not made the mistake of equating the 1960s solely with protest or social movements.

Our collection joins a spate of recent books that have popularized the idea of a uniquely Canadian moment. Dimitry Anastakis has edited a collection of essays (2008) that explore several themes commonly associated with this period, such as the Vietnam War and the Quiet Revolution, and several less common topics, such as masculinity and architecture.[6] In contrast, Athena Palaeologue's 2009 collection, with a few exceptions, mainly pays homage to student radicals and the New Left.[7] In the same year, a group of historians in Canada edited an immense collection of essays, with several Canadian contributions, in which they posit the emergence of a global 1960s consciousness.[8] Bryan Palmer's *Canada's 1960s* (2009), which is the most comprehensive account of the 1960s to date, offers an original interpretation of the decade as a fulcrum in the struggle over Canadian identity: 'The irony of Canadian identity in the 1960s was that as the old attachment to British Canada was finally and decisively shed it was replaced only with uncertainty.'[9]

These texts represent the beginning of an exciting debate about the issues and events that define this moment in history.[10] But many focus primarily on social protest or youth, whereas the following collection embraces a more expansive approach to historicizing the 1960s. In particular, we critically explore ideas surrounding periodization and generations. This book also makes a comprehensive effort to place the Canadian experience in an international context. Finally, *Debating Dissent* is far from a disparate collection of chapters: it is a deeply integrated account where each of the essays speaks to the others. Still, this is certainly not the last word on this topic.[11] The proliferation of texts on the 1960s in Canada presents a rare opportunity to challenge the commonly accepted idea of a monolithic 'post-1945' or 'post–Second World War' Canadian history. Perhaps it is time to recognize that the postwar period ends where the sixties era begins?

This collection is unique in many ways. We critically examine the idea of the 'sixties' and engage in debates on periodization. The 'long sixties,' discussed below, inform our scholarship. Each chapter is an original contribution from one of the leading experts in the field in Canada. French Canadians and English Canadians, as well as most regions, have a voice in this book. In several cases, the authors have also sought to reveal the transnational ties or influences that informed the Canadian experience. Moreover, although themes such as youth, social protest, and the New Left appear in these pages, they do not dominate the narrative. Our goal is to confront stereotypical accounts. One of the greatest flaws in our understanding of the 1960s is the idea that it was the boomers' historical moment. No single generational cohort was at the heart of the sixties experience. Without denying the obvious passion and excitement of this period, we have approached this topic as history rather than as a lived experience of a particular generation. Several contributors remind us that it was, in fact, a moment of intergenerational cooperation. The Black United Front, examined in James Walker's essay, articulated its vision in generational terms. Two different visions of the 'race problem' emerged in 1960s Nova Scotia, one rooted in an older church-based constituency seeking compromise and accommodation and another emerging from a youth movement committed to radical change and community participation. But ultimately they worked together to mobilize black Nova Scotians and campaign for social change.

This book itself, in fact, is built along an intergenerational vision. Canadian historians searching for literature on the 1960s continue to rely heavily on first-person accounts or literature produced by former activists.[12] These accounts, while invaluable contributions to our understanding of the sixties, are increasingly being challenged by a new generation of historians.[13] Jean-Philippe Warren's 2008 book *Une douce anarchie: Les année 68 au Québec* is an excellent example. In Quebec, at least, students were far less radical than accounts of former activists have suggested: 'Bien sûr, les moins de 30 ans formaient alors un groupe dont l'éthique activiste et la vision du monde différaient de celles de leurs parents; néanmoins, leur militantisme politique ne devrait pas être exagéré par ceux qui s'ennuient d'un temps où la jeunesse aspirait à changer le monde.'[14] Many of these new scholars are present in this collection; their work appears alongside submissions from established scholars, several of whom are former activists.

The following chapters suggest several ways in which we might think about the myriad meanings and legacies of the 1960s. The sixties were an historical moment that fomented a revolution in education, racial divisions, anxieties about national security, consumerism, Aboriginal mobilization, anti-Americanism, the search for national identity, clashes between capital and labour, innovations in public policy, and debates surrounding the family, health, and the environment. It was an era deeply shaped by the Cold War, and by unprecedented, albeit unequally distributed, prosperity, an uncommonly youthful population, a shift to post-industrialism, and a new cultural politics.

In this chapter we hope, first, to present a picture of the common narrative that pervades the literature, in order to demonstrate how other chapters in this book contest or deepen our understanding of the narrative. The 1960s in Canada were about much more than youth, social protest, and the Cold War.[15] Moreover, the recent spate of books in Canada on this topic focuses exclusively on domestic developments, while the international literature rarely mentions Canada.[16] In the first part of this introduction, we explore Canada's social, cultural, and political history in the 1960s and argue that Canada was often a key player, if somewhat reluctant at times, in global developments.

Our second objective in this chapter, and throughout this entire volume, is to develop a framework for future studies on the 1960s without reifying or idealizing the decade. We reject the decadal approach and embrace the idea of the 'long sixties.'[17] While periodization, the division of the past into self-contained periods, is an essential tool for historians, the concept implies that a period contains a unity of experience defined by events, values, and political and social hierarchies. The 1960s, as Alice Echols suggests, is 'best illuminated when embedded in a discussion of the past fifty years. Viewed in this fashion we can see how the conflicts and confusion about race, sexuality, gender and generation have played out over time.'[18] A confluence of factors, some predating the decade, had a profound impact on Canadian society.[19] We believe that using the framework of the 'long sixties' complicates the idea of the period as a 'rupture' from an earlier period, avoids the mistake of too closely associating the spirit of the 1960s with one or two dominant organizations or movements, and challenges the assumption that there ever was a unified or cohesive 1960s 'generation.'[20]

But, if historians reject both the decadal approach and the explanation of rupture, what characterizes the sixties as a particular period of study? We present the 'sixties' as an *idea,* linked only roughly to a moment in time, without borders. The last part of this introduction attempts to answer this question by examining the complicated meaning of the sixties as a moment of questioning authority, grappling with modernity, and rethinking nationhood and the permeability of national borders. The sixties constitute, in this sense, a useful category of historical analysis and an idea worthy of study.

Canada and the 1960s

A common narrative pervades histories of the 1960s. It is one deeply embedded in the Cold War, social and political ferment, a revolution in popular culture, youthfulness, and economic prosperity.[21] Despite the lack of recognition in the international literature on the 1960s, Canada played an important role on the world stage, and it was no less a transformative period within Canada than anywhere else. Moreover, these developments were not limited to the decade itself, and they cannot be understood without placing the 1960s in the context of the broader postwar period.

Depending on one's point of view, the world was either entering a period of relative prosperity and stability in 1960 or descending into strife and widespread devastation. Nikita Khrushchev ascended to the leadership of the Communist Party of the Soviet Union following

Joseph Stalin's death in 1953, and Khrushchev soon distanced himself from his predecessor by publicly denouncing the atrocities committed under Stalin's regime. McCarthyism was on the decline in the United States. The young and charismatic John F. Kennedy, campaigning on a domestic platform titled 'the Rights of Man,' replaced President Dwight D. Eisenhower, the stalwart Cold War general determined to block communist expansion.

But the Cold War and the race to build weapons of mass destruction threatened to lead the world into another global catastrophe. Canada's military budget was $1.5 billion in the early 1960s (a substantial sum, although slightly less than its high of $1.9 billion in 1953), and its armed forces counted more than 120,000 personnel, a peacetime record.[22] The United States spent more than $5 billion to create an air defence system in the 1960s while maintaining an armoury of 1,710 intercontinental ballistic missiles. The United Nations 1968 Treaty on Non-Proliferation of Nuclear Weapons was a landmark achievement, albeit an imperfect step: France and China refused to sign it. Still, it was an important symbolic moment that recognized worldwide fears of the potential for the complete destruction of the human race. Unfortunately, nuclear weapons tests continued and the arms race led to ballooning defence budgets. Canada had been a key player in the development of the atomic bomb in the Second World War, and Lester B. Pearson allowed the United States to place nuclear weapons on Canadian soil after becoming prime minister in 1963.[23]

Canada became entangled in a series of military alliances that would have profound consequences for the country's own security. Canada was a founding member of the North Atlantic Treaty Organization (NATO) in 1949, and joined a continental military pact with the United States (NORAD) in 1958. These alliances drew the country into the most dangerous confrontation of the Cold War, when nuclear war appeared, for a moment, inevitable. In 1962, Khrushchev attempted to park nuclear weapons ninety miles off the coast of Florida. Kennedy responded with a naval blockade of Cuba while Americans built bomb shelters in their backyards. In Ottawa, Prime Minister Diefenbaker dithered over whether or not to support the American blockade, while his minister of defence quietly placed Canadian troops on alert without his knowledge.[24] The crisis was resolved, but the terrifying possibility of future confrontations between the superpowers remained.

Tensions between the East and West continued to mount, and space became the latest battleground. The Soviet Union was the first country to send a man to orbit the earth (in 1961), and in 1969, the Americans landed the first man on the moon. Canada launched its own man-made satellite into space in 1962, only the third country to do so, and a domestic space industry emerged. A fledgling military aviation industry was also developing in Canada. But staggering cost overruns convinced Diefenbaker to eliminate government contracts in 1959 for a high-tech supersonic fighter jet, the Avro Arrow, essentially killing the industry in Canada.[25] Many nationalists never forgave him.

For many historians of the period, the defining theme of the 1960s was the war in Vietnam. American troops began moving into Vietnam in the 1950s and remained until 1975; U.S. involvement reached its peak soon after Kennedy's assassination in 1963. Canada, a member of the failed International Control Commission (1954–73) to oversee the partition of Vietnam, refused to send troops, but did not hesitate to supply American troops with arms or provide a home for American draft dodgers.[26] For the next five years the American government supplied the South Vietnamese with more than half a million soldiers and millions of dollars in economic aid for a conflict destined to end with no discernible winner. At no time did the United States officially declare war on the communist regime of North Vietnam, yet at the close of the decade, America had lost more than forty thousand soldiers in Southeast Asia. Canada, meanwhile, profited enormously from the conflict: Canadian industry furnished $2.47 billion of war materiel to the United States between 1965 and 1972 under the Defence Production Sharing Agreements.[27] As the two superpowers clashed, and democracies emerged in Turkey and South Korea in 1960, decolonization movements in the 1960s destroyed the final vestiges of European imperialism.[28] The process of decolonization was rarely smooth. Tens of thousands of people, for example, died as a result of violence between French troops and Algerian nationalists until Algeria was granted independence in 1962. In truth, Canada had very little presence in Africa at this time. Pearson, though, began to reach out to francophone African countries (as a precursor to the Francophonie), and Canada was a major contributor to the Colombo Plan (1950), which provided aid to poor countries in the British Commonwealth.[29] Canada did, however, take a strong stand on apartheid. The Union of

South Africa, which had been an independent Dominion since 1910, became a republic and an international pariah in the 1960s. Apartheid policies included bans on interracial marriage, separate institutions for blacks, and episodes of brutal repression against blacks.[30] Canada fought to include a statement on racial equality as a requisite for membership in the Commonwealth, which led to South Africa's withdrawal in 1961 and its increasing international isolation.[31]

Meanwhile, violent clashes within and between nation states racked the Asian continent, including China's Cultural Revolution, a war between India and Pakistan, and conflicts between Vietnam, Laos, and Cambodia. Canada's presence in Asia was little better than in Africa, although by 1975, Japan surpassed Britain as Canada's second-largest trading partner (Canada also had a weak presence in the Middle East, which suffered several violent conflicts during this period, including the Six Day War in June 1967 between Israel and Egypt).[32] Still, at a time when the United States refused to recognize the communist government in China, Diefenbaker's decision to allow Canadian wheat exports to China in 1961, and Trudeau's decision to recognize and visit China in the early 1970s, were bold foreign policy initiatives.[33]

Historians of the 1960s invariably turn to social movements. It was, without a doubt, a transformative period. New Left movements emerged in Europe, North America, and South America. Socialist movements gained momentum in France and Italy. Canadians listened on the radio, or watched on their new television sets, as 250,000 people marched on Washington in 1963. The American civil rights movement, which has become an iconic symbol for the American 1960s, gained momentum in the 1950s and had a significant impact on social movements across the United States for decades. Meanwhile, worldwide protests were organized against the Vietnam War. A protest in front of the United States embassy in Montreal led to twenty people being wounded and forty-six behind bars.[34] Student movements flourished. An alliance of students and workers in France in May 1968, calling for extensive social, economic, and political reform, nearly toppled the government.

Canada, too often portrayed as the 'peaceable kingdom,' was no less a hotbed of activism. The student movement and the New

Left peaked in the 1960s; the number of women's rights groups in British Columbia increased from fewer than a dozen in 1969 to over two hundred by 1974; the first gay rights organizations were formed in Vancouver and Toronto; and the founding of Greenpeace in Vancouver in 1971 symbolized the birth of the modern environmental movement (inspired, in part, by Rachel Carson's seminal 1962 book, *Silent Spring*). The federal government's ban on Aboriginal political organizing for land claims, instituted in 1927, was removed in 1951, and within a decade the Aboriginal rights movement began to flourish. African-Canadian organizations spread across the country while advocates for children's rights, prisoners' rights, animal rights, peace, poverty, and official languages organized in unprecedented numbers.[35]

Many of these movements, however, were marred by failure, violence, or repression. The French alliance of May 1968 was shattered when workers decided to abandon the movement in return for minor concessions from the government; student protests in Canada peaked in the late 1960s but declined soon after; the assassination of Martin Luther King Jr in 1968 precipitated riots and looting across the United States; and the shooting deaths of five students at Kent State University in 1970 at the hands of the Ohio National Guard symbolized the struggles and obstacles facing peace activists and the student movement. A terrorist organization dedicated to an independent and socialist Quebec state, the Front de libération du Québec (inspired by movements in Algeria and Cuba), was responsible for widespread bombings, thefts, vandalism, and other acts of violence throughout the 1960s. In its ultimate act, the organization kidnapped a Quebec Cabinet minister and a British diplomat in 1970, precipitating a national crisis that led to the imposition of the War Measures Act, the suspension of civil liberties across the country, and numerous human rights abuses.[36]

And, of course, how can we speak of the 1960s without talking about sex, drugs and rock 'n roll? Folk music was still popular, but it was soon eclipsed by rock 'n roll. Elvis, the Rolling Stones, and the Beatles became household names. When Bob Dylan used an electric guitar for the first time at the Newport Folk Festival in 1965, it was, for many people, the symbol of a new era. Canada's music industry flourished and produced international sensations like Gordon Lightfoot, Neil Young, The Guess Who, and Joni Mitchell.[37] Canada's market was far too small for successful artists, though, and eventually they all sought their fortunes in the United States. Meanwhile, Timothy Leary was experimenting with LSD at Harvard University until he was dismissed in 1963, and the United States government criminalized LSD in 1966. Canada's Narcotic Control Act (1961) was the first major revision of laws dealing with illegal narcotics since the 1920s. In 1965, there were only sixty convictions for possessing marijuana in Canada; more than six thousand people were prosecuted for the same offence in 1970.[38] The rising popularity of drugs, especially among white middle-class youth in the 1960s, convinced Nixon to declare a war on drugs in 1971. It is easy to overlook the possibility, however, that the 'rise' in illegal drug use may be attributed to the dramatic expansion of police forces. The Metropolitan Toronto Police Force was created in 1957 and grew to more than five thousand members (about one thousand of them civilians) by 1977; the cost of policing Toronto alone had risen from $58,129,000 in 1971 to $140,520,000 by 1977.[39] More police walking the streets invariably resulted in more arrests.

Drugs, music, and sexual revolution have shaped public perception of the 1960s. The birth control pill was introduced in 1961, and students at McGill University produced a controversial (but highly sought-after) *Birth Control Handbook* in 1968, a year before birth control was legalized in Canada.[40] The Woodstock Festival of 1969 and controversies surrounding youth 'ghettos' in cities like Toronto (Yorkville) and Vancouver (Gastown) appeared to exemplify a generation's attachment to new forms of cultural expression.

The 1960s were also, for many Canadians, a period of national celebration and reflection. The country celebrated its centennial in 1967, a new flag was unveiled in 1965, Expo '67 in Montreal showcased the country to the world, and Trudeaumania in 1968 galvanized many Canadians. George Grant wrote one of the most famous books on Canadian history, *Lament for a Nation,* in which he closed the book on Canadian nationhood after the pro-American Lester B. Pearson replaced Diefenbaker as prime minister in 1963.[41]

Important political changes were underway. The Liberal Party formed the federal government for the next sixteen years. In the provinces, Progressive Conservatives ruled in Ontario, Nova Scotia, Manitoba, and in Prince Edward Island (until 1966). Joey Smallwood's unstoppable electoral machine entrenched the Liberal Party in Newfoundland (1949–72), and the Liberals formed governments in New Brunswick, Saskatchewan (after defeating the New Democrats in 1964), and Quebec (under Jean Lesage, 1960–64). Right-wing conservative governments ruled with large majorities in British Columbia (1953–72) and Alberta (1935–71) under the banner of the Social Credit Party, and in Quebec after 1966 under the Union Nationale.

Two developments, in particular, marked the 1960s as a turning point in Canadian political history. Jean Lesage ushered in a new era of Quebec politics as well as widespread social and economic reform, a process commonly known as the Quiet Revolution. In the midst of this fundamental realignment of Québécois society, many Quebeckers rallied around a fledgling political movement for Quebec independence.[42] Several new separatist parties were formed in the 1960s: the Action socialiste pour l'indépendance du Québec (1960), the Rassemblement pour l'indépendence nationale (1960), the Comité de libération nationale (1962), and the Ralliement national (1966). René Lévesque united the movement under the banner of the Parti Québécois in 1968; nine years later they formed the government.[43] The New Democratic Party (NDP) emerged from the ashes of the Co-operative Commonwealth Federation (CCF) in 1961, and Tommy Douglas, the former premier of Saskatchewan, was elected party leader. And yet, the 1960s failed to produce an upsurge in support for the NDP.[44] Party stalwarts such as David Lewis also found themselves threatened by a new movement within the party: the Waffle. The Waffle movement sought to shift the NDP back to its socialist roots and was strongly anti-American, particularly in the context of foreign investment. The Waffle was eventually defeated, but not before posing a serious challenge to David Lewis's leadership ambitions in the early 1970s.[45]

Many innovative public policy initiatives were undertaken during this period, far too many to account for in this small space. But one of the most notable is the omnibus bill of 1969. The massive bill, containing 120 clauses in 126 pages, tightened restrictions on firearms, increased penalties for drunk drivers, regulated lotteries, introduced new rules for young offenders, and placed limits on the ability of the police to forcibly detain material witnesses. The two most controversial clauses involved legalizing homosexuality and abortion (albeit by requiring hospitals to create a strict and unwieldy regulatory mechanism called a Therapeutic Abortion Committee). Earlier the same year the federal government had passed a controversial bill on divorce. For the first time in history divorce became accessible to most Canadians. In both cases the ramifications of the laws lasted far beyond the 1960s. Thousands of people flocked to secure a divorce in the 1970s (many of them women), and thousands of women across Canada mobilized to protest the abortion law.[46]

Riots in Vancouver and police attacks on peaceful demonstrators in the U.S. state of Georgia were brought home to millions of people in the 1960s with the popularization of a new technology. North America was entering the age of television. Television was introduced in Canada in the 1950s and blossomed in the 1960s; television stations (including the Canadian Broadcasting Corporation) proliferated in major cities. New fads captured the attention of baby boomers. Davy Crockett (1955), hula hoops (1958), Barbie dolls (1959), and G.I. Joe (1965) became quick successes in Canada and the United States. Consumer products such as washing machines and refrigerators were increasingly affordable, modernized telephones improved communications, and far more people were travelling by airplane than ever before.[47]

It was a period of intense economic growth. The gross domestic product grew on average by 5 per cent annually throughout the 1960s. Unemployment remained low, usually around 4.5 per cent to 5 per cent. Although inflation would reach 5 per cent by the late 1960s, in general, inflation was 1 to 2 per cent annually. Canada's strong economic performance was abetted by a similar trend on a global scale: world trade expanded six-fold between 1948 and 1973 at an annual rate of 7 per cent, and the U.S. economy grew at an average rate of 2.6 per cent. The most successful economic achievement during this period for Canada was unquestionably the Auto Pact, essentially a free trade agreement between Canada and the United States for auto parts and vehicles. Almost instantly the agreement changed the face of the Canadian economy. Auto sales surpassed pulp and paper as the country's primary industry, and vehicles exported to the United States accounted for 40 per cent of Canadian trade in 1968 (compared with 3 per cent in 1963).[48] But the postwar prosperity that, for many, defined the 1960s era did not last forever; an international oil embargo imposed in 1973 battered Western economies and contributed to the emergence of a global recession.

Postwar economic growth financed the modern welfare state. Several major social programs in education, health, and income security were established in the 1960s. The federal government established a universal medical insurance program in 1966, and by the early 1970s every province had implemented universal health care. It was a prosperous time for many Canadians. People were consuming more (retail sales rose more than $20 billion), buying more cars (registrations were up 40 per cent), purchasing more homes, and going to school in record numbers. Between 1963 and 1968, university enrolment in Canada increased more than in the previous fifty years; dozens of new institutions were born, hundreds of faculty members were hired, tens of thousands of students swelled the ranks of undergraduate programs, and capital expenditures on universities across the country rose from $100 million in 1955 to over $1.5 billion by the end of the 1960s. The standard of living for most Canadians increased dramatically: central heating, electric appliances, and hot and cold running water became accessible in all but the poorest of regions (Third World epidemics were still widespread at the end of the decade but smallpox and tuberculosis, major killers in poor countries, were on the wane thanks to widespread international vaccination programs). Automobile registration soared to the point that most people had their own vehicle, some with two or three. Life expectancy rose 5.5 per cent for men and 9.5 per cent for women, thanks, in part, to new medical technologies and discoveries such as polio vaccines.[49]

This, then, is a basic portrait of the 1960s familiar to most people. Social protest, youth, affluence, and the Cold War, in particular, are the predominant themes in the literature (and, we would suggest, in the popular imagination as well).[50] The 1960s became the fulcrum for transformations in politics, social life, culture, and the economy; but these transformations often originated in an earlier period and, in almost every case, continued into the 1970s. To offer one example: the narrative often emphasizes youth and the explosion of social movement activism. To be sure, youth were at the forefront of social movements at this time, but 'older' activists, such as Gus Wedderburn and George Manuel, were essential to the success of these movements. These experienced activists 'fought tirelessly in the 1950s to set the groundwork for the work of future SMOs, and they continued to play a critical role in shaping the activism of these movements.'[51] If there is something remarkable about the 1960s it has little to do with an unfulfilled revolutionary moment; it is the way in which these developments coincided with many other crucial transformations that influenced and interacted with each other during a particular moment in history.

Without a doubt we have left many issues unexplored: the illegal activities of Royal Canadian Mounted Police; the Munsinger affair; the crusade to 'Canadianize' postsecondary education; Rochdale College; economic nationalism; Canadian literature, from the proliferation of publishing houses in Quebec to the rise of new literary icons such as Margaret Atwood (*The Edible Woman,* 1969) and Jacques Godbout (*Salut Galarneau!,* 1967); nationalization and secularization in the labour movement; the Montreal Canadiens' and Toronto Maple Leafs' combined eight Stanley Cups in ten years; the 1960 Canadian Bill of Rights and the Supreme Court of Canada's lacklustre response; immigration; widespread legal reforms instigated in Ontario and Quebec dealing with the administration of law; the first Human Rights Code (Ontario, 1962) and the proliferation of similar legislation across the nation.[52] And the essays in this collection explore even more themes, from women's liberation to Red Power.

This collection includes several chapters that engage with many of the themes associated with the 1960s while, at the same time, recasting them in a new light. Michael Boudreau and Marcel Martel revisit the theme of social protest by drawing on case studies that we know little about: the Gastown riot and the riot at Sir George Williams University. Both authors place their case studies in the context of the counterculture movement and rising tensions between youth and the expanding police forces in Canadian cities. Roberta Lexier and Catherine Gidney offer fresh perspectives on education: the former forwards a strong critique of the student movement, while the latter reminds us that faculty power, and not only student power, helped to change the structure and governance of the modern university. José Igartua, who was living in Montreal during the Sir George Williams riot, guides us through the most important developments associated with the Quiet Revolution, while Matthew Hayday places the Quiet Revolution in a broader national context and revisits the national unity debates that dominated intergovernmental politics. Stephen

Azzi proposes an original interpretation of the nationalism we often associate with Diefenbaker and the cultural politics of the 1960s and 1970s. The anti-American discourses that pervaded Canadian nationalist rhetoric originated, according to Azzi, in the United States. These contributions move well beyond the stereotype of the 1960s narrative of youth, affluence, and social protest.

In addition, there are several chapters that chart completely new directions for the future historiography on the 1960s. Bryan Palmer offers a rare glimpse into the Red Power movement; despite the growing literature on social movements in Canada, very little has been written about the history of Aboriginal activism. James Walker's essay on Black Power in Nova Scotia also fills a significant omission in the literature on social movements, while at the same time speaking to the 1960s experience in Nova Scotia. Erika Dyck presents LSD use in the context of Humphry Osmond's research in Saskatchewan, as a tool of medical experimentation and a case study in the professionalizing of medicine. Catherine Carstairs's essay on health food and the environment illuminates an important debate, and a part of daily life, that rarely finds its way in the literature on this period. Peter S. McInnis's contribution ensures that workers have a voice in this collection, not as members of large bureaucratic unions, but as wildcat strikers challenging the labour leadership's power. Steve Hewitt and Christabelle Sethna expose the inner workings of the RCMP while offering original insights on second-wave feminism.

As we read these chapters, it became increasingly clear how this moment in history profoundly shaped modern Canada.[53] True, Canadians did not experience any upheaval comparable to May 1968 in France,[54] and current political debates do not share the American penchant for using 1960s imagery to denigrate partisan opponents. But within these chapters it is not difficult to see the lasting impact of the 1960s on Canada. Faculty and student activism created a model for university governance and research that still dominates Canada's postsecondary institutions. The RCMP's crude tactics in the surveillance of feminist activists have evolved into sophisticated surveillance policing that targets domestic as well as international activists. Fears surrounding illegal narcotics such as LSD are as common today as they were in the 1960s; even minor attempts to legalize marijuana spark intense debate. The Aboriginal organizations established in the 1960s have become a

powerful lobby, and they have been at the forefront of campaigns dealing with land claims, residential schools, and constitutional change.
Health food stores are ubiquitous in Canadian cities, and what was
a nascent movement in the 1960s is now a multibillion dollar industry. And who could deny the lasting legacy of the Quiet Revolution,
Québécois nationalism, and the constitutional debates of the 1960s?
Canadians have spent decades struggling over the constitutional question and official bilingualism, while the Parti Québécois has become a
powerful political force in that province as the Bloc Québécois claimed
its place in the federal government. The 1960s, or more accurately the
historical moment we define herein as the sixties, has undoubtedly had
a profound legacy for Canada.

Historicizing the Sixties: Continuity and Fracture

In rejecting the decadal approach to the study of the sixties, we
challenge the stereotype of a quiescent 1950s or a co-opted 1970s.
Catherine Carstairs, for instance, in her contribution to this volume, discusses health food stores in the context of the 'long sixties':
'Concern about the safety of the food supply began in the 1950s, and
peaked in the 1970s...This chapter thus concurs with a growing body
of literature in both the United States and Canada that argues that
the changes associated with the 1960s...often had their roots in the
1950s or earlier and frequently came to fruition only in the 1970s.'[55]
In truth, the boundaries between these years are far more fluid than
commonly assumed.

Finding a way to periodize the sixties is a complicated and fractious
process. Any attempt to impose structural unity on a topic or period
is by nature arbitrary, and the decision that a historian makes in this
realm is an explicit choice that shapes the types of questions asked
and how historical evidence is assessed. Yet, all historians attempt
to periodize in some manner. Are, for example, the sixties best
understood in 'decadal' terms? We disagree. As historians Catherine
Gidney and Mike Dawson argue elsewhere, this decadal approach is
itself rooted in an earlier twentieth-century historiographical project,
and it is an approach that can limit the possibilities of studying continuities between eras and social processes.[56] Certainly, there is one
strand of thought that laments the 'end' of the sixties, a sense that as

the decade ended, so too, did something larger and deeper, such as a feeling of hope for social and political transformation or a passionate commitment to ending inequality. Anastakis argues, for example, that 'the passion and irreverence of the decade ended imperceptibly and quietly, and lamentably seems to have been lost forever.'[57] But, as several authors demonstrate in this collection, political commitment did not die or go out of fashion at the end of the 1960s, nor was it missing in earlier periods. The passion for social justice, evidenced in the struggle for women's full reproductive freedom; the ongoing battle over bilingualism, language rights, and national identity; and protest against environmental degradation are only three examples of ongoing social movements that continued after the 1960s. While the nature and style of political engagement changed over time, these chapters demonstrate that the 1960s must be understood within a larger framework of time.

Related to periodization is the question of continuity and fracture. Is there anything useful in retaining an idea of the 1960s that poses a clear beginning, middle, and end to the period? We find this approach highly problematic. Such a narrative may be possible when studying a specific organization or social movement, whether Students for a Democratic Society (SDS) or the Student Non-Violent Co-ordinating Committee (SNCC) in the United States or, in Canada, the Student Union for Peace Action (SUPA) or the Company of Young Canadians (CYC). It is an approach that also favours the idea that the 1960s was characterized, on many levels, by a break from an earlier period marked by quiescence and conformity.[58] As Magda Fahrni and Robert Rutherdale have pointed out elsewhere, however, Canadian historians have long been attentive to the dangers of assuming that the postwar period can simply be categorized by straightforward domestic conformity and political quiescence in the 1950s and radical dissent in the 1960s.[59] Numerous historians have also made clear the dangers of equating one organization or particular social movement with the 'spirit' or 'generation' of a period, pointing out that such an analysis ultimately privileges what generally ends up being a youthful, male, middle-class, student elite. American historians have argued that this type of periodization can easily result in a declension narrative, which assumes not only a simple beginning and end to the period, but also a tendency to assume that 'good 1960s' movements, once characterized by unity of purpose, fractured into identity politics, violence, anger, and disillusionment.[60] As Alice Echols argues, the narrative of the sixties is still presented in such a way as to see women, Black Power, or the gay liberation movement as 'pesky subplots that eventually overwhelm the sixties dream of the beloved community, that upend the dream of We-ness.'[61] The essays in this collection challenge those narratives that locate authentic political engagement or activism within movements dominated by white, generally male, middle-class university students. Rather, they tell the story of a sixties where important transformational moments are located in a range of social movements, regions, political styles and ideologies, and age groups, and where the unity of categories such as age, youth, student, or woman is fundamentally questioned.

We see the sixties as a period representing a confluence of ideas and historical trends, not restricted to a specific beginning and end, and with a legacy that continues today. As the authors in this collection demonstrate, understanding any particular moment necessitates a reach backward or forward in time, to both historical antecedents and unintended legacies. Erika Dyck's chapter, for example, takes the drug most associated with the counterculture, LSD, and shows how its complicated history is rooted in clinical experimentation in North America in the late 1950s and early 1960s. That LSD and the 'psychedelic' came to be associated with dissent, protest, and freedom from authority was partly attributable to Timothy Leary, whose own work was initially rooted in an earlier model of clinical research and who was not particularly 'young' in the 1960s.

Finally, as historians, we need to consider how social actors in the 1960s saw themselves. How they thought about youth, age, and generation must be assessed within a critical and complicated historical framework.[62] As several chapters in this collection demonstrate, so-called generational cohorts were never unified entities, but always contested. For example, Marcel Martel's examination of the response to the Sir George Williams riot reminds us that the category of 'student' was contested. Furthermore, intergenerational cooperation and relationships existed throughout the 1960s. Is it just coincidence, for example, that the students in Roberta Lexier's chapter on student movements are using discourses of representation, accountability, and democratic governance similar to those of the faculty in Catherine Gidney's chapter on the activism of and formation of the Canadian

Association of University Teachers? Or that wildcat strikes, portrayed at the time as manifestations of youthful exuberance, in fact, included older as well as younger workers?

Meaning and Legacy

One of the great challenges of this study was constructing the sixties as a coherent unit of analysis. One common theme that emerges from these chapters is that the sixties can be partially characterized by a questioning of established and hierarchical authority. That questioning occurs along a political continuum, however, including liberal demands for dialogue and greater representation within existing bureaucratic, institutional structures, challenges to hierarchy within personal, individual relationships, and demands to restructure the entire social and political system. We can see the interplay of many of these challenges to authority in the case study of the Abortion Caravan. Steve Hewitt and Christabelle Sethna draw a vivid picture of the ways in which feminist activism confronted the paternalism embedded in the Therapeutic Abortion Committees established by Trudeau's Liberal government in 1969, as well as the patriarchal notions of women's responsibility for reproduction upheld by the state and medical professionals. In Gidney's and Lexier's accounts of university activism, both faculty and students organized and argued for greater power sharing and accountability on campus among students, faculty, and administration. And Matthew Hayday situates the Royal Commission on Bilingualism and Biculturalism within the context of dissent inside the framework of political power. According to Hayday, policy changes relating to bilingualism and national unity were rooted in fundamental debates about English-Canadian identity, Quebec nationalism, and the particularities of Canadian federalism, themes that are visited again in José Igartua's overview of the Quiet Revolution. In contrast, Peter McInnis examines the grassroots anger and activism of 'hotheads' who struggled against both employers and the bureaucracy of unions within the legal framework of the postwar labour accord. Meanwhile, Bryan Palmer's Red Power activists rejected cultural assimilation and state concessions for Aboriginal peoples, and tapped into the politics and language of international decolonization movements.

The chapters in this collection demonstrate that Canadians were grappling at this time with the conditions of modernity. In particular, people struggled with the ambiguous effect of progress, ambivalence towards scientific 'expert' authority, and alienation from a rationalized and bureaucratic postwar welfare state and labour accord. New Left activists and members of the counterculture spoke of alienation arising from these processes with modern industrial capitalism. But they were not the only groups to struggle with the dehumanizing effects of the period and the underlying uncertainties of the postwar nuclear age.[63] That these stories of struggle range widely is not surprising, for the nature of engagement with these concerns rested on social, economic, and cultural location, which in turn, shaped that which seemed possible at the time. We see youth in the Vancouver's Gastown riot of 1971 protesting against what Michael Boudreau calls the 'alienation of modern life,' and McInnis's 'hotheads,' young working-class men, rebelling against both labour leadership and the state. McInnis argues that the conflict must be understood in a framework of a modern industrial relations regime, itself a hierarchical process, which attempted to rationalize and modernize workplace disputes with its own set of 'experts' who stood apart from the workers. Feelings of distrust and ambivalence in this period can be seen through stories about 'expert' regulation of bodies through drugs and technology. Erika Dyck's examination of the origins of LSD as firmly rooted in medical experimentation for therapeutic purposes illustrates how the terms 'normal' and 'drug-taking' shifted when youth adopted the practice, whether they were poor street youth, activists in the Gastown smoke-in, or acid-dropping hippies of the counterculture. While some youth challenged the state's regulation of drug use and its association with immorality, others challenged the power of the state and of medical authorities to safely regulate the health and nutrition of the population. The development of consumer activism, the health food movement and alternative medicine, as Catherine Carstairs points out, was rooted in concerns over the negative effects of technology, fear over the healthiness of food additives and processed foods, and suspicion regarding the ability of regulatory agencies to keep food safe. These concerns, she argues, rose in large part from uncertainty regarding the long-term health concerns resulting from living in the nuclear age. Could experts keep Canadians safe? And what if the very

tools used to keep society safe, such as drugs, additives, preservatives, chemicals, or weapons, ultimately harmed or destroyed the very
people they were meant to protect?

Finally, one does not have to accept the argument that the period
prior to the 1960s was cohesive or quiescent to see that questions
about the identity of the Canadian nation, including its historical
ties to Great Britain, its political and economic relationship with
the United States, and its positioning vis-à-vis francophone and
Aboriginal peoples, were of central importance during this period.
What was Canada? What was the meaning of citizenship? What role
should state policy play in creating, sustaining, or rebuilding a modern Canadian nation? Bryan Palmer's attempt to theorize the 1960s
in Canada offers another helpful lens. He argues that it was a water-
shed period in which the identity of Canada as a British nation, tied
unquestionably to order and progress, was eroded. His argument is
evocative not only because he suggests that Canada emerged from
the 1960s without a new, cohesive identity, but because he claims
that the 1960s asked a much larger question about the usefulness of
national identity or even of a nation state itself.[64] Finally, in questioning the fundamental nature of Canada, questions about the relationship between Canada and the Cold War superpower to the south were
of central importance. Historian Ian McKay has argued that Canadian
left social movements were simultaneously 'derivative of' American
movements, yet also original, rooted in the 'particularities' of specific
local factors and of Canadian national political structures.[65]

The chapters in this collection speak to the complicated ways in
which Canadians viewed themselves and the United States, the sharing
of ideas, organizations, and peoples across the border, and the influence of American ideas of liberation on Canadian social movements.
James Walker's study of the Black United Front, for example, demonstrates the growing influence of the United States; specifically, the
impact of the American civil rights movement on social movements in
Canada. Azzi's chapter on the development of nationalism is illustrative of the complex story of changes to the notion of Canadian identity. While defining Canada in opposition to the United States was not
a new phenomenon, North American and global politics, particularly
assassinations of American political leaders and American foreign policy in Vietnam, provided a powerful critique of American imperialism

rooted in left nationalist politics. Arguing, however, that this critique of American global empire was rooted in America's own critiques of power, Azzi suggests that left Canadian nationalism was deeply embedded in transnational movements and ideas. Critiques of nationalism were also central to the ongoing debates about the future of Quebec and Canada. Marcel Martel's chapter on the riot at Sir George Williams takes an infamous incident of campus radicalism and locates its importance not just in the context of the student movement, but in the changing and dynamic milieu of Quebec's Quiet Revolution, as well as the racial politics of Montreal's black population. What happened in the computer room at one downtown university campus was connected to questions about the English-French relationship and the future of Quebec, but also to transnational protest and the politics of decolonization.

It will be clear, after reading through this collection, that not every author is in agreement as to the importance or legacy of the sixties, nor do the authors agree on the best way to conceptualize or periodize this era. As this collection makes evident, the 1960s in Canada is not one story, but many.[66] And not only were there many stories, there are many interpretations of their meaning. Race, ethnicity, age, gender, religion, class, region: these all framed one's relationship to structures of power and also one's cultural view, sensibilities, possibilities, choices, and options. Ongoing debates about how to characterize, understand, and theorize the sixties make clear that Canadian historians have much yet to say on the topic. Debate and disagreement will ultimately create a rich, lively, and ongoing assessment of this era.

FURTHER READING

One of the great challenges of editing a collection of essays is struggling to decide what topics to cover within the covers of a single book. Obviously, we could not address every possible topic. The following are some suggested readings of 1960s scholarship in Canada on topics not covered in this collection:

Chenier, Elise. 'Rethinking Class in Lesbian Bar Culture: Living the "Gay Life" in Toronto, 1955–1965.' In Mona Gleason and Adele Perry, eds., *Rethinking Canada: The Promise of Women's History,* 301–22. Toronto: Oxford University Press, 2006.

Clément, Dominique. '"Rights without the Sword Are but Mere Words": The Limits of Canada's Rights Revolution.' In Janet Miron, ed., *A History of Human Rights in Canada,* 43–60. Toronto: Canadian Scholars' Press, 2009.

Clément, Dominique. 'The October Crisis of 1970: Human Rights Abuses under the War Measures Act.' *Journal of Canadian Studies* 42/2 (2008), 160–86.

Devriese, Marc. 'Approche sociologique de la génération.' *Vingtième Siècle: Revue d'histoire* 22 (1989), 11–16.

Dubinsky, Karen. '"We Adopted a Negro": Interracial Adoption and the Hybrid Baby in 1960s Canada.' In Magda Fahrni and Robert Rutherdale, eds., *Creating Postwar Canada: Community, Diversity, and Dissent, 1945–75,* 268–88. Vancouver: UBC Press, 2007.

Dummitt, Christopher. 'A Crash Course in Manhood: Men, Cars, and Risk in Postwar Vancouver.' In Dimitry Anastakis, ed., *The Sixties: Passion, Politics and Style,* 71–98. Montreal and Kingston: McGill-Queen's University Press, 2008.

Henderson, Stuart. 'Toronto's Hippie Disease: End Days in the Yorkville Scene, August 1968.' *Journal of the Canadian Historical Association* 17/1 (2006), 205–34.

Igartua, José. *The Other Quiet Revolution: National Identities in English Canada, 1945–1971.* Vancouver: UBC Press, 2006.

Ireland, Kristin. 'Our True North Strong and Free: The Sixties and Transsexual Sex in Ontario.' In M. Athena Palaeologue, ed., *The Sixties in Canada: A Turbulent and Creative Decade,* 270–85. Montreal: Black Rose Books, 2009.

Kealey, Linda, and Heather Molyneux. 'On the Road to Medicare: Newfoundland in the 1960s.' *Journal of Canadian Studies* 41/3 (2007), 90–111.

Little, Margaret Hillyard. 'Militant Mothers Fight Poverty: The Just Society Movement, 1968–1971.' *Labour/Le Travail* 59 (2007), 179–98.

Marquis, Greg. 'From Beverage to Drug: Alcohol and Other Drugs in 1960s and 1970s Canada.' *Journal of Canadian Studies* 39/2 (2005), 57–79.

Martel, Marcel. 'Law versus Medicine: The Debate over Drug Use in the 1960s.' In Magda Fahrni and Robert Rutherdale, eds., *Creating Postwar Canada: Community, Diversity, and Dissent, 1945–75,* 315–33. Vancouver: UBC Press, 2007.

Raboy, Marc. 'The Future of Montréal and the MCM.' In Dimitrios
    Roussopoulos, ed., *The City and Radical Social Change,* 235–59.
    Montreal: Black Rose Books, 1982.
Robbins, Wendy, Margrit Eichler, Meg Luxton, and Francine Descarries,
    eds. *Minds of Our Own: Inventing Feminist Scholarship and Women's
    Studies in Canada and Quebec, 1966–76.* Waterloo: Wilfrid Laurier
    University Press, 2008.
Rutherdale, Robert. 'Fatherhood, Masculinity, and the Good Life during
    Canada's Baby Boom, 1945–1965.' *Journal of Family History* 24/3
    (1999), 351–73.
Sethna, Christabelle. '"Chastity Outmoded": *The Ubyssey,* Sex, and the
    Single Girl, 1960–1970.' In Magda Fahrni and Robert Rutherdale, eds.,
    *Creating Postwar Canada: Community, Diversity, and Dissent, 1945–
    75,* 289–314. Vancouver: UBC Press, 2007.
Vipond, Robert. 'The Civil Rights Movement Comes to Winnipeg:
    American Influence On "Rights Talk" in Canada, 1968–1971.' In
    Stephen L. Newman, ed., *Constitutional Politics in Canada and
    the United States,* 89–107. Albany: State University of New York
    Press, 2004.
Zelko, Frank. 'Making Greenpeace: The Development of Direct Action
    Environmentalism in British Columbia.' *BC Studies* 142–3 (Summer/
    Autumn 2004), 197–239.

PART ONE

Drugs, Health, and the Environment

Author Rachel Carson wrote *Silent Spring*, a book about the negative environmental impact of synthetic pesticides, in 1962.

U.S. Fish and Wildlife Service (1944). Public Domain.

1

Food, Fear, and the Environment in the Long Sixties

Catherine Carstairs

In 1969, the journalist Marjorie Harris complained about the 'bland and mushy-textured food' in Canadian supermarkets, and wondered if all of the food technologists, nutritionists, and agricultural scientists really had our best interests at heart.[1] She mused: 'Many people today are worried about all the chemicals being added to the soil, as well as to the water and air. Nobody seems to feel particularly great, especially in urban areas.' Experts at the Food and Drug Directorate told her that there was no way of determining the cumulative effects of all of the chemicals Canadians consumed but assured her that the situation was being carefully monitored and that Canadian food was safe. Her response: 'I found it rather chilling that tons of chemicals are dumped annually into our basic life resources and there is no way of checking on cumulative effects.' For another view, she turned to the best-seller *Let's Get Well* (1965) by Adelle Davis, who warned that American soil was poor, fruits and vegetables were grown with dangerous pesticides, and packaged food was deprived of vitamins and minerals. Harris began keeping track of what her family was eating. Finding it 'woefully deficient in vitamins,' she put her family on a regime of yeast, vitamin B6, and insolitin. A few days later, she wound up in a hospital emergency room, covered in hives. Even so, she took Davis's protein-heavy advice to heart and began eating liver for breakfast every day. She concluded: 'I avoid all the snappy packaged foods I can; I put wheat germ instead of flour into most of the food I cook; we eat as close to whole wheat bread as I can find; we all drink lots of milk; we munch away on carrots, celery and apples.'[2]

Harris was not alone. An extensive consumer survey by Health and Welfare Canada in 1979 showed that 87 per cent of Canadians were worried about the additives in their food.[3] By the end of the 1970s, there were more than five hundred health food stores across Canada, and mainstream supermarkets and drug stores had opened health food sections.[4] A growing number of Canadians worried that the food processing industry and agribusiness was making food less nutritious and wondered if their arthritis, hyperactivity, and even cancer, could be prevented or cured by eating more nutritiously. They were also concerned that nuclear fallout, pesticides, and cancer-causing food additives had made food unsafe to eat.

This fear about food was part of a larger shift taking place in people's attitudes towards science, medicine, and expertise. As Erika Dyck points out, the years immediately following the Second World War are often seen as a high point in terms of people's faith in medicine, science, and technology.[5] Indeed, there were some remarkable scientific breakthroughs in the 1940s and 1950s and reasons to feel optimistic about the promises of modernity. Antibiotics cured many previously life-threatening illnesses. Freezing made it easier to eat a wide variety of fruits and vegetables year round. Thanks to aerial pesticide spraying, it was possible to enjoy a pleasant summer evening outdoors in June. But as Paul Boyer showed in his book about the nuclear bomb, there was also some anxiety about these technological breakthroughs.[6] The nuclear bomb had ended the Second World War, but it could also end life on the planet. From the 1950s onwards, Canadians wondered if these new technologies might have harmful effects that were not yet known. The sociologist Ulrich Beck has argued that the development of nuclear and other technologies, with their potentially disastrous consequences for the planet, ushered in a new era of modernity, the 'risk society,' in which we worried less about the class inequalities produced by industrialization and, instead, focused more on avoiding its risks.[7]

This chapter refers to the 'long sixties,' because concern about the safety of the food supply arguably began in the 1950s and peaked in the 1970s. In Canada, as in the United States, the story begins with concern over nuclear fallout in the late 1950s and early 1960s. As the fallout problem diminished, Canadians began to worry about pesticide contamination and mercury poisoning. By the early 1970s, fears about food additives took central stage. This chapter, thus, concurs with a growing body of literature in both the United States and Canada that argues that the changes associated with the 1960s, including the civil rights movement, changes in sexual practices, the feminist movement, and the environmental movement often had their roots in the 1950s or earlier and frequently came to fruition only in the 1970s.[8] It will also argue, as Stephen Azzi shows in his chapter, that Canadians who were interested in food and the environment were influenced by what was happening in the United States. Indeed, many of their concerns were international – as Ulrich Beck has argued, the risk society is a global society.

History of Canadian Foodways in a Few Quick Bites

Over the past two centuries, Canadian foodways have changed dramatically. In *Roughing It in the Bush,* a classic account of settlement in Ontario in the mid-nineteenth century, Susanna Moodie describes living on milk, potatoes, and bread for months on end; squirrel, deer, fish, and dandelion were welcome additions to this monotonous fare. Even so, rural people in nineteenth-century Canada could buy tea, coffee, candy, spices, raisins, and mustard from country stores; their urban counterparts purchased milk, cheese, meat, fruits, and vegetables. By the late nineteenth century, people purchased wrapped packages of flour, biscuits, and oats instead of scooping them out of a barrel. With some justification, advertisers promoted packaged foods as cleaner and healthier than bulk foods. From the manufacturers' perspective, these products could also be branded, meaning that they could be marketed nationally or even internationally. At the same time, refrigeration and commercial canning permitted year-round consumption of a wider variety of fruits and vegetables. Mass supermarkets like Dominion and Loblaws emerged in the early 1920s, and by the late 1950s they would dominate the grocery industry in most of English Canada.[9]

While many people welcomed the convenience of packaged and canned foods, others worried that we were destroying the nutritional value of our food. In the 1830s, the American Sylvester Graham campaigned against bakery bread, arguing that home-made bread, made with unrefined grains, was healthier and that a bland, vegetarian diet would provide a pathway to health and spiritual advancement. In the late nineteenth century, John Harvey Kellogg argued that a natural food diet and vegetarianism would counter modernity's excessive stimulation and stress. In Canada, Robert Jackson promulgated these ideas in *How to Always Be Well* (1927), which lauded the diets of 'primitive peoples' and decried the horrors of 'bolted bread,' cooked meat, and refined sugar.[10]

Paying their critics little heed, food scientists and mainstream nutritionists continued to discover new and more exciting ways of preserving and delivering foods.[11] For the most part, Canadians welcomed these developments. Newspapers and magazines celebrated the bonanza of frozen, instant, and prepared foods. In 1955, an article in *Maclean's* touting the rise of instant foods, the end of home baking, and the increase in fruit and vegetable consumption prophesied that 'the day may come when food can be manufactured chemically in large quantities.'[12] In an Alice Munro story, set at a dinner party in the early 1950s, a normally silent man blurts out that frozen vegetables 'were better than fresh. The color, the flavor, everything was better than fresh. He said it was remarkable what they could do now.'[13] By the 1960s, Canadians were eating a much broader variety of foods and were in less danger of food-borne illness than ever before. Although there was some concern about the nutritional status of the very young and the very old, most nutritionists thought that obesity was the biggest nutritional problem facing Canadians.[14]

Nonetheless, the critique of the industrial food system mounted in both the United States and Canada. By the interwar years, a number of health food stores had sprung up in Canadian cities, selling vitamins, herbs, and 'wonder foods' such as yogurt, molasses, and wheat germ. In the 1950s, health food books by Gaylord Hauser and Adelle Davis, among others, sold well on both sides of the border.[15] These authors claimed that the quality of our food was abominable and that a varied diet of home-cooked foods would make people healthier, thinner, and more energetic. By the late 1960s, a growing number of Canadians, worried about pollution and food additives, and distrustful of big business, they began to take heed of their critique. There was an explosion of interest in health food in the popular media and a growing number of health food stores and restaurants.

The Main Course: Fallout, Pollution, and Frightening Additives

So, why were food fears mounting? As the arms race escalated in the early 1950s, the United States, the Soviet Union, Britain, and France began testing more powerful nuclear weapons. In 1954, the United States exploded a hydrogen bomb at Bikini Atoll in the Marshall Islands. The fallout rained on a nearby Japanese fishing vessel, killing one man, and causing severe radiation sickness is twenty-three others. This incident attracted front-page headlines across the world. In 1957, Albert Schweitzer (a physician and philosopher who won the Nobel Prize for Peace in 1952 and a famed global citizen) broadcast a plea to the 'world's peoples' to bring an end to the tests, warning that fallout would lead to blood cancers and birth defects. The following year, Nobel Prize – winning chemist Linus Pauling submitted a petition to the United Nations signed by more than nine thousand scientists, including twenty-six Nobel Prize winners, calling for an end to nuclear bomb testing. They warned: 'each nuclear bomb test spreads an added burden of radioactive elements over every part of the world' and threatened an 'increase in the number of seriously defective children.'[16] Pauling won the Nobel Peace Prize for this work in 1963.

That same year, a group of scientists and local activists, including Barry Commoner, formed the Greater St Louis Citizens Committee for Nuclear Information (CNI) to raise awareness about nuclear fallout. In late 1958, the CNI began collecting baby teeth to determine the extent to which fallout from nuclear tests was being absorbed into the bodies of growing children. Funded by the American Cancer Society, the U.S. Public Health Service, and other groups, the Baby Tooth campaign collected teeth from tens of thousands of children. The results showed that strontium-90 had begun accumulating after 1952, the year of the first hydrogen bomb. Over the next four years, the teeth showed a 300 per cent increase in strontium-90.[17]

By the late 1950s, opposition members in the House of Commons kept up a regular stream of questions about strontium-90 in milk, wheat, fish, water, and the bones of children. In 1960, a group of prominent Canadians formed the Canadian Committee for the Control of Radiation Hazards. The *Toronto Star* warned: 'strontium-90 – the unseen assassin of our days – will still kill thousands of children, or turn them into cretins.' The influential women's peace group, the Voice of Women (VOW), collected more than twenty thousand baby teeth for University of Toronto dentist Dr Murray Hunt and for the CNI study.[18] After the signing of the Limited Test Ban Treaty in the summer of 1963, levels of strontium-90 and other radioactive material began to decline, and concern over fallout diminished. But, in the meantime, the birth of severely deformed babies whose mothers had taken thalidomide shook Canadians' confidence in the ability of the experts to keep them safe from harm.

The tranquilizer thalidomide first went on sale in Canada in April 1961. Because it helped to prevent nausea, doctors frequently prescribed the drug to women in the first months of pregnancy. A few months after it was introduced in Canada, German authorities noted a dramatic increase in rare congenital deformities among children whose mothers who had taken thalidomide. Later that year, the pharmaceutical company marketing the drug in Canada warned Canadian physicians that there was a link between the drug and birth defects, and in March 1962, the company withdrew the drug from the market. It was too late; in the summer of 1962, Canadian newspapers reported that children had been born with legs fused to their buttocks and truncated arms. The stories often focused on their distraught mothers. Thalidomide served as a dramatic warning of the devastating potential of new technologies and shook Canadians' confidence in their regulatory authorities, especially since officials in the United States had delayed approval of thalidomide because of concerns over its safety.[19]

At the same time that the thalidomide story unfolded, there was also growing press attention to the problems of pesticides. In 1962, the popular American science writer, Rachel Carson, published *Silent Spring,* a poetic and passionate account of the dangers of synthetic pesticides. Her book begins with the eerie account of a bucolic farm town that had fallen silent – the birds were gone, the fish had died, farm animals were stillborn, and children were dying unexpectedly. The cause was a granular white powder. Carson admitted that no community had experienced all of these disasters, but all of them had happened somewhere – 'a grim spectre has crept upon us almost unnoticed.'[20] She warned that mankind was engaged in an unprecedented experiment. Since the Second World War, scientists had developed two hundred new chemicals to kill insects, and these chemicals were accumulating in the bodies of fish, birds, reptiles, animals, and humans.

Much of the ensuing publicity focused on DDT. DDT had initially been held up as a safe, almost miraculous substance. During the Second World War, the pesticide protected American soldiers from malaria and typhus in the South Pacific. After the war, homeowners employed it to rid themselves of unwanted pests, while farmers used it to increase crop yields, and cities did aerial spraying of DDT to cut down on summer mosquitoes. But in the aftermath of Carson's book, attitudes towards DDT began to change. In the summer of 1965, hundreds of dead seagulls turned up on the shore of Lake Ontario. A University of Guelph researcher declared that DDT had killed them. The following summer, a study revealed that dying fish in Lake Muskoka had extremely high levels of DDT, and it questioned if they were safe for human consumption. In the summer of 1968, the federal government banned the use of DDT in National Parks.[21]

Ontario became the first provincial jurisdiction to impose restrictions on DDT use after the death of four ducks and six ducklings on Toronto Island led to a public outcry. In the summer of 1969, a Toronto Island resident found the ducks and brought them to University of Toronto zoologist and prominent environmentalist Donald Chant, who had them autopsied. He reported that the ducks had high levels of the pesticide diazinon. Pollution Probe, an environmental group formed at the University of Toronto four months earlier, convened a two-day hearing into the deaths of the ducks. The Superintendent of Parks admitted (incorrectly) that it had used diazinon on the island in May. The commissioners of the hearing included: Marshall McLuhan, the University of Toronto professor famed for his pioneering work on communications, Dr Robert McLure, moderator of the United Church of Canada; and Dr Ernest Sirluck, University of Toronto vice-president. During the hearing, McLuhan and Chant joked that humans were not fit for consumption because of the high levels of DDT in their bodies, while a young University of Toronto 'co-ed' expressed fear that the pesticides were going to make her sterile, an issue also raised by Rachel Carson in *Silent Spring*. The commissioners recommended that public agencies should have to notify the public before using pesticides. The day after the hearing, NDP members of the House of Commons asked the government whether the amount of

DDT in food was unsafe, and they asked for further study of the issue, while in Ontario the Liberals called for a ban on DDT. That same day, the U.S. Department of Agriculture announced a thirty-day suspension of the use of DDT.[22]

At a conference that September, Donald Chant threatened to sue the provincial government's pesticide advisory board, complaining that it was a rubber stamp for the pesticide industry. Just two weeks later, the Ontario government announced that it would limit the use of DDT to tobacco and apple growers. Still, the federal government insisted that while all Canadians had residues of DDT in their bodies, the amount was well within the margins of safety. The *Globe and Mail* retorted that levels of radiation once thought to be safe were no longer thought to be harmless and that DDT had already been shown to be toxic. Two days later, Prime Minister Pierre Trudeau made headlines with his warning that DDT could 'wipe out humanity' if ships carrying DDT were to accidentally release their cargo into the ocean. In early November 1969, the federal government restricted DDT use to twelve crops and reduced the maximum level allowed in foodstuffs.[23]

Soon afterwards, the media began expressing concern about mercury pollution and its impact on fish and birds. Mercury-based compounds were used as a fungicide on crops and in the manufacture of pulp and paper and electrical appliances. In the late 1960s, industries released approximately two hundred thousand pounds into Canadian waterways every year. Mercury poisoning initially causes vague symptoms such as fatigue and headache, but in the later stages it can lead to numbness in the limbs, loss of muscular coordination, and tunnel vision. Eventually, it can kill. In 1969, the Alberta provincial government banned the hunting of pheasants, partridge, and grouse because high mercury levels made the birds unfit to eat. The following year, the federal Department of Fisheries forbade fishing on Lake St Clair and the St Clair and Detroit rivers because pickerel and perch were found to contain forty times the allowed amount of mercury. High levels of mercury contamination also led to the closure of the commercial fishery on Lake Winnipeg. University of Toronto Professor Robert Jervis warned that mercury levels in all foods were rising and that Canadians were probably exceeding the limits of safety established by the World Health Organization. Ultimately, those most seriously affected were Ojibway people on the Whitedog and Grassy Narrows Reserve, where mercury waste from the Reed Paper company led to health problems and devastated the local tourist economy.[24]

If pesticide residues on fruits and vegetables and mercury contamination of fish were not enough to alarm people about the safety of their food, the press then began drawing attention to the serious impact of polychlorinated biphenyls (PCBs) on birds, other wildlife, and fish. Companies producing paints, plastics, printing ink, and electrical transformers used PCBs until 1971, when Monsanto, the manufacturer, voluntarily limited their sale after U.S. studies showed increased levels of PCBs in wildlife. Nonetheless, PCBs continued to be used as fire retardants in a more limited range of products, and they were leaching into groundwater from waste disposal sites. By the early 1970s, some scientists speculated that some of the negative effects attributed to DDT might actually have been caused by PCBs, and they cautioned that PCB-contaminated fish were unsafe to eat. Studies in the mid-1970s showed high levels of PCBs in fish from the Great Lakes, while American researchers linked PCBs to cancer. In 1975, the Canadian government announced that PCBs in fish would not be allowed to exceed two parts per million and in 1977 the import, manufacture, and sale of PCBs was banned in Canada. Even so, PCBs continue to be released into the environment through spills and fires and are a significant problem in the Canadian Arctic.[25]

Nuclear fallout, pesticides, mercury, and PCBs all raised alarm about the safety of the food supply. But it was food additives that caused Canadians the most concern, perhaps because they seemed more immediate. After all, food additives, with their frightening, multisyllabic names, were listed right on the box.[26] Also, they were easier to avoid. One could buy products that did not have additives; fighting pesticide use and pollution required a different type of activism. Food additives, of course, were nothing new. Sulphur dioxide has preserved wine and rennet has preserved cheese for centuries, but the rapid increase in processed foods in the years after the Second World War resulted in the vastly increased use of artificial colours, emulsifiers, artificial sweeteners, and preservatives. Although health food writers spoke out against additives in the 1950s, they received little mainstream press attention until 1960, when the Food and Drug Directorate banned the use of two coal-tar colour additives after new studies showed that they were carcinogenic. Oil yellow AB and oil yellow OB were used to colour butter, margarine, and cheese. The *Toronto Star* published an outraged article entitled 'Look What They're Doing to Our Food!' while *Maclean's* declared 'we're poisoning ourselves with pesticides, preservatives and "improvers."'[27]

This was followed by the shocking story of twenty deaths in Quebec City. In 1965, Dow Brewery began adding cobalt sulphate to their beer to make the foam last longer. Over the next year, fifty beer drinkers appeared in local hospitals suffering from nausea and shortness of breath. In many cases, their faces and necks had turned blue. Quebec's deputy minister of health established a committee to investigate. The committee found that the men had all been heavy drinkers and ate a poor diet. Due to their protein deficiencies, they were unable to absorb the cobalt. In March 1966, Dow removed cobalt sulphate from the beer and later that year, the Food and Drug Directorate banned the use of cobalt sulphate. While the case received intense publicity in Quebec, and especially in Quebec City, where Dow beer accounted for 80 per cent of the beer market, the scandal attracted relatively little attention across the country, perhaps because it was only breweries in Quebec that were using the additive, and the patients, all severe alcoholics, were not the most sympathetic victims.[28]

It was the cyclamate ban in 1969 that would really raise public alarm about food additives. Cyclamates are an artificial sweetener that came into widespread use in the 1950s, when the demand for diet soft drinks exploded. In the mid-1960s, two Japanese studies suggested that cyclamates might lead to miscarriage, prompting the U.S. Food and Drug Administration (FDA) to begin its own studies. In 1967, the FDA said that they had found no evidence of the harmfulness of cyclamates, but by 1968, they recommended that consumers limit their consumption of the artificial sweetener. In the fall of 1969, FDA scientist Jacqueline Verret reported that cyclamates injected into chicken eggs caused birth defects. Then a small study showed that rats being fed large amounts of cyclamates developed bladder cancer. This triggered the Delaney clause, a 1958 amendment to the U.S. Food and Drug Act, which banned any chemical food additive which caused cancer in animals, and on 19 October 1969 the United States announced a ban of the artificial sweetener. In Canada, Health

Minister John Munro told Canadians that they should not be alarmed; his department was studying the matter. He pointed out that the U.S. studies were based on very large amounts of cyclamate use. But, a few days later, the Canadian government ordered soft drink manufacturers to remove cyclamates by the end of November 1969, while the makers of special diabetic foods would have six months to find substitutes. In the case of diabetic foods, it was thought that the benefits of the product outweighed the potential risks posed by cyclamates. Not everyone was alarmed. Journalists and letters to the editor countered that there was no evidence that cyclamates caused cancer in humans, suggested that the 'sugar interests' might be behind the ban, and worried that diabetics were being left with relatively few food choices. Sweet lovers wrote letters complaining: 'why should we care about what happened to a few rats?' But others applauded the government for acting quickly to protect public health.[29]

The cyclamate issue attracted the attention of the famed U.S. consumer activist Ralph Nader. His book, *Unsafe at Any Speed* (1965), excoriated the automobile industry for ignoring safety and led to significant safety improvements including shoulder straps for front-seat passengers and shatter-proof windshields. Next, Nader turned his attention to the meat-processing industry. Imitating one of his heroes, the muckraking journalist Upton Sinclair, whose book *The Jungle* precipitated the passage of the Meat Inspection Act of 1906, Nader revealed that diseased cattle and pigs were still part of the food supply. Meat packers also used a banned additive (sulphite) in order to give the flesh a pink and fresh-looking appearance. Nader's revelations led to a stronger meat inspection bill in 1967. Building on this success, Nader hired vast teams of summer students (Nader's Raiders) in Washington to investigate the workings of the regulatory bodies of the federal government. In the summer of 1969, sixteen students were hired to investigate the Food and Drug Administration. The result was *The Chemical Feast* (1970), which condemned the incompetence of the FDA, accused it of having too cozy a relationship with industry, muzzling their own employees when it came to evidence that would be harmful to manufacturing interests, and wasting their attention on prosecuting small vitamin manufacturers instead of focusing on the violations of the large food processors. The book warned consumers that there were hundreds of potentially dangerous additives in their food and insisted that 'Americans might be sitting on a mutagenic time bomb.'[30]

Numerous other exposés followed. Gene Marine and Judith Van Allen's *Food Pollution: The Violation of Our Inner Ecology* (1972) provided an amusing and sarcastic account of the failure of the FDA to protect the public. In *Eating May Be Hazardous to Your Health* (1974), FDA scientist Jacqueline Verret cautioned: 'All of us are involved in a gigantic experiment of which we shall never know the outcome – at least in our lifetime.' In Canada, McMaster University biochemist Ross Hume Hall, a frequent media commentator on food and environmental issues, published *Food for Nought: The Decline in Nutrition* (1974), in which he condemned our 'lifeless bread,' the use of food additives and commercial fertilizers, and the influence of agribusiness. Linda Pim of Pollution Probe, one of the most active environmental groups in 1970s Canada, published a booklet entitled *Additive Alert* (1979). It listed forty-six additives that might have harmful effects but were still allowed in Canadian foods.[31]

As it turns out, the cyclamate ban was just the beginning; it seemed that the critics were right. In the early 1970s, research showed that quite a few food additives had the potential to cause cancer, heart disease, and other ailments. In 1970, Canada's Food and Drug Directorate reduced the allowed amount of brominated vegetable oils (which were used in citrus-flavoured soft drinks) after studies showed that they impaired heart functioning in rats. A few years later, after scientists revealed that nitrites could be carcinogenic, the federal government prohibited the use of nitrites in cooked sausage products, canned meats, fish, and cheese, and limited the amounts of addititves that could be added to cooked sausages, canned meats, and bacon. In 1977, a study by the Health Protection Branch (Canada) revealed that the artificial sweetener saccharin caused bladder cancers in mice, and banned it as a food additive, although it continued to be available for purchase as a table-top sweetener.[32]

Another banned substance was diethylstilbestrol (DES), a synthetic estrogen, which first came on the market in the 1940s. It was used to prevent miscarriages, but doctors also prescribed it to prevent girls from becoming 'too tall,' to prevent hot flashes during menopause, and as a 'morning-after' contraceptive. In the 1950s, researchers at Iowa State University discovered that DES caused cattle to gain weight faster and made their meat taste better. DES began to be used extensively in animal feed. But in the early 1970s, studies showed that young women whose mothers had taken DES during pregnancy had significantly higher rates of vaginal cancers than other women their age, while rats fed DES developed mammary tumours. In July 1972, the U.S. FDA banned DES from animal feed and eight months later outlawed the use of DES implants. Canada followed suit, not because authorities believed that DES was dangerous, but because it would make it more difficult to market Canadian beef in the United States.[33]

The public was also alarmed about the flavour enhancer monosodium glutamate (MSG). In 1968, two researchers showed that MSG could produce headaches, abdominal discomfort, and chest pain. This became known in both the scientific and popular press as 'Chinese restaurant syndrome' because MSG was said to be extensively used in Chinese cookery. In fact, packaged soups, mayonnaise, salad dressing, and meat tenderizers frequently contained MSG, and as Ian Mosby has argued, the association of MSG with Chinese restaurants had more to do with racist stereotypes about exotic Chinese cooking than it did with the excessive use of the food additive. Just after the cyclamates ban, two scientists announced that MSG damaged the brains of baby mice. This was particularly alarming because MSG was extensively used in baby foods, and while the pro-natalism of the baby boom years had begun to decline, health threats to children were still taken very seriously. The next day, a number of major manufacturers including Heinz, Gerber, and Beechout said that while they were still convinced of the safety of MSG, they would stop using it in baby foods.[34]

The concern about food additives and children's health grew after the publication of Dr Ben Feingold's 1974 best-seller, *Why Your Child Is Hyperactive,* which blamed food additives, especially artificial colours, for what he and many others saw as a rapid increase in hyperactivity among children. Feingold claimed that 50 per cent of hyperactive children placed on a restrictive diet improved markedly in less than a month. Parents across North America began eliminating food additives from the children's diets in the hope of improving their behaviour and keeping them off Ritalin, an amphetamine-type stimulant used to reduce hyperactivity in children. In the House of Commons, Dr Paul Yewchuk, a Progressive Conservative Member of Parliament from Alberta, became a proponent of Feingold's theory.

He complained that as many as 40 per cent of children were hyper-active in some areas and warned that hyperactivity frequently led to delinquency and crime. He demanded that the government research the impact of food additives on children's behaviour.[35]

One of the most controversial colours, Red Dye no. 2, was banned in the United States in 1976. This famously led Mars to get rid of red M&Ms, even though they had never actually contained Red Dye no. 2. In Canada, the Food and Drug Directorate was not persuaded that Red Dye no. 2 (or amaranth, as it was known in Canada) was unsafe. The study that led to the ban in the United States had mixed up some of the rats in the control group, and the experimental group and many of the dead rats' bodies were so decomposed that a proper analysis could not be conducted. *Science* condemned it as a 'ludi-crously botched experiment.' The Canadian government claimed that: 'Every day a person would have to eat more than 1,600 pounds of food containing approximately 100 parts per million of amaranth' to receive the same amount of red dye as the rats in the study. Adding to the confusion was the fact that the Americans suggested that food manufacturers replace Red Dye no. 2, with Red Dye no. 40, which Canadian authorities believed was unsafe.[36]

The large number of food additive bans and what seemed to be scientific uncertainty over safety led to public outrage and anxiety. In the House of Commons, NDP member Lorne Nystrom argued that 90 per cent of cancers were caused by environmental factors, including food: 'This is what happens in a modern man's diet. There is more processing, more artificial food, more fabricated and phony foods…Over 1,800 chemicals are put into our food supply on a rou-tine basis, and probably another 1,000 chemicals are used from time to time…We are teaching people to eat crappy food, junk food.'[37] When the *Globe and Mail* consumer columnist Ellen Roseman asked her readers if they were concerned about chemicals in their food, she received an 'overwhelming yes.' Christine M. Steele of Mississauga wrote: 'I really think that nature intended us to eat a fresh orange, not reconstituted vitaminized, coloured, orange-flavoured crystals.' Betty Gardner of Don Mills worried: 'I avoid highly processed food, but even if we stick to meat and fresh vegetables it seems we are in danger from antibiotic residues and chemical pesticides. HELP.'[38] In 1979, the Health Protection Branch surveyed nearly 25,000 Canadians about their attitudes towards food additives. Forty-seven per cent of all Canadians approached in malls agreed to fill out a survey – a remarkably high response rate. Only 19 per cent thought that the addition of colours to foods was justifiable, and 70 per cent said that food additives did not improve the quality of the food; 76 per cent said that they were making an effort to eat food with fewer additives.[39]

To counter the fear, mainstream nutritionists and the Department of National Health and Welfare cautioned that food additives had improved the safety of the food supply and that the risks were small compared with the problems of food-borne illness. Assistant Deputy Minister Alex Morrison of the Health Protection Branch told Canadian audiences that, while it was important to be vigilant about food additives, they helped to protect the safety of the food supply by keeping food fresh.[40] He emphasized that there were 'complex trade-offs' between the risks posed by food chemicals and the risks of food-borne disease and food shortages. He urged people to understand that tests in animals were not the same as tests in people. 'People believe that safety is absolute rather than relative. They want a zero risk food supply, which is not achievable. Safety is always a relative term.'[41] Industry representatives also tried to quell the alarm. The president of Canada Packers claimed that food additives had increased the safety of the food supply and decreased the incidence of nutritional deficiencies.[42] In 1972, the Canadian Institute of Food Science and Technology invited Richard Hall, president of the U.S. Institute of Food Technologists, to give the keynote address at their annual conference. He condemned the 'hysterical concern' over food additives, which he said 'have an essentially unblemished record of safety.'[43] Still, it was hard not to feel uneasy when people like biochemist Ross Hume Hall warned that a 'typical supermarket diet' consisted of '5,500 different chemicals a day; 2,500 of these chemicals are deliberately added and the rest arrive there through contamination.'[44]

Digesting Fear

By the end of the 1970s, many Canadians were feeling the same confusion over their food as Marjorie Harris had described in 1969. They wondered if their headaches, digestive problems, or more seriously, cancer, had been caused by food additives, pesticide residues, or fallout contamination in their food. While most people shrugged their concerns off and purchased food that was convenient and tasty, some tried to radically transform the way that they were eating to avoid at least some of these man-made risks. Many converted to the teachings of the American nutritionist Adelle Davis. The nutrition establishment condemned her, but she was a pop-culture icon with her recommendation that people heavily supplement their diets with vitamins and minerals to make up for the devitalized soil, pesticide residues, and other dangers in food.[45] Some young people adopted a 'macrobiotic' diet, which also eschewed all 'unnatural' foods in favour of brown rice and organically grown fruits and vegetables.[46] In Canada, some turned to the Finnish writer Paavo Airola, the author of *There Is A Cure for Arthritis* (1968), *Are You Confused?* (1971), *How to Get Well* (1974), *How to Keep Slim, Healthy and Young with Juice Fasting* (1971), who was the featured columnist in Canada's most widely circulated health food magazine, *Alive*. Airola recommended a vegetarian, whole food, organic diet with regular fasting to rid the body of impurities. All of these writers promised that you could be healthy even in a chemically laden age, although it would take considerable sacrifice and effort to get there.[47] Interestingly, eating differently had appeal across the generational spectrum; as McInnis, Palmer, Walker, and Hayday also show in this volume, many of the social movements of the 1960s achieved support from the young, old, and middle-aged.

Very few Canadians followed these recommendations of health food writers religiously. But the fact that health food stores vastly increased in number and that the number of books on health and nutrition exploded, speaks to the impact of the years of concern over fallout, pesticides, mercury, and food additives. While the threat of an all-out nuclear war had declined since the early years of the Cold War, there were other, more insidious, threats afoot. The new technologies that made our lives easier appeared to have some hidden costs. As in the case of DDT, DES, and mercury, it seemed that it often took years before the harmful effects emerged. The regulatory authorities did not appear to be doing a good job of protecting the public. Were these substances dangerous or safe? Why was there so much disagreement? To what extent were the regulatory authorities in the pocket of industry? One of the legacies of the long sixties was a growing sense of fear that science and technology had grown so complicated that no one, not even the experts, could determine safety. In the face of this fear and uncertainty, one of few options was to try to shop and eat differently and, hopefully, keep yourself and your loved ones as healthy as possible.

FURTHER READING

Dummitt, Chris. *Manly Modern: Masculinity in Postwar Canada.* Vancouver: UBC Press, 2007.

Egan, Michael. *Barry Commoner and the Science of Survival.* Cambridge, MA: MIT Press, 2007.

Loo, Tina. *States of Nature: Conserving Canada's Wildlife in the Twentieth Century.* Vancouver: UBC Press, 2006.

Parr, Joy. 'Smells Like? Sources of Uncertainty in the History of the Great Lakes Environment.' *Environmental History* 11/2 (April 2006), 269–99.

Zelko, Frank. 'Making Greenpeace: The Development of Direct Action in British Columbia.' *BC Studies* 142–3 (Summer/Autumn 2004), 197–240.

Journalist Sidney Katz swallows a dose of LSD with Drs Chuck Jillings, Humphry Osmond, Ben Stefaniuk, and Elaine Cumming looking on. The photograph accompanied Katz's subsequent article about his LSD experience in *Maclean's* magazine, October 1953.

Permission of Michael Kesterton.

2

The Psychedelic Sixties in North America: Drugs and Identity

Erika Dyck

The 1960s have often been depicted by groovy terms, tie-dyed fashions, and trippy music. These kinds of expressions have often been attributed to the influence of mind-bending drugs that encouraged engagement with unorthodox spirituality and philosophy, some of the most iconic images of the 1960s. It was this association between hallucinogenic drug use and displays of nonconformity that has characterized this period, that of the so-called 1960s generation, as psychedelic. However, the word 'psychedelic' was coined in 1957 by psychiatrist Humphry Osmond, then working at the Saskatchewan Provincial Mental Hospital, as he attempted to pull together different linguistic strands from 'psyche,' meaning mind, and 'delos,' with its Greek roots meaning to bring to light. Osmond blended these two concepts to create a term that described the sensations he felt when he experimented with d-lysergic acid diethylamide (LSD) in an effort to understand schizophrenia. Given this clinical past, where, then, did the connection between LSD and hippies come from? Who or what produced the social identification with countercultural activities stimulated by mind-altering drugs? Focusing on the history of LSD, this chapter examines these questions and considers how the meaning of 'psychedelic' evolved, from a term evoking clinical connotations to a nostalgic shorthand for a broader set of ideas associated with the 1960s.

In the mid-1960s the cultural reputation of LSD underwent a dramatic shift. It went from a psychoactive substance that formed part of state-funded psychopharmacological research carried out by white-coated, male scientists (and a few female scientists) in a clinical environment to a recreational drug abused by long-haired college students dressed in bright clothing who listened to contemporary musical compilations often inspired by drug consumption. The objectives behind LSD consumption had also changed. The clinicians in Canadian research on the drug were part of a government-supported medical research establishment, and they contributed to developments in psychiatry in the 1950s. By contrast, the recreational users, who embraced LSD more than a decade after the medical experiments began, allegedly adopted an anti-authority attitude and attracted criminal attention. While the change in the population of users partly explains the different conceptualizations of the psychedelic cultures, it does not fully account for this transition.

Some authors in this volume have demonstrated the way that the 1960s have been characterized as a period defined in part by a particular generation. Others have emphasized the reform-minded political mood of that decade that fed into the emergence of newly politicized collective identities and their associated movements that tended to spill into the 1970s. Some contributors, however, have looked for precedents in the 1950s, rather than extending the 1960s into the 1970s. From the perspective of the 1950s, the 1960s represent an extension, and perhaps an adaptation, of Cold War posturing, scientific rationalization, or English-French tensions. For example, Catherine Carstairs demonstrates (in this volume) that faith in scientific and medical experts reached a peak in the 1950s, after which a number of crises, such as thalidomide and toxic pollution, indicated growing popular disillusionment in the ability of experts to forecast the side effects of science and technology.

Examining this decade from these different angles helps to give better definition to the periodization and sociopolitical characterization of what has generically been simply called 'the sixties.' By examining the psychedelic drug use in both the 1950s and 1960s, this chapter attempts to contribute to these debates, using LSD as the common element, while the people, the contexts, and the decades present changing variables. The characterization of a psychedelic era is somewhat ironic, since the psychedelic pioneers of the 1950s were white-coated, middle-aged, male scientists who represented a more typical image of the establishment, while those who followed in the 1960s self-consciously embraced an identity that stood in stark opposition.

These kinds of ideas emphasize the importance of considering the stereotypical linkages between hippies and LSD use that has become an iconic image of the 1960s. At times the connection between LSD and the hippies relied upon a politicized image of youth as a radical other, poised to upset the conventional social order. Indeed, as fellow contributors in this book show, the 1960s were also a period identified with political movements, but the relationship between radicalism and psychedelic drugs is less convincing. Indeed, as authors Boudreau and Hewitt and Sethna, suggest, drug users are often summarily dismissed as deviant members of society, whose lifestyles forfeit their right to otherwise normal rights of citizenship, including political protest.

The 'hippies' were not confined to one geopolitical region, although concerted efforts to constrain their activities seemed to concentrate on particular areas where these groups were most visible. In Canada that often meant urban destinations such as Toronto's Yorkville or Vancouver's Gastown, although the term applied generically to individuals and groups who fit a particular description as young, long-haired, diseased, listless, and unhygienic sorts.[1] The characterization of the North American hippie crossed national borders, but the psychedelic dimension had important Canadian roots that fed into this conceptualization.

The Psychedelic Fifties

Although LSD was originally synthesized in the late 1930s, it did not attract serious attention until the 1950s. First capturing interest from military and medical investigators, LSD remained confined to the domain of scientists in research laboratories throughout that decade. Within that context the drug acquired a reputation for its potential as a pharmacological agent. By the end of the 1950s, over a thousand medical and scientific publications about LSD were in circulation. Applications ranged from its use as a truth serum for military interrogation, primarily in the United States; to its consumption in Canada by mental health professionals to produce a model psychosis from which individuals might better empathize with their psychotic patients; to its prescription by North American psychoanalysts and psychotherapists for easing patients into therapy sessions that required intense periods of self-reflection; to its use as a therapy for a range of disorders then associated with mental illness, including depression, alcoholism, and homosexuality. Although it is difficult to quantify the rates of use during this period, it seems clear that several medical authorities were familiar with, and even enthusiastic about, LSD's potential as a tool in medical science.

One such enthusiast was Humphry Osmond, who originally coined the term 'psychedelic' amid his own investigations with LSD. Working at the Saskatchewan Provincial Mental Hospital in Weyburn from 1951 to 1961, Osmond first published the term in 1957. The word originally grew out of his medical experiments with LSD (and mescaline, the active constituent in the peyote cactus) and referred to the sensations cultivated under clinical conditions. Osmond created the word to refer to the 'mind-manifesting' effects of the drug; he intentionally avoided a word that sounded overly medicalized. His own experiences with the drug convinced him that LSD created a temporary state of psychosis that matched descriptions from patients with schizophrenia, a chronic disease characterized in part by delusions, hallucinations, and a break from reality. Psychedelic, used in the context of schizophrenia studies was first published in a leading scientific journal, *Annals of the New York Academy of Sciences*.[2]

Osmond introduced his new term at a time that historian John Burnham has referred to as the 'golden age of medicine,' referring to a period of unprecedented medical authority, largely stemming from the development of new medical technologies.[3] New pharmaceutical therapies were among some of the technologies introduced during the 1950s and, as scholar David Healy has described, this decade witnessed an intense period of pharmacological investigation that gave rise to our modern fascination with pharmaceuticals.[4] Prescription drugs entered mainstream society at an unprecedented rate, launching a pill-popping phenomenon that dovetailed with emerging conceptualizations of normalcy; gradually, taking pills became part of normal behaviour, rather than an indication of abnormal behaviour.[5] Medical scientists and medical practitioners rose in esteem as new technological and pharmacological advancements promised to conquer an expanding list of complaints: pain, menstruation, anxiety, depression, hypertensive disorder, alcoholism, and schizophrenia.

Within the context of 1950s medico-scientific investigations, LSD was therefore unremarkable. But the drug quickly attracted interest from people beyond the medical context. For example, Osmond travelled to Los Angeles, California in 1953 and provided author Aldous Huxley with samples of another hallucinogenic drug, mescaline. Huxley published *The Doors of Perception* a year after his mescaline trip, which subsequently attracted popular attention from recreational users, but which medical investigators also lauded for its articulation of an experience that had defied clinical explanations.[6]

The psychedelic reaction, according to its proponents, distinguished LSD from many other contemporary pharmacological substances, such as tranquillizers or sedatives, because of its capacity to provide users with a powerful consciousness-raising experience. The drug did not simply produce a chemical reaction with subjective responses; users described the LSD trip as causing philosophical, epistemological, and ontological changes in perspective. Patients who underwent these experiences during trials in Saskatchewan had complained about the difficulties in finding appropriate language to describe the LSD reaction. The intense and consciousness-raising aspect of the LSD experience encouraged clinicians to distribute the drug more widely in the population to amass a larger collection of reactions.[7]

In search of better ways to measure the LSD reaction, the Saskatchewan-based investigators expanded their project and linked up with a research team in British Columbia to test the drug's capacity to enhance creativity and spirituality, which explicitly moved them outside the boundaries of orthodox medicine.[8] Now working more closely with a group of researchers connected to Hollywood Hospital in New Westminster, British Columbia, the circle of middle-class experimenters widened to include priests, professors, architects, graduate students, psychologists, anthropologists, authors, pilots, and artists, whose reports stimulated the growing curiosity about the consciousness-raising qualities of the drug.[9]

Throughout these experiments (whether official or unofficial), the clinical investigators continued to publish their results in medical journals and sustained research grants, largely from federal and provincial government sources. Access to the drug remained legal in Canada for clinical investigators, who received supplies from the drug's sole manufacturer, Sandoz Pharmaceuticals (headquartered in Switzerland). By the end of the 1950s, however, the experiments entered non-clinical territory, and the expanded set of investigators began exploring different applications for LSD, such as its use in enhancing creativity or inspiring it in the first place. Some experimenters employed a similar approach with spirituality. Reports from patients and non-patients alike suggested that an LSD reaction often caused the user to experience a psychological reaction that many described in spiritual terms, whether the individual hallucinated and confronted God, or found a new appreciation for an orderly design of nature, one which they realized could only exist through the imagination of a higher being. These kinds of observations not only defied rational, clinical evaluation, but also suggested that the drug might actually have the capacity to change or enhance attitudes, beliefs, or even morals. In one report Osmond and his Saskatchewan colleague Abram Hoffer described some of their findings on the question of LSD and its stimulation of spiritual beliefs: 'The LSD experience has been compared to Zen Mysticism...Recently Hoffer gave LSD to a man aged 88. He had an excellent transcendental experience in which his faith in atheism was revivified.'[10]

In the case of LSD use in the 1950s, its consumption by medical scientists, and later by patients, authors, artists, and intellectuals did not raise alarms. Students who volunteered to participate in LSD experiments during this decade did not attract suspicion from state authorities worried that their mind-manifesting experiences would contribute to a breakdown in social order. Many of those drug-consuming individuals also experimented with new ideas, including radical psychological theories of the boundaries between sanity and insanity.[11] Many of their ideas were published in academic journals and in the mainstream media. As a result of their social standing and respected positions as medical and cultural authorities, the psychedelic drug users of the 1950s were arguably in a much better position to influence social changes than the baby boom generation that followed. Yet, the image of white-coated men tripping on the fluid chords of Mozart, entranced by a photograph, or lost in the swirl of colours on a painting has been overshadowed by a similar image replacing Mozart with the Grateful Dead, photographs with concert posters and classical paintings with day-glow art.

In 1961, news of the thalidomide tragedy surfaced, which drew significant attention to the medico-scientific enterprise and the need for stricter standards and regulations for determining the safety of a drug before it reached the market.[12] As Barbara Clow has described, 'more than four million tablets had made their way into Canadian homes and hospitals during eleven months of legitimate sales and at least another million pills had been distributed as samples.' Clow also explains that 'U.S. officials [had] refused to approve the drug for sale because they were dissatisfied with the details of toxicity studies, [while] Canadian regulators apparently felt that the safety of thalidomide had been well established by European experience and the five hundred pages of documentation submitted by the company.'[13] This international event brought significant public attention to the kinds of medical experiments that were taking place and raised alarms about the unanticipated side effects of chemical substances. In Canada, it drew particular attention to the way in which drugs were being approved and regulated, and gave policy makers occasion to reconsider other substances that might require additional regulatory attention. At that time, Canadian officials at the Department of Health singled out LSD as another drug that should join thalidomide on the banned substances list, but medical researchers in the Canadian Psychiatric Association successfully lobbied the federal government to retain research access to the drug, while promising to conduct more careful experiments and to assiduously monitor their supplies.[14]

Timothy Learyism

In 1962, another newcomer to psychedelic studies entered the fray. Harvard psychologist Timothy Leary began studying psilocybin (mushrooms), which he later introduced to his graduate students.[15] Although Leary at first resisted LSD studies, which he felt were too subjective, his name would later become synonymous with the drug, along with his famous catch phrase, 'tune in, turn on, and drop out.'[16] Leary's attitude towards drug experimentation, and indeed personal drug use, was even more cavalier than that of his psychedelic predecessors. Within a year he lost his position at Harvard for conducting 'unscientific' research, but soon afterwards he was catapulted into the media spotlight promoting LSD use.

Through a host of financially lucrative connections and an overwhelming dose of charisma, Leary inherited an estate in upstate New

York, Millbrook, after losing his position at Harvard. From there he continued his drug exploits and entertained a steady stream of America's intellectuals and anyone else who would make the trip, including Ken Kesey and his band of Merry Pranksters. For authorities, Leary represented the epitome of a breakdown of moral order, while for admirers Leary symbolized a higher form of freedom – mind freedom. For his admirers, Leary became a cultural guru.

Although Leary cannot be blamed (or credited) with introducing LSD to North American youth, his social connections and his personal ambitions placed him in an unusual position to operate in society as a moral entrepreneur, or an influential cultural figure.[17] Leary did not belong to the under-thirty generation in the 1960s, but became one of its self-appointed leaders. Capitalizing on the drug's capacity to enhance spirituality, he welcomed the opportunity to fuse non-Christian religious beliefs with his own LSD-inspired renderings of spirituality. He identified himself as a radical nonconformist, while tacitly relying on his former professional position as a Harvard psychologist to bolster his credibility. Osmond, though, was concerned about Leary's claims to spirituality, and wrote to him that if he sought to use LSD for non-medical purposes 'I would, as a good member of my profession *strongly* oppose you.'[18] Osmond remained convinced that ethical, scientific research with psychedelics had real potential for clinical advancements.

Leary's contribution to the history of LSD is somewhat disproportionate, but it undoubtedly enlarged the frame under which psychedelic activities fell. He influenced the characterization of psychedelic drugs, and the associated attitudes, by linking LSD use with nonconformist behaviour, spiritual explorations, and an alternative lifestyle. None of these characteristics were particularly unique to Leary, but his high-profile activities forged a popular association between Learyism and LSD, which served to distort popular conceptions of what it meant to experience something psychedelic.

Leary's public profile also reached Canadians. Coverage of him in the media, often for criminal charges for drug possession (usually marijuana-related), enraged Canadian LSD investigators, who felt that their research would suffer further harm because of Leary's discrediting antics. For example, in February 1967 the *Globe and Mail* reported that the federal government was entertaining the idea of criminalizing LSD altogether, claiming that 'exponents of its use, such as Timothy Leary in the United States, have raised the use of the drug almost to the status of a religious cult.' The article goes on to say: 'In Canada, LSD takers seem to be centred in Toronto, Montreal and Vancouver. The practice apparently has a vogue among university students.'[19]

A year later Leary appeared on the front page of the *National Enquirer* pictured alongside photographs of Regina psychologist Duncan Blewett and Saskatoon psychiatrist Abram Hoffer under a headline exclaiming: 'The Most Important – And Most Dangerous – Drugs of Our Time: The New Psychedelics.' The tabloid newspaper described Leary as 'the messiah of the "psychedelic movement"' and went on to draw on medical authorities such as Blewett and Hoffer to corroborate the healthful effects of this drug in an attempt to mix heightened spiritual awareness and nonconformist views with medically sanctioned uses of the drug.[20]

Around the same time that Leary's name splashed onto the pages of Canadian newspapers, an underground market in LSD attracted media and police attention. Until 1963, the Sandoz Pharmaceutical Company in Switzerland had remained the only legal manufacturer and distributor of LSD, and it only supplied the drug to qualified medical investigators, including people like Osmond and Hoffer. By 1963, however, it became clear to police authorities throughout North America that either the regulations governing distribution were being ignored or that there were illegal manufacturers in operation. Regardless of the source, the outcome was an identifiable rise in the recreational use of the drug, particularly among university students. In British Columbia the Vancouver School Board published a bulletin on the 'Dangers of LSD (Lysergic Acid Diethylamide),' which played upon the growing stereotypes associated with its use. For example, the bulletin explained that 'persons who use LSD are often young. They cannot cope with the overpowering effects of the drug...Case histories show a slipping in achievement in every phase of life. Secrecy that surrounds the use of LSD and all illicit drugs tends to drive young people into groups separated from the rest of society.'[21]

Had authorities pressed the clinical investigators, they might have more readily found a number of illegitimate sources, but instead they focused first on identifying criminal activities on campuses.[22]

Public education campaigns reinforced this connection between drug use (often undifferentiated, meaning that speed, heroin, LSD, marijuana, and even alcohol evoked the generic phrase 'drug abuse') and youth, with pamphlets and posters distributed to high schools and published in varsity newspapers outlining the dangers of drug abuse. Newspaper articles also focused on this agenda, printing front-page stories reminding readers of the dangerous and unpredictable behaviour unleashed by drugs; a surprising number of individuals depicted in these stories ended as fatalities – either suicide or murder.[23]

This kind of publicity further expanded the connotations attached to the word 'psychedelic.' The term now moved from a clinical reaction referring to a mind-manifesting experience, to something associated with a nonconformist attitude (epitomized by Timothy Leary), to a criminal and dangerous activity that could result in death. By the end of the 1960s, LSD fit into a cascading list of narcotic substances that supposedly led to a criminal and immoral lifestyle. While authorities debated over which particular drug functioned as the gateway substance, usually focusing on marijuana, many assumed that soft drug use could lead to experimentation with harder drugs, including LSD, amphetamines (speed), and heroin. No longer concerned simply with changes in attitudes, the escalation of drug use associated with this theory meant that recreational drug users would embark on a path that would inevitably lead to crime, addiction, and violence.

Although Canada did not produce a Leary-like figure, or a comparable individual embodiment of this bridge between the medical establishment and the youth counterculture, a number of individuals played formative roles in the escalation of debates over LSD use in Canada in the 1960s. Many of these individuals, like Leary, first encountered LSD in a clinical context. For some, including psychologist Duncan Blewett, the increasing reports of recreational LSD use on campuses did not raise alarms. Rather, Blewett quietly supported this activity believing that, taken responsibly, LSD might indeed heighten intellectual pursuits and should therefore be encouraged at Canadian universities.

Leary and Blewett shared a reputation for charisma, charm, and an infectious curiosity for probing the psychological depths of the psychedelic experience. In a handbook describing the therapeutic uses of LSD,[24] Blewett and colleague Nick Chwelos in Regina boldly claimed that 'the psychedelics are the strongest tools ever dreamed of for man's betterment. They can make humanitarians out of fanatics, friends out of enemies, effective people out of neurotics.'[25] Although Blewett's actions sometimes bordered on the margins of professionalism, he belonged to a larger community of psychedelic researchers in Canada, which in part shielded him from individual attention, and also stimulated him to continue his slightly more academic investigations.

Rather than cultivate a psychedelic revolution among Canadian youth, Canada's psychedelic experts seemed caught between the medical establishment and the youth counterculture. Most of the Canadian experiments were arranged through the clinical investigations.[26] The university students who first encountered LSD did so through these clinical studies. The investigators themselves were often sympathetic to the claims of new insights into creativity, philosophy, religion, and governance that the student drug takers used to defend their recreational use of the drug. The potential for radical ideation did not alarm the original investigators, but concerns about political consequences for their own research did. Leary did not face this problem; with no future prospects of resuming clinical studies, Leary was not caught between these two perspectives.

The Psychedelic Sixties

By the mid-1960s psychedelics had become part of an even different vocabulary, one associated with student rebellions, counterculture activities, jazz and folk music, bohemian fashions, and urban destinations like Haight-Ashbury in San Francisco, Yorkville in Toronto, or Gastown in Vancouver.[27] Musicians, poets, writers, and artists glamourized psychedelic drugs by publicly admitting to their use and flirting with the law by embroidering drugs in their cultural products. Bands famously popularized the language of the drug culture, such as Jefferson Airplane in their 1960s hit 'White Rabbit,' which exposed an intimate appreciation for pills, mushrooms, hookah pipes, and 'chasing rabbits' crescendoing in a chorus encouraging listeners to 'feed your head.' When *Rolling Stone* magazine asked former Beatle John Lennon about LSD, he admitted that 'he used to eat it all the time.' He went on to explain that he 'got a message on acid that you should destroy your ego, and I did, you know. I was reading that stupid book of Leary's and all that shit.'[28]

Drug use, especially that of illicit substances, had deep roots within the artistic community, but its presence had largely remained private until this point. Although access to LSD remained legal for qualified medical scientists, state, provincial, and federal laws across North America strictly prohibited its use outside that context. Consequences ranged from fines to jail terms, and by the mid-1960s government authorities also looked to ban the substance from the medical arena. Popular artists had, unsurprisingly, a significant influence on the consumption of cultural products and ideas, which in this case included a growing tolerance for the notion that you could achieve mind expansion through drug use. Political or social opposition to drugs was held up by such popular figures as further evidence of the entrenched conservatism of the older generation. These messages linked sobriety with conservatism and drug use with liberalism, thus creating a false generational dichotomy that was increasingly politicized along these lines.

In this context 'psychedelic' often referred to an attitude, rather than a particular reaction to a specific drug. It no longer mattered whether individuals actually consumed drugs, or which ones; the word itself gradually acquired a new cultural meaning. In the 1967 cult classic, *The Electric Kool-Aid Acid Test,* American author Tom Wolfe articulated the expanded conceptualization of the term: 'thousands of kids were moving into San Francisco for a life based on LSD and the psychedelic thing. *Thing* was the major abstract word in Haight-Ashbury. It could mean *any*thing, isms, life styles, habits, leanings, causes, sexual organs.'[29] Wolfe's popular pseudo-journalistic accounts of life in the Haight, or the adventures of Ken Kesey,[30] offered readers an insider's view of the heartland of the American hippie scene; an alluring bohemian lifestyle, which according to Wolfe, was intimately entwined with drug use.[31]

But drug use among this community did not inspire fears of abuse, addiction, or violence, as it did in the contemporary newspaper reports. Instead, as the musical tributes to the drug culture suggest, here drugs cultivated new avenues of thinking or provided users with an opportunity to demonstrate their disregard for the law. They regarded the criminalization of drug use as an abuse of state power or as a legal encroachment on individual (and psychological) freedoms. Psychedelics were fused with anti-authority attitudes in the public imagination. From the perspective of the lawmakers the impression that a sizeable portion of the population refused to comply with the rules suggested that stricter measures needed to be put in place to avoid civil chaos. Furthermore, by refocusing attention away from youth, in general, and onto drug use, in particular, authorities might be able to divide this potentially explosive community, whose strength appeared to emanate from its force as a collective.

In Canada, the threat posed by hippies raised concerns from the Royal Canadian Mounted Police (RCMP). Marcel Martel has argued that RCMP officers used the alleged connection between drug use and political radicalism to target hippies as criminals. He states that in the 1960s 'the RCMP targeted a specific group among drug users: the hippies. Hippies constituted a threat because they challenged morality and established social values with their ideology, lifestyle, and values.'[32]

The subsequent criminalization of LSD symbolized the state's disapproval of the activities of the hippies. The focus on drugs as one of the primary illegal or immoral elements in the hippie attitude provided lawmakers with an opportunity to reinsert authority in a traditional arena, and in a manner that generated public support for anti-drug legislation and also created internal divisions within the more broadly defined counterculture. As long as psychedelic attitudes simply referred to an open attitude, liberal beliefs, tolerance, and a general desire to question authority or critique the status quo, the psychedelic age appealed to a wide range of individuals, from activists to scientists as well as heads and seekers. This meant that terms such as 'hippies,' 'counterculture,' and 'student radicals' could all be collapsed under a psychedelic umbrella. However, as governments imposed new laws criminalizing the sale and consumption of LSD, splinters appeared along the lines of users and non-users, and legal versus illegal users. The change in the legal status of LSD realigned the term 'psychedelic' with a particular psychoactive substance, rather than a loose coalition of ideas and attitudes.

For the psychedelic community, however, drugs were part reality and part metaphor. For many users, the new laws represented a fundamental misunderstanding of the drug culture; many felt that recreational drug use, particularly of marijuana and LSD, was no more harmful than the social consumption of legally regulated alcohol.[33]

Others consumed products of the psychedelic era without necessarily endorsing drug use. Commercial products of the decade represented links with the drug culture and blurred the division between actual and associate members of a psychedelic community. New genres of psychedelic music, or psychedelic art, especially in the form of concert posters, commoditized a psychedelic mood that mixed drug use with artistic expression. Consumers of these items did not need to actually engage in drug use to display their affiliation with that culture. Toronto had become one of the favoured Canadian hippie destinations; Yorkville, as Stuart Henderson explains, had by the late 1960s become the epicentre of countercultural activity in Canada and home to a collection of hippies, greasers, bikers, students, and artists.[34] An educational experiment fed the Canadian hippie project with students and new counterculture recruits from the nearby high rise of Rochdale College. Rochdale, in some ways, seemed to be Toronto's response to Montreal's Sir George Williams University, or Simon Fraser University in British Columbia, institutions whose occupants – both students and faculty – engaged in new forms of governance and education that they felt better suited the mood of the sixties. Rochdale, however, also attracted media attention as a drug haven. Its popular journalists cum historians Mietkiewicz and Mackowycz claimed that 'the drugs were acid, some speed, some peyote and mescaline, and always alcohol and marijuana. I don't recall ever running into heroin or cocaine. It was mainly hallucinogenics, marijuana and alcohol.'[35]

The idea that 'psychedelic' was increasingly meant to describe a broader set of activities frustrated clinical investigators. Users generically applied the term 'acid' to substances based on the mode of consumption and/or the anticipated and real effects, namely, the presence of hallucinations. Scientists felt that the word had been co-opted by curious thrill-seeking youths, who did not or could not appreciate the seriousness of psychedelic explorations if they merely consumed the drug as a recreational form of escapism. While researchers had not encountered issues of addiction or flashbacks in the course of their clinical studies with LSD in the 1950s, the widespread consumption of hallucinogenic substances of unknown doses and origins created new challenges for them. Users themselves were often ignorant about the drugs they had consumed. The popular tolerance towards drug use within certain communities also gave rise to poly-drug use, where consumers potentially mixed alcohol, acid, marijuana, amphetamines (speed), heroin, and other substances, producing a reaction that stymied authorities in their ability to sort out the constituents of a drug cocktail.[36]

The escalating problems associated with drugs, in general, including overdoses, addictions, crime, and prostitution, gradually eroded the temporarily more positive image of a colourful, playful, and even politically empowering association with psychedelics. Serious health problems arose and presented new challenges for addictions specialists and health professionals. Overdoses, suicides, and violent behaviour captured front-page attention, reinforcing the idea that drug users were dangerous and that drugs themselves were toxic.[37] The medical profession and addictions specialists also tended to see the more severe cases, because casual users were less likely to end up in emergency rooms, which further distorted the conceptualization of the scale of associated harms. Most medical researchers abandoned their legal studies of LSD during the mid-1960s, and by 1968 the American and Canadian governments closed that window definitively by placing LSD under the Narcotic Control Act, making it illegal for any use.[38]

Although medical studies had never concluded that LSD was addictive, seekers continued to obtain illegal supplies of the drug. The illegal traffic in LSD exposed additional complications and pushed the black-market manufacture, distribution, and consumption of LSD (and other drugs) deeper underground. While estimated rates of LSD use continued to rise into the 1970s, users were more often defined as belonging to a drug community than a generational collective, and as such they were identified as generic drug users rather than as a countercultural social force or as political radicals.

By the end of the decade, tolerance towards drug use within the generational cohort dissipated and was replaced by more aggressive internal policing that treasured sobriety among its members. By the 1970s, pop icons existed on both sides of the drug equation. Elvis Presley in the United States, for example, ceremoniously joined Richard Nixon's 'war on drugs' by becoming a federal agent.[39] Meanwhile, so-called psychedelic guru Timothy Leary sat in the Orange County Jail in California on charges of drug possession.[40] In Canada, acid-rock enthusiasts tried to reconnect LSD with a more romantic image of free love and groovy tunes in a music festival set to commence in Toronto and tour by train to Vancouver in the summer of 1970. Although there were no Canadian headlining acts, the Toronto-based organizers identified well-known American artists, such as the Grateful Dead, the Band, and Janis Joplin, and added Canadian content with the likes of Sylvia and Ian Tyson to round out the tour.[41] The tour ended in disaster, plagued with financial difficulties, anti-hippie protests, police surveillance, and for Joplin, the end of her career; she died that October. The newspaper coverage of the event also highlighted the kinds of splinters that had deepened within the so-called psychedelic culture, capitalizing on the nature of the anti-hippie protests that had developed out of leftist groups, which used to be lumped together in a generational mix.[42]

Although it is too simplistic to argue that by 1970 the sixties were over, in the case of LSD and its psychedelic offshoots, the party had ended. Legally, LSD had lost its unique status as a consciousness-raising drug and, instead, joined the ranks of other narcotics, as an illegal and abusive substance, albeit one that produced a distinctive high. Drug overdoses claimed the lives of popular icons who had previously embraced psychedelics, which further contributed to the publicity of the fatal consequences of illicit drug use, psychedelic or otherwise. After Joplin's fatal drug overdose in 1970, Jim Morrison, whose band name 'The Doors,' was allegedly borrowed from Aldous Huxley's mescaline-inspired novel *Doors of Perception,* overdosed in Paris in 1971. These kinds of high-profile drug-related deaths signalled another decisive shift in the conceptualization of psychedelics to a term that reunited drugs with images of psychosis, insanity, and now death.

Conclusion

As part of a larger trend towards the disaggregation of what had once been considered a more homogeneous collective, the baby boomers, hippies, or counterculture members passed through the psychedelic age in a characteristically dramatic fashion. Over a short period, the word 'psychedelic' had come to hold a variety of different meanings, which were embraced or resisted by various factions in an attempt to signal a cultural disposition towards moral authority. However, that disposition differed significantly as the term moved from one community to another. Among the scientists, 'psychedelic' offered a vocabulary that aided in the mobilization of a critique of medical language, clinical trials, and a pharmacological tradition that downplayed subjectivity in medicine. Within a few years, the drugs appealed to other intellectuals who used them as tools for exploring spirituality and creativity in ways that presented alternative interpretations of orthodox religious authority and medical understandings of the boundaries between sanity and insanity. This move placed psychedelic studies on the margins of professional medicine, but continued to advance the idea that psychedelic substances themselves cultivated a desire to challenge fixed ideas.

The hippies retained this feature of the psychedelic ethic, but also pushed it in new directions. As the term evolved and absorbed ideological trappings of liberalism and collective action, it became disconnected from drug use itself and applied more broadly to a group of people and of drugs, defined variously and conveniently through concepts of youth, hippies, counterculture, student radicals, and simply, radicals. The disjointed application of the term, in combination with a glamourization of drug use, in general, led to the degradation of the psychedelic age, the fracturing of the psychedelic community, and the stagnation of psychedelic medicine.

FURTHER READING

Dyck, Erika. *Psychedelic Psychiatry: LSD from Clinic to Campus.*
   Baltimore: Johns Hopkins University Press, 2008.
Henderson, Stuart. *Making the Scene: Yorkville and Hip Toronto in the Sixties.* Toronto: University of Toronto Press, 2011.
Herzberg, David. *Happy Pills in America: From Miltown to Prozac.*
   Baltimore: Johns Hopkins University Press, 2008.
Hoffer, Abram. *Adventures in Psychiatry: The Scientific Memoirs of Dr Abram Hoffer.* Caledon: KOS Publishing, 2005.
Martel, Marcel. *Not This Time: Canadians, Public Policy, and the Marijuana Question, 1961–1975.* Toronto: University of Toronto Press, 2006.

PART TWO

Higher Education

Special Issue

The C.A.U.T. *Bulletin*

A Publication

Of The

CANADIAN ASSOCIATION

OF

UNIVERSITY TEACHERS

Report on the Crowe Case

VOLUME 7 NUMBER 3
JANUARY 1959

The Crowe case occurred at United College (now the University of Winnipeg) in September 1958. It helped to establish CAUT's work on academic freedom in Canadian universities.

Permission of Canadian Association of University Teachers.

3

The Canadian Association of University Teachers and the Rise of Faculty Power, 1951–1970

Catherine Gidney

In the years after the Second World War Canadian universities underwent a significant transformation. A growing belief in the importance of universities to the economic and cultural success of Canadian society resulted in the initiation of massive provincial and federal grants. Canadian universities expanded in number and size: from twenty-eight in 1945 to forty-seven by 1970, with enrolment rising from 64,731 to over 300,000 during the same period. And they expanded in scope, offering a broader range of programs and becoming increasingly focused on research.[1]

These changes would have a significant impact on how faculty members experienced the university as a workplace and upon their expectations about their role within these institutions. In the university of the 1940s and 1950s, power radiated downward from within a hierarchically structured institution. The board of governors functioned as the supreme governing body and the chairman of such a board wielded enormous power. Not surprisingly, then, individual faculty members had little direct role in the governance of their institutions. They usually played no part in the selection of a president and often had little control over the appointment of other administrators such as deans or department heads. They could not negotiate salaries or workplace conditions. Moreover, many universities had no formal policies regarding procedures for hiring or firing faculty members, on tenure (appointment without a term limitation), or on academic freedom (the right to intellectual work free from interference).

Beginning in the late 1960s, and continuing through the next several decades, faculty members gradually gained greater access to governing structures at all university levels. Today, departments are fully involved in hiring their own members. Faculty either receive set travel and research grants or these are approved by faculty-led committees. In general, universities assure academic freedom, and faculty associations maintain a keen eye on its enforcement. Moreover, faculty-administration relations are now shaped by an ongoing process of collective bargaining. These elements of university governance now seem basic to the very nature of most Canadian universities. Yet, throughout the 1950s and 1960s, many faculty members worked hard, institution by institution, to gain basic control over the governance of their workplaces. The creation, in 1951, of a national organization, the Canadian Association of University Teachers (CAUT), was central to this long-term process.

In this chapter, I examine the activities of CAUT, through its *Bulletin,* in the first two decades of the organization's existence. The general characterization of CAUT's origins in the current literature is of a cautious, moderate organization whose founders were motivated by a desire to reverse 'a general decline in the economic and social status of the academic profession.'[2] In 1958, CAUT became involved in the Crowe case – the first major case in Canada in which the profession made efforts to protect the academic freedom of individual professors. That case, it is argued, was pivotal in the evolution of CAUT.[3]

The general picture of CAUT's origins is certainly not wrong. Yet, there is also another story to be told. The 1950s and 1960s marked what political scientist David Cameron has termed 'a virtual revolution...in the internal structures and operations' of Canadian universities.[4] Here I argue that despite CAUT's seemingly cautious nature, its early attention to workplace issues gradually helped produce a demand for the fundamental reshaping of the role of faculty within the university. In making this argument, I root the transformation in the role of faculty members within the university not in the late 1960s and its aftermath but rather in the spirit of change already underway in the early to mid-1950s. In doing so, I raise questions about our historical understanding of the 1950s and 1960s and the role of the professoriate in the emerging radicalism of the 1960s. Although Canadian historians are beginning to focus attention on the postwar period, work in the history of higher education for this period remains limited. The 1950s have at times been characterized as a period of quietude, in particular, in contrast to a more radical sixties.[5] This is a characterization that is indirectly reinforced by studies that, for good reason, focus on the mid- to late 1960s, but which, as a result, do not provide a longer view of campus activity. The result is that the 1960s are often understood as a period on its own and campus activism a phenomenon of that period.

Some of the rethinking about the relationship between the 1950s and 1960s has been underway for some time. In the past several decades, historians in the United States have begun to challenge the view of the 1960s as rupture, focusing instead on the ideological developments and political events of the 1940s and 1950s which helped lay the groundwork for the radicalism of the 1960s.[6] Similarly, historians of Quebec have traced the origins of the Quiet Revolution (see Igartua, in this collection) back to the 1930s or even earlier. Drawing on this literature, historians of student culture have rejected the characterization of the 1950s as a period of *grande noirceur* (great darkness) in contrast to the Quiet Revolution of the 1960s. For students in Quebec, they suggest, the 1950s marked a period of transition, with student leaders committed to social and university reform.[7] This examination of CAUT activities fits within this broader literature: I argue for the need to see a more fluid relationship between the two decades and to begin to place the activism of the 1960s within a broader framework, as the outgrowth of a longer period of demand for change.

The Creation of CAUT

The Canadian Association of University Teachers was founded in 1951, at a point of transition within Canadian universities. Postwar prosperity had already begun to translate into a campus building boom. Faculty salaries, however, remained low. Indeed, because of inflation, they were lower in 1950 in real terms than at any point in the century other than 1914–18. Faculty salaries also remained significantly lower than those in other professions. Concern about low salaries reflected not only faculty's economic grievances but also a more general sense of being considered an undervalued component of Canadian society.[8]

CAUT's first goal after its creation was to mobilize support for the organization. F.S. Howes, the president of CAUT in the early 1950s, saw the organization as a 'National Body' that could 'provide a valuable service to local units, not only as an information centre and liaison...but also in representing the University Teaching Profession as a whole on national issues.'[9] In 1953, he established a newsletter, the *Bulletin,* to help facilitate 'professional consciousness.'[10]

Through the 1950s, Howes and a committee of committed individuals at his home institution McGill University produced, collected, or edited most of the material for the *Bulletin.*[11] It was distributed to the CAUT membership, which by 1958 included 78 per cent of Canadian university teachers and twenty-six affiliated faculty associations.[12] The newsletter became the central means by which CAUT publicized the information it collected, and it served as a forum for discussion.

Workplace Conditions

In the early 1950s, CAUT leaders initiated studies on salaries, tenure, sabbatical leave, income tax exemptions, retirement plans, and hospitalization and health insurance schemes. In the process they uncovered disparities in working conditions across the country.[13] The CAUT executive established a national salary scale, which it believed all Canadian universities ought to embrace, and in 1956 it presented a brief to the Royal Commission on Canada's Economic Prospects (the Gordon Commission), demanding greater federal funding for universities. A decade later, it wrote a major brief in response to the report of the Bladen Commission on University Funding. It also lobbied provincial and federal governments for greater funding for higher education.[14]

As early as 1954, CAUT demanded 'greater faculty participation in the running of Canada's universities.'[15] As mentioned earlier, the governance of these institutions operated – at least in the ideal case – as a form of benevolent paternalism. Within many Canadian universities power was divided between an academic body, the senate, responsible for academic affairs, and a lay body – a board of governors, trustees, or regents – in charge of finances. At others, power flowed more directly from a single governing board.[16] In general, the board of governors appointed the president or principal, who held office without a fixed term and at the pleasure of the board. In 1955, Donald Rowat, a member of the School of Public Administration at Carleton College, undertook a survey of faculty involvement in university governance. He found that decision-making bodies were composed 'primarily of administrators and academic officials appointed and controlled by the president and governing board.'[17] Faculty usually had no representation on governing boards. A few institutions allowed faculty members

to sit in the senate, but it had limited power. Responsible for the academic program of the university, the senate played no role in deciding
the financial direction of the university. As a result, faculty had little
real power to develop new program offerings or create new departments or faculties. Moreover, while some universities had established
practices for consulting the faculty about the appointment of deans and
department heads, the practice was not universal.[18] Vice-presidents,
deans, and department heads often 'held office for an indefinite period
at the president's pleasure.'[19] In general, faculty members had little
say in the selection of the highest administrative office, the president,
who was chosen by, and responsible to, the governing board.[20]

Faculty members also played little role in hirings, firings, or setting
the conditions of the workplace. With the advice of department heads
and deans, presidents usually appointed faculty, set their salaries, and,
in conjunction with the board of governors, had the right, although
it was rarely executed, to dismiss them.[21] Faculty had little ability to
negotiate different terms. At many institutions, demands for increased
salaries could only be presented to governing boards as a brief, and
without expectation of a reply.[22] The case of the University of Toronto
is illustrative. At their annual meeting in November 1950, faculty
members passed a resolution calling for an increase in salary to reflect
the high cost of living. A committee, chaired by prominent scientist
Tuzo Wilson, requested a meeting with President Sidney Smith. In an
experimental move, Smith arranged for a meeting with leading members of the board of governors. Impressed by the case put forward by
Wilson and his colleagues, the board of governors approved significant increases in the salary scale. In his history of the University of
Toronto faculty association, William Nelson argues that in subsequent
years, when faculty made their pleas for increased salaries, Smith
often evaded their requests that he support the faculty position during
his meetings with the board. Moreover, Smith never again convened a
meeting between faculty and members of the board. Nelson notes that
salaries did increase through the 1950s but that by 1958 full professors
had just barely regained the purchasing power of their 1939 salaries.[23]

Faculty members, then, had limited influence over the economic
dimension of university governance. This is not to say that they had
no power within their own institutions. At some universities, for
example, faculty sat on department committees that recommended
promotions or general committees recommending travel grants.
President W.P. Thompson of the University of Saskatchewan argued

that faculty relations committees (forerunners of faculty associations) could also provide some relief to faculty concerns. He noted that at the University of Saskatchewan, where one was created in 1945, the chairman of the faculty association had access to committees making decisions on such things as travel grants or promotions in order to ensure fair treatment of faculty across departments.[24] Moreover, individual faculty members often had significant influence, especially in smaller institutions where personal relationships continued to exist between administrators and staff. In order to run their institutions effectively presidents and deans sought the advice of faculty.[25]

While CAUT executive members recognized this type of indirect influence they also found it problematic. They noted, for example, that while a number of 'internal bodies regulate and control many academic matters,' these bodies generally consisted 'of administrative and academic officials appointed by the president and the governing board' rather than by elected faculty.[26] They also worried about the role of the existing faculty relations committees. In addition to faculty members, such committees often included presidents and other administrators. As one 1956 article in the *Bulletin* stated, 'how the conditions of employment can be candidly discussed in meetings of the latter groups is a matter of some perplexity to members of the former!'[27]

CAUT's leaders, therefore, demanded a greater share of control over the workplace. A 1957 editorial in the *Bulletin* argued that 'academic staff should have control of admission of students, curricula, appointment and tenure, [and] allocation of income.'[28] Eight years later, H.B. Mayo, a political scientist at the University of Alberta, also condemned the existing system. Mayo argued that at provincial universities boards of governors were neither directly accountable to the government for their funding nor to the faculty who 'may have no more share in governing a university than if the "colonial" or corporation models were followed.'[29]

Tenure and Academic Freedom

Faculty members' lack of role in university governance and inability to influence their workplace conditions extended, not surprisingly, to the issue of tenure and academic freedom. While most Canadian universities recognized the principle of tenure, only three had written policies on the issue. Moreover, few universities had formal regulations regarding termination of a permanent position. Where such

policies did exist faculty had not been consulted regarding regulations on tenure, dismissal, or other matters of conduct.[30] Historians
agree that CAUT was slow to establish principles regarding academic
freedom. The issue came to a head in 1958. In that year the board of
regents of United College, Winnipeg, fired Henry Crowe, a professor
of history, after the president of the college intercepted a letter from
Crowe to a colleague which impugned the character of the president
and condemned Christianity as 'a "corrosive force."'[31] CAUT set up
an enquiry in 1958, which found that Crowe had indeed been dismissed unjustly.[32] Shortly after hearing from its own ad hoc committee on academic freedom and tenure in June 1959, CAUT established
a permanent committee on academic freedom and tenure to deal with
future cases. By 1962, fourteen tenure cases had appeared before
CAUT's national office. Most of the cases emerged from institutions
that did not have any established tenure agreements, and the executive secretary of CAUT was able to help settle most of these through
informal intervention.[33]

In its support of academic freedom, CAUT played a role in fur-
thering the secularizing trend already underway within Canadian
universities.[34] The tensions between professors' right to academic
freedom and the denominational priorities of church-sponsored
institutions can be seen in the Crowe case. The immediate cause of
Principal Lockhart's move to dismiss Crowe arose in part from the
latter's attack on the religious purpose of the college.[35] The conflict
between academic freedom and denominational aims arose again in
1965, at Acadia University, when the United Baptist Convention of
the Atlantic Provinces resolved that future faculty members at Acadia
be required to be Christians. In that case, the Associated Alumni of
Acadia University brought their weight to bear against the convention
resolution and ultimately, in February 1966, the province removed
Acadia from convention control. Prior to that act the CAUT executive
publicized a resolution condemning the actions of the convention as a
'violation of the intellectual integrity and academic freedom essential
to the well-being of the university community and to the common
good.'[36] Through the resolution, CAUT leaders emphasized their support for secular priorities – part of a broader transformation occurring
within Canadian universities.

CAUT leaders' concern about academic freedom reinforced their
belief about the need for faculty to gain a greater role in university
governance. Indeed, it ignited further activities in this area. A 1960

editorial in the *Bulletin* stated: 'questions of academic freedom and tenure...bring up, in its most fundamental form, the question of whether university professors are merely hired hands or are the members of an academic community with rights and obligations which are settled in an atmosphere of law.'[37] As we have seen, this was a concern that predated the Crowe case. For example, the Rowat Report on university governance had already gained faculty attention. Yet, as David Cameron notes, the Crowe affair 'added impetus to a campaign already gaining ground among Canadian educators.'[38]

As a result, in subsequent years numerous debates on the issue of governance appeared in the *Bulletin*. These led to the publication in 1964 of a collection of articles by prominent academics and members of CAUT which collectively urged the reform of university governance.[39] At the same time, in the early 1960s, J. Percy Smith, executive secretary of CAUT, had been seeking funding for a large-scale study on the issue. After receiving a large grant from the American Ford Foundation in 1963, CAUT and the National Conference of Canadian Universities and Colleges (NCCUC) co-sponsored a commission on university governance. The subsequent report, popularly referred to as the Duff-Berdahl Report, called for sweeping changes in the governance of Canadian universities.[40]

Transformations in Faculty Power

In the 1950s and 1960s CAUT leaders worked to expand the role of faculty within their institutions and to legitimize the right of faculty to speak without repercussions on issues affecting the university and society. Thanks in part to the efforts of the Canadian Association of University Teachers, in the late 1960s, and even more so in the 1970s, faculty began to play a greater role within their universities' governance structures. David Cameron notes that whereas in 1955 only three of thirty-five boards of governors had faculty representation, in 1965 'on the eve of the Duff-Berhahl Report, the number of boards containing faculty members had increased to 18, out of a total of 56. Over the next five years this increased to 43 out of 59 and by 1975 stood at 58 out of 63.'[41] No university had open senate or board meetings in 1967. By 1969, eleven had opened their senate meetings. Two years later, of sixty-four universities, more than half had open senate meetings while ten had open meetings of their boards of governors. In addition, power within universities had become much more decentralized and democratized, with more decisions occurring at the department level, through faculty committees, and with administrative appointments made at least in consultation with faculty if not through faculty election. In contrast to the earlier period, by 1970 at least half of Canadian universities had adopted the CAUT policy of tenure granted after a set probationary period, and significantly more universities had instituted formal rules for dismissal.[42]

Still, the change in governance was often uneven. While faculty members gained power on boards of governors, they usually formed a minority that could be outvoted. Similarly, although senates became more representative, they continued to contain many non-faculty members.[43] At some institutions restructuring may have reduced faculty power. At the University of Toronto, for example, university governance was restructured in 1971 from a bicameral system where power was divided between a senate and a board of governors to a unicameral system that integrated the two bodies. According to one critic, 'the academic staff seem to have exchanged their virtual control of the academic program for 12 seats on a 50-man council.'[44] At other places, progress was often slow. The University of Saskatchewan did not have any faculty on its board of governors until 1974, when one faculty member was added to a twelve-person board. Dalhousie University's charter prohibited faculty representation on its board of governors until 1988.[45] Indeed, even in the first decades of the twenty-first century, boards of governors of some institutions continue to have closed meetings, sometimes refusing to disclose the time and location of their meetings. These boards have even required elected faculty representatives to sign non-disclosure statements.[46]

In general, however, faculty's role in university governance changed significantly. This development occurred within the context of a broader transformation of the university. Many newly created faculty associations appeared on campus, reinforcing CAUT's aims. In 1950, only a handful of faculty associations existed in Canada. By 1968, at least forty-four such organizations had emerged.[47] Provincial faculty associations also developed. For example, in 1963 faculty created the Ontario Confederation of University Faculty Associations, consisting of one member of each university association along with the executive secretary of CAUT. It lobbied for better salaries, increased resources, and for government recognition of the importance of university autonomy and academic freedom.[48] At the same time, many Catholic universities, both French and English, underwent a process of deconfessionalization, resulting not only in greater lay control but new governance structures which gave greater voice to faculty.[49]

Some university presidents also supported the aims of CAUT. Frank Abbott notes that F. Cyril James, principal and vice-chancellor at McGill University, and Sidney Smith, president of the University of Toronto, both vocally lamented faculty working conditions such as low salaries, large classes, and lack of leaves. At the University of British Columbia, Norman MacKenzie believed that for faculty to do their best work they needed some security. He supported increased salaries, sufficient pension plans, and the implementation of sickness and disability insurance. W.P. Thompson, president of the University of Saskatchewan, supported the creation of faculty associations and believed that faculty should be represented on the committee recommending a presidential appointment.[50] Presidents, of course, did not support all of CAUT's aims. For example, MacKenzie, who did not see the aims of administrators and teaching staff to be at odds, believed that as president, he was best suited to present faculty concerns to the board of governors. Nor did he believe in the automatic right to travel grants or sabbatical leaves.[51] For his part, Thompson believed that faculty already had representation, arguing that when a business matter appears before the board of governors which has 'academic implications, the views of the faculty or of an appropriate section of it are secured either directly or through the senate.'[52] Although not in agreement on some basic issues, presidents' support for even limited improvements in workplace conditions and faculty representation on university committees gave weight to CAUT's demands.

The demands of the Canadian Association of University Teachers for better conditions also fit within administrators' broader agenda to secure more funding for their institutions and to secure for universities a more central place within Canadian society. In the 1940s and 1950s, educators endorsed the right of all Canadians to higher education and emphasized the importance of institutions of higher education to the well-being of the nation. In the context of the Cold War and the technological advances of the Soviet Union, university presidents helped create the image of the university as a site of salvation for Western civilization. They considered the liberal arts, in particular, as key to the moral and cultural development of the nation. At the same time, the business community and government officials worried about the shortage of workers with the professional and technical skills needed to fill positions in the growing white-collar sector. Government commissions recognized the importance of increasing funding to universities. In light of the impending teacher shortage and the difficulty of recruiting and retaining faculty, the Gordon Commission explicitly recognized the need to increase faculty salaries. As a result, through the 1950s and 1960s the federal government began to significantly increase funding to universities.[53]

By the mid to late-1960s, students would also come to play a significant role in the transformation of the university. As Roberta Lexier's and Marcel Martel's chapters in this collection illustrate, the student movement, and accompanying counterculture, dramatically changed the political and social culture of campus life. Students held teach-ins and sit-ins on issues ranging from the Vietnam War to the state of the environment. They organized psychedelic festivals exploring the cultural impact of the emerging drug scene and produced and distributed material on birth control. They also questioned existing university governance. Students protested their lack of representation on everything from department committees to governing boards, challenging the undemocratic structure of university governance and arguing for students' right to play a meaningful role in the nature of their education and the running of their institutions.[54]

Historians have too often overlooked the role of faculty, and even administrators, in raising and even initiating issues that became central to the student movement.[55] Still, many faculty who helped initiate a process of university reform balked at the prospect of sharing power with students. In 1967, the president of CAUT worried that 'it appears that the students by taking the initiative may profit most from Duff-Berdahl.'[56] Indeed, in some cases this appeared to be true. When the new governing council was formed at University of Toronto in 1972, student representation fell just four members short of parity with faculty. Despite their disappointment with this shortfall, students had made enormous strides, particularly in comparison with faculty.[57]

Conclusion

The Canadian Association of University Teachers was not the only group attempting to reshape the modern university in the 1950s and early 1960s. It did, however, play a significant role. Historians have tended to characterize CAUT, in its origins, as primarily interested in 'bread-and-butter issues' such as salaries and pensions.[58] Yet, I would argue that the aim of improving their institutional and social position was part of a broader goal of achieving control over workplace conditions. CAUT's demands were certainly gradual and tentative. In 1956, for instance, after receiving a brief on the state of the teaching profession, Walter Gordon, chairman of the Royal Commission on Economic Prosperity, chastised faculty for setting their sights too low and encouraged them to begin aggressive action.[59] Indeed, in establishing their national minimum salary scale, faculty rates failed to keep pace with inflation.[60]

Still, if members of CAUT were cautious, even tentative in their purposes, the end result of their activity helped transform the Canadian university. The days of professors petitioning (sometimes) benevolent presidents and their governors disappeared. Individual professors gained more freedom within their departments as did departments from their deans. Regulations became increasingly codified. CAUT leaders supported, and helped ignite, faculty demands for a greater role within their institutions.

CAUT's early efforts to change the nature of the role of professors on campus points to the need for a continued reconceptualization of the relationship between the 1950s and the 1960s. David Cameron notes that in 1967 Sir James Duff, in a conference paper on the Duff-Berdahl Report, commented on the rapidity with which the recommendations had been taken up. Duff attributed this phenomenon to the fact that 'the report reflected views that were already taking shape in most Canadian universities.'[61] Reflecting on the events of the 1960s more generally, historian Arthur Marwick has argued that the activities of the decade became a revolution not because of a radical minority but because of the support of a significant majority.[62] Within the pages of the *Bulletin,* support for change in the university and beyond marks an early expression of what would become a larger social movement. Within the field of postsecondary education, this would result in the transformation of the university.

In 1966, Percy Smith, executive secretary of CAUT, argued that CAUT's growth and 'discovery of its deeper purpose' was 'nothing less than the working of a revolution in Canadian university life.' That revolution, he wrote, involved 'the demand, insistent but never irresponsible, that the idea of the community should displace the idea of the corporation in the organization of our universities,' that faculty should hold a place at the centre of university education and governance.[63] By the 1970s, much had changed in the structure of Canadian universities. Faculty and students had gained direct representation on many academic and governing bodies. Administrators, faculty, and their unions, had begun to codify rules and procedures governing hiring, firing, and academic freedom. Faculty associations had grown in number and, despite early calls for the creation of a professional association rather than a trade union, many would begin turning to collective bargaining as a means to secure rights. All of this was a significant shift from the university of the 1950s. It marked the turn towards a more democratic university where faculty would play a greater role in shaping their institutions and would have direct control over departmental affairs. Moreover, faculty gained increased independence from the priorities set out by administrators and greater control over their own workplace conditions. Although the transformation of university governance and of faculty-administration relations did not begin to occur until the late 1960s, much of the groundwork for such change was laid by the Canadian Association of University Teachers and individual professors in the 1950s and early 1960s.

FURTHER READING

Axelrod, Paul. *Scholars and Dollars: Politics, Economics, and the Universities of Ontario, 1945–1980.* Toronto: University of Toronto Press, 1982.

Cameron, David M. *More Than an Academic Question: University, Government, and Public Policy in Canada.* Halifax: Institute for Research on Public Policy, 1991.

Gidney, Catherine. *A Long Eclipse: The Liberal Protestant Establishment and the Canadian University, 1920–1970.* Montreal and Kingston: McGill-Queen's University Press, 2004.

Gosse, Van. *Rethinking the New Left: An Interpretative History.* New York: Palgrave, 2005.

Stortz, Paul, and E. Lisa Panayotidis, eds. *Historical Identities: The Professoriate in Canada.* Toronto: University of Toronto Press, 2008.

Canadian students in the sixties hoped to symbolically, or perhaps literally, stamp out existing authority structures on university campuses.

Permission of *The Carillon,* 13 October 1967.

4

To Struggle Together or Fracture Apart: The Sixties Student Movements at English-Canadian Universities

Roberta Lexier

Universities underwent significant transformations in the 1960s. Before the Second World War, institutions of higher learning were, generally speaking, relatively small, offering a classical liberal arts education to the political and economic elite of Canadian society. In response to contributions made to the war effort and the emerging requirements of a modern, technological workforce, Canadian commentators increasingly perceived postsecondary education as central to the cultural and economic development of the nation and to the personal advancement of individuals into the middle class by the 1960s.[1] Universities soon became large, complex, state-funded institutions that offered a more utilitarian and applied education to an ever-expanding proportion of young people. Such developments are reflected in the massive expansion of existing campuses, the opening of new schools in communities throughout the country, the growing importance of professional programs, and the doubling of the student population in the 1960s.[2] These changing circumstances facilitated the development of a powerful student movement. Students mobilized in large numbers in order to exert considerable influence over the discussions taking place on their campuses and spearhead efforts to transform their institutions. This chapter analyses how and why a student movement gained momentum and influence at English-Canadian universities in the 1960s.

Surprisingly, except for a small amount of literature on students and the New Left in the 1960s,[3] little has been written on the movement that brought students together in an effort to transform postsecondary education.[4] Prior to the 1960s, students were not considered responsible adults, either by the university or the wider society, especially since the legal age of majority was twenty-one.[5] As such, they had little official political engagement in the university community, and they did not have any role in the decision-making structures of their institutions. Moreover, their own organizations were subject to oversight and control by university officials and remained mostly apolitical, primarily responsible for organizing yearbooks, dances, clubs, athletics, and other social events. A minority of students participated in political organizations and activities, including youth wings of political parties, national student associations, and wider 'efforts to transform the political and social order of Canadian society.'[6] Yet, such activism, despite its success in provoking discussion, 'largely failed to elicit the active involvement of the vast majority of students in reform, let alone revolutionary causes.'[7]

The sixties in Canada were a particularly turbulent era characterized, as the chapters in this collection illustrate, by nationalist movements, demands for racial and gender equality, opposition to the war in Vietnam, and a revolution in postsecondary education. The focus here is on the student movement in English Canada during the 1960s. In particular, it is based on research at three institutions – Simon Fraser University, the University of Saskatchewan, Regina Campus (now University of Regina), and the University of Toronto – where the student movement remained active and influential throughout the period. Although events and issues played out differently at each of these institutions as a result of their very unique situation, there are nevertheless remarkable similarities in the dynamics of this movement at all three universities.

This essay explores the student movement in the context of the 'long sixties,' with the movement's rise to prominence and its sudden decline. For a brief moment, the student body, which was incredibly diverse across Canada, found common ground on issues such as university governance. Students identified themselves as a distinctive group on campus with collective interests and positions that differed considerably from those of university administrators and faculty members. However, because ideologies and identities constantly shifted, the student movement remained temporary and fragile and frequently fractured and divided. When a sizeable number of students could not support their leaders' positions, and refused to accept that as students they should inherently adopt a radical critique of the status quo, the movement splintered. Furthermore, deeper divisions between students and student leaders emerged by the early 1970s, when many activists prioritized particular ideological perspectives and focused on issues external to the university. The student movement was rooted in the formation of a set of common concerns about increasing the roles and responsibilities of students within the university system.

Origins of the Student Movement

Alliances between student leaders and the larger student population began to emerge in the mid-1960s, when students began to develop a set of common concerns and interests centred around their identity as a distinct group on campus. Prior to the 1960s, university administrators were charged with regulating the behaviour of their supposedly immature and dependent students. 'For decades – indeed for centuries,' American historian David Allyn explains, 'school administrators had served as foster parents, entrusted with the responsibility of guiding and governing their charges as they made the transition from adolescence into adulthood.'[8] In other words, the university 'exercised the prerogatives of a strict but judicious parent.'[9] This relationship was known as *in loco parentis,* in the place of the parent, and through it administrators regulated both the academic and personal conduct of their students. Rules were therefore put in place covering sexual relations, alcohol consumption, swearing, and smoking.[10]

In addition, as children, students had no political role to play within the university. They did not participate in any meaningful way in governing structures, and student governments, under the gaze of administrators, were responsible primarily for social activities. In addition, few students saw themselves as a distinct group on campus, even though there existed clearly demarcated boundaries between students, faculty members, and administrators, especially in the classroom and in existing disciplinary structures. These conditions prior to the 1960s were not particularly conducive to the development of a mass movement among university students.

All of this began to change in the mid-1960s when university administrators decided to abandon the principle of *in loco parentis* and recognize students as mature adults within the university community. This decision was taken for a number of reasons in response to changes in the wider society and in the university. For example, as some scholars argue, societal values, especially those regarding premarital sex and individual freedom and responsibility, were in a state of flux, especially as a result of the advent of the birth control pill in the early 1960s.[11] As Michiel Horn explains, 'The growing permissiveness of society made the parental role less relevant.'[12] At the same time, notions of adolescence and adulthood were subject to sustained discussion and debate as young people became more numerous and powerful members of society.[13] It became difficult for university administrators to regulate the behaviour of young people who were increasingly viewed by many individuals as adults.

Perhaps even more important than these external changes were the developments taking place within the universities themselves. Charged with more utilitarian tasks, including training students for entry into a modern and technological workforce, universities were largely unable to maintain their traditional role as the 'central spiritual and cultural institution in society.'[14] As a result, according to historian Catherine Gidney, university administrators 'lost the ability to control students' behaviour on moral grounds,' and the responsibility of university administrators to regulate the personal behaviour of students began to erode.[15] At the same time, universities were increasingly involved in training future citizens in a democratic society and were, therefore, expected to foster 'responsibility, maturity, and citizenship.'[16] This required that students regulate their own behaviour. In addition, by the mid-1960s, enrolments at English-Canadian universities were expanding dramatically, more than doubling between 1960 and 1966.[17] With significantly more students at university, and fewer living in residences, 'old administrative structures became insufficient.'[18] There were more students in proportion to the number of administrators and faculty members, and it became unwieldy and expensive to oversee the conduct of each individual on campus.[19] These practical concerns were foremost in the minds of university administrators by the mid-1960s and convinced them to abandon *in loco parentis*.

The dismantling of paternalistic disciplinary structures was important to the development of the student movement because it dramatically altered the identity of students from children to adult members of the university community.[20] As a result, most students found themselves with increased personal freedom and individual responsibilities. Yet, for many students, these changes did not go far enough. Student leaders increasingly debated the nature of their new identity and concluded that, as adults, students should have greater responsibility within the university community: though recognizing that they were relatively insulated from the world outside their institutions, these students, nevertheless, insisted upon the rights and responsibilities generally associated with adulthood. They demanded that their new individual responsibility be extended to student organizations, especially to the student governments with which they were increasingly involved. Furthermore, these student leaders defined responsibility in two different ways: first, as accountability to their electors and, second, as political engagement within the university.[21] Student leaders increasingly viewed students as a separate and unified group on campus and began to mobilize students on campuses across Canada. While never fully cohesive, the desire for a more meaningful voice within the institution did help bring students together as a separate group united around a common set of concerns.

Coming Together: The Example of Student Participation in University Governance

Within a short time, student leaders developed alliances with a significant proportion of the student body. This alliance was most apparent in the campaign for student participation in university governance. Inspired by their professors, who, as Catherine Gidney explains in her contribution to this collection, were, by the late 1950s and early 1960s, demanding a greater voice in the decision-making process within their institutions, student leaders increasingly insisted upon the same rights for students. In particular, they pressed for direct representation on the board of governors, the senate, departmental councils, and most other governing bodies within the university. To a significant degree, these demands were framed in terms of a new conception of student identity. Many activists maintained that students had different concerns from other members of the university community, including faculty members and administrators, and that these must be considered by decision makers.[22] As those most immediately affected by policy decisions, they argued, students have a 'unique perspective' to contribute to the decision-making process.[23] Thus, while encouraged by the demands presented by their professors, these student leaders increasingly conceived of students as a separate group with their own interests and concerns.

In addition, the campaign for student participation in university governance was grounded in a particular world view rooted in the importance of democracy. Democracy was central to the ideological framework in Canada, and much of the Western world, in the postwar period. Politicians, journalists, and other political, cultural, and religious commentators of the time had framed the Second World War as a battle to protect democracy from the threat of totalitarianism. As well, Western leaders employed such rhetoric within the context of the Cold War, which, they insisted, was being fought to guard against the oppressive communists. Young people born after the war, some of whom became university students during the 1960s, were raised in the midst of this overt ideological warfare and generally internalized ideas about equality, justice, and participation that their elders insisted were central to the democratic system.[24]

Inspired by this world view, many student leaders asserted that direct participation in the university decision-making process was their democratic right. They argued that students, as members of a democratic community both nationally and within individual universities, had the inherent right to make the decisions that affected their lives.[25] 'We seek the political rights of free human beings to have a say in those decisions that affect them,'[26] argued one student. An editorial in the University of Toronto student newspaper the *Varsity* explained that 'students not only have the right to know about decisions which affect their activities, they have a right to participate in the making of these decisions ... [T]here is no question that they should participate in making decisions affecting their own activities.'[27]

Student leaders at the University of Toronto, the University of Saskatchewan, Regina Campus, and Simon Fraser University were able to mobilize a significant number of students to campaign for direct student representation on university governing structures, including the board of governors, the senate, the president's council, and departmental decision-making bodies. According to Cyril Levitt, this issue created 'a sentiment of solidarity among...students.'[28] As well, university administrators felt that large numbers of students backed these demands. 'Many of our students,' University of Toronto Registrar Robin Ross claimed, 'have a general dissatisfaction with the "system" i.e. the process by which decisions are made in the university.'[29] Similarly, at Simon Fraser University there was the feeling that 'most students would welcome the establishment of new governing bodies so that student members might present the student point of view and expedite the implementation of their suggestions.'[30] There was, Toronto student Greg Kealey later recalled, 'a fairly broad consensus on more student involvement in things like university governance.'[31] As a further indication of student support for these issues, most demands were presented by the student governments at each university, which depend, to a large extent, on the student body to remain in power. Despite occasional opposition to the tactics employed by activists, including the use of a sit-in at SFU,[32] no significant opposition to these demands developed at any of the three universities. Ultimately, these campaigns helped convince a significant proportion of the student body that they were distinct from other groups on campus, including administrators and faculty members, and that they could only achieve a more meaningful voice in university government if they worked together.

As a result, throughout the late 1960s, students successfully struggled together to organize campaigns aimed at achieving greater participation in university governing structures. University administrators at Simon Fraser University granted students seats on the senate in 1967, making it the first university in Canada with student representatives on that body.[33] At the University of Toronto, President Claude Bissell offered students seats on the president's council and on the senate and membership on a number of committees as well as on faculty, department, and college boards.[34] In Regina, Principal William Riddell actively encouraged the various faculties and departments to find ways of involving students in the decision-making process,[35] although this approach was 'exploratory and on an ad hoc experimental basis'[36] and led to the introduction of a myriad of policies across campus. Nevertheless, by the late 1960s, at all three universities included in

this study, students were granted representation on university governing bodies.

While there are many possible explanations as to why administrators reformed their policies, their own records indicate that they
believed that offering students positions on governing bodies would
prevent further tensions or conflicts from developing on campus.[37]
Such concessions were relatively minor and insignificant and would
not threaten existing structures but might satisfy a substantial proportion of the student body and mitigate against further conflict. This
decision, then, might have been a simple case of divide and rule;
while student leaders might continue to escalate their demands and
tactics, administrators may have been betting that a large number of
students would be happy with these concessions and would refuse to
participate in other campaigns. By the late 1960s, university officials
were well aware of the potential for confrontation with their students,
both as a result of events at other universities throughout Canada
and the United States including the events at Sir George Williams
University (discussed by Marcel Martel, in this collection), but also
because of their experiences with student leaders during other debates
over student government autonomy and discipline. As such, they may
have hoped that a few simple reforms, which did not require a major
overhaul of structures or power relations on campus, would limit
additional hostilities.[38]

Splitting Apart: Campaigns for Accessibility and Debates over the Purpose of the University

The alliance that developed regarding the issue of participation in the
decision-making process, however, proved relatively fragile. Although
student leaders continued to assert their ability to speak on behalf of
the entire student body, some of the issues they raised highlighted
divergent political ideologies among students and made it increasingly difficult to sustain a mass movement on campus. For example,
at the same time that activists pressed for increased student involvement in governing structures, they also spearheaded campaigns to
remove the perceived financial obstacles to higher education, including tuition fees and student loans, which they contended excluded
academically qualified individuals who could not afford university.

These students had largely internalized a belief in the centrality of postsecondary education for national development, including economic expansion and cultural advancement, and insisted that the only reason people would not attend universities was because of the high costs involved.[39] They maintained that governments should take on a greater responsibility for funding postsecondary education because of its stated national importance.[40]

The response of the student body to these actions varied dramatically. Some students participated in campaigns aimed at increasing accessibility to universities, though mostly likely for personal reasons because their own costs for higher education were also rising. Other students actively opposed the position taken by their leaders; they insisted that students must pay for their own education because they would benefit directly from a university degree.[41] As such, student leaders had to contend with deep ideological divisions that did not emerge during campaigns for greater participation in university governance. Similar to other social movements, where ideological fractures frequently splinter alliances, divergent positions regarding governmental versus individual responsibilities limited the ability of student leaders to sustain a unified student movement on this issue.

Similarly, debates regarding the purpose of universities in Canadian society exposed entrenched ideological divisions within the student body. In order to keep up with the technological and material developments of the postwar period and satisfy the demands of the modern workforce, postsecondary education shifted from a traditional liberal arts orientation to a greater focus on utilitarian scientific research and practical job training. In response to these changes, the purpose of higher education became a central part of public and on-campus debates.[42] Student leaders, especially those located in the arts faculties, attempted to present a unique student perspective in these discussions, insisting that dramatic actions were required to make the world a more equitable and just place and that higher education should directly contribute to social change. They argued that the emerging practical orientation of the university, focused increasingly on job training rather than on critical thinking, limited its ability to accomplish this task.[43] 'There was a sense,' Toronto student Joel Lexchin recalled when reflecting upon his experiences of the sixties, 'that the universities were a place where new ideas would come from and that the universities would lead the way in changing society.'[44]

In response to this argument, many other students, mainly members of professional schools and programs, took a more conservative stance. They generally accepted the evolving functions of their universities and frequently refused to adopt or, on occasion, actively opposed the social justice positions presented by their leaders. These students rarely engaged in the political discussions and activities surrounding the purpose of the university. One particular incident at the University of Toronto, however, demonstrated that many of these students fundamentally disagreed with their leaders.

In November 1967, some student leaders participated in a protest over the use of the University Placement Service, an employment service on campus, by the Dow Chemical Company, which manufactured napalm for use in the war in Vietnam. They argued that the university should actively oppose the war and reject any association with a company involved in the slaughter of innocent Vietnamese civilians. 'U of T,' an article in the student newspaper explained, 'should have nothing whatsoever to do with a company that profits from such a crime.'[45] The engineering students being recruited by Dow opposed the actions taken by this relatively small group of anti-war activists. Engineering students, the Engineering Society insisted, 'should themselves have the right to make moral decisions about their employers' without interference from any other group or individual on campus.[46] For a significant proportion of engineering students, the university existed to train them for employment and assist them in obtaining a good job upon graduation; the protests against the use of the Placement Service by the Dow Chemical Company thus directly challenged their vision of the purpose of higher education. As such, they engaged in counter-protests and even spearheaded a campaign to impeach Students Administrative Council (SAC) President Tom Faulkner because of his support for the initial protests.[47] Faulkner ultimately received the support of the majority of students on campus,[48] but such conflicts reveal that conflicting perspectives, rooted in different ideological beliefs, emerged during debates surrounding the purpose of higher education and, ultimately, restricted the formation of student alliances.

Decline and Difference

Despite these various divisions within the student body, which frequently limited the unity and power of the student movement, student leaders nevertheless remained at the forefront of many of the debates on their campuses. In part, this was a result of the continued unity of the student leadership throughout the 1960s. Though differences of opinion often developed, and some individuals organized independent groups that could focus on their specific concerns, significant issues and events on campus usually brought most student leaders together into a coalition that could present a common front. However, by the late 1960s and early 1970s, the student leadership began to fracture along ideological lines, signalling the end of a powerful student movement at English-Canadian universities. As well, the movement's accomplishments throughout the 1960s contributed to its ultimate decline.

In the first place, as former Canadian Union of Students (CUS) President Peter Warrian recalled, 'the student movement became factionalized, largely over political ideologies.'[49] For example, by 1969, University of Toronto student Andy Wernick could point to at least eight separate groups of what he called 'activists' on campus, including the Young Socialists, the youth wing of the Trotskyist League for Socialist Action; the Canadian Party of Labour, a militant group connected with the Progressive Labor Party in the United States; the Maoist Canadian Student Movement; and the anti-capitalist and anti-imperialist New Left Caucus. In explaining the distinctions between these groups, Wernick said that they each gave different answers to questions of how imperialism was to be defeated, how to build socialism in Canada, what kind of socialism to construct, and how groups should operate on campus.[50] In other words, while different political perspectives had always existed, by the late 1960s, student leaders at the university were increasingly divided over revolutionary theories: who, they debated, would lead the desired revolution, and how would it be achieved? These competing factions made it difficult for student leaders to work together and limited their ability to attract support from a significant proportion of the student body.

At the same time, a significant number of politically active individuals at these universities became ever more concerned with a variety of 'non-student' issues and began to develop or join other social movements that could address their specific interests. Examples include English-Canadian nationalism, the Waffle, the environmental movement, the women's movement, and gay and lesbian liberation movements.[51] In each of these cases, the perspectives and tactics employed by the student movement became less relevant as people focused more and more on off-campus problems and prioritized their non-student identities. For instance, many politically active female students began to join with other women within the university and in the non-academic community by the late 1960s and early 1970s to struggle against women's oppression. In doing so, these women drew upon a collective gendered identity that united them with a broad range of women.[52] While gender was always a constituent part of female students' identity and their educational status remained important, they increasingly associated more with individuals who shared their concern for women's issues than with those focused on student interests. At the same time, the students who became active in the English-Canadian nationalist movement raised alarm regarding the influence of the United States over the politics, economics, and culture of Canada. While these individuals occasionally related such anxieties to the universities themselves, through campaigns for more Canadian courses, programs, and professors, they frequently shifted their focus to the wider national context.[53] Ultimately, the decline of the relatively powerful, though always fragile, sixties student movement was largely a result of ideological splinters within its leadership, along with different opinions on the relationship of students to larger social concerns outside the university community.

Furthermore, the student movement may have fallen victim to its own success. Having achieved many of their initial goals, a significant number of students may have been satisfied with their accomplishments and were unwilling to continue to press for further changes within their institutions. Student governments, increasingly secure in their positions on campus, became bureaucratized and lost much of the energy and activism that had emerged in the mid-1960s when student leaders had to fight for autonomy. As well, while many students seemed to accept the importance of democracy and participation in governing structures, the decision to allow for student involvement on decision-making bodies may have been a satisfactory concession for a sizeable proportion of the student population. Thus, efforts by student leaders to push for parity, or equal representation with faculty members, failed to attract the same level of support as earlier campaigns to reform the governing bodies on campus.[54] These achievements, ironically, further emphasized divisions within the movement and may have contributed to its decline.

Conclusion

In public perception, there is often an assumption that identity politics developed in the wake of the 1960s, when formerly united mass movements supposedly fractured into a variety of disconnected groups. For students on English-Canadian university campuses, the sixties were a moment when they were able to overcome their differences, find common ground on what defined student issues, and create a relatively cohesive movement. Demanding that their identity as adults include greater responsibility within the university community, students increasingly viewed themselves as a separate group on campus with their own interests and concerns. As such, they united and forced dramatic changes within the university. However, these alliances proved temporary as students continued to negotiate their conceptions of themselves and the world around them. Issues such as access to and the purpose of higher education demonstrated that divergent and already existing ideological positions were present within the student body. By the late 1960s and early 1970s, even the student leadership was fracturing into various political ideologies, and furthermore, the achievements of the movement highlighted the different world views held by students. Understanding the student movement in the sixties may provide greater insight into the dynamics of other social movements, helping to explain why and how such movements develop, attract mass support, and ultimately dissolve.

FURTHER READING

Boren, Mark Edelman. *Student Resistance: A History of the Unruly Subject.* New York: Routledge, 2001.
DeGroot, Gerard J., ed. *Student Protest: The Sixties and After.* London: Longman, 1998.

Jasen, Patricia. "'In Pursuit of Human Values (or Laugh When You Say That)": The Student Critique of the Arts Curriculum in the 1960s.' In Paul Axelrod and John G. Reid, eds., *Youth, University, and Canadian Society,* 247–71. Kingston and Montreal: McGill-Queen's University Press, 1989.

Levitt, Cyril. *Children of Privilege: Student Revolt in the Sixties, A Study of Student Movements in Canada, the United States, and West Germany.* Toronto: University of Toronto Press, 1984.

Owram, Doug. *Born at the Right Time: A History of the Baby Boom Generation.*Toronto: University of Toronto Press, 1996.

A picture taken of the computer centre located on the ninth floor of
the Hall building after the February events.
Permission of Service des archives de l'Université Concordia–Concordia
University Archives.

5

'Riot' at Sir George Williams: Giving Meaning to Student Dissent

Marcel Martel

On 29 January 1969 some two hundred students occupied the ninth floor of the Hall Building, which housed the campus's computer centre at Sir George Williams University (later part of Concordia University), in Montreal. In a show of solidarity, other students occupied the university's Faculty Club eight days later, claiming that the university continued to ignore students' complains of faculty racism. What began as a peaceful occupation ended violently, however. A fire caused an estimated $1 million worth of damage to the computer centre, street protests developed outside the university, and ninety-seven individuals were arrested. Although most of those arrested were white, the media focused on forty-eight black protesters, many of whom were non-citizens who had come from the Caribbean to study.[1]

This chapter focuses on how these events were interpreted by various social actors: student unions, the Sir George Williams Faculty Union and university administrators, federal politicians, the Royal Canadian Mounted Police, and Montreal's black communities. Because of the occupation, the way it ended, and the dramatic nature of the police intervention, these social actors had to make sense of the meaning of the occupation and the riot. How they interpreted the riot either justified radical protest and social change, or conversely, justified repression of groups attempting to foment dissent and social change. University students, and especially their leaders, were determined not to let their opponents use these events as a means to dismiss students' agenda of campus reforms. Campus leaders (with the notable exception of Union générale des étudiants du Québec) distanced themselves from these events because they desired increased participation in university governance. Federal officials, in particular the RCMP, denounced the violent sit-in, linking this dissent to 'foreigners' and using the incident to call for increased restrictions against immigration. Finally, for the black communities in Montreal, these events provided an impetus to organize and challenge their marginalization. Ultimately, the riot is a case study of student activism in the sixties and the limits of dissent in the context of widespread opposition to the protestors.

The Sir George Williams riot was deeply rooted in the sixties. It was, as Walker and Palmer document in other chapters in this volume, a period of acute racial confrontation. And as Gidney and Lexier also reveal in their chapters, the sixties were a revolutionary period in postsecondary education. Sir George Williams changed from a degree-granting college to a university in 1959, and around the same time several new universities such as Brock, Simon Fraser, Trent, York, and the Université du Québec network were created. Many of these institutions were confronted with students who sought a direct voice in university governance. But, as part of the broader reinterpretation of the sixties in this book, examination of the riot demonstrates the complexities of the student movement, which did not speak with one voice and struggled, at times, to find common ground.

Sit-ins and demonstrations characterized campus life in the 1960s, and they took place in an atmosphere of ideological turmoil that had a significant impact on the student movement. Students not only used the campus as a forum to foment a change in university governance, they also sought to make society more responsive to the unique needs, concerns, and expectations of university students. Students, as Lexier explains (in this volume), claimed a group identity based on a set of common interests. For worried university administrators, parents, experts on youth, politicians, and police officers, the events at Sir George Williams University were hardly reassuring.

In the Line of Fire: University Students, University Administrators, and the Faculty Union at Sir George Williams

The events at Sir George Williams initially dealt with the issue of racial discrimination. The university admitted many black and immigrant students and offered a diversity of academic programs and evening classes that accommodated the needs of those working during the day. In April 1968, eight students – six from the West Indies and two from East India and Asia – complained that their biology instructor, Perry Anderson, was giving lower grades to visible minority students. At the time the Faculty of Science had no established process to handle complaints, but the university would develop such a policy during the fall term. In May 1968, students met with Dean of the Faculty of Science Samuel Madras, who, after hearing from the biology instructor and the plaintiffs, rejected the complaint. However, the plaintiffs were not informed of the results of the dean's inquiry.

In the fall of 1968, Anderson was back at work and was promoted to the rank of assistant professor. This led the plaintiffs to believe that the investigation conducted by the dean of science in the previous spring had ignored their complaints. An emerging sense of mistrust among the students was fuelled by a belief that their complaint was not being taken seriously and that the inquest conducted by the dean of science was an attempt by faculty to diffuse the controversy and protect the reputation of the institution. In December, one of the plaintiffs presented the dean with a request to dismiss Professor Anderson. Confronted with the escalating tone and demands of the complainants, the Science Faculty Council proposed the creation of a five-person hearing committee. The plaintiffs supported the initiative because the committee's members had to be approved by all parties – that is, the plaintiffs, Professor Anderson, and the university.

In January 1969, Anderson announced that he would resume teaching. Vice-Principal (Academic) John W. O'Brien wrote to Anderson encouraging him to reconsider his decision, fearing 'the risk of violence.'[2] Black students reacted to O'Brien's warning with outrage. His fear that black students would resort to violence was, according to these students, another example of institutional racism.[3] Upon reconsideration, Anderson decided not to resume teaching.

On 10 January, the original six black West Indian students presented a written complaint against Anderson to new Acting Principal D.B. Clarke. Furthermore, they expressed concerns that the hearing committee was composed of only faculty members. Meanwhile, two black professors resigned from the committee. In reaction, the university administration appointed two more members, an act that displeased the six plaintiffs, and decided to proceed anyway with the hearing on 26 January. Students rejected the committee and left the hearing. On 29 January, along with 194 others, they occupied the computer centre on the ninth floor of the Hall Building. If, for some participants, the occupation of the computer centre was a way of denouncing technology that was dehumanizing society, strategic considerations influenced the decision to take control of this particular place. Since the university administration had moved its headquarters to an adjacent hotel, students targeted the computer centre. Although the university increased security on campus, including at the computer centre, it did not deter students from taking control of this strategic target.

The faculty association was divided over how to handle the issue. At a general meeting of their association at the end of January, most faculty members sided with the university's administration and its handling of the students' complaint. A faction of faculty members nevertheless dissented and sided with the occupiers. Perhaps in reaction to the position taken by the faculty association, students decided to occupy the faculty club (or 'liberate' it, to use the occupiers' words). By contrast, the RCMP argued that the students occupied the faculty club because the hearing committee met behind closed doors. In another report, filed in May 1969, the RCMP claimed that the occupation of the faculty club resulted from a rally held on 4 February. At this rally, after seven individuals including Roosevelt Bernard (Rosie) Douglas spoke, Leo Barker invited the 'white students' present to occupy the faculty club 'in support of the black students' demands.' According to the author of the highly censored memorandum released by the Access to Information Office, between one hundred and two hundred students ended up occupying the faculty club. However, this protest movement declined over time, and some of the participants joined those who occupied the computer centre.[4]

During the occupation of the computer centre, the hearing committee proceeded with its investigation despite the plaintiffs' boycott. Meanwhile, negotiations between the administration and the occupiers led to an agreement to create a new hearing committee. The administration hoped that this agreement would end the occupation, but the faculty association rejected the solution because Anderson had not been consulted.[5] Without resorting to violence, the faculty association became a force opposed to students, at least in the view of the occupiers.

The occupation quickly turned violent. According to the administration, the occupiers ransacked the premises on 11 February, and those students who had been occupying the faculty club joined the occupiers on the ninth floor of the Hall Building. When police stormed the premises, barricades blocked them. Later that day, a fire broke out in the computer centre. Police officers and firefighters were called in to put an end to the occupation. As suggested by Michael Boudreau (in his chapter about the Gastown riot in Vancouver), it was police intervention that turned the demonstration into a riot.

At the time, there were approximately seventeen thousand students at Sir George Williams. Based on mainstream and student newspapers accounts, fewer than 10 per cent of the student population took part in the demonstrations inside and outside the university, and in the occupation of the computer centre and faculty club. As Neatby and McEown have stressed in their study on university students, students who directly participated in protest activities usually represented only a minority of the student population.[6]

Student Responses

As the reactions to the events at Sir George Williams University demonstrate, student unions during this period were far from united. For the students, or at least for their official spokespersons, these events constituted a violent incident that had to be denounced. Why such denunciations? Given what had happened, the leaders of student associations feared that university administrators would reject their requests for participation in governing bodies. There was also a fear that more militant elements would be perceived as the true voice of the student movement and would undermine demands put forward by the students' elected representatives.

Although student leaders used various channels to express their demands, the events at Sir George Williams did raise the issue of how to handle violence as a means of protest. Since media coverage stressed the violence of the February events, student leaders felt compelled to react. If protest as a form of dissent did not garner a great deal of support among students – with some exceptions – those who took part in them believed that collective action was part of an international movement.[7] Student activism, especially in 1968, was spreading in the

Western hemisphere (France, Italy, Mexico, Spain, Germany, and the United States), in Asia, and in countries behind the Iron Curtain, such as Poland and Czechoslovakia. History was putting wind in their sails. Students felt that their battles were, therefore, legitimate and were part of the protests, sit-ins, and strikes taking place in many institutions in the Western hemisphere in the second half of the 1960s.[8]

Initially, the Sir George Williams Students Legislative Council did not support or condemn the occupation, a position denounced by the occupiers.[9] However, the end of the occupation provided an opportunity for the student body to make some important moves. First, it fired David Bowman, the editor-in-chief of the *Georgian,* the student newspaper, on the ground that he had supported the occupation. Second, it condemned the Canadian University Press for its 'distorted' coverage of the Sir George Williams events, arguing that it misled 'Canadian students about what really happened here and why.' *The Georgian* withdrew from the organization.[10] Finally, it withdrew from the UGEQ, the Quebec student union, an event that marked the culmination of a latent conflict between the two organizations. These two organizations did not share the same views on Quebec's political situation and aspirations. At the time, Quebec, as documented in José Igartua's essay in this collection, was in the midst of the Quiet Revolution, which created an atmosphere of popular ferment. It was not, however, free from tensions, as measures to strengthen the French language as the main language of communication in the province forced English-speaking people and immigrants to adjust to increasingly politicized views of how individuals should demonstrate their attachment to a new Quebec identity centred on the use of the French language. The transformation of French-Canadian identity and nationalism into a Quebec-territorial one led some nationalists to equate the struggle of French Canadians to the quest of Third World countries to throw off colonial political and economic rule. The political positions taken by the predominately francophone UGEQ in favour of the working class, its support for Quebec independence, and its opposition to provincial language legislation – Bill 63 – that gave parents in Quebec the right to send their children to English-speaking schools, antagonized a number of those in the Sir George Williams students' association. The final straw was UGEQ's sympathy for the occupiers.[11]

For its part, the Canadian Union of Students did not excuse the use of violence. However, when it came time to identify those responsible, CUS blamed the university administration because it had left the file to rot, arguing that its 'refusal to negotiate in good faith' ultimately provoked the violence.[12] CUS, nevertheless, condemned the events because it felt that being labelled as a supporter of the rioters might damage its credibility on other issues. For their part, students' councils at McGill, Ryerson, the University of Waterloo, and the University of Windsor condemned the destruction and violence by students in Montreal. However, with the exception of McGill, the councils agreed to make a financial contribution to the fund established to help those arrested and facing criminal charges.[13]

Not everyone embraced a strategic position of condemning the occupiers and violent dissent. From the start, UGEQ, which spoke on behalf of Quebec students, supported the occupiers.[14] For UGEQ, the events at Sir George Williams University demonstrated how the establishment resorted to violence when threatened. In short, the recourse to violence by the occupiers was a response to the institutionalized violence to which they were subjected. Furthermore, UGEQ condemned the media coverage that targeted non-Canadian citizens as being responsible for the violence that marked the end of the occupation of the computer centre.[15]

UGEQ's position reflected its leadership's concern for the struggle against racial discrimination in the United States. Since its inception in 1964, UGEQ had been concerned with the civil rights struggle of African Americans. In March 1965, the Quebec student union organized a sit-in in front of the United States consulate in Montreal to protest racial discrimination. Thousands took part. The events at Sir George Williams provided some activists with the opportunity to cast the union as part of the struggle for racial equality, and this probably led, in turn, to UGEQ support for the occupiers. At the same time, UGEQ adhered to the 'decolonization struggle' framework and used these events as an example of the struggle and difficulties that students faced when attacking the establishment and fighting for their rights and a better world. The events at Sir George Williams University, and in particular the way in which the media interpreted them, reinforced UGEQ leaders' depiction of the student as an exploited intellectual worker. The rattling of the chain of exploitation triggered repressive reactions on the part of the establishment.[16]

Attributing Dissent and Violence to Foreigners

Politics and the House of Commons

The events at Sir George Williams generated numerous reactions outside of the university. Although Montreal municipal and Quebec provincial politicians were silent on the issue in the days following the crisis (or at least the newspapers used for this study did not report any of their comments), several Progressive Conservative and two Social Credit Members of Parliament asked pointed questions in the House of Commons. They hoped to embarrass the Trudeau government by questioning Cabinet ministers on issues related to immigration. They attributed the protest's violent end – the destruction of the computer centre – to the presence of foreign students. The former leader of the Social Credit Party, Robert Norman Thompson, did not hesitate to attribute the crisis to Chinese communist influence. Consequently, dissent could be expunged from Canadian society by expelling foreigners who had participated in the sit-in and preventing potential foreign agitators from coming in. Thus, MPs pressed the federal government to explain what it was doing to put an end to the influence of foreigners on Canadian student movements. Alberta Progressive Conservative MP Paul Yewchuk suggested cutting funding to non-Canadian university students active in creating unrest, while Ontario Progressive Conservative MP A.D. Hales went a step further by recommending cutting or withholding student loans to any students taking part in what he called 'campus riots.' Other MPs suggested using the country's immigration policy to put an end to these external influences by keeping potential agitators out of Canada. For his part, Montreal Liberal MP Marcel Prud'homme demanded to know if non-Canadian citizens arrested and convicted would be deported. Most MPs who intervened pressed the government to appoint a commission of inquiry, a suggestion that Prime Minister Trudeau quickly rejected.[17]

The possibility of expulsion expressed by MPs was inspired by several newspapers that blamed foreigners for contributing to the riot. For instance, the leading French-language newspaper *La Presse* force-fully condemned the events at Sir George Williams and denounced the violence in an editorial penned by Renaude Lapointe. From her title 'Le banditisme universitaire' to her description of the occupiers as a *'bande de voyous,'* Lapointe did not hold back. The foreigners abused the institution's *'hospitalité'* because Sir George Williams welcomed a number of foreign students. Since these students had abused this hospitality, they should be sent back home.[18]

The Royal Canadian Mounted Police

MPs and newspapers were not the only ones who blamed external influence in their explanation of the Sir George Williams crisis. The RCMP, which had gathered intelligence on university students over the years, reached a similar conclusion. According to Steve Hewitt's study of RCMP activities on university campuses, the RCMP was not well prepared to understand the nature of the new conflicts on university campuses and within youth organizations. In their chapter in this book, Steve Hewitt and Christabelle Sethna argue that this unpreparedness was also reflected in their dealings with feminist organizations. The ideological context of the Cold War shaped the RCMP's approach to most situations, leading it to cast communists as the primary threat in most of its analyses of dissent and protest. In the 1960s, the RCMP broadened the scope of its definition of what con-stituted a national threat by including activists from the Black Power movement, the Red Power movement, the Quebec Independence movement, anarchists, members of feminist groups, and student orga-nizations. In this last case, RCMP infiltration of university campuses had a specific goal: to detect and measure communist influence on university campuses – among faculty, in the student press, and within other organizations. With the emergence of the counterculture move-ment (Black Power, Red Power, and student activism), the RCMP was caught unprepared. It lacked the resources and the training to understand the nature, demands, and actions of the students, particu-larly those at Sir George Williams University. Moreover, the RCMP had few agents who came from minority ethnic or racial groups. It was, therefore, difficult for a police force dominated by white officers to infiltrate black student circles. In 1973, the RCMP acknowledged its own difficulties by stating in a memorandum later released by the Access to Information Office (in a highly censored form) that it did not have such 'valuable resources' at the time.[19]

Despite these investigative shortcomings, the RCMP believed that the activities and militancy of students at Sir George Williams were the result of the increasing presence of black activists and, in particular, the influence of the Black Panther movement. In an assessment written about the university in September 1968, the reporting officer warned his superiors that the quality of the gathered intelligence was somewhat questionable. He wrote that 'a few times when I did ask discreet questions to moderate students, I usually received evasive or non-committal answers. Therefore, the information contained in this paper should be taken for what it is; my own opinion, formed from a restricted position. Most of the information collected came to me second-hand.' Despite his limitations, the officer did warn about student activism in the Faculty of Arts but reassured his superiors by stating that students at Sir George Williams were 'much less radical than' those at Simon Fraser University.[20]

In another assessment, sent to RCMP headquarters at the end of January 1969, an officer alerted the force to the threatening influence of the Black Panthers in Montreal and at Sir George Williams, in particular. Writing before the beginning of the occupation, the officer did not allude to the possibility of what ensued. However, he did label the Black Panthers as an 'extreme threat to the national security.' Why such a label? According to the officer, this movement constituted a threat to Canadian universities, and he predicted that it could threaten the federal government as well. He concluded his report with a warning: there could be a significant increase in threatening activities by this movement during the remainder of the year. This report only increased the concerns of the RCMP, especially since a series of conferences had recently been held in Montreal: the Congress of Black Writers that took place at McGill University, 11–14 October 1968 and the Hemispheric Conference to End the War in Vietnam held in November 1968. The presence of Stokely Carmichael, the 'Honorary' Prime Minister of the Black Panther Party at the Congress of Black Writers, and his call for 'aggressive violence' to change the status of blacks, worried RCMP officials. [21] An internal report on 18 February 1969 shows that before using his speech at the October Conference to encourage 'negroes to take up arms,' the Panther leader was referred as the 'famous Stokely Carmichael.' While in Canada, Carmichael had planned to go to Halifax but he had to return to the United States. Instead, he sent 'a capable team of Panthers [...] to foment racial unrest and violence in the Halifax Negro community.' According to the RCMP, this team was made up of two American Black Panthers who ended up playing a decisive role in organizing black militants in Halifax and increasing the tensions between blacks and whites in that city. [22]

While the students occupied the computer centre, the RCMP head-quarters received a report on 3 February 1969. According to its author, it was still 'impossible to make a full assessment of the University's situation' but a general strike was not out of the question. This was considered a possibility because many students, even those who did not agree with the black students' strategy, had criticisms of the university administration and wanted 'more student freedom.' Furthermore, the author insisted that the occupiers were less concerned about the complaint of racism and more about the university administration in general. Discontent was, in fact, so intense that 'a few extreme radical groups' and 'many students' were 'advocating the complete destruction of the Administration, which in turn would destroy the University.' The situation 'could get out of hand,' not only at Sir George Williams, but also at other universities, although the author did not specify which institutions he was referring to. At the time, the RCMP expected UGEQ to exploit these events and create turmoil at McGill University and Université de Montréal. Commenting on the report, headquarters concluded that Black Panthers and the Internationalists were involved.[23]

In an internal report submitted at the end of the occupation, on 18 February 1969, the RCMP presented its understanding of the causes of the Sir George Williams incident. The report warned that the intelligence gathered on these events was 'incomplete' and 'inconclusive' because of the restrictions on information collection being imposed on the RCMP by the federal government. Despite the 'incomplete' information, however, leftists and foreigners were blamed for both the occupation and the resulting violence. The RCMP identified a series of individuals who belonged to one of the following groups: Black Power activists, anarchists, Trotskyists, separatists, the Sir George

Williams Movement, the Internationalists, and other pro-Chinese communist groups. With regard to the Internationalists, the RCMP noted that its leader, Hardial Bains, had graduated from the University of British Columbia in 1964, starting a small branch of the movement in that province before leaving for Dublin to teach at Trinity College. Back in Montreal by 1968, Bains started working closely with Bob Cruise, a McGill student labelled as a communist 'active in subversive movements.' Instrumental in the dissemination of communism, they also both helped create the Sir George Williams Movement, a group linked to the Internationalists. [24] In addition, the RCMP's February 1969 report gave the names of those who took part in the occupation and those who were arrested, noting that most of them were social sciences students. Seven faculty members, including Léandre Bergeron, were also identified as sympathetic to communist and separatist ideologies. In the eyes of the RCMP, these faculty members had contributed to the atmosphere of dissent through both the content of their teaching and their invitation of public speakers, like Jewish American draft dodger Ronald Rosen.[25]

The February report also identified Rosie Douglas as a key player and 'one of the prime agitators in the Montreal negro community.' Listing a series of events in which Douglas took a leading role, the RCMP demonstrated that he constituted a threat. Not only had he helped the black community get organized but he had advocated violence as a means of expression. Additionally in October 1968, Douglas became one of the key organizers of the Congress of Black Writers in Montreal, an event that was well attended by Caribbean students and black nationalists and 'left a lasting impression on militants.' According to the RCMP, Douglas later managed to get arrested in Halifax so that he could allege 'police harassment of blacks.' Finally, with reference to the Black University Conference held at Howard University in Washington, DC, the RCMP believed that Douglas ended his speech by saying that 'the time for the revolution is now.' [26]

Based on the gathered intelligence, the RCMP constructed a narrative about international influence upon the student movement. The RCMP feared that foreigners from the United States and the Caribbean would create subversive organizations like the Internationalists, while foreign organizations like the Black Panthers would infiltrate Canadian-based student movements. Also, by looking back on past events and focusing on where many of the occupants came from, they tried to demonstrate that these events were shaped by foreigners who chose Sir George Williams University as a place to pursue radical and subversive activities. With the university serving as a playground for these leaders and organizations, the RCMP's solution was to keep them out of the country and hope their influence would diminish.

Therefore, Rosie Douglas was arrested, convicted for his participation in the occupation, and deported in 1976.[27] He was convicted and deported on the basis of reports and investigation about the level of influence of the Black Panthers among Montreal's black population, a community and actor in the crisis that I will now turn to in more detail.

The Many Voices of the Montreal Black Community

More than fifteen thousand blacks lived in Montreal when the crisis took place. Throughout the 1960s, the media provided extensive coverage of the American Civil Rights movement, including radical wings such as the Black Panthers. Black communities in Montreal watched with great interest the events happening in the United States and in the civil rights movement. Through media coverage and conferences attended by American civil rights activists in Montreal, members of local black communities questioned race relations in a broader North American context.

Despite the media's tendency to generalize reactions from the black community, in fact, reactions were varied. The idea of a uniform and unanimous black community was a media and state construction; there were several black communities in Montreal in the 1960s. Montreal was home to a diverse black community, including individuals from other Canadian provinces, black immigrants from a variety of islands in the Caribbean (notably, students and women who worked as domestics), African Americans, and recent immigrants from other parts of the world. Furthermore, ethnicity, language, and the date of arrival in Montreal provided even more points of difference and distinctiveness within the black community. While some were foreigners who had come with a visa to attend an educational institution, others had settled in the city many decades earlier.

Despite this diversity, however, many black individuals were active in the creation of an institutional network that included the Negro

Citizenship Association and its journal *Expression*. Immigrants and students from the Caribbean who came to study were instrumental in the formation of the Caribbean Conference Committee in 1965. Although black activism in Montreal was inspired by African-American struggle, the institutional network played a role as well. By 1968, a turning point had arrived for the city's black communities, and in particular for the Caribbean community, according to David Austin. The Caribbean Conference Committee became the Canadian Conference Committee, and its mandate shifted to focus on the social and economic reality of black people in Montreal. In truth, this shift was largely moved forward by the influence of the American Black Panther movement as well as the conferences that had been organized that year in Montreal.[28]

Two conferences held in October 1968 – the Congress of Black Writers at McGill University and the Conference on Blacks in Canada at Sir George Williams University – brought blacks together to reflect on their social, economic, and political experiences in Montreal. Although their grievances and struggles were prompted by local circumstances, black people depicted their battle as part of a larger one that had, at least in North America, no national boundaries. One of the participants stated: 'this conference has proven to be the biggest event in the lives of Blacks in Montreal. The overall effect on the Black psyche was to inculcate a feeling of exhilaration and uplift; we had been christened in the holy cause,' an assessment shared by the RCMP as previously mentioned.[29] As Sean Mills explains, black activism in Montreal was part of an international movement but it was 'deeply imbedded in the lived realities of Montreal.'[30]

In reaction to the portrayal of the Sir George Williams crisis as a foreign disturbance, some witnesses of the events published a collection of essays entitled *Let the Niggers Burn!* The authors of this book portrayed the event as a turning point for the black community. According to them, the revolt illustrated the racism that characterized ethnic relations in Montreal as revealed in the actions of the police, the media, and the crowd standing outside of the Hall Building. It helped black people become aware of their blackness and to relate to all other black people who were struggling, regardless of where they lived in the world, to assert their identity and their rights as individuals. Their interpretation of these events was based on the fact that they were the victims of police repression, perceived media bias, politicians who accepted the media's characterization of the riot as foreign-led, and the crowd of spectators who had uttered racist insults. The events that took place at Sir George Williams University illustrated for Montreal's blacks the racism of white society. They helped in the development of 'blackness' as a source of pride and as a category of identity, which could be broadly defined as the rising awareness of various forms of oppression based on skin colour characterizing the common experience of blacks, regardless of the ethnic, language, and class differences within the community.[31]

The behaviour of the crowd, gathered outside the Hall Building and estimated by the *Gazette* at two thousand to four thousand people, reinforced the view of the authors of *Let the Niggers Burn!* that racism was prevalent in Montreal. However, the makeup of the assembled demonstrators was not homogeneous, nor was the interpretation of events. Some commentators noted that certain members of the crowd expressed hostility to the occupiers in racist language. For example, the authors of *Let the Niggers Burn!* stated that the crowd was hostile towards students and shouted racist comments such as 'kill the niggers' or 'get rid of the niggers.'[32] The *Gazette* claimed that the majority of those gathered encouraged the police to intervene by yelling 'Go Cops Go' and 'Let's get it over with.' The article went on to point out that individuals in the crowd who supported the work of the police officers chanted 'Burn, Burn,' back at the occupiers.[33] According to Martin O'Malley, writing in the 15 February 1969 edition of the *Globe and Mail,* someone yelled 'Go back to Biafra!' at black occupiers.[34] Furthermore, another journalist from the *Globe and Mail* reported the racist remarks of those assembled outside the Hall Building. While most of these people denounced the occupation and showed their indignation, 'at a tense moment on the street someone shouted: "Get rid of the niggers."'[35]

Conversely, some members of the crowd denounced the police violence, and were deeply critical of both the actions of the state and the racism underlying the reasons for the occupation. For example, the *Globe and Mail* reported that the marchers passed by, one carrying a sign reading 'This is Montreal, Alabama,'[36] and the *Gazette* mentioned that while in the minority, many 'protesters raised their hands in the fascist salute and hissed.'

The fundamental divisions in the crowd, and in the interpretation of the riot, are reflected in the observations of RCMP Inspector D.G. Cobb, who reported that on 11 February 1969, two hundred students from different groups walked down Maisonneuve Boulevard. These demonstrators 'carried no signs or placard' but supported those inside the Hall Building. Meanwhile, thousands of bystanders and students 'were watching' on the sidewalks during the demonstration. According to Cobb, hostilities between bystanders and protestors increased to the point of both verbal and physical violence. Amidst chants of 'Go cops go,' a 'few scuffles broke loose between them and the demonstrators.' Not understanding 'why the Montreal City Police did not attempt to dislodge the insurgents,' some of the bystanders volunteered 'their help to crash in' because they did not tolerate 'vandalism.' In the end, Cobb praised the work of the Montreal City Police by stating that they 'were calm, efficient, and avoided to worsen by their repression, an already deteriorating situation.'[37]

Was the crowd there because there was 'a generalized belief present among crowd participants,' as stated by the RCMP, or did 'the crowd activity intend to be collectively instrumental in achieving some desired end'?[38] Based on various accounts, the crowd's behaviour was not homogeneous. Some supported the protesters inside the Hall Building and others did not, which could explain the shouts of 'kill the niggers,' and other racist comments. Others were frustrated with police inaction since they wanted officers to 'dislodge the insurgents,' as stated by the RCMP. Others were critical of state repression, which could explain the fascist salute of certain individuals in the crowd.

Other black leaders used these events to ask why so many black Montrealers were not involved in the protest and were not attending universities.[39] The under-representation of Montreal- and Quebec-born black people at university illustrated the problem of access to higher education for blacks. As part of becoming aware of what being black means, some black educators put together the Quebec Black Board of Educators, whose main goal was to change the school curriculum in order to make it responsive to the needs of black students and to reduce drop-out rates. The events of 1969 also helped create new organizations, such as the Coalition of Black People of Quebec, to endow black communities with leadership, and to fight racism.

Some activists founded the newspaper named the *UHURU,* which became a means to express their understanding of oppression while locating the struggle of Montreal blacks in the larger international context of imperialism. In their eyes, Black Power became a theoretical analytical framework for race relations.

Conclusion

Because it was students who occupied the computer science centre at Sir George Williams University in Montreal, student unions reacted, as student representatives, either by condemning or condoning the occupation. Student unions disassociated themselves from the Sir George Williams events for fear of undermining their quest for access to university governance. Although dissent among university students would eventually decline, others, mostly UGEQ, used the Sir George Williams event as an opportunity to reinforce their construction of students as exploited individuals, but also as agents of change. For the politicians, the presence of foreigners allowed them to ask the government to review the mechanisms regulating immigration in order to keep troublemakers on the other side of Canada's borders. By focusing on foreigners, politicians and the RCMP allowed the government to reassure potentially worried Canadians that the student protests occurring elsewhere in the Western hemisphere would not occur here, despite the fact that most of the occupiers were Canadian. By identifying the threat as external to Canada, it could be extirpated from society by keeping people who took part in the events, and those who questioned racism, out of the country. Finally, the black community had various reactions. For some, Sir George Williams inspired and increased their sense of pride, while for others, it underlined the fact that black people were under-represented in Canadian universities.

The events at Sir George Williams University also revealed much about the relationships among the state, social dissent, and the use of violence. The events that unfolded there have similarities with other movements of social agitation that result in violence and the intervention of law enforcement. Often, as was the case in the Winnipeg General Strike of 1919, the 'foreign influences' angle was pursued. As in 1919, some of those arrested in 1969, in particular Rosie Douglas, were deported from Canada on the ground that they constituted a menace to national security. The Sir George Williams case invites us to analyse the state's actions and its recourse to repression, because the forces of order, to use Max Weber's terminology, exert a part of the state's monopoly on legitimate physical violence.

FURTHER READING

David Austin, 'All Roads Led to Montreal: Black Power, the Caribbean, and the Black Radical.' *The Journal of African American History*, 92/4 (Fall 2007), 516–39.

Eber, Dorothy. *The Computer Centre Party: Canada Meets Black Power.* Montreal: Tundra Books, 1969.

Forsythe, Dennis, ed. *Let the Niggers Burn! The Sir George Williams University Affair and Its Caribbean Aftermath.* Montreal: Our Generation Press, 1971.

Mills, Sean. *The Empire Within: Postcolonial Thought and Political Activism in Sixties Montreal.* Montreal and Kingston: McGill-Queen's University Press, 2010.

Palmer, Bryan D. *Canada's 1960s: The Ironies of Identity in a Rebellious Era.* Toronto: University of Toronto Press, 2009.

Warren, Jean-Philippe. *Une douce anarchie: Les années 68 au Québec.* Montreal: Boréal, 2008.

PART THREE

Authority and Social Protest

An image from the Gastown Riot, Vancouver, 7 August 1971.
Courtesy of Dave Patterson, *The Province.*

6

'The Struggle for a Different World': The 1971 Gastown Riot in Vancouver

Michael Boudreau

Canada first criminalized drugs in 1908 when the federal government passed the Opium Act, which made it an indictable offence to manufacture, possess, or sell opium for non-medical purposes. Marijuana was added to the list of illegal substances in 1923. Under the Narcotic Control Act, which replaced the Opium Act in 1961, anyone convicted of possessing marijuana could face up to seven years in prison. This relatively stiff penalty for what some Canadians considered to be a minor offence highlights the moral tone that permeated Canada's drug laws. By the Second World War, alcohol had gained widespread social and cultural acceptance, but drugs were deemed to be a direct threat to the moral fibre of Canadian society. Drug users were depicted as deviants, 'fiends,' and criminals. In this sense, drugs have long been encased in a discourse of 'moral panic' in Canada, a panic that reached its nadir in the 1920s, when many of the country's stringent drug laws were created, and then gradually subsided. But the fear and the stigma that were associated with drugs never disappeared.[1]

The debate in Canada over drug use resurfaced in the 1960s. Many young Canadians, notably 'hippies,' publicly flouted and mocked conventional behaviour. Marijuana became a potent symbol of the counterculture and the social rebellion that it encapsulated. The federal minister of health declared in the early 1970s that marijuana was representative of youth 'alienation' across the country.[2] As 'weed' gained popularity in the 1960s, so too did the call for its legalization. Those who advocated legalizing drugs, or at least reducing the penalties for possession, argued that marijuana was a harmless recreational drug similar to alcohol. Canadians should not have to endure the burden of a criminal record for using a small amount of marijuana.[3]

A majority of Canadians, however, especially the police, opposed legalization. A public opinion survey in April of 1970 revealed that 77 per cent of Canadians did not support the removal of criminal sanctions against marijuana. They believed that drugs were a threat to users' health and would lead to a breakdown in social order. The RCMP and municipal police forces in Toronto and Vancouver cracked down on drugs and drug users. Beginning in 1965, the number of arrests under the Narcotic Control Act for possession, cultivation, and trafficking, increased dramatically: 162 people were charged in 1965, 398 the next year, and 1,678 in 1967–68. Most of these arrests, which resulted in prison sentences for those convicted, occurred in southwestern Ontario and British Columbia.[4] It would not be until 1969 that the penalties for possession were reduced, which meant that by 1972, 95 per cent of those who were convicted of marijuana possession paid fines instead of being sent to jail. But police efforts to rid Canadian society of drugs continued into the 1970s, as did the backlash against their actions and the demand for legalization.[5] The tensions that arose from this situation, at times, led to clashes between hippies and young people and the police. One such clash, which turned from a peaceful protest against police enforcement of drug laws into a violent affair, was the 1971 Gastown riot in Vancouver. This riot, along with the public's reaction to it and the resulting public inquiry, is the subject of this chapter.

One of Vancouver's most controversial protests was the 1971 'Gastown Smoke-In & Street Jamboree.' Organized by the Yippies – the Youth International Party – the Jamboree took place on Saturday, 7 August 1971, in Vancouver's Gastown district. The Smoke-In was intended to be a public display of civil disobedience by Vancouver's 'hippies' and disaffected youth against Canada's drug laws, as well as a forum to denounce the police department's crackdown on 'soft' drugs. But as a result of the intervention by the police to break up the demonstration, this largely peaceful gathering quickly became a violent riot, leaving several people severely hurt, dozens arrested, and thousands of dollars in property damage in its wake. A public inquiry was quickly convened to investigate the cause of the riot and the allegations of police brutality. In the end, the Gastown riot eroded the already limited trust that many young residents of Vancouver had in their police force. It also exposed the growing chasm between a segment of the city's population, primarily the young, who supported legalizing drug use, and the city's advocates of 'law and order.'

The riot was a symbol of the mounting tensions between state authorities and youth during the sixties in Canada. It represented, first and foremost, what many considered to be a harsh police response to social protest. The Gastown riot also illustrates that social and political dissent in the 1960s, in addition to the spirit and discourse that underpinned that dissent, did not end with the conclusion of the decade. The Youth International Party, and its 'struggle for a different world' in the 'angry seventies,' underscores that the fight for social justice, which was one of the key hallmarks of the 1960s, continued into the early 1970s.

Gastown and the Spirit of the Sixties

Rebellion, protests, and the struggle for change and social justice are synonymous with the sixties. This is evident not only in the Gastown riot, but also in Martel's and Lexier's case studies in this collection. *Time* magazine described the impact that many young people had upon the culture, politics, protests, and social movements of the 1960s as a 'youthquake.'[6] And as the editors of the journal *The Sixties* note, no recent decade 'has been so powerfully transformative in much of the world…The era's social movements…dramatically changed the political culture in the developed West and beyond.'[7] Young people 'truly believed they could create a new and better world.'[8] Underpinning the intensity and the spirit of the sixties was the 'counterculture.' Doug Owram has aptly observed that the counterculture in Canada helped to politicize the non-political. Music, clothing, hair (including beards), and language became forums for young Canadians, those under the age of thirty, to express themselves and their difference from and opposition to materialism and the culture of conformity that their parents represented and much of society espoused.[9] The counterculture valued 'creativity, rebellion, novelty, self-expression, anti-materialism, and vivid experience.'[10] Age itself became an important indicator of identity; to be young was to identify with this counterculture and to embody a sense of alienation.

A passion for challenging accepted norms remained a central part of the sixties counterculture. And confrontations with institutions and individuals of authority often led to violence. Yet, in comparison with the United States, the 1960s in Canada were generally non-violent.[11] Nonetheless, the intensity of the era was very much evident in Canada, as many of the events detailed in this volume, including the Gastown riot, attest. But the fact that the Gastown Smoke-In failed to change Canada's drug laws does suggest that, like the sixties, the 'aspiration for change was so much greater than the consequences' for some protests and social movements in the angry seventies.[12]

Gastown, named for Gassy Jack Deighton who opened Vancouver's first saloon, was an 'area of free exchange in a milieu of corporate cannibalism.'[13] Located in the city's downtown core (primarily Water, Alexander, Powell, and Carrall streets), Gastown was home to an eclectic mix of restaurants and bars. The district catered to middle-class residents and tourists, alongside 'freak bars' – the Alcazar and Gassy Jack's Place (which were 'comfortable places in which to drink and rub shoulders with old winos, to deal and to score')[14] – and hip stores such as Junior Jelly Beans for Jeans and the Tin Ear (a record store). Gastown was a symbol of 'hip consumerism,' and in the opinion of the *Vancouver Sun,* the area was 'vibrant and interesting,' with a European flair.[15]

Gastown attracted a number of 'dissatisfied' youth who came to Vancouver from across Canada craving new experiences and a fresh start. But many of these young Canadians quickly joined the swollen ranks of British Columbia's unemployed.[16] Some of these youth lived in the cheap hotels and hostels that were scattered throughout the district, and many hung out in the plethora of stores, restaurants, clubs, and bars that lined the streets of Gastown in search of food, work, and friends. The city's alternative paper, the *Georgia Straight,* urged the residents of Gastown to decide what they wanted their community to be. They needed to 'build a sense of a particular community with a set of values different and worth preserving in the midst of another, larger, homogenizing society.' Gastown was a place where consumerism, poverty, and a spirit of community and rebellion lived in awkward coexistence.

'Long hairs' (as hippies were often referred to in the Vancouver media and by the police), and most young people (by virtue of their alleged association with the counterculture of drugs, music, and clothing), were not always welcome in some retail establishments or in certain parts of the city. But the efforts to harass and intimidate Vancouver's youth elicited a quick, and organized, response. In 1968, for instance, the Hudson's Bay Store on Georgia and Granville streets instituted a 'No "Hippies" Allowed' policy at its Round Table Restaurant. Uniformed guards were stationed at the entrance to the restaurant with instructions to prevent anyone who looked liked a hippie, essentially young people who had long hair and/or beards, from entering. According to the Bay, hippies were only buying a few items and occupying tables in the restaurant for too long and thereby denying the tables to 'straight' paying customers.[17] In addition, the Bay claimed that hippies were blocking the aisles of the store and inconveniencing shoppers. To protest against this policy, the Yippies staged a 'sit-in' at the Bay. The protesters asserted that the Bay reaped huge profits from the sale of clothing to the young, including hippies, but hypocritically refused to serve hippies in its restaurant.[18]

There were numerous confrontations between public authorities, including the police, and hippies and youths. Young people often congregated on the grounds in front of the Vancouver Courthouse on Smithe Street. But the city council viewed their presence as unsightly and disruptive, and in 1968 it decided to prosecute them using a provincial order-in-council that prohibited loitering in areas near government buildings. Close to two hundred people gathered at the courthouse on 6 March 1968 in a show of defiance against the law. The police arrested a group of people and charged them with loitering. At the trial of one of the demonstrators, Judge Lawrence Eckhardt declared that the order-in-council was discriminatory, but that he had no choice but to apply the law. In an effort to publicly mock Eckhardt, the *Georgia Straight* awarded him its 'Pontius Pilate Certificate for Justice.'[19] Two years later, in June 1970, a group of hippies occupied the Four Seasons waterfront redevelopment site near Stanley Park and proclaimed the area to be a people's park and a campsite for the homeless. The Vancouver police quickly mobilized to break up the occupation. A few months later, in October, the police donned riot gear and forcibly removed a group of youths who had refused to obey an eviction order to leave the Jericho Youth Hostel in

Kitsilano. The clash turned violent and was dubbed by the media the 'Battle of Jericho.'[20]

The Youth International Party was a key feature in these confrontations. The Yippies, the so-called angry hippies, were non-authoritarian, communal, cooperative, and anti-hierarchal. They were also considered by some Vancouver residents to be drug-using 'anarchists.'[21] The Yippies were involved in a number of protests and social causes in Vancouver in the late 1960s and early 1970s. For example, the Yippies tried to alleviate poverty by opening a food co-op. And, in April of 1970, the Yippies burned an effigy of George Shrum, the head of B.C. Hydro, which at the time operated the city's trolley buses, to denounce a hike in bus fares due to excessive electrical costs associated with running the buses.[22] The Yippies appeared to be, in the eyes of the media and the police, a sheer nuisance.

Gastown, or 'Grasstown,' as it had become widely known, was considered by some to be the 'soft-drug capital' of Canada. The Vancouver police estimated that in October of 1969 there were two thousand 'known' soft drug users in Vancouver and another twenty-five hundred suspected users.[23] On average, most users were twenty-four years of age or younger. Many of them were so-called non-criminal addicts. According to the police, their drug use stemmed 'from the fascination of youth for the sub-culture of the hip movement and the new cult of the "free thinkers" bent on ridding the community of what they consider to be "hang-ups" and false values.'[24] Equally troubling for the Vancouver police was that soft drugs users were 'more disposed to become heroin addicts than persons without drug experience.' This claim seemed to be supported by police statistics, which indicated that from 1968 to 1972, the number of persons charged with trafficking in heroin in Vancouver had risen from sixteen to 222 and those charged with trafficking in soft drugs, over the same period, rose from thirty-one to 348.[25]

To address the drug problem, the Vancouver police launched 'Operation Dustpan' in July 1971. Twenty undercover police officers were assigned to this operation. The primary focus of Operation Dustpan was Gastown and, within ten days, the police had arrested fifty-nine young men and women in Gastown on charges of possession and trafficking.[26] Even prior to the start of Operation Dustpan, the Vancouver police had taken a vigorous approach to tackling the illegal drug trade in Vancouver. In the first six months of 1971, the police had arrested 574 people for possession of LSD and marijuana. This compares with 800 arrests for possession for all of 1970. Many youths within Gastown's counterculture community remained defiant in the face of these arrests. They were also opposed to what they considered to be unjust drug laws. As one young man told the *Vancouver Sun* following a police raid on the Last Chance Saloon in Gastown: 'At [certain] times in history there have been laws that didn't make sense. Then people break it until it's changed.'[27]

Of all the forms of harassment and intimidation that hippies and young people encountered in Vancouver during the late 1960s and early 1970s, Operation Dustpan provoked the greatest outrage. Operation Dustpan convinced many young people that the Vancouver police were determined to drive them out of Gastown. Fifty-nine of the 109 arrests in the first ten days occurred in Gastown.[28] In the eyes of many young people, the police did not enforce the drug laws in a uniform fashion. Rather than target all drug users, including people in suburbia who smoked 'weed,' the police zeroed in on the 'hip sub-culture, the most visible and vulnerable,' meaning that they bore the 'brunt of...legal persecution.'[29]

The Gastown Smoke-In and Street Jamboree

Eventually the Yippies, and many Vancouver youth, had had enough of Operation Dustpan and what they considered to be the 'Gestapo practices' of the police. The Smoke-In and Street Jamboree was youth's way of voicing their displeasure with the police's 'Gestapo practices.' They wanted 'an immediate end to the harassment and intimidation campaign which is being carried out in Gastown by [Mayor] Tom Campbell's police [and] an end to arbitrary police questioning and illegal searches,' as well as 'the physical brutality currently used by Vancouver police against long hairs...Native People...Hip People...and poor people generally.' The Smoke-In was also meant to be a show of solidarity with the individuals who had been arrested during Operation Dustpan. Finally, the Yippies used the Jamboree to call for the legalization of marijuana to prevent the law from being used 'as a weapon to drive poor hip people out of Gastown...while more affluent people who may also smoke marijuana are made welcome in the area's emporiums of plastic.'[30] The *Georgia Straight* reminded all those who planned to attend the Jamboree that trouble could occur because the 'police have a monopoly on how to create violence, so we should be on our guard not to get sucked into their game...[The] SMOKE-IN is an act of civil disobedience and commitment ...The alternative is to do nothing, to remain silent and abandon the dozens of brothers and sisters who are still in jail for dealing in dreams, good and bad.'[31]

Between fifteen hundred and two thousand people attended the Jamboree, which began at 8:30 p.m. in Maple Tree Square. The music of the Grateful Dead, Jefferson Airplane, and Led Zeppelin filled the air, and many people took part in a street dance, ate ice-cream sandwiches, and chanted 'power to the people.' A few in attendance smoked marijuana and a ten-foot 'joint' was paraded through the crowd, much to everyone's delight. This ritualized, theatrical sharing of public space, which included 'smoke-ins,' 'be-ins,' and 'love-ins,' was, as George Lipsitz has claimed, at the core of the sixties experience.[32] Most first-hand accounts of the Jamboree convey the impression that this was a festive, and peaceful, occasion. David Gibson, a public relations consultant, stated that the 'mood of the crowd was generally friendly.' Gary Girvan, from West Vancouver, recalled that the crowd was not in the mood for violence; most just enjoyed listening to people play guitars, drums, and flutes, and they wanted to meet friends and take in the atmosphere; 'violence was just not in the air.' The same conclusion was drawn by Douglas Grant who, along with his wife, had come to Gastown after they had eaten dinner in Chinatown. According to Grant, he and his wife, who was six months' pregnant, had encountered a peaceful crowd, so they decided to stay for the festivities: 'This [the Jamboree] seemed to me to be an appropriate thing to encounter in Gastown as it is an area dedicated to friendship and getting together.'[33]

At the same time, however, the Yippies also wanted the Jamboree to be a political protest. Gary Girvan remembers that the only individuals who seemed to be protesting were the Yippies. They read petitions calling for the repeal of the country's drug laws and burned copies of the federal Narcotic Control Act. At one point, three protesters climbed up to the roof of the Europe Hotel overlooking Maple Tree Square, and ceremoniously 'mooned' the police.

This, by most accounts, was the extent of the Yippies' civil disobedience.[34] The Jamboree was part of a broader 'protest *culture*'
that was a product of the alienating experiences of modern life.[35]
However, for Vancouver Police Inspector Robert Abercrombie, who
was in charge of the police officers on the scene that night, the
antics of the Yippies, and the other 'long hairs' in attendance, were
an affront to decency and to law and order. Abercrombie believed
that he had to act in order to quell their disrespect for public
decency: 'Decency – the way I like to see it.'[36] At 10:00 p.m., 'acting on his own judgement and on reports given to him by junior officers,' Inspector Abercrombie decided to halt the Jamboree. He also
wanted to clear the streets to allow cars and transit buses to pass
through the district unobstructed. Using an antiquated 'loud-hailer'
(megaphone), Abercrombie announced to the crowd that they had
two minutes to disperse. But, as witnesses later testified, because of
the noise from the Jamboree and the poor quality of the sound ema-
nating from the megaphone, not many people heard Abercrombie's
proclamation. As a result, few people heeded the order to leave the
area. So, when the throng failed to move, twenty-eight riot police,
equipped with helmets and thirty-six-inch-long riot sticks, and
four officers on horseback, also with riot sticks, charged towards
the crowd. At this point, so one person remarked, 'pandemonium
broke loose.' Shortly after the first charge, it became evident to the
police that they needed reinforcements. An additional thirty-six
officers were dispatched to the scene, bringing the total police presence that night to sixty-eight. In the words of one person who had
attended the Jamboree, the riot police 'were brutal...They came in
swinging. They didn't ask people to move.'[37] Most of the officers,
both on horseback and on foot, swung their riot sticks indiscrimi-
nately at men, women, and children who were attempting to flee.
Similarly, the officers on horseback used their horses to trap people
in the doorways of stores and residences, where they had fled for
safety, and then hit these individuals with their riot sticks. A pregnant woman was one of the many people who were struck while
being trapped by the horses. The Mounted Squad repeated this practice, on what the police called a 'wall to wall basis,' until the streets
had been cleared of people.[38]

The police failed to account for the hundreds of citizens who were caught up in the melee as they left the restaurants and bars in Gastown to investigate the source of the ruckus. They were unable to distinguish between demonstrators and spectators. Moreover, the physical geography of Gastown contributed to the mayhem. The Jamboree was held where four streets (Water, Alexander, Powell, and Carrall) converged and Carrall Street ended in Gastown. This meant that people could not easily exit the area via Carrrall, which left only the three other streets as escape routes and each of them quickly became congested with cars and pedestrians.[39]

Chaos erupted. The crowd responded by hurling rocks, bottles, pieces of cement, and firecrackers at the officers. The firecrackers, in particular, only made the horses more agitated and the officers more determined to break up the demonstration and detain anyone who refused to leave the area. This clash, which the chair of the public inquiry characterized as 'street combat,' resulted in eleven civilians and six police officers being injured. The police later admitted that prior to this outburst, the crowd had been peaceful and that projectiles were only thrown after the riot police had charged into the throng of people who were standing in Maple Tree Square.[40]

Of the seventy 'street demonstrations' that had occurred in Vancouver from August of 1970 to August of 1971, the Gastown riot led to the worst forms of police brutality against innocent protesters and bystanders.[41] After witnessing the police strike people at random with their riot sticks and throw two people through plate glass windows, David Gibson concluded: 'This was one of the most vicious examples of police action I have ever had the misfortune to witness.' Patricia Bacon, a student at Simon Fraser University in nearby Burnaby, claimed that at first the police did not harass her because she was not 'dressed as a hippy.' But when she informed the police that if they were going to arrest innocent people, then they should arrest her as well, she was escorted to a police van: 'As I was entering the van a billy club was shoved between my legs in an obvious sexual assault.'[42] Other women were also abused by the police. One young woman, who called herself 'Sunshine,' wrote a letter to Mayor Campbell and described for him how several riot police had attacked her: 'he hit me on the head with his riot stick [and] the other police [officer] came behind me and got me across the back and shoulders.'[43] Others viewed a group of riot police drag a young woman by her hair for a quarter of a block, through broken glass, to a paddy wagon. Terry Young, a student visiting from Quebec, saw three officers hit a young, pregnant woman on the back and on her head with their riot sticks. 'I have never been more sickened or disgusted in my entire life,' he said after seeing this attack. Some of these attacks were performed by undercover police officers who were part of Operation Dustpan. Fifteen undercover officers were present that night with orders to mingle among the crowd, identify the leaders of the protest, and arrest them if necessary. When the riot began, at least four undercover policemen, who were wearing 'regular tourist-type clothing,' donned helmets, grabbed riot sticks, and waded into the crowd. An internal police investigation into the riot later concluded that the actions of 'certain members of this [undercover] Squad were over-aggressive.'[44]

According to many witnesses, the police were simply 'swinging first and asking questions later.' This sentiment was echoed by a Gastown business owner who told the *Globe and Mail* that there was 'almost a satanic arrogance' to the police's actions. Don Shary, who called the police 'storm troopers,' reported that he 'was hit maliciously with an official police penis extension [a riot stick].'[45] Vancouver City Alderman Ed Sweeney, who came to the riot after he was called at home by a *Vancouver Province* reporter, criticized the tactics of the police. In Sweeney's words, the police used their riot sticks 'like you would use a stick to beat a dog.'[46] When the riot had ended, seventy-nine people had been arrested, thirty-eight of whom were charged with offences ranging from causing a disturbance and possession of a dangerous weapon, to obstructing a police officer. Most of these charges were later dropped. Ironically, the police had decided, prior to the Jamboree, not to arrest anyone for the possession or use of marijuana. As one of those arrested later recalled, perhaps naively, 'My youth dropped away completely...I certainly lost my idealistic notions about the system being...inherently right...I guess it quashed my notion that justice would always prevail in the world, because it very clearly hadn't in this case.'[47] *Vancouver Sun* columnist Allan Fotheringham captured the mood of many observers the following Monday: 'Pigs is a dirty word and no one likes to use it, but there were some pigs loose in Gastown on Saturday night.'[48]

'I Am Totally Shocked That Something of This Sort Could Happen in Canada': The Public Reaction to the Gastown Riot

The public's reaction to the riot revealed that many residents of Vancouver reviled hippies and young people who used drugs. Morlaine Hawer of Burnaby, for example, wrote to Mayor Campbell and stated unequivocally that 'my only criticism of the police action is that they were too lenient – they should have used their clubs more on the heads of some of the mindless weirdos!'[49] Her comment was echoed by many others who wrote to the mayor to express their support for the police. For them, the police applied remarkable restraint when faced by a group of people (hippies) whose actions and language were deplorable. As the Fraser Valley District of the Women's Christian Temperance Union concluded, those who 'support people who challenge authority and resist law enforcement [like the Yippies] are promoting anarchy.'[50] They vigorously opposed any charges against the police officers for abuses during the riot.

This endorsement of the actions of the police against those who had participated in the Jamboree was in keeping with the general level of disdain for hippies in Vancouver in the 1960s. The police felt that the 'Hip' movement had jarred parents into realizing that drugs, in particular, had become a serious social issue. Parents apparently saw their children growing their hair and dressing in 'unorthodox fashions' to become part of a new 'subculture.' All of this made parents, so the Vancouver police suggested, 'against hippies [and] against drugs and [they] want[ed] the police to do something about both.'[51] That the Jamboree was intended to be a platform to call for the legalization of marijuana only reinforced the perceived threat that hippies, who one Vancouver resident called 'dirty, drug-ridden tramps,' posed to Canadian society.[52] Another observer, who described himself as a home owner and taxpayer, fully supported the police and was tired of paying taxes for 'youth on welfare, Opportunities for youth handouts & half a dozen other half-baked ideas.' In this sense, many who sided with the Vancouver police felt that the Gastown riot represented an ongoing struggle between decent, hardworking citizens and what Inspector Robert Abercrombie, in a letter to Campbell, called the 'bleeding hearts and marijuana lovers.'[53]

The fervour with which some individuals supported the police was matched by those who felt that the police had used excessive force. Gary Smith, a twenty-eight-year-old businessman and self-described 'small r right-wing follower of whatever party I believe best at the time,' berated Mayor Campbell for calling the Jamboree's organizers a 'bunch of thugs' who would not be allowed to run the city. Such rhetoric, Smith maintained, would only further inflame the situation and widen the chasm between Vancouver's youth and the rest of the city: 'You are acting like a tyrannical, idiotic schoolteacher and it is safe to say [that] your pupils will rebel.'[54] F. Pratt, in a letter to the *Vancouver Sun,* indicated that she or he had not thought much about the riot until they had read the newspaper accounts and then felt a mixture of anger at the police and sadness for Vancouver. Although Pratt did not believe in communism or drugs, she or he also did not believe in 'Mussolini Hitler type armed thugs masquerading as my police force and I care not against whom they are operating.'[55]

The Vancouver Police Department offered its own interpretation of what had transpired in Gastown. Chief of Police Fisk formed an internal investigative team to draw conclusions about how the police department had planned for this event and the nature of the police response to what Fisk dubbed the 'Gastown Disturbance.' The final report claimed that the ability of the police to contain the situation was complicated by the number of 'straight' citizens who were visiting Gastown that night. Moreover, the department did not put a great deal of planning into how it would police the Smoke-In because it 'was not anticipated that the Smoke-In...would develop into a major incident.' Inspector Abercrombie's decision to clear the crowd was endorsed by the report because if he had not done so, 'there is a strong possibility that the situation could have become riotous.' The report concluded that the police had fallen into an expertly laid trap, with a crowd that was whipped into a frenzy by 'professionals to the point where the situation became highly explosive' and confrontation could not have been avoided.[56]

'The Common Good Must Be Given Top Priority in These Matters': The Public Inquiry into the Gastown Riot and the Aftermath

The Yippies, the British Columbia Civil Liberties Association (BCCLA), the provincial New Democratic Party, four city aldermen, and the *Vancouver Sun* led the call for a public inquiry into the Gastown riot. In response to mounting public pressure, the attorney general appointed an inquiry, which began hearings less than a month after the riot. The inquiry was mandated by the attorney general to investigate the 'nature of the said disturbance, the motivation of the persons involved, whether the purpose of the disturbance was in the public interest, the conduct of the members of the public present and whether any such conduct was in defiance of law and order.' The chair of the inquiry, Justice Thomas Dohm of the British Columbia Supreme Court, was also asked to determine the 'nature of police intervention and whether or not such intervention was appropriate in the circumstances.'[57]

Dohm concluded that the police had used 'unnecessary, unwarranted, and excessive force' against the people who had assembled that night in Gastown, turning a peaceful gathering into a 'riot.' The arrival of the riot squad, Dohm argued, 'caused panic, terror and resentment. The violence erupted only when the police intervened.' Dohm believed that the Vancouver police had inappropriately used officers on horseback as a first resort to control the crowd, thereby endangering public safety. And it was obvious to Justice Dohm that some of the police officers were not well trained, particularly those who had inflicted undue harm on protesters. Nevertheless, the inquiry did exonerate most of the policemen who were involved in the riot; they had 'acted in an exemplary manner' and as such they 'deserve and need the respect of the citizens they serve.'[58]

The Yippies did not escape unscathed in his report. Dohm denounced the organizers of the Jamboree as 'agitators' who were determined to initiate a confrontation with the police. Two key agitators that Dohm singled out for criticism were Eric Sommers, a social worker and writer for the *Georgia Straight,* and Kenneth Lester, a freelance writer and a landed immigrant from the United States. Dohm described these members of the Yippies as 'intelligent and dangerous, radical young men' who had organized the Jamboree out of their 'desire to challenge authority in every possible way.' All that Sommers, Lester, and the Yippies wanted to do in Gastown that night, Dohm surmised, was to whip the crowd of 'gullible young people' into a frenzy, and when the police 'over-reacted,' they gave Sommers and Lester the confrontation that they had sought.[59] Dohm's point underscores the fact that the Gastown riot was a central part of the ongoing conflict between local authorities and youth in Vancouver.

In a response printed in the *Georgia Straight* following the release of Dohm's report, Kenneth Lester boldly asserted that 'if a person becomes dangerous in the eyes of the Establishment for standing up for their beliefs in the face of injustice, then indeed we are dangerous young men. A danger to a dying society.'[60] Lester also maintained that the Jamboree was an act of peaceful civil disobedience and the only thing about the gathering that was unlawful was the police response. But Dohm considered the reasons for the Jamboree to be a 'sham.' To him, the Smoke-In was not an example of civil disobedience, but an act of 'criminal disobedience.' Dohm believed that civil disobedience should only be used to reform a law that is 'intrinsically reprehensible,' and only then after all constitutional attempts to change that law had been exhausted. Otherwise, in Dohm's words, civil disobedience is tantamount to 'anarchy.'[61] Dohm's views about civil disobedience were the product of, and perhaps reflected, a growing concern among police officials in Vancouver over the prevalence of social protests and clashes between the police and young people.

In the eyes of Justice Dohm, Mayor Tom Campbell, the police, and possibly much of middle-class society in Vancouver, the Yippies, and their 'struggle for a different world,' epitomized anarchy. The Yippies, on the other hand, felt that the time had indeed come to challenge authority and change social attitudes towards marijuana, the country's drug laws, young peoples' lifestyles, and the poor. In order to counteract this sentiment and prevent any further conflagrations on Vancouver's streets, Justice Dohm believed that city council should adopt a policy of no longer allowing demonstrators to take over the city's streets.

The *Georgia Straight* denounced the Dohm inquiry as a 'white wash' because it essentially exonerated the police and dismissed the Jamboree's attempt to change public opinion about Canada's archaic drug laws.[62] Other critics of the Vancouver police, notably the BCCLA, were not as harsh in their criticism of Dohm's report, but insisted that the inquiry should have established a process whereby relations between the police and the community could be improved. In December of 1971, the BCCLA released its own report into the Gastown riot and police-community relations. *The Police and the Community* argued that the police came to Gastown that night with 'very negative, and perhaps for some even spiteful, attitudes' towards 'hippies' and youth, which inevitably led to conflict. These attitudes resulted from the police isolating themselves from the community, evident in the scaling back of foot patrols and their increasing use of cars to patrol the city. So, it is not surprising, the BCCLA report concluded, that for the police, protest groups, and the young people who belonged to them, were 'strangers' and 'weirdos' who posed a risk to social order. [63] The BCCLA urged the police, politicians, and the community to look beyond the Jamboree and recognize that the attitudes and beliefs of the youth who had organized the Smoke-In were grounded in social and economic problems that society must address.

The Vancouver Police Department eventually assigned four constables to Gastown, not necessarily to establish better relations with youth, but to bring about 'a more positive approach by the resident and business community [to]...controlling the increasing drug distribution problem.'[64] No criminal charges were brought against the police officers; Attorney General Peterson cited a lack of evidence and the poor calibre of the witnesses. The BCCLA condemned Peterson's decision, in part, because it reinforced the public's perception that one set of laws existed for the police and another set of laws for youth.[65] The charges against the civilians who were arrested during the riot yielded mixed results. Some, like Sham Williams, were fined for creating a disturbance. Others were found guilty of performing an indecent act and obstructing a police officer. In a majority of the cases, however, the charges were dismissed or stayed, mainly because of insufficient evidence or because the arresting officers did not properly identify themselves.[66]

In some respects, the Dohm inquiry was a 'white wash' because it failed to deal with the underlying causes of the riot, namely, the poor social and economic conditions faced by many young people in Gastown, and elsewhere in Vancouver, along with the police harassment of 'long hairs' in the city. Nor did Dohm entertain the possibility that Canada's drug laws, and their enforcement by the Vancouver drug squad, notably Operation Dustpan, might in fact, be unjust. In this sense, the inquiry contributed little to the public debate over the legalization of marijuana and the treatment of society's disgruntled youth. The Yippies' voice had not so much been silenced by the police's actions, as discredited by the public inquiry and eventually ignored by the mainstream media. But the resolve that was behind the Gastown Smoke-In and Street Jamboree, and the concomitant social malaise and youth dissatisfaction with modern society, so reminiscent of the 1960s and which the riot brought once again to the surface, continued to thrive in Vancouver in the early 1970s. As several of the chapters in this book indicate, riots, protests, and 'wild cat' strikes were evident across Canada in the 1960s and early 1970s. And while not all of these confrontations with authorities achieved their desired goals, this should not diminish the fact that groups like the Yippies had the courage of their convictions and challenged what they considered to be social injustices in Vancouver.

FURTHER READING

Aronsen, Lawrence. *City of Love and Revolution: Vancouver in the Sixties.* Vancouver: New Star Books, 2010.

Barnholden, Michael. *Reading the Riot Act: A Brief History of Riots in Vancouver.* Vancouver: Anvil, 2005.

Hunt, Andrew. '"When Did the Sixties Happen?" Searching for New Directions.' *Journal of Social History* 33/1 (1999), 147–61.

Lipsitz, George. '"Who'll Stop the Rain?" Youth Culture, Rock 'n' Roll, and Social Crises.' In David Farber, ed., *The Sixties: From Memory to History,* 206–34. Chapel Hill: University of North Carolina Press, 1994.

Martel, Marcel. 'Law versus Medicine: The Debate over Drug Use in the 1960s.' In Magda Fahrni and Robert Rutherdale, eds., *Creating Postwar Canada: Community, Diversity, and Dissent, 1945–75,* 315–33. Vancouver: UBC Press, 2008.

– 'They Smell Bad, Have Diseases, and Are Lazy: RCMP officers Reporting on Hippies in the Late Sixties.' *Canadian Historical Review* 90/2 (2009), 215–45.

The Abortion Caravan was organized by the Vancouver Women's Caucus to protest Canada's restrictive abortion laws. The Caravan travelled across the country,
stopping in various locations on its way to Ottawa.
Abortion for Women Caravan Tour, Calgary, Alberta, April 1970. NA-2864-5986.
Permission of Glenbow Museum Archives.

7

Sex Spying: The RCMP Framing of English-Canadian Women's Liberation Groups during the Cold War

Steve Hewitt and Christabelle Sethna

Women's liberation emerged as one of the defining issues of the sixties.[1] Growing numbers of women were working outside of the home; Doris Anderson, editor of *Chatelaine,* upped the feminist content of the popular women's magazine; and the government of Prime Minister Lester B. Pearson struck the Royal Commission on the Status of Women (RCSW) in 1967. By the end of the decade, fledging women's liberation groups composed mainly of young, white, middle-class university women disillusioned with the male dominance of New Left student politics challenged women's inferior position in society and began organizing on their own.[2] Unlike older, more established women's organizations, which were willing to work with the government, women's liberation groups asserted that women's oppression could be overcome only through fundamental changes to society. These changes would result in equality between men and women. Canadian women's liberation groups viewed their struggle as parallel to that of oppressed peoples seeking liberation. Wars of decolonization, the civil rights movement, anti-war, Native, student, and labour activism, as well as American feminist organizing were major influences. However, Canadian women's liberation groups were far keener on a class-based analysis of women's oppression than were their American counterparts, reflecting the importance of socialism to feminism in Canada. Still others were inspired by the radical feminist politics of those American women's liberationists who understood the oppression of women as rooted in biological differences between men and women. In Quebec, women's liberation politics were deeply connected to nationalist struggles for independence from Canada.[3]

Throughout the country, women's liberation groups with names such as the Vancouver Women's Caucus (VWC), Front pour la libération des femmes (FLF), Toronto Women's Liberation (TWL), and New Feminists (NF) adopted the non-violent, non-conformist, and anti-capitalist values common to the New Left counterculture. They also displayed an affinity for public spectacles such as marches, demonstrations, sit-ins, and street theatre performances. Women's liberation groups concerned themselves with access to safe and legal abortion, day care, violence against women, the role of women in labour unions, and equal pay for work of equal value. A familial metaphor equated feminism with a sisterhood based on women's global solidarity. However, from the early 1970s onward, as women's liberation groups began to wrestle with internal splits and factions that cut deeply across personal and political lines over matters such as ideology, organization, class, sexuality, and race, this romanticized notion was cast into doubt. By the mid-1970s, many women's liberation groups dissolved under the weight of these fractures or morphed into larger coalitions. Nevertheless, the concerns they raised remained an integral part of what came to be known as second-wave feminist politics.[4]

Despite their short shelf life, women's liberation groups quickly come to the attention of the Canadian state. The Royal Canadian Mounted Police (RCMP) Security Service, the name commonly applied to the RCMP's intelligence branch which went through a variety of names throughout its history, began spying on these groups because the state perceived them to represent a left-wing subversive threat. Subversion emerged in the twentieth century as a convenient justification for directing the powers of the state against domestic targets. Framing left-wing activity as subversive allowed the state, in the words of Colin Leys and Elizabeth Grace, to 'delegitimize activities and ideas opposed to the established order, and hence to legitimize the state in acting against them, even though the activities are legal.'[5] At work was what the late historian Frank Donner described in the American context as the 'the agitator-subversion thesis,' in which, he argued, there was a denial of 'the relevance of social and economic factors as the cause of unrest' with the emphasis for causation instead being placed on the role of individuals.[6]

Hampered by the belief that communism was not just the main threat but the *only* national security threat, the RCMP initially responded as did the Federal Bureau of Investigation (FBI) in the United States, by interpreting all left-wing activism as somehow communist-led or communist-inspired. This consistent pattern of understanding security threats to the Canadian state within a communist versus anti-communist binary frame of reference grew cumbersome in the context of the emergence of Québecois nationalism, student power at high schools and universities, the American civil rights movement, Red Power, Black Power, and anti-Vietnam War agitation concomitant with the rise of the New Left in the 1960s.[7] Only in the latter half of the decade did the RCMP Security Service begin to abandon this rigid framework. By 1967, a year in which the counter-subversion branch of the RCMP held active files on forty-eight thousand individuals and six thousand organizations,[8] the Security Service had dramatically expanded its definition of a subversive to include any of the following: 'CP of C [Communist Party of Canada] member, suspected Trotskyist, self-admitted Marxist, black nationalist, student agitator, anarchist, red power advocate, or an associate of communists.'[9] The involvement of women on the left in some women's liberation groups meant that both individuals and groups were constructed as a subversive threat deserving of police attention.

In previous decades, the RCMP selected a wide range of women's organizations for scrutiny because of their political activities, their relationship to unions, and/or the class, racial, or ethnic background of their members.[10] Beginning in the latter half of the 1960s, an explosive mix of Cold War and New Left politics sparked the RCMP Security Service to cast their surveillance net over women's liberation groups. The Mounties' interest in women's liberation groups was partly based on their overall focus during this period on domestic social movements as a threat to social order. Women's liberation groups represented just some of the numerous newly emerging associations caught in the Mounties' crosshairs. But the RCMP also targeted women's liberation groups out of fear that first communists and then later other radical left-wing interests could infiltrate and use any of these new associations to undermine the Canadian state.

Surveillance of domestic social movements had become one of the RCMP's key activities in the 1960s; it was inevitable that the force would eventually focus on the women's liberation movement. And yet, despite the Mounties' growing political sophistication and their increasing recognition of the varieties of left-wing radicalism, what we call 'sex spying' stymied the RCMP. Their inability to understand the gendered implications of the women's liberation movement outside an established Cold War anti-communist framework is indicative of how developments in the 1960s continued after the end of the decade. The RCMP established a pattern of surveillance against feminists in the 1960s that continued into the 1980s.

Intelligence services and police forces have historically been all-male institutions.[11] This was especially true of the Mounted Police. By the twentieth century, the Mounties' identity was based on a 'hegemonic masculinity'[12] that stressed physicality, size, and violence.[13] Before 1974, women toiled in the RCMP only in clerical positions. The perception of women in the RCMP before 1974 is perhaps best exemplified by the Miss RCMP Pageant, a regular occurrence for a number of years.[14] With such an ornamental view of the female sex, it is not surprising that the force would take a dim view of women participating in various kinds of protest movements.

Gender was the key variable at work. However, the interaction of gender with other variables such as the class position, racial and ethnic origins, age, sexuality, and political ideologies of those being spied upon *and* those doing the spying factored significantly into the surveillance reports generated by sex spying.[15] For example, when nearly 250 members of women's liberation groups across Canada gathered in Winnipeg in the spring of 1972, a female informer provided the RCMP with far more than dozens of names of those in attendance accompanied by brief biographical sketches. In addition to noting that a young woman named 'Rita MacNeil' described as 'from Toronto Women's Caucus (TWC). She's the one who composes and sings women's lib songs,' the informer relayed details of meetings, speeches, and even social gatherings. Through salacious comments tinged with homophobia, she revealed what she believed her secret employers wanted to know: 'One hundred sweating uncombed women [were] standing around in the middle of the floor with their arms around each other crying sisterhood and dancing. The church had banned the "wine and cheese" part of the party so they all got bombed on vodka. Two dykes had been imported from the U.S. to show everyone how it was done which they proceeded to do in the middle of the floor.'[16] In effect, sex spying meant that an all-male, all-white, homosocial[17] police force found itself spying on women's liberation groups whose members often rejected conventional white, middle-class roles for women that were steeped in attention to heteronormative feminine appearance and demeanour. Therefore, sex spying presented an unprecedented challenge to the RCMP. Like the FBI, which had extensively infiltrated the American women's liberation movement,[18] the Mounties found themselves struggling to understand the structure, tactics, and goals of Canadian women's liberation groups and the potential threat they posed to national security.[19]

Targeting Women's Liberation Groups

Older, more established women's organizations such as the Voice of Women (VOW), had long been portrayed as threats to national security because of their potential to influence national and international government policy and, as a result, were subjected to surveillance. In the case of women's liberation groups, the Mounties presumed that these groups, or some of their members, had connections to New Left interests and thus represented a subversive threat to Canada's liberal-democratic political system. In particular, given the political fracturing of the Old Left, the popularity of the New Left and the appearance of women's liberation groups, the RCMP shifted its attention to the relationship of Trotskyism to the women's liberation movement. The widespread belief among security officials was that Trotskyists were employing what has been contentiously labelled 'entryism' (a term also adopted by the RCMP), meaning the tactic of infiltrating wider social movements, such as women's liberation, by extremists in order to further their own subversive agendas.[20] As such, went the argument, small-scale Trotskyist interests in the form of groups such as the League for Socialist Action (LSA) and its youth arm, the Young Socialists (YS), could exert a disproportionately greater influence than if they operated openly on their own. The Mounties were not completely out in left field in linking together women's liberationists and Trotskyists. FBI surveillance was also designed to monitor 'groups that were believed to be infiltrating and attempting to exert control over [the women's movement].'[21] Moreover, many women's liberation groups did slant left, reflecting the importance of socialism to feminism in Canada.[22] In addition, some LSA and YS members joined women's liberation groups seeking to co-opt issues such as access to safe and legal abortion in order to win a broader section of women over to Trotskyism.[23] Finally, the powerful appeal of the women's liberation movement enticed women in the LSA and the YS to commit personally and politically to spread feminist ideas within these organizations.[24]

Nevertheless, the RCMP's characterization of the Trotskyist threat did not differ largely from the frame of reference the force had used to explain the communist menace. The Trotskyists may have been a potentially different group of left-wing radicals but, from the point of view of the RCMP, they still functioned in exactly the same manner as had the communists. This point of view complicated the Mounties' efforts at sex spying. Women's liberation groups differed profoundly from the left-wing radical masculine protest template in terms of structure, tactics, and goals. When it came to structure, many women's liberation groups explicitly rejected hierarchical leadership modes that were crucial to protest organizations dominated by men. Not surprisingly, the Mounties interpreted one Saskatoon women's liberation group in October 1969 as appearing 'to be in a disorganized state, having no executive or leader as such with [three members] forming the nucleus of the group, calling meetings on an irregular basis.'[25] In contrast to the sometimes physically violent nature of men's uprisings, women's liberation groups adopted tactics such as position papers, marches, consciousness-raising meetings, and street theatre characterized by humour and irony to get across their message. As a result, RCMP surveillance of Women's International Terrorist Conspiracy from Hell (WITCH) and the Purple Penis Avengers, both active in Canada in the late 1960s, required a profoundly different understanding than did typical male unrest.[26] Finally, the goal of women's liberation groups was to work towards gender equality. This lofty ambition differed from the more materialist demands of left-male movements, including those involved in, for example, the labour movement.[27] The RCMP may have had expertise when it came to understanding the machinations of communists, but it had no similar experience in dealing with women who called not for the overthrow of government per se but of a status quo that was predicated on gender inequality.[28]

Under the RCMP Gaze

Although the RCMP began surveilling individual women's liberation groups operating on university campuses when they first materialized in the late 1960s, sex spying commenced on a national scale in May 1969 with the opening of a general file entitled 'Women's Liberation Groups – Canada.'[29] The Security Service would later describe these groups as having been established 'to publicize the role of women in society and to stop so-called exploitation of women.' The comment seemed to acknowledge that women's liberation groups had a political mandate to better women's lives. Still, the RCMP remained on alert.

An August 1969 report on the newly formed Vancouver Women's Caucus described its membership within the familiar frame of reference: 'the aims of the organization appear to be purely social in nature, but a definite extreme left and political radical undercurrent is prevailing.'[30] By 1971, a Mountie or a Mountie informer operating out of Regina felt confident enough to offer a detailed, albeit confused, distinction between women liberationists and feminists by making crude comparisons of feminists with lesbians in the aftermath of a Young Socialists conference held in Waterloo, Ontario:

> The Women's Liberation organization is distinguished from a feminist organization in that the feminist organizations hate men because they're men. In other words, they are Lesbians or homosexuals. Women's Liberation on the other hand wants to destroy the feeling of male superiority and the dependence that women feel on men. They want to establish a role for themselves as women or as people in their own right, with their own goals, and their own proficiency. They want to be free to exercise this degree of freedom any time they choose to do so. The Young Socialists aren't as interested in the feminists or the men haters as they are interested in Women's Liberation. The reason for this is that Women's Liberation will and does attract a broad cross section of the population more so than the feminists do.[31]

Another report on the National Convention of the Young Socialists, held in October 1969 in Montreal, further reinforced the RCMP's assessment of the linkage between women's liberation and Trotskyism. It was noted that a panel discussion about women's liberation outlined the creation of Trotskyist groups in Toronto, Winnipeg, Brandon,

Saskatoon, Calgary, Regina, Ottawa, Edmonton, and Vancouver.[32] The VWC and the Toronto Women's Caucus, both of which absorbed members from the League for Socialist Action and the Young Socialists, received special attention and detailed analysis.[33]

In particular, a vigorous VWC kept the RCMP on its toes. Angered by the restrictions on access to abortion, VWC members and supporters travelled in a van followed by a convoy of cars from Vancouver to Ottawa to demand reforms to the abortion law in the spring of 1970. The RCMP followed the 'Abortion Caravan,' as it was known colloquially, from province to province all the way to Parliament Hill. Although the force had repeatedly voiced its anxieties about the possibility of Trotskyist involvement in the VWC, the Mounties on the ground downplayed the threat posed by the women. Expecting women's liberationists to look and act in ways that transgressed white, middle-class, heteronormative roles for women, the noted 'ladylike' behaviour of the protesters threw the force off-guard. Eventually, the RCMP in the capital found themselves completely unprepared when the VWC led an occupation of the lawn of the residence of Prime Minister Pierre Trudeau by approximately three hundred women. Two days later, a much smaller contingent of approximately eighteen women sneaked into the public galleries of the House of Commons to condemn loudly the unfairness of the abortion law. In the aftermath of these two security breaches, the force's main concern was not whether the VWC had endangered the seat of government because of the group's putative Trotskyist connections but whether the protesters had 'embarrassed' Parliament and the prime minister.[34]

Still, ensuing coverage of women's liberation groups illustrates that it became increasingly convenient for the RCMP to attribute the rise of the women's liberation movement not to gender inequality but to the efforts of Trotskyist radicals. A senior member of the Security Service conveyed this very point to the federal government in April 1972, following a national conference of women's liberation groups in March:

> The Trotskyists, who are known to be great opportunists, have been instrumental in organizing several women's groups around many issues since 1970. The prominence of the Trotskyists in these organizations is usually only temporary...

Our analysis of the Trotskyist involvement in women's liberation, which is based on intelligence received over a period of two years from 1970 to 1972, is that there is no political or physical threat presented by them in this area of endeavour.[35]

The clear undertone to this report and to others was that women's liberation groups were a subversive menace to Canada because of the Trotskyist factor. The leadership of the RCMP was aware of the incongruity of spying on organizations that were not in actual fact guilty of subversion. A senior Mountie, in 1972, pointed out that a wide variety of interests, including proponents of women's liberation, were 'legitimate pressure groups in the main, and have to be viewed as such.' However, he added that police interest in individuals with subversive agendas operating within the said groups justified continued surveillance of these groups by Canada's national police force.[36] This rationale was further on display in an August 1973 summary of women's liberation projects at the University of Toronto:

The concept of women's liberation is now firmly established as a fact on campus. There has been a successful series of women's courses and the administration has also set up an ad hoc committee on the status of women at the U. of T. to examine areas of discrimination against women. This shows that women's liberation is accepted as a truism on the campus and is an example of what was considered a few years ago as a major plank of the New Left's program has now become accepted by the majority of society. It should be added that there is still a small vocal minority who are attempting to use women's liberation as a means to radically alter society.[37]

Systems of Surveillance

By 1977, the RCMP had institutionally made the following conclusion about what women's liberation groups represented while justifying ongoing monitoring: 'Women's Liberation, like all other mass movements, is directed at, and appeals to the lower echelon of society (the worker, the disfavoured) and thus provides fertile ground for the left wing element in which to grow its revolutionary seeds and achieve its own ends. The movement is spotted, throughout with red (from the executive down).'[38] The possibility of endless scrutiny necessitated putting into place vast systems of surveillance. At the best of times, espionage was not an easy task for the simple reason that members of the RCMP often differed greatly from the members of the groups that they tracked. The contrast could not have been any greater when it came to sex spying that involved a predominantly male organization surveilling women's liberation groups that obviously excluded men.

The force relied upon a variety of surveillance methods to generate reports on women's liberation groups. Although many of these reports contained inaccuracies and trivia, the RCMP managed to collect copious amounts of material on the women's liberation movement. Open source material, including mainstream and left-wing newspaper and magazine accounts as well as other kinds of media coverage, served the police's information needs. Mounties themselves would have conducted physical observation and would have taken photographs during public protests where the presence of men would not have appeared unusual. Less likely, but not completely inconceivable, was technological surveillance in the form of telephone taps and planted microphones. The use of such technology is frequently exaggerated by those monitored by the state. It was used infrequently, however, because of the amount of resources involved and the difficulty of gaining physical access to a property to install the equipment.[39]

There was another crucial method of intelligence gathering employed by security agencies that reveals an uncomfortable truth: human intelligence. State security forces deliberately planted agents into the ranks of targeted organizations. Because the RCMP had no female members before the mid-1970s, the force either relied on individuals who were already active members of the targeted groups or they recruited women on the outside and had them infiltrate the women's organizations.[40]

Whatever their personal or political beliefs, women informers were absolutely crucial to sex spying. These women may have been members of women's liberation groups who attended closed-door meetings or members of the general public who were present at larger events involving these groups. Without their assistance, RCMP surveillance reports would not have contained lists of the names, addresses, and telephone numbers of women's liberation group members, speeches given by invited speakers, plans for demonstrations, summaries of meetings, correspondence with other groups, and dissension among participants. Some reports were remarkably specific. In an RCMP report on a conference organized by the VWC at the University of British Columbia in November 1969 the informer provided a statistical breakdown of those in attendance by city.[41] Others revealed a tone of antipathy towards women who did not live up to conventional standards of feminine appearance and demeanour.[42] In one November 1969 report, an informer described Margaret Mitchell, who in 1979 would be elected as a New Democratic Party Member of Parliament for the riding of Vancouver East, having a 'heavy build.'[43] In May 1970, a report of a gathering in Saskatoon to welcome the VWC's Abortion Caravan asserted: 'The mixed audience consisted of about 1/3 "hippy," 1/3 high school and university students, and 1/3 nondescript average persons.'[44]

Informers had a front-row seat at the very infighting that led to splits and factions within women's liberation groups. Nowhere was this more evident than during the April 1971 Indochinese Conference. Organized by various Canadian and American women's liberation groups and held in Vancouver and Toronto, the conference featured five Indochinese women who had journeyed across the Pacific Ocean to discuss the Vietnam War. Signalling their awareness that they were under watch, the organizers took it for granted that the conference would be an irresistible draw for state surveillance. Indeed, when Cora Weiss, a co-founder of Women Strike for Peace, arrived in Toronto from the United States in April 1971 for the conference, she welcomed the crowd with the address: 'sisters, friends and members of the FBI.'[45]

The RCMP was an interested party at the conference. Mountie reports based on informer accounts dutifully captured the tensions there. Some Canadian women resented the American women for their ignorance about Canada. Differences emerged between older and younger peace activists. At odds were straight women and lesbian women and white women and women of colour. These divisions were a stark indication of just how difficult it was to unite women with competing interests and identities within one mass movement. Yet, the information was relayed without any hint of analysis; rather, the informers couched their reports in prurient language that marked the women as deviant not only because of their leftist leanings and law-breaking activities but also because their race, class, age, sexuality, and citizenship underscored their unfeminine appearance and demeanour. The following surveillance report demonstrates that the RCMP informers were more obsessed with the unfeminine appearance of the participants, than their political activities or beliefs, even though the latter were the purpose of the Mounties' surveillance. The RCMP informers clearly failed to grasp the aims of the women's movement, and continued to interpret what they saw through a lens shaped by conventional stereotypes of gender, race, and sexuality:

> 5. [deleted under Access Information Act: Source reported] the mood of both meetings was that there was not complete agreement... Some women present were boldly displaying the publication 'Lesbianism is Revolution.' [deleted: name of woman] of Calgary appeared to have spent the afternoon with the Gay Liberation women. In the evening, she was boldly displaying a copy of 'Lesbianism is Revolution.' Source also noted that earlier in the afternoon, she appeared to have been quite drunk...
>
> 28. [deleted] approximately 400 individuals attended the Plenary meeting held during the afternoon of 2-4-71. The crowd was made up of many Americans, including many coloured people, some lesbians, and many young 'hippie' women. Copies of lesbian literature were evident everywhere...A W. Lib. [women's liberation] girl sang about freeing herself from the chains of being a wife...The odour of marihuana was definite as the evening progressed, and people smoked it openly. A Negro woman talked and sang against NIXON and U.S. imperialism... [deleted: name of woman described] [the] scene as sickening and expressed the opinion that the Americans were particularly poorly behaved.[46]

The political divisions evident among the women depicted in this passage would spell a bitter end to the conference. These divisions, coupled with the perceived deviant aspect of the women present, must have guaranteed the Mounties a steady supply of willing informers.

Informers could also use their role or influence within an organization to disrupt the group from within. In her study of the American women's movement, historian Ruth Rosen discovered that the FBI recruited, some for pay and others on a volunteer basis, dozens and possibly hundreds of women to spy on other women in women's liberation groups: 'Porous and inviting, the movement permitted easy access and infiltration. For feminists, it was next to impossible to distinguish between informers and ordinary women who behaved oddly, suggested weird actions, held rigid positions, had poor judgment, or created dissension every time they opened their mouths.'[47] Famed American feminist Betty Friedan went so far as to blame divisions in the women's liberation movement on the FBI, although Rosen downplays the ultimate impact of the FBI beyond its ability to damage 'trust' among women.[48]

While there is overwhelming evidence that state agencies deliberately destroyed individuals' careers and personal lives during the Cold War, the ultimate impact of state surveillance on the women's liberation movement is yet to be determined.[49] Whatever the case, surveillance and/or the threat of surveillance can affect behaviour and encourage paranoia and fear. There is also the psychological impact of the knowledge that one had been subjected to state surveillance. As American feminist Letty Pogrebin noted in 1977: 'The important fact is that they tailed us and invaded our privacy, both psychic and physical. They snooped. They pressed their candid camera against a one-way mirror to our private lives. It seems impossible not to feel outrage at these flagrant violations of the rights of free speech, association and assembly.'[50]

Leaving aside the wider impact of state surveillance, RCMP sex spying included attempts to damage deliberately the work of various women's liberation groups. In the case of the Vancouver Women's Caucus, the then head of the RCMP Security Service, Assistant Commissioner J.E.M. Barrette, wrote to D.B. Beavis, the secretary of the Security Sub-Panel, an important body within the Privy Council Office in Ottawa, to emphasize the involvement of Trotskyists with the group's Abortion Caravan. Barrette advised the minister that the Trotskyist angle 'may be disseminated at your discretion, however, the R.C.M.P. is not to be named as the source.'[51] The intent, which dovetailed with FBI practices, was to provide the federal government with evidence of links between the VMC and Trotskyists in order to discredit the VWC through the media.[52]

Tracking funds allotted to women's liberation groups from government coffers was another strategy the Mounties used in their surveillance efforts. In June 1971, Barrette's successor as head of the Security Service, John Starnes, wrote to Solicitor General Jean-Pierre Goyer to warn him that 'funds have been allotted to various individuals and groups of interest to the Security Service by the Secretary of State Department's Opportunities for Youth Program. [deleted]... The foregoing information indicates that radical and subversive elements view the Opportunities for Youth Program as a readily available source of funds to finance their activities.'[53] Women's liberation groups were among those receiving government funding. Later in December that same year, the Security Service provided the Department of Manpower and Immigration with a list of applications for funding various grassroots projects, information on how much government money was sought in each application, and secret RCMP information on those involved in each application.

Project 51107, a women's centre in Vancouver, was heavily scrutinized for its connections to Trotskyists, university activists, and other radicals. Once again, as the following excerpt demonstrates, the RCMP remained trapped in an anti-communist framework, and sought only to link women's liberationists to Trotskyists and other radicals:

14. It came to our attention in August of this year that the Vancouver Women's Caucus, a radical New Left women's liberation movement, had outlived its purpose and would disband. It was suggested that their meeting place, 511 Carral Street, be turned into a drop-in centre for women...

15. The co-ordinator of this project [deleted: name] was a teaching assistant at Simon Fraser University... She was one of 114 persons arrested following the occupation of Simon Fraser University [deleted] During 1970 she became actively involved in the VWC with, amongst others, the two individuals who forwarded letters of recommendation on behalf of this project [deleted]

16. [deleted: name] was known in 1969/70 to be a sympathizer of the Progressive Workers Movement [deleted: file number], however, her activities since have been almost solely confined to the VWC.

17. [deleted: name] as with [deleted: name], was a campus activist during the Simon Fraser University upheaval but has since been mostly involved with the VWC while maintaining her contacts with known Marxist revolutionaries.

18. Although their backgrounds and activities are somewhat condemning through the duration of the VWC's activities, these three women seem to have remained apart from the two more militant groups involved. This

organisation suffered attempts by both the Trotskyists and revolutionary youth groups for control of the VWC but it was, in part, due to the efforts of these individuals that these elements were removed from the organization. It is difficult for us on the basis of information at hand to predict what may result from the financing of this project.[54]

Clearly, the aims of the women's liberation movement continued to stymie the RCMP. Just over two weeks later, the Security Service warned about another application, this one by the Toronto Women's Caucus, for the same reason:

> We are providing for your consideration, information concerning a project application from Toronto, the Women's Involvement Program (a Division of the Toronto Women's Caucus)...
> 2. The Toronto Women's Caucus is a Trotskyist controlled front organization...It is our feeling that a large percentage of the money granted to the project would filter into the L.S.A. and Y.S. coffers, and as the Canadian Trotskyist movement has strong international ties, may also be used to finance international ventures. [deleted] Although we have no substantial information, there is little doubt that the majority of the twenty jobs that this project will create will be held by L.S.A. and Y.S. members. It is suggested therefore, that if this project is approved, consideration might be given to closely scrutinizing its progress to ensure that funds are not being diverted from the actual reasons for which they were intended.[55]

Despite the Mounties' intervention, the application was approved. The Department of Manpower and Immigration would subsequently contact the RCMP for information on whether the funds it had awarded were being used properly.[56]

Conclusion

Sex spying continued through the 1970s and into the 1980s. In 1982, the RCMP appeared to return to the more traditional Cold War binary framework in a report filed under the title: 'Communist Party of Canada (CP of C) Policy and Activity Re: Women's Group.' The report noted that the Communist Party was sending two delegates to the annual meeting of the National Action Committee on the Status of

Women, an umbrella women's organization then funded primarily by the federal government.[57] The pursuit of subversives by the Canadian security state would continue even after the Canadian Security Intelligence Service (CSIS) replaced the RCMP Security Service in 1984. Official counter-subversion, increasingly embarrassing to the federal government, would finally end in 1988, a year before the Berlin Wall was toppled.[58]

During the 1960s, where women's liberation groups were concerned, the RCMP emulated the approach of the FBI. Like the FBI, the RCMP Security Service attempted to frame women's liberation groups as a subversive menace to the state that justified continued surveillance. The force insisted that although women's liberation groups might not represent a national security threat per se, their connections to the left, namely, Trotskyists, could. While there were some links between women's liberation groups and the League for Socialist Action and the Young Socialists, this approach made it impossible for Canada's national police force to interpret accurately the structure, tactics, and goals of women's liberation groups. Despite many years of espionage, the RCMP Security Service uncovered nothing more subversive than a rejection of conventional white, middle-class heteronormative roles for women and the pursuit of gender equality in society.

Thus, sex spying proved to be a failure. Herein, the RCMP differed little from its American security cousins. As Ruth Rosen illustrates, the FBI could not see the forest for the trees: 'Ironically, the FBI searched for signs of subversion in the women's movement but couldn't recognize what was truly dangerous. While they looked for communists and bombs, the women's movement was shattering traditional ideas about work, customs, education, sexuality, and the family. Ultimately, this movement would prove far more revolutionary than the FBI could ever imagine.'[59] Even when the RCMP's own intelligence indicated that women's liberation groups were primarily concerned with the exploitation of women in society, the Mounties did not abandon the belief that radical leftist subversion underlay the rise of the women's liberation movement. In so doing, the Royal Canadian Mounted Police failed to recognize how radically this movement, which would outlive the Security Service, was beginning to alter Canadian society on personal, political, and institutional levels. Indeed, the RCMP itself, in the midst of spying on women's groups, would open up its own ranks to women members in 1974.

FURTHER READING

Brownmiller, Susan. *In Our Time: Memoir of a Revolution*. New York: Dell, 1999.

Cunningham, David. *There's Something Happening Here: The New Left, the Klan, and FBI Counterintelligence*. Berkeley: University of California Press, 2005.

Echols, Alice. *Daring to Be Bad: Radical Feminism in America, 1967–1975*. Minneapolis: University of Minnesota Press, 1989.

Freeman, Barbara M. *The Satellite Sex: The Media and Women's Issues in English Canada, 1966–1971*. Waterloo: Wilfrid Laurier University Press, 2001.

Hewitt, Steve. *Spying 101: The RCMP's Secret Activities at Canadian Universities, 1917–1997*. Toronto: University of Toronto Press, 2002.

PART FOUR

Race and Working-Class Movements

Major strike at Lenkurt Electric, Burnaby, British Columbia, May 1966.
Courtesy of George Diack, *Vancouver Sun.*

8

'Hothead Troubles': Sixties-Era Wildcat Strikes in Canada

Peter S. McInnis

For organized labour the 1960s began with little fanfare. In the 1963 inaugural year of the magazine *Canadian Dimension,* economist Cy Gonick ruminated on the state of Canada's unions. Charging that trade unions were in serious decline, having squandered momentum as defenders of social justice, Gonick pinpointed the 'growing obsolescence of the strike as labour's ultimate weapon.'[1] The rapidly unfolding events of the mid-1960s would force revisions to this pensive assessment as an outburst of unauthorized 'wildcat' strikes shook the confidence of Canadian society. These actions were staged by a cadre of protesters who, because of their critical stance towards employers, government, and union officials alike, had earned the disparaging epithet 'hotheads.' The flare-up of spontaneous job actions, the unseating of long-time labour leaders, the refusal to ratify collective agreements, inter-union raiding, and breakaway movements were all cited as evidence of growing labour unrest.[2] The rise of this militant union culture brought with it a reassessment of Canada's 'postwar settlement.' Critics claimed that the settlement was, by the 1960s, discredited by those impatient for substantive change.[3]

The phrase 'postwar settlement' had entered the lexicon as the descriptor for the informal accord between labour, business, and the state designed to secure workplace harmony.[4] Under this new regime, all parties were to abide by certain rules or 'best practices' designed not only to reduce strikes and lockouts, but also establish the basis for mutual goals in the increasingly competitive world of global capitalism. This settlement was, in part, outlined in a 1946 landmark ruling by Mr Justice Ivan C. Rand. The 'Rand formula' set out a balance of rights and obligations and established the tone for future industrial relations policy. Unions obtained the right to organize and bargain collectively, and this offered them a measure of social credibility and financial stability. In return, labour acceded to business demands for uninterrupted production and the concept of 'management rights' – the latter gave employers residual control over any workplace matter not specifically addressed in the language of a written contract. The entire settlement was constructed on the edifice of an ever-expanding capitalist mass production and mass consumption society, with inherent gendered assumptions that privileged male over female workers.

With the attainment of formal recognition, many trade unions were careful to reinforce their new-found legitimacy. During strikes those walking the picket lines traditionally held aloft placards stating 'on legal strike,' or 'our strike is legal,' lest observers get the impression that unions would countenance illegality. There was good reason for this caution. One of the sacrosanct regulations Rand stipulated was that all labour stoppages during the legal term of a contract were prohibited. Unions assumed the responsibility to prevent illegal strikes and police their memberships from disrupting routine work schedules. Failure to curtail obstreperous workers could result in heavy fines and jail sentences for labour leaders. Added to this was the fact that many unions were under covert surveillance by the Royal Canadian Mounted Police, anxious to expose any wrongdoing which might undermine labour's credibility.[5] Wildcat actions, because of their inherent illegality, represented precisely the type of internal protest that respectable union officials most feared, because they contained the potential to undermine the procedural stability upon which the postwar settlement was premised. Commentators noted that the United States experienced a decisive swing to the political right in the immediate postwar era, and this had brought about the passage of the exceedingly anti-labour legislation known as the Taft-Hartley Act.[6] The Canadian situation was never as reactionary, but unions were careful to play by the established rules so as to avoid any similar backlash.

The federal Department of Labour's 'Strikes and Lockouts' files for the mid-1960s reveal a startling inventory of workplace disturbances. These monthly computations indicate sustained activity of an 'illegal' or unsanctioned nature. Of the more than 1,100 strikes recorded for 1965–66, fully 53 per cent were deemed wildcat actions.[7] Even this figure likely undercounts the true extent of the disruptions as stoppages of very short duration were often not recorded officially. The total working time lost overall reached a twenty-five-year high.[8]

Many of these so-called quickie strikes, lasting days or merely hours, represented effective guerilla tactics against the ponderous bureaucracy of Canadian industrial relations. They were brief, incisive job actions just long enough to register dissent without engaging the procedural machinery of retribution. While most stoppages were ostensibly fought over higher wages and benefits, they were also launched for a host of seemingly trivial reasons: the refusal to provide free lemonade during a humid summertime work shift, or frustration with a surly foreman who treated workers with less than their due respect, or to protest arcane shop-floor regulations.[9] Some workers went so far as to improvise their own work schedules. At the Oshawa plant of General Motors, twenty-eight autoworkers were suspended after an impromptu decision to forgo the clamour of the assembly line in favour of an extended lunch break at a nearby tavern.[10] Remarkably, and against all considered advice, the sudden noncompliance of workers proved effective, as neither management nor union officials could counteract such widespread indiscipline.

These impetuous actions echoed the nineteenth century, a time long before constraints of industrial legality stifled the raw emotions of the workplace, when the only true test of power was the resolve of workers to stand up to the boss. Although some of these actions may be judged as ill-considered, instinctual reactions to the workplace environment, it may argued the 'hotheads' were, in fact, articulating their claim to a moral economy which demanded a 'fair' wage and 'just' conditions.[11] The controlling paternalism of employers and union officials alike was to be resisted. If some actions appeared spontaneous, they had a basis in long-simmering critiques of 'the system.'

Protests were initially characterized as typical cyclic strike patterns which if given sufficient time would dissipate. As this strike wave coincided with a thriving domestic economy, economists speculated that a tight labour market had bolstered the material expectations of many trade unionists while spiralling inflation rates added a sense of urgency. In 1965, the 'big strike,' a wildcat of postal workers, the first such action in forty years, forced the federal government to offer substantial wage hikes and the right to bargain collectively. The postal strike was a transformative experience: two previously ineffective organizations emerged as bona fide trade unions – one of which, the Canadian Union of Postal Workers, became synonymous with militancy. The 1965 strike, and subsequent job actions linked to postal unions, raised significant challenges on matters such as collective bargaining, technological change, health/safety protections, and gender equality. It also positioned Canadian public sector unions in the forefront of labour militancy.

Without doubt, economic motivations were central to the emboldened actions of labour, but this in itself is an insufficient explanation. Close analysis suggests that the wildcats served as a stinging rebuke not only of capital, but also of elected labour representatives and their American-dominated 'international' unions.[12] Organized labour in Canada had helped launch a new political collaboration with formation of the New Democratic Party in 1961, a move that it was hoped would bring about significant federal reforms for working people. Wildcat strikes, it was argued, would only serve to undermine these efforts by allowing detractors to label the activities of so-called big labour as inherently irresponsible.

Trouble in the Ranks

Labour bureaucrats were quick to condemn this internal rancour. Tellingly, international unions – the Steelworkers, Mineworkers, and the Teamsters, organizations with decidedly autocratic reputations – incurred much of this internal dissent. These same unions actively participated in the Cold War purges of communist labour and were quite adept at quashing dissident voices. The standard anti-communist metaphor of spreading contagion was now applied to union militancy. Assuming the role of disgruntled labour official, William Mahoney, Canadian director of the United Steel Workers of America, warned that 'wildcat strikes carry with them an atmosphere of irresponsibility,

a defiance of constituted authority and organization which can easily spread. They threaten not only management but properly organized labour as well.'[13] In a round-table interview, however, four of
Canada's most senior labour officials downplayed the 1965–66 strikes
as sporadic incidents of an inexperienced rank and file, actions that
in no way threatened the basis of the industrial relations system premised on the 'free' collective bargaining between unions and employers.[14] A similar line of argument was offered by the Canadian Labour
Congress (CLC), anxious to downplay any potential obstacle to ami-
cable relations with the federal government. CLC President Claude
Jodoin in his annual presentation to the federal government noted the
obvious surge in strikes and placed the blame on employers and rising
inflation: 'It is natural and inevitable that trade unions should exploit
the advantage or relatively good times to obtain higher wages.'[15] What
Mahoney, Jodoin, and other labour executives failed to understand
was that a substantial cross-section of their membership had come
to interpret industrial relations procedure as less a bulwark for basic
union rights and more as an impediment to the effective application of
workers' self-determination. The system of Canadian labour relations
was not the solution to the problem – it was the problem.

Industrial relations experts John Crispo and Harry Arthurs commented that an undisciplined layer of 'newly organized groups of
workers possessed of unrealistic expectations about the potential
of concerted strike actions to solve their problems, can produce an
unhealthy combination of naïveté and strike-happiness.'[16] Bewildered
union officials complained, 'younger workers just want more without appearing to be concerned how they get it. The consensus seems
to be that their dues simply buy a service and they are not satisfied
with the service.'[17] Newspaper editorials chided labour bureaucrats to
constrain their membership by warning that 'defiance of the law is a
communicable disease.'[18] Unions hardly needed an excuse to clamp
down on militancy. From the start of the 1965–66 wildcats, labour
officials made concerted efforts to manage their ranks and protect the
sanctity of the contract. Yet, repeated threats to bar militants from
negotiations, withhold strike pay, and impose other punitive sanctions
all failed to achieve the desired results.

As a direct result, organized labour was tightly constrained to an industrial relations system designed in the narrow sense for the maintenance

of workplace peace rather than to address broader issues of injustice or fairness. Participation in an elaborate, multistage conciliation process – including a mandatory 'cooling-off' period – infuriated those seeking immediate resolution of disputes through direct action. The adage 'obey now; grieve later' meant that employees could only legitimately complain about management directives by submitting official grievance claims, a tediously slow step-by-step process that could take months to resolve with no guarantee of satisfaction. In the meantime, job activities, however unpleasant or unfair, were to continue unabated. This placed union officials in the unenviable position of having to defend a flawed industrial relations process to their membership. Added to this was the potential for an employer's unilateral imposition of new technology during the life of an existing contract – something that could lead to sudden and irrevocable job loss.

Violence on the Line

These wildcat strikes were often violent and unpredictable. Reports of police intervention and vandalism of company premises featured prominently on newspaper headlines.[19] Verbal and physical assaults on trade union officials were becoming commonplace as angry members were no longer willing to accept the highly formalized and rigid constraints of modern industrial relations practices. Stuart Jamieson, an economist with extensive experience in this field, later commented that the persistence of violence and illegality in this decade was much more pervasive than even he himself had first realized. If one seeks to trace the demise of the postwar settlement, noted Jamieson, the 1960s might be the place to start looking.[20]

That the many youthful dissidents were male, often with less than a high school diploma, may have accounted for their particular expressions of anger and frustration.[21] Exaggerated verbal and physical posturing was their preferred form of collective statement. The highly gendered language of wildcat strike rhetoric, with allusions to 'smashing,' 'pounding,' 'kicking,' and 'destroying' opponents, suggests an overtly masculine ethos of physical confrontation to much of these job actions, and an implicit (and often explicit) sexism to this strategy. Although the connections between masculinity and physicality had long been associated with strike actions, by the 1960s, such incidents had certainly dissipated when compared with earlier decades of the century. This sudden surge of violence in the mid-1960s caught many by surprise. Here, the generational demographic may have been significant, as less experienced workers had not yet learned, or been coerced, to follow established industrial relations procedures.[22]

Linking organized labour to violent activities was a particularly sensitive matter. Throughout the early 1960s Canadians followed extensive media coverage of the sordid internal politics and corruption of some trade unions, including corruption in the Seafarers' International Union, the construction sector, and Jimmy Hoffa's Teamsters. Gun battles among striking pulp cutters in the northern Ontario woods and bombings of Quebec textile factories added to the sensationalism.[23] It was easy to conflate these reports of labour troubles and unfairly denounce all Canadian unions as corrupt, disruptive, and anti-social.

In May 1966, a major strike occurred at Lenkurt Electric, a manufacturer of telecommunications equipment, based in Burnaby, British Columbia. Lenkurt had fired 257 union members for participating in a wildcat action that April, and things soured further when members of the International Brotherhood of Electrical Workers refused to comply with union officials who had initialed a back-to-work settlement. The ensuing suspension of the local business agent was met with angry protests and over sixty resignations from union Local 213. A New Westminster deputy sheriff sent to serve a legal injunction was encircled by picketers who physically assaulted him, threw the injunction to ground, and trampled on it.[24] The *Vancouver Sun* reported the deputy sheriff's claims that it was his worst experience in eighteen years on the job. Instead of a well-ordered picket line, there was 'just an unruly, threatening crowd.'[25] That spring, delegates to the national convention of the Canadian Labour Congress adopted a policy of 'massive civil disobedience' against such anti-union injunctions, while other resolutions sought to reassert the right to strike during the life of a contract. Clearly, in terms of radical intent, the membership was running ahead of pragmatic CLC officials.

Were the 1965–66 wildcat strikes a continuation of this unlawful trend, or was there something new to this story? It is obvious that the hothead rebels, while unruly, were not hardened criminals. Their activism took the form of improvised disruptions, more the expression of an inchoate alienation with the workaday world rather than predetermined scheme to sabotage the economy. In this respect the militancy was not anti-capitalist, as few concrete alternatives were debated. However, allusions to broader campaigns for social justice and equality were cited, and in this respect, the wildcats should be considered as an important element of the emergent global 1960s protest culture. Indeed, because analysis of the working class itself is curiously absent from most North American studies of the era, this raises challenging interpretive questions. There was much more to the decade than the exploits of rancorous middle-class college students, a point raised repeatedly in this volume of collected essays and, in particular, in the chapters by Roberta Lexier and Michael Boudreau, who note the potential for convergence between middle- and working-class dissent. If we are to address the persistent clichés of the sixties as a largely narcissistic era in which one should (as Erika Dyck notes earlier in this volume, quoting Timothy Leary's oft-misunderstood phrase) 'turn on, tune in, drop out,' the sharp rise in militancy suggests a propensity for confrontation over acquiesce. Canada's 1960s brought awareness, however imperfectly articulated, that society should, and indeed would, change to better reflect a new generation coming of age.

A New Generation?

The actions of rowdy workers spoke to a sense of alienation, resentment, and class tension that had its partial roots in generational expectations. Generational conflicts, as several other contributors in this collection note, were a common theme in 1960s protest. Erased from memory were the heroic years of labour's struggle for basic recognition; also forgotten was the 'ten lost years' of the Great Depression, when mere possession of a job was cause for thanksgiving. This postwar generation wanted it all (income, material possessions, and career satisfaction), and they expected it straight away. Sociologists quickly coined the term, 'affluent worker' to characterize this syndrome.[26] A five-part series appearing in the *Montreal Star* included one segment on labour. McGill University industrial relations specialist H.D. Woods analysed the problem: 'Perhaps for the first time in history, the public not only has expectations that the "world owes me a living," but "it owes me a good living." In the 1930s we would have been satisfied with job security. Now almost everyone has a kind of security built automatically into the growth of the community. The good life, therefore, means not only security but a higher and higher income.'[27]

As the centennial year approached, the comfortable material life Professor Woods spoke of was still restricted to a minority of working-class Canadians. Those in the highly unionized resource and manufacturing sectors expected to see tangible evidence of the nation's growing postwar affluence. A convergence of economic and demographic conditions presented the opportunity to push hard for a bounty of wages and benefits their predecessors could only imagine. Contracts brimmed with perks such as paid training leave, full prescription services, or extended vacation packages, all of which made this upper echelon of unionists among the best remunerated in the industrial world.[28] The majority of workers, however, relegated to tangential industries in weakly unionized or non-union settings were told to expect much less. This may have been Canada in the prosperous 1960s but the gap between the haves and have-nots remained a persistent problem.

Middle-class social movements, as other chapters in this collection document, were a defining feature of the sixties, but expressions of inter-class communication remained sporadic. As both Roberta Lexier and James Walker argue in this book, university-age Canadians turned their studies to critiquing the legacy of neo-colonialism and championing the spread of civil rights. Some younger trade unionists similarly studied the principles of economics, industrial relations, labour law, and history at one of several 'labour colleges' established to prepare them for careers in union institutions. The progress of second-wave feminism also offered its own set of challenges to male assumptions, irrespective of class. By the 1960s, these movements had not coalesced into a unified expression of militancy. The linkage between specific labour rights and broader citizen rights was only weakly established.

Still, the sheer numbers of postwar baby boomers coming into the job stream were changing the scene for organized labour in Canada. Some of the anger and frustration evident by the mid-1960s was due to the obvious prejudice of a legal system that commonly issued ex parte injunctions (judicial restraining orders typically requested by employers without the union's input) against picketers regardless of whether or not the strike action was legal. In this respect, workers just starting their careers immediately saw the transparent inequality of the legal system and, consequently, pushed their union leaderships for reform. It was argued that the opportunity for reform must be seized. While redress for injustices against organized labour might be pursued through legal channels, such an approach was inherently problematic because it tended to blunt the potential for grassroots activism. Canadian union bureaucracies were viewed as partially complicit in supporting a flawed industrial relations regime and obliged to face the reality that the status quo was no longer tolerable for many of their membership. Without doubt, the tensions evident within the labour movement entailed generational issues, but to suggest that this was simply a clash of the old and new overlooks the persistence of many experienced workers in the wildcat actions. In 1965–66, a major impasse between the Teamsters and Ontario-based trucking firms tied up the province's transport sector until a new master contract was conceded by management. The truckers' strike was a thoroughly nasty affair with incidents of fire-bombing of tractor trailers, tire slashing, and frequent arrests for common assault. These members of the Teamsters Union were less fresh-faced youth than grizzled old-timers who had learned effective, but hardly subtle, methods to convey their displeasure.

There were other incidents of cross-generational activism. During the summer of 1966, two major strikes drew public attention. In July, eighteen thousand workers at the International Nickel Company (Inco) operations in the Sudbury region launched a week-long blockade of company premises. So complete was the illegal stoppage that Inco was reduced to ferrying in management personnel by helicopter. The following month witnessed a halt to the Hamilton operations of the Steel Company of Canada (Stelco), as sixteen thousand employees ceased work. Press reports noted: 'The strike appeared to have been well organized, but neither the union nor the company could identify those behind it. Some attributed it to hotheads, others to communists, and still others to a group of Canadian autonomists with the union.'[29] Details of the Stelco and Inco strikes show that a sizeable number of the militants were, in fact, workplace veterans whose intimate knowledge of company operations and the job site itself were key in the initial success of the protests.[30] The coordination of picket lines and maintaining solidarity were attributable in no small measure to those whose careers preceded the 1960s generation. The oft-repeated cliché that youth distrusted anyone over the age of thirty, while capturing some of the frisson of the times, unnecessarily accentuates the generational element over the primacy of class. The wildcat strikes were about working-class militancy and not simply generational angst.

The new militancy also signalled a rejection of the 'old left' unionism of the previous decades with its emphasis on the ideologically based project of social transformation. This new generation, representing a transitional phase to an emergent sixties counterculture, was diverse, less focused, and more inclined to undisciplined initiatives. In this milieu, things happened quickly, and even a year or two represented significant difference. Workplaces that were relatively quiescent in 1964 might become hotbeds of wildcat actions by 1966. The use of wildcat strikes, while not unique to this period, signalled a serious disconnect between workers and the constraints within which they were forced to operate. Workers were faced with the daunting prospect of breaking down the existing industrial relations system while at the same time having to operate within its parameters.

Task Force on Labour Relations

Finally, an exasperated federal government undertook the responsibility to study the nature of postwar labour-management relations by establishing the Task Force on Labour Relations, under the direction of H.D. Woods. By the time the task force reported to the government, in late 1968, it had sponsored the preparation of no less than seventy-three ancillary reports studying all aspects of Canadian industrial relations. Coming at this critical juncture the project had the potential to be the most influential labour-management investigation since the 1889 Royal Commission on the Relations of Labour and Capital.[31] The results, however, were inconclusive at best.

By the time the Woods task force reported back to the government, in December 1968, it had formulated an extensive list of recommendations. The task force had been granted a broad mandate to explore revisions to Canadian industrial relations practice. Committee members corresponded with leading experts and visited American and

European centres. In this 1960s atmosphere of crisis and experimentation, concepts were floated by labour relations experts. Issuing his 263-page report for the Ontario Royal Commission on Labour Disputes, Mr Justice Ivan C. Rand broached the idea of a 'Director of Enforcement' to serve as a final arbitrator of industrial disputes. Chief Justice Bora Laskin of the Supreme Court of Canada had earlier suggested a standing committee of labour experts on call to resolve deadlocks. Discussions of a Canadian labour court similar to those used in Sweden or Australia were also vetted.[32]

The task force's conclusions were remarkably similar to those of the Donovan Royal Commission on British Trade Unions and Employers Associations – published that same year. Both government reports supported the principle of 'industrial plurality' and noted that conflict was intrinsic to the process of union-management relations. In others words, the system was not broken and with the passage of time youthful exuberance would yield to common sense pragmatism. In retrospect, these opinions may have been correct but not before the ideological challenges ushered in by this decade resulted in profound reform within organized labour in Canada, the United Kingdom, and the United States. Many of labour's dissidents refused to accept these soothing reassurances, and some would later pursue this cause within the ranks of the labour leadership.

From Consent to Coercion

The state responded to the proliferation of wildcat strikes and labour militancy with a new weapon: back-to-work-legislation.

It was a national railway strike of 110,000 non-operating workers affiliated with sixteen unions, led by the Canadian Brotherhood of Railway Employees (CBRT), that led directly to the formation of the Task Force on Labour Relations. The strike against both Canadian National Railways and the Canadian Pacific Railway began as a series of wildcat actions starting in Montreal and Toronto and moving west until a nationwide halt was called on 26 August 1966. Because railways came under federal jurisdiction, intense pressure was placed on the minority Liberal government of Lester Pearson to find a quick resolution. Bill C-230 was pushed through the House of Commons in the early hours of 1 September 1966.[33] Although federal back-to-work legislation had been invoked previously, such as during a rail stoppage in 1950, it was an option rarely used because it undermined the government's own assertions that it functioned as an 'impartial umpire' between labour and capital. With the predictability of a Newtonian law, the force of illegal strikes met the counterforce of legal barriers. The mid-1960s wildcat wave had thus begun the process of what analysts have termed the advent of 'permanent exceptionalism,' whereby state neutrality gives way to the routine (and predictable) use of anti-union emergency legislation to curtail the exercise of labour democracy.[34]

Even before the workers succumbed to legislative sanctions, internal correspondence within the CBRT makes it clear many union members were scathingly critical of national president William J. Smith. It was Smith who boldly predicted that CBRT would never yield to the politicians or the courts and stated that he himself preferred jail rather than conceding defeat. Smith's bellicose remarks proved insincere, and he quickly backtracked on this tough talk once Bill C-230 became law. The membership was furious, describing these actions as a 'betrayal' and a 'denial of democratic rights.' Unofficial 'strike continuation polls,' taken in September, indicated severe rifts within the CBRT over compliance with or defiance of any of the legislation.[35] 'Ordering us to return,' wrote a Kamloops-based worker, 'did more to weaken and destroy our strike effort than any other action ... you must resign forthwith.'[36] The non-ops had earlier staged similar wildcats in June 1965 and 1966, only to be told by their leadership that the time was not right.[37] Following the 1966 action, a hastily commissioned report prepared by a CBRT official described a 'deep resentment of the imposed settlement ... much of it directed at the union rather than the federal government.'[38]

Breakaway Movements

By the mid-1960s organized labour was compelled to address two strands of internal dissent that threatened to fracture class unity. The forces of Québécois nationalism during the years of the Quiet Revolution are well documented generally, and in this volume with José Igartua and Matthew Hayday's chapters. Arguably indicative of an insular expression of Québécois culture, the province's trade unions had undergone rapid transformation to become dynamic entities willing to challenge the dominance of both foreigners and English Canadians. The relinquishing of overt religious connections with the comparatively conservative Catholic 'confessional' unions resulted in the emergence of the Confederation of National Trade Unions. The CNTU, in turn, pushed the well-established Quebec Federation of Labour to compete in the same ideologically charged territory as their militant counterparts. Less evident is the appeal of a resurgent Quebec labour movement outside the province. The upstart CNTU found new adherents in the ranks of younger workers, largely because of the novelty of joining a movement that was deemed progressive and even subversive. The CNTU linked workplace issues with broader social concerns in a synthesis that transcended narrow class politics. In the words of one British Columbian activist, just converted to the CNTU, 'we needed someone to shake things up and they looked like the ones to do it.'[39] The mix of a Quebec-based union congress, which espoused separatism and a grassroots democratic process, was a formidable test for the established unions.

In English Canada, similar discontent brewed. An underlying theme to most of the job actions was frustration with the inherent constraints of 'international' unions. For decades, Canadian workers had drawn on the inspirational, monetary, and organizational support of American trade unions. The resulting bureaucratic structures resembled an extension of the branch-plant economy that dominated Canadian business. Observers had long complained that unions headquartered in the United States failed to comprehend the unique political and ideological circumstances of their cross-border affiliates. The latter 1960s would signal the start of an ongoing breakaway movement by which a significant number of Canadian union locals obtained autonomy from their American counterparts. Soon Canadian-led trade unions would decide uniquely made-in-Canada solutions to the challenges posed by industrial relations practices. For organized labour, renewed expressions of Canadian nationalism fed into a burgeoning mood of anti-Americanism, as Canadians of all ideological stripes questioned the increasingly problematic relationship between the two nations. The rapid expansion of the Vietnam War after 1964 further heightened public scepticism of American institutions. This burgeoning Canadian nationalism (or anti-Americanism), which is examined in Stephen Azzi's chapter, raised important questions about what it meant to be Canadian in the sixties and why it was important to make this differentiation.

Assessing the Implications

Why these events happened and what they tell us of the nature of postwar industrial relations suggests that even a buoyant 1960s economy could not hide a serious systemic weakness both in the Canadian industrial relations apparatus and the underlying ideological values on which it was premised. The focus on a mostly younger generation of unionists – those who came of age after the consolidation of industrial pluralism in the late 1940s and variously described as privileged, affluent, educated, listless, and insolent – raises important questions as to what organized labour had actually achieved in the decades following the Second World War. The protracted struggle for collective bargaining rights had, by the mid-1960s, given way to a postwar generation raised in unprecedented prosperity who may have taken these material benefits for granted.

Wildcat strikes and the intrinsic challenges these illegal actions posed for unions, employers, and governments suggest a revision to the ways in which Canadians understand the nature of the working-class experience. Evidence of a rapid disintegration of the postwar settlement is clearly suggested by the widespread militancy in the lower ranks of unionized workers. Although there is general acceptance that, by the 1970s, the nature of labour relations had taken a decided turn for the worse, evidence from the 1960s should readjust this timeline as the roots of 'permanent exceptionalism,' the systematic removal of assumed labour protections and prerogatives, appears to stretch back further into the earlier decade.

The hothead troubles of the 1960s make a definitive statement that there was much more to this tumultuous decade than typically invoked stereotypes. The anti-establishment stance of many protest groups, regardless of class, coalesced on the need for greater accountability of their elected representatives. Clearly, this coincided with the rise of student protests, anti – nuclear war action committees, and New Left movements generally, but the self-activity of a militant working class must now be added to this mix. Some of these protests involved regrettable actions of violence, but most episodes brought forth exuberance indicative of true grassroots mobilizations. It all came down to the fundamental adage that labour would never secure rights which it was not prepared to actively defend. If this lesson had been somewhat obscured in the immediate postwar years with the promise of orderly industrial relations practices, the events of the 1960s wildcat strikes reasserted 'the salience of class' for a new generation of Canadians.[40]

FURTHER READING

High, Steven. *Industrial Sunset: The Making of North America's Rust Belt, 1969–1984*. Toronto: University of Toronto Press, 2003.

McInnis, Peter S. *Harnessing Labour Confrontation: Shaping the Postwar Settlement in Canada, 1943–1950*. Toronto: University of Toronto Press, 2002.

Palmer, Bryan. *Working-Class Experience: Rethinking the History of Canadian Labour, 1800–1991*. 2nd ed. Toronto: McClelland and Stewart, 1992.

Panitch, Leo, and Donald Swartz. *From Consent to Coercion: The Assault on Trade Union Freedoms*. 3rd ed. Aurora: Garamond, 2003.

Russell, Bob. *'Back to Work?' Labour, State, and Industrial Relations in Canada*. Toronto: Nelson, 1990.

About fifteen Africville houses, with a well and nearby sign reading, 'Please boil this water before drinking and cooking.' Africville, Halifax, Nova Scotia, 1965.

Courtesy of Bob Brooks NSARM Acc. 1989–468.

9

Black Confrontation in Sixties Halifax

James W. St G. Walker

African and African-descended people have been a part of Canadian history since the beginnings of transatlantic settlement. The first recorded visitor with African roots was Mathieu de Coste (or da Costa), who served the governor of Acadia in 1608 as guide and interpreter. His employment suggests that he was already familiar with the territory and its Aboriginal inhabitants. At least one other African, unidentified by name, died of scurvy at Port Royal in 1606, and it is possible that one of Jacques Cartier's crew members came originally from Africa. The first person recorded as coming directly from Africa, and the first enslaved African known in Canada, was a child sold to a Quebec family in 1628. At his baptism in 1633 the young man was given the name Olivier Le Jeune. From that time until the British conquest about 1,400 Africans were enslaved in New France, and another 2,000 were brought into the British colonies by American Loyalists at the close of the American Revolution. Outnumbering their enslaved brethren were 3,500 free Black Loyalists who had escaped from American enslavement to the British during the war, and offered their services to the Loyalist cause. Promised not only their freedom but full equality as British subjects, the Black Loyalists were transported to British North America, chiefly to Nova Scotia, in 1783. Equality, however, was withheld. The formerly enslaved Loyalists were either denied land entirely or settled on the poorest soil, with farms of inadequate size, and without implements or provisions. They were forced into labouring for white farmers or in the emerging urban centres, and in their desperation they were prepared to accept low wages. This earned them the resentment and hostility of white labourers who were in competition for some of the same jobs.

Black Loyalist communities have long existed on the outskirts of many towns in Nova Scotia and a few in New Brunswick. Poverty was built into their very structure, but they were able to develop churches and schools essentially under their own control, and a distinct black culture evolved that was different from their white neighbours and different, too, from the slave culture they had left behind. As slavery was gradually abolished in British North America in the 1790s and early 1800s, formerly enslaved African Canadians added to the population and geographical distribution of the free black communities. Another burst of population arrived during the War of 1812, when Britain again promised enslaved Americans the opportunity of a free life in British territory. About two thousand of them, known to history as the Black Refugees, were settled in Nova Scotia and New Brunswick after the war. In subsequent decades, the descendants of those enslaved in Canada, Black Loyalists, and Black Refugees merged as an African-Canadian community, physically segregated, economically disadvantaged, and socially restricted, but sustained by their religious and cultural identity in their confidence that they were equal and deserved equal treatment in Canada. Because of their isolation, living in segregated all-black communities, their economic dependence on the mainstream society, and because their small numbers dictated non-confrontational tactics in their ongoing campaign for racial equality, African Canadians in the Maritimes remained out of sight and out of mind for most of their fellow Canadians.

This entire situation would undergo a dramatic change in the 1960s, in all parts of Canada. With about half the total African-Canadian population in 1961,[1] black Nova Scotians were prominent in launching a more confrontational phase in their history and a new definition of their place in Canadian society. How that movement began, in Halifax, is the subject of this chapter.

In the 1960s, the black community of Nova Scotia experienced a shift in consciousness that threatened to erupt in 1968, with an impending and multifaceted confrontation between black and white communities, between African-Canadian citizens and their government, and between two political visions within the black community itself. An apparent resolution to all these potential conflicts was promised with the formation of the Black United Front, which seemed to maintain the community's traditional non-confrontational approach to mainstream racism while incorporating a radical innovation: the people themselves would take charge of their own affairs and set the terms of their community's future development.

Black Power!

The signature episode of the decade lasted only eighteen hours, when Stokely Carmichael visited Halifax in October 1968. He came as the guest of Burnley 'Rocky' Jones, a black Halifax youth leader, following the Black Writers Congress in Montreal, where both had been invited speakers.[2] The visiting American was prime minister of the Black Panther Party and the most prominent exponent of black radicalism in the United States. In his Montreal speech he said that 'aggressive violence was essential if the blacks were to change their status. In performing such violence the blacks would do to the whites only what had been done to the blacks many times in the past.'[3] Jones himself had told the Montreal audience that a revolution was necessary in Canadian race relations, and while he claimed to reject an armed insurrection, he added, 'if you think those who control this society will allow a non-violent minority to take over, you're crazy.'[4] Not surprisingly the presence of Black Power's chief advocate, staying in the home of the city's own leading black militant, created considerable alarm in Halifax. In a story bound to increase the tension, the local newspaper quoted from Carmichael's Montreal speech: 'get all the guns you can and be prepared to kill for your people.' In Halifax Carmichael was more circumspect: 'We are internationalizing black power. We recognize all the problems that black people of Halifax have and we wanted to begin some coordination so that we can move against racism and capitalism.'[5] The president of the moderate Nova Scotia Association for the Advancement of Coloured People, H.A.J. 'Gus' Wedderburn, warned Haligonians: 'Time is running out, let's start finding solutions to the problems of the Negro.'[6]

Carmichael promised that more Panthers would follow him, and they did, meeting with local black people, analysing the racial situation in Halifax, and preaching a message of black pride and self-direction. One of the Panthers was stopped by police and found to have an illegal firearm in his possession; since he was driving Rocky Jones's car at the time, Jones too was arrested. This accentuated the sense of impending violence, and also seemed to confirm the feeling among younger African Canadians that the police were persecuting them and had them under surveillance. Jones referred to the jailed Panther George Sams as 'a political prisoner.'[7] But contrary to the media stir, the Panthers did not try to provoke violence in Nova Scotia. Their purpose was to encourage the local black population to consider its own dilemma and produce a program of action suitable to its circumstances. To that end they suggested a community-wide 'Black Family Meeting,' where African Canadians could gather on their own with no media or government witnesses, for an intimate discussion of their problems. The meeting was arranged for 30 November 1968 in the North End branch of the public library, in the heart of the black district. The prominent black churchman Rev. Dr W.P. Oliver agreed to chair the meeting.[8]

The announcement of the meeting electrified black Halifax. As many as five hundred people attended, listening to the Panthers' and local militants' analysis but reassured by the presence of Dr Oliver in the chair. To the question 'What now?' the Panthers described an organizational model operating in Washington, DC, a black 'united front' representing all organizations, neighbourhoods, and opinions, that permitted communication and consensus building in the community and greatly increased their influence with the white power structure. The assembly decided to adopt this model, creating that night the Black United Front of Nova Scotia (BUF). An eclectic interim committee was selected, with Dr Oliver as chair and including radicals Rocky Jones and Denny Grant but also moderates such as Gus Wedderburn, Buddy Daye, and Edith Gray. Their three-point mandate was to design a program relevant to the needs of black Nova Scotians, suggest a permanent structure for the new organization, and explore sources of funding for its programs. The interim committee was to carry its proposals back to another Family Meeting for approval. Oliver recorded that the theme of the meeting was 'mutual respect and unity among Black people. They were urged to strive for dignity as Canadian citizens.' The new organization, he explained, 'is based on the philosophy of self-determination and recognizes that every cultural group in Canada should be able to maintain its identity without any sense of inferiority or that it is a subservient group.' To the anxious Halifax press he announced that 'the mood of the meeting was one of anti-violence, in favour of a "new firmness," dignity, aggressiveness, even militance...wanting action in the immediate future.' Relieved that violence had been avoided, the *Chronicle-Herald* welcomed the 'N.S. Black United Front: Common Purpose, A New Dignity,' and called it 'a magnificent opportunity to resolve in an exemplary way the differences between white majority and black minority...It is here, perhaps more than any other place, where the Canadian solution to this issue will be worked out.'[9]

A Canadian Solution

For almost two hundred years, African Nova Scotians had been trying to work out a 'Canadian solution' to the problems imposed by mainstream racism. As a poor and politically powerless community, they developed an unaggressive strategy, seeking cooperation from sympathetic officials and concentrating their votes behind candidates who would support their interests. This approach did produce many significant victories, but the pace was excruciatingly slow. An attempt to increase the rate of progress within that prevailing tradition was initiated in 1945, when W.P. Oliver, then pastor of the Cornwallis Street African Baptist Church, called for the creation of the Nova Scotia Association for the Advancement of Coloured People, designed to unite African Nova Scotians in a concerted campaign against discrimination in employment, education, and housing. Convinced that discrimination could be overcome if his people acquired skills and attributes that were valued by the mainstream society, Oliver urged them to ensure that they and their children gained a decent education. The association conducted surveys of housing and employment conditions, using the results to press for corrective action by government. Delegations visited employers in efforts to gain openings for black workers and break the discriminatory patterns that held African Canadians in a hammerlock of poverty. Their tactics revealed a basic faith in white society, an expectation that if they could 'prove' themselves worthy, they would be accepted as equals.[10]

This tactical orientation was enhanced following a visit by Alan Borovoy to Halifax in 1962, on behalf of the Jewish Labour Committee. Borovoy's intention was to assist the people of Africville in organizing resistance to the threat of expulsion from their community, and to that end he gathered some Halifax residents already involved in various human rights–related issues to form the Halifax Citizens Advisory Committee on Human Rights. Their initial purpose was 'to advise in matters related to an anticipated clearance of the Africville land area,' and they also undertook 'to advise local groups or individuals...concerning protection or advancement of human rights, and to submit briefs as from time to time may be required, to appropriate government authorities.' Borovoy drafted briefs for the committee to submit, on Africville and on fair employment and fair accommodations practices (FAP), and provided a set of procedures for 'testing' local establishments to see if they were honouring the provincial FAP law. Black and white teams tried to rent apartments, apply for a job, or get service in a barber shop; when discrimination occurred, they wrote up a detailed report and incorporated their findings in briefs to the provincial government, asking for an educational program informing the public of the existence of human rights laws and for improvements in their enforcement. Committee chair Gus Wedderburn, president of the NSAACP and, beginning 1 March 1964, the Jewish Labour Committee's part-time staff person in Halifax, was receiving advice and submitting monthly reports to the JLC leadership.[11]

Over the next several years, the committee sought to ameliorate the terms and conditions of the destruction of Africville, and armed with the results of their testing, urged the provincial government to improve the enforcement of human rights laws. They pursued the standard tactics followed by the NSAACP since 1945, with some refinements and connections coming through the Jewish Labour Committee. For example, in 1965, following repeated rebuffs from the Nova Scotian Hotel over the hiring of black personnel, the NSAACP appealed to the JLC's national director David Orlikow in Ottawa, who spoke with the national vice-president of CN hotels and who, in turn, contacted the Halifax manager asking him to hire an African Canadian for the hotel dining room.[12] The association continued to press its usual concerns, for greater access to employment and housing and, particularly, for improved educational opportunities. In November 1964, Nova Scotia Welfare Minister James Harding submitted to their demands by establishing a $25,000 bursary program for African-Canadian students, which he announced as the first part of a plan 'to help Negroes keep their children at school, men at work, and improve housing.' Because the bursaries amounted to $25 to $100 per recipient, they were not calculated to make a major difference in the capacities of impoverished families. Nevertheless, Wedderburn graciously welcomed the program as 'one of the best things that ever happened to the Negro in Nova Scotia,' on the grounds that it could give black youth a new sense of purpose and overcome defeatism. After 'a century or more of de facto segregation,' he explained, black Nova Scotians had become 'apathetic and just about beaten. They feel they've lost their fight.'[13]

New Strategies

The community dynamic began to change in the summer of 1965, when Burnley 'Rocky' Jones returned to Nova Scotia. Jones, just turning twenty-four, was born and raised in Truro, and after service in the Canadian Army moved to Toronto where he joined the Canadian support groups involved with the American civil rights movement. One of those groups, the Student Union for Peace Action, sponsored his move to Halifax, together with his wife Joan. They were to inaugurate the 'Nova Scotia Project,' a grassroots community development program aimed at involving African-Canadian youth in defining their needs and organizing for change. In its headquarters known as Kwacha ('Freedom') House, the project held sessions in leadership training and strategies for community organization, with cooperation at first from the NSAACP and the African United Baptist Association, and with assistance from the Company of Young Canadians. The Africville removal was just getting underway, and Black Power emerged that summer among some of the younger members of the African-American movement. Using Africville as the counter-example, Kwacha House stressed participation: nothing should be done without the compliance and active involvement of the people to be affected by the action. But as this principle was put into practice, the young participants and their leader, too, grew more militant, meeting resistance from both black and white establishments because they seemed to be 'rocking the boat.'[14]

For years, the NSAACP had maintained that black people had it in their power to make changes: get an education, become presentable, earn your stripes. It was a 'bootstraps' philosophy and could exist only with a parallel belief that effort would be rewarded, that the system worked. Jones fashioned a profound shift in this understanding. 'Doing something' need not mean becoming acceptable to white society; it could mean that no one else is going to fix things for you, and you have to take it into your own hands. Do not rely on big brother or big sister. And anyway, winning one case would simply move you on to the next case. It was not the occasional apple that was rotten, but the barrel itself. In tandem with this evolving analysis, Jones was developing new tactics for its implementation. His aim was to target people with his message, not elites, and he identified systemic discrimination as the fundamental flaw in contemporary society. He sought to change the consciousness of his Kwacha House members, with lessons in black pride and African culture, equipping them for a broader attack on the disadvantages they experienced. A glimpse into the shifting African-Canadian youth attitude is provided by the NFB film *Encounter at Kwacha House,* made in 1967.[15] By this time Jones was advocating confrontation, boycotts, or occupations of discriminatory businesses, even hinting at violence. 'If you can show the kids that the system out there is a racist system, then you can do something,' he argued to the camera. Many, but not all, of the young people gathered for the filming were agreeing with him.

Events seemed to confirm Jones's contention that piecemeal reform was ineffective. White neighbours threatened violence against former Africville residents who relocated in their neighbourhoods, police regularly harassed 'mixed' couples in the streets of Halifax, tests of employment discrimination showed that five of six agencies would exclude black applicants from job competitions. The report of the Negro Employment Interim Committee, submitted to Mayor Allan O'Brien of Halifax in September 1968 by Jules Oliver, son of W.P., contained damaging evidence of ongoing discrimination. Describing his own experience with racist humiliation while job seeking, one eighteen-year-old told the committee: 'I'm beginning to think there's something in that bloodletting that's going on in the States.'[16]

Organizing the Black United Front

These incidents make it apparent that African Canadians were not so much 'apathetic,' as Wedderburn had suggested, but intimidated and frustrated; they were losing their faith in the system, in the officials set up to protect their rights. They were trying to behave 'normally,' but were confronted with racism and an indifference that seemed to be invincible. There was, therefore, a tremendous receptivity to the inauguration of the Black United Front, at least in younger circles. They saw W.P. Oliver's interpretation of the new organization as representing a coming together of the moderate and radical streams in recent Nova Scotian history, for so it seemed when Dr Oliver said that BUF 'will permit the Black man to develop and mature as a contributing member of the Canadian society, eliminate paternalism and result in a pluralistic society wherein all will have justice.'[17] The radicals themselves were hopeful, since the BUF council was to consist of two members from each black community in the province, and in them would reside the final authority for the direction of the organization. Letters went out over Dr Oliver's signature in December 1968, inviting communities to name their representatives.

On the weekend following the Black Family Meeting, the Committee on Human Rights, now called the Nova Scotia Human Rights Federation, held its annual conference to commemorate Human Rights Day. There was a special interest in the 1968 conference because it was intended to celebrate the International Year for Human Rights, and its importance was compounded by the recent Panthers' visit, the delivery of Jules Oliver's report, the Black Family Meeting, and the formation of BUF. In preparation, an NSAACP delegation met with Premier G.I. Smith, on 26 October, at which time they 'tried to get across that the ranks of the militants are increasing.' What was happening in the United States could happen here, as the recent visit of Stokely Carmichael indicated. The underlying understanding was that if the government would only act to enforce existing legislation and, in particular, appoint a full-time administrator for provincial human rights, the problem of discrimination would be overcome and violence would thus be avoided.[18] Inflating the concern just at that moment was an incident in St Croix, near Windsor, Nova Scotia, where the local cemetery refused to bury the body of three-year-old Jennifer States because of a

1907 by-law prohibiting the burial of African Canadians. Cemetery official Irene Ross said, 'I see no reason for changing the by-law at present. We have enough white people to cope with.'[19] The St Croix cemetery became the immediate symbol of the entrenchment of racist attitudes and the inability of the authorities to do anything about it. Anxieties and expectations for the Human Rights Conference were high.

As president of the NSAACP and conference chair Gus Wedderburn sent out the invitation to the December gathering. Addressed to 'Concerned Nova Scotians,' the letter said: 'You have seen on your TV and in the newspapers, the tragic consequences of the denial of human rights to fair housing, fair employment, education and human dignity in the United States and in many other countries too. Need I say more about why we are holding this conference and why it is important that you attend?' This was the problem. The solution was also anticipated in the letter, promising that Premier G.I. Smith would be addressing the conference, and 'we are hoping that he will have an important announcement to make concerning the appointment of a full time human rights co-ordinator for the province.' Also on the platform for Saturday morning, 7 December, was Rocky Jones.[20] On Friday the Halifax paper carried a report, 'No Plans to Disrupt Conference – Jones,' clearly implying that he might. The story presented an interview with Jones:

> People are afraid of the fact that Black people here are beginning to organize and to realize the seriousness of their plight, he said. 'An outsider came here and stated certain facts. Those facts here are…poor housing, inadequate jobs, a whole history of oppression.'He said Black people have come together to define their role in society, to redefine their whole cultural heritage, and to exert pressure to make society responsive to their needs.
>
> The White community has two choices – either to continue to suppress the Negro and risk confrontation, or to help open doors to let the Black people become a dynamic community, Mr Jones said.[21]

In this analysis, the appointment of a full-time human rights commissioner was far from a satisfactory solution.

On Saturday, 7 December, Premier Smith did indeed announce the appointment of a human rights director: Ontario journalist Marvin Schiff, a thirty-one-year-old white man. A perceptible groan arose from certain quarters in the audience of over eight hundred people. Jones immediately interjected. The black community had not been adequately consulted about this appointment, he charged, and further-more a qualified black candidate had not even received a formal reply to his application. The conference erupted, many people utilizing this failure of courtesy to criticize the appointment itself. The premier pleaded ignorance; Schiff expressed his anger at the procedural lapse but vowed to stay on the job. The rest of the conference was anti-climax, although clearly the agenda had been captured by the radi-cals and the rhetorical level had been elevated. When Professor John Cartwright from Boston University spoke, later in the afternoon, he received a standing ovation when he raised his fist and cried 'Freedom Now.' But apart from some apologies over the details of Schiff's selection, the institutional response remained fixed: with appropriate enforcement, the human rights structure could eliminate the 'Negro problem' from above.[22] The following Monday, on CBC television, Gus Wedderburn said: 'For the time being, I am quite prepared to accept the Premier's promises and good faith to see what happens. And if his promises are not kept, then we just have to keep working and pushing some more.'[23]

Obviously, there were two quite different perspectives on the prob-lem and on the appropriate solution, and both were represented in the BUF interim committee that began meeting in December 1968 to formulate its structure and purpose. One view hoped that BUF would provide an opportunity for an increasingly militant black com-munity to mobilize, express itself, and design grassroots programs to 'do something' from the bottom up. The other expected it to enhance their bargaining power with government, to further the institutionally driven programs of the NSAACP and the Human Rights Committee. Using his prerogative as chair, Dr Oliver added several new mem-bers to the interim committee, including his son Jules, people who would support a more moderate and top-down approach. This group drew up 'A Pilot Project in Self Determination on the Part of Nova Scotia's Negroes' and, without the knowledge of some interim com-mittee members, the senior Oliver and Gus Wedderburn carried it to Ottawa in January 1969 to win federal government financing for their plan. The document briefly outlined the history and current condi-tions of the African Canadians in Nova Scotia and referred to the recent appearance of Black Power, which 'is still free from violence,' but perhaps not for long. Their proposal incorporated much of the rhetoric of the radical group, stressing black participation in developing their own goals and programs, but the 'umbrella' structure and community control were omitted.[24]

In Ottawa, the delegation met fellow Nova Scotian and Manpower Minister Allan MacEachen and Jean Leger, deputy minister to Secretary of State Gérard Pelletier. Both were encouraging. MacEachen said, 'None of us here can deny the truth of what you've said. We are in full accord with you.' Leger added, 'I will go a step further. I have talked with the Hon. Mr Pelletier about this ... He is a socially conscious man. This involves citizenship, people, the position, the status, of non-white people in Canada – not only Canada but the entire continent. I am prepared to say that he will support this presentation. You go back home, define your needs, be a little more specific, and we will take care of it.'[25]

Some members of the interim committee were appalled by these developments, fearing that government money would mean government control and outraged that the commitment to report back to another Family Meeting before taking action had been neglected. Shortly after the delegation returned to Halifax, the radical element established a new group, the Afro-Canadian Liberation Movement, and issued a pamphlet proclaiming: 'The time has come for Black People to unite. We must come together as a race of people, and work towards solving of our problems collectively.' The ACLM aimed to revolutionize the black community from within, to effect 'a Black consciousness and identity through the awareness of our history and the revival of our culture,' and a 'liberation of the mind from the deliberately imposed conditioning by white society in order to enable a proper re-evaluation and a true definition of ourselves.' The final goal would be 'the elimination of all forms of racial oppression, social and economic injustices against Black People – by whatever means necessary ... To this end we pledge our lives.'[26] Since BUF was designed as an 'umbrella,' the foundation of the ACLM did not necessarily imply rejection; it could coexist, along with the NSAACP and other organizations, within a broader BUF coalition. At a teach-in at St Francis Xavier University in Antigonish, at the end of January, Jones was emphatically encouraging young African Canadians to become involved in BUF and to participate in the selection of community delegates.[27] But, clearly, the radicals were declaring their non-confidence in the direction BUF was taking.

Jones's reputation as a radical continued to grow. He was invited to Montreal to speak to a demonstration at Sir George Williams University protesting alleged racism by a professor, and almost immediately afterwards his student audience occupied the university's computer centre.[28] Two weeks later, the weekend *Globe Magazine* ran a feature article on 'Rocky the Revolutionary.'[29] But rather than interfering with the moderates' plans, as Wedderburn feared, this attention undoubtedly ensured government support. Furthermore, the debt to the radicals was evident in the rhetorical tones of BUF's formal submission to the federal government, which was ready in March 1969. The document announced that the general objective was 'to assist the Black community of Nova Scotia to achieve a level of self-determination that will enable the community to have a major role in identifying the nature of its social and economic problems, to plan for the approaches to solving these problems and to organize in such a way that maximum use will be made of available community resources including its own inner resources. The organization is to be controlled and directed by members of the Black community. Professional staff and indigenous workers will be employed to work with local communities.'

BUF proposed to conduct surveys and other research to illuminate African-Canadian problems, develop effective communications among all black communities, promote programs in 'Afro-history and culture,' work with existing organizations and government departments so that services could be delivered effectively to black people, and to build an effective system of record-keeping and evaluation to account for their expenditures. Communities would be encouraged to study their own problems, so that BUF could design appropriate programs or submit briefs on their behalf to government departments. The submission proposed a staff of nine persons, headed by an executive director who should be 'a member of the Black race' with a university degree and postgraduate training in social work or community development, have demonstrated management skills, an understanding of local black culture, and experience in the area of race relations. They asked for an initial budget of $70,000 for the first year of a five-year plan.[30]

Government Involvement

While the BUF proposal was being rewritten, a new funding program was developed in Ottawa designed 'to allow for the citizens to have a major role in the identification, planning and solution of problems' and 'to improve the quality and effectiveness of the federal government's delivery of welfare services.' The BUF application was the first to be considered under the new rules.[31] Health and Welfare Minister John Munro and Secretary of State Gérard Pelletier jointly made a submission to the Cabinet Committee on Social Policy, warning that racial unrest and violence threatened Nova Scotia and that extremists planned to disrupt the Canada Summer Games scheduled for Halifax in August. If Dr Oliver and the moderates took control of BUF, the radicals would be discredited and the violence avoided, and this could be accomplished through government funding of the BUF application. The Cabinet committee agreed that 'absence of support might enable black militants to take over from the moderates,' and sent a recommendation to the full Cabinet to accept the BUF proposal.[32] But when the Cabinet discussed this recommendation, Prime Minister Trudeau objected to 'supporting separately and treating with special status one section of the population when government policy was moving in the opposite direction with respect to Indians.' The proposal was sent back to the Social Policy Committee for further consideration.[33] Munro and Pelletier reformulated their argument, explaining that the grant was not a unique project or a sop to a particular group, but an application of a general principle to involve recipients in designing their own welfare programs. On this basis the Cabinet approved a grant of up to $100,000 per year over a period of five years to the Black United Front.[34]

There had been a rather basic transformation in the BUF objective, from the 'self-directed community program' sought by the Family Meeting to a 'self-administered welfare grant' as awarded by the federal Cabinet. Nevertheless, Munro announced publicly that 'the Federal government is giving money to the Negro community (in Halifax) to structure themselves so they can protest, and to "raise hell."'[35] And hell was raised. Munro's office received letters from every part of the country protesting the grant. One citizen expressed 'deep concern as there are signs this organization is itself racist, revolutionary and under the manipulation of communists. Apparently "Rocky Jones," who publicly advocates violence against our society, is the leader of the organization.' Many letters linked BUF to the Black Panthers and blamed the 'moral cowardice' of the government for giving in to blackmail and threats of violence by 'black agitators.' 'Hearing of this reminds one of the bread shops and blood curdling circuses arranged for in the times of the Roman empire to mollify the multiple throngs of savages and barbarians.' None of the letters approved of the government's proposal to support BUF. Although Munro insisted that he had been misquoted, the impression remained that BUF was a radical organization and that the government had legitimized it with half a million dollars in funding.[36]

The provincial government, too, grew alarmed about what forms of 'community involvement' might emerge under BUF stimulation, and so a 'liaison committee' was established with membership from BUF and the province to 'assist BUF...in reaching sound decisions on the scope and nature of the specific detailed program.' When this condition was revealed to the interim committee, in August, the radicals protested vigorously, but the moderates prevailed and the liaison committee was accepted.[37] This structure was quite consistent with W.P. Oliver's long-developed philosophy of cooperating with government authority in order to win advantages for the community. On 15 August 1969, the official announcement was released by Munro and Pelletier. The public explanation was that the money would assist 'the establishment of the Black United Front as a representative body with a council elected by the black people of Nova Scotia on a community-by-community basis,' and 'finance the BUF program of community self-help which will include such things as family life education, housing assistance, consumer economics and educational and job opportunities.' Munro added that the grant was intended 'not to fight a racial problem – but a poverty problem.'[38]

The Radical Legacy

The disillusionment of the ACLM radicals can be easily understood. Conservatives within the African-Canadian community were also distressed. Despite the involvement of W.P. Oliver, elder statesman of the African United Baptist Association and of the NSAACP, both of those bodies were initially suspicious of BUF. The moderator of the AUBA, Ross Kinney, refused to endorse BUF and said that his membership resented the intrusions of the Black Panthers into the province's affairs. Many objected to the label 'Black' in the organization's name, and its implications of Black Power and radicalism. At a meeting of the NSAACP, Wedderburn called for a motion to endorse BUF, but when the 'verbal crossfire...reached the shouting stage,' amid accusations of 'association with the Black Panthers,' he declared from the chair that he would not put it to a vote. But, as the officials had predicted, once the grant was received the organization gained legitimacy, and both the AUBA and the NSAACP embraced BUF as a partner in black community affairs. And they were no doubt consoled by the appointment, in April 1970, of Jules Oliver as the executive director. Rocky Jones would not be running the organization after all.[39]

Although outvoted, Jones and the ACLM had deeply infected the way the new organization would be interpreted to the Canadian people, in general, and to the black people of Nova Scotia, in particular. The institutional goal, at least as articulated in public, had been confirmed as 'self-direction' and 'participation.' When Jules Oliver became BUF's first executive director, he issued a statement serving notice that the organization 'will not tolerate any more infringement on the human rights and dignity of the Black communities of Nova Scotia. It is the conviction of the Front that if the Black people are to acquire pride in themselves, dignity as human beings, a sense of self-worth and respect as a race of people, we must be united as one family...The basis of our philosophy [is] self-determination.'[40] However, real authority rested in the executive director and the honorary chairman, W.P. Oliver. An 'umbrella' function never evolved, and the council, with two representatives from every black community, never functioned as a decision-making body. Internally, the organization developed a hierarchical management structure, and even the staff were discouraged from open discussion or dissent. 'Bottom up' was no more than a bitter memory. This does not mean that BUF failed to have significant accomplishments, but they tended to fall within the NSAACP tradition of facilitating government programs for the benefit of the black population. BUF staff helped communities apply successfully for Local

Initiatives Project and Opportunities For Youth grants amounting to several hundred thousand dollars, worked with Canada Mortgage and Housing Corporation to fund cooperative housing projects, intervened on behalf of welfare applicants, responded to instances of discrimination and helped submit complaints to the appropriate authorities, and amassed useful survey information on the state of housing, health, and education in the black communities. A monthly newspaper, *Grasp,* provided a link among communities and gave an outlet to a black 'voice' in the province.[41]

Yet, BUF's most important contribution has been less tangible. According to a 1972 assessment by an uncommitted academic, Peter Paris, BUF gave the black population 'a new sense of worth and power...in fighting social injustice.' Individuals knew that, for the first time, there existed an institution with some resources that would speak exclusively for them and an institution that, formally at least, belonged to them. This, in turn, improved the black people's self-image and sense of confidence, Paris reported.[42] BUF's 'Cultural Awakening Program' introduced black history, showing that the African Canadians of Nova Scotia were part of an enormous African populace and heritage, all of which produced black pride and participated in a genuine shift of consciousness from 'oppressed minority' to 'Black Community.' The new language of 'blackness' proved liberating for many young people. Even the Halifax *Chronicle-Herald* recognized, as early as October 1970, that as a result of BUF programs 'individual problems are now seen as community problems which has an effect of enabling communities to act as cohesive organizations.'[43] This is precisely the message that had been articulated by Rocky Jones and his colleagues. If BUF's programs reflected the NSAACP and Human Rights Committee orientation, the consciousness and spiritual impact it conveyed were closer to Kwacha House or the ACLM. The consequences are incalculable, but assuredly the stirrings of black consciousness generated in the late 1960s, of which BUF was an immediate product, also fed the 'Black Renaissance' that subsequently occurred in black Nova Scotian culture – in poetry, literature, art, and film – and is occurring still.[44]

It has been suggested that the creation of the Black United Front of Nova Scotia 'produced the demise of Black protest,' and as a deliberate government strategy, black militancy was pulled 'into normal political channels' and its leaders absorbed 'into stable institutional roles.'[45] In one sense this is undoubtedly true: the government did 'purchase' BUF and monitored its activities, motivated in no small way by an intention to eliminate the radicalism. But the individuals who were absorbed into institutional roles with BUF already held views that were consistent with normal political channels and cooperating with government. They were less duped than victorious, gaining a platform and federal funding for which they had dreamed for years. BUF was, indeed, a triumph for the strategy of the NSAACP and Human Rights Committee. Nor were the radicals 'eliminated.' Realizing that they had been outmanoeuvred for control of BUF, the radical group decided not to disrupt the unity of their community any further, particularly in view of a crisis in the spring of 1970 over the appointment of an allegedly racist city manager for Halifax.[46] Many of their number and Dr Jones, in particular, have remained a thorn in the side of the establishment, their militancy undiminished, and a continuing inspiration to many.[47] Militancy was not discredited in the minds of the black population. On the contrary, militancy could be recognized as the author of BUF's very existence. Not only were the NSAACP and Human Rights Committee leaders expressing themselves in the language of self-direction, participation, and community control, but so were ministers of the federal government! In the eyes of an observer at the time, the government had not rejected but had conceded to black demands.

Conclusion

As Alan Borovoy had done for the NSAACP, the Panthers reinforced a trend already existing within the black community in Nova Scotia, represented by Kwacha House and other signals of increasing black frustration with current solutions and an emerging redefinition of the problem. They catalysed that feeling and created a sense of 'crisis' without which the Black United Front of Nova Scotia would not have been established, and as federal Cabinet documents show, government funding would never have been forthcoming. Whatever the government's intention, the public – both supporters and opponents – accepted BUF as an organization intended to foster black participation, and it did so, even though BUF itself did not develop as a participatory body. For generations black Nova Scotians had been deliberately excluded, physically, socially, culturally, economically, politically. Now their participation was being acknowledged and extolled, not just as a moral good but as a public principle and part of their normal rights as citizens. The sixties black confrontation in Nova Scotia had extended the meaning of Canadian citizenship and Canadian diversity.

FURTHER READING

Clairmont, Donald, and Dennis Magill. *Africville: The Life and Death of a Canadian Community*. 3rd ed. Toronto: Canadian Scholars' Press, 1999.

Mackenzie, Shelagh. *Remember Africville*. 35 min. Montreal: National Film Board, 1991.

Pachai, Bridglal. *Beneath the Clouds of the Promised Land: The Survival of Nova Scotia's Blacks*. 2 vols. Halifax: The Black Educators Association of Nova Scotia, 1987, 1991.

Walker, James W. St G. *The Black Loyalists: The Search for a Promised Land in Nova Scotia and Sierra Leone*. 2nd ed. Toronto: University of Toronto Press, 1997.

Whitfield, Harvey Amani. *Blacks on the Border: The Black Refugees in British North America, 1815–1860*. Hanover, VT: University Press of New England, 2006.

Winks, Robin. *The Blacks in Canada: A History*. 2nd ed. Montreal and Kingston: McGill-Queen's University Press, 1997.

Premier Harry Strom, Harold Cardinal, and Jean Chrétien, minister of
Indian Affairs, 18 December 1970.
Courtesy of PAA, J-547

10

'Indians of All Tribes': The Birth of Red Power

Bryan D. Palmer

There is no denying that something changed as the sixties placed its stamp on Indigenous peoples.[1] They, in turn, left their mark indelibly on it. There are, of course, profound continuities in the history of Canadian Aboriginal resistance to colonization, struggles against oppression and injustice reaching back centuries. This essay highlights the undeniable change that occurred in the mid-1960s as Native protest became more aggressive. It was led by a youthful contingent of militants whose demands for redress, by 1968–69, were growing in both their willingness to challenge colonization directly and their refusals to countenance any longer the practices of the past.[2]

Native political organizing, of course, predated the 1960s. Situating the rise of Red Power in the 1960s, it is crucial to recognize both the historical continuities in Indigenous political protest and organizing and the extent to which a new and militant politics of demand animated a youth-led and increasingly radical set of Aboriginal mobilizations between 1965 and 1975.

Kiera L. Ladner's blunt conclusion that successful Aboriginal political organizations in Canada were little more than 'puppet regimes which were to aid in the goal of "civilizing" the Indian' may well be unduly dismissive. Yet, her general stress on the Canadian state's sorry record of dealing with Native peoples is hardly open to challenge, nor should the extent to which this circumscribed Aboriginal militancy and curtailed organizational possibilities be understated. Few pre-1950 Native movements and political bodies embraced tactics and strategies of militant opposition. Even F.O. Loft's trade union–influenced League of the Indians of Canada, founded at the end of the First World War from a base on the Six Nations Reserve near Brantford and spreading across the country in the 1920s, premised itself on cultivating government sympathy and assistance. Yet, it proved too much a thorn in the side of Duncan Campbell Scott's Indian Administration. Amid state fears of alien-endorsed revolution in the epoch of the Winnipeg General Strike, Indian Agents accused Loft and his co-workers in the cause of Aboriginal mobilization of 'Bolshevism.' Police vigilance and the 'unrelenting opposition of Indian Affairs' played their part in helping to bring the League of the Indians of Canada to a state of 'near collapse by the early 1930s.' This was but one instance of the federal state severely constraining Aboriginal mobilizations, to the point of even banning 'Indian' organizing. It is thus impossible to understand the limitations of pre-1950s Native activism, as the struggles of the radical Communist Party and Co-operative Commonwealth Federation aligned Métis organizers Malcolm Norris and Jim Brady make abundantly clear, without appreciating the colonial state's capacity to constrain it in a variety of ways.[3]

By the late 1950s and early 1960s, however, a new day of Native political organizing was dawning. Veteran organizer Andrew Paull is a case in point. Paull's activism began in the first third of the twentieth century. He founded British Columbia's Allied Tribes movement in 1916 and helped establish the Native Brotherhood of British Columbia in 1931. In the 1940s, Paull was involved in the formation of the North American Indian Brotherhood (NAIB), which championed land claims and Native rights, spearheading a drive to forge a cross-country mobilization of Indigenous peoples.[4]

One of Paull's protégés in the 1950s was George Manuel, a rising activist in the interior of British Columbia. Manuel emerged as a powerful regional voice in the NAIB. From there, the west coast spokesman struggled to bring Native organizations together. He believed that a unified Indigenous movement would be more effective in prying concessions and change from Ottawa. Such efforts resulted in an Aboriginal Rights Committee presenting submissions to the federal government in 1960 and, eventually, a broader-based NAIB under Manuel's leadership. These B.C.-based mobilizations were paralleled by developments in Manitoba leading to the formation of the National

Indian Council in August 1961. Manuel would come to embrace radical, anti-colonial ideas and situate Canadian Aboriginal peoples in a generalized 'Fourth World' struggle for independence.[5]

In this kind of ongoing political struggle, which reached from the eighteenth century into the mid-twentieth century and beyond, differences of region and identity proliferate. For Norris and Brady the 1950s were, according to their biographer Murray Dobbin, a decade of 'political stagnation.' Yet, for the Kahnawake, as Alfred details, a break with 'the Indian Act mentality' and its reliance on colonial institutions heightened in this period as Mohawk resistance to the expropriation of Aboriginal lands associated with the development of the St Lawrence Seaway produced a tangible shift in consciousness. 'No surrender' became the watchword of a rising Native nationalism as the Seaway development project 'drove Kahnawake away from a position of trust in the Canadian government.' The stage was set for a new politics of Aboriginal organization and challenge in the 1960s. Ideas and answers began to surface that would have been 'inconceivable to Mohawk leaders in the 1950s.'[6]

The 1960s were thus years of self-discovery as Aboriginal people themselves charted new paths of opposition, demand, and protest.[7] As George Erasmus told *Canadian Dimension*'s Fred Gudmundson in 1984, 'It really wasn't until the very late 1960s that things started to change. Younger leaders started coming forth, finally being able to clearly analyze the position of Native people in the Canadian context, and they began speaking out loudly and publicly expressing our discontent. What we started to see happening was that the squeaky wheel gets the grease, and the grease, in this case, was government programs that were supposed to remedy the situation.'[8] Native Studies scholar Peter Kulchyski confirms this centrality of the 1960s in the changing relations of Aboriginal peoples and the Canadian state: 'In Indian Country, the sixties was a time when sea changes led to crises and conflict, and ultimately a new paradigm in Indian-government relations...For just over 100 years policies were developed at the whim of officials; after 1970 Aboriginal people became major players in policy development.'[9]

It is no accident that Native writers such as Jeanette C. Armstrong, Lee Maracle, and Eden Robinson have worked their recent prose around young Aboriginal militants of the 1960s, born in British

Columbia, who found inspiration and new direction for their lives
in the United States – based American Indian Movement (AIM) and
Vancouver's Native Alliance of Red Power (NARP).[10] Lee Maracle's
radical odyssey begins as a Yorkville hippie; encounters anti-war
demonstrations and Trotskyist organizers in Toronto; encompasses
readings of Malcolm X, Frantz Fanon, Marx, and Mao; and finds its
culmination in West Coast fish-ins and the Skid Row proselytizing
of NARP in Vancouver. Bobbi Lee initially felt like she was being
bombarded with 'all the talk,' worrying that she was being 'sucked
into this great wave of whatever it was' that these leftists were doing.
But gradually she was transformed by this 'new world' that she had
entered; a love of Red Power was rooted in a love of learning, reading, political engagement, and struggling to 'Think Native.' By the
end of the 1960s, 'youth everywhere were holding conferences, chiefs
were meeting, everyone was talking about our rights; rights we didn't
dare to believe existed in the 1950s.' She recalled: 'We had minds;
we could think.'[11] Anything but mundane, this discovery was a break-
through, in which past barriers were transcended, and new possibilities embraced passionately.

The emergence of Red Power in the 1960s is a little studied phenomenon. Like many other 'sixties' movements and mobilizations,
Red Power addressed old grievances in ways that broke from the past.
Drawing on the sensibilities of the youth radicalism of the 1960s,
Native movements of the decade were increasingly vocal and militant. If Red Power's message could well be delivered in the dialect
of locale and regional experience, it was influenced profoundly by
international currents and was premised on the fundamental idea that
all Native peoples shared a common history of dispossession that
required immediate and forceful redress. Red Power thus drew inspiration from the radicalism of the period, seeing its cause as linked to
the Black Power movement in the United States, the rise of revolutionary nationalism in Quebec, and the general anti-imperialist agitations
of the decade. Youthful Native militants came to appreciate and seek
sustenance through developing connections with elders, a phenomenon that existed in the history of white New Leftists, but in entirely
different, and perhaps weaker, ways. This meant that what was new
in the Red Power movement was always dialectically related, indeed
inseparable from, what was old in Native experience.

What follows is an attempt to contextualize Red Power and detail some of its manifestations. This chapter suggests, albeit all too briefly, that Red Power emerged at the end of the 1960s at the interface of the historical actuality of Native dispossession, the colonial state's blundering attempts to redress Aboriginal grievance, and the self-activity of Indigenous peoples themselves. Moreover, the legacy of Red Power is appreciated as fundamental to an understanding of how sixties sensibilities helped to set a stage on which future generations grappled with the ongoing meanings of the colonization of Canada's First Nations.

Material Legacies of Dispossession: The Dialectics of Sixties 'Discoveries'

As the 1960s unfolded, the Canadian state came to pride itself on reform and the expansion of welfare services that were often heralded as a War on Poverty and the creation of the Just Society. The material legacies of dispossession that were central to Aboriginal experience took on new salience, as it became apparent that the country's Indigenous population was mired in poverty.[12] Journalists such as Heather Robertson decried the deplorable conditions prevailing on many Native reserves.[13]

If the reserve was, for many Native peoples, a place of protection and solace, in which the traditional ways of the elders were passed on to the young and guarantees against the discriminatory marginalization of the colonizing experience preserved, it was also regarded by a growing contingent of Aboriginal youth as a cul-de-sac of entrapment. The discontented understandably left the reserves in droves in the 1960s, but the exodus merely swelled the ranks of urban 'Skid Rows.' There Native youth quickly fell prey to unemployment, substandard housing, and a cycle of substance abuse that fed into criminalization.[14]

These general trends were exacerbated by an assault on Indigenous ways of life as the colonial state exacerbated an already dire situation with a two-pronged initiative. First, the state continued its practice of reserve relocation and, as the tragic destruction of the Ojibwa Grassy Narrows reserve in northern Ontario over the course of the 1960s revealed, severed Native peoples from their long-standing connection to lands and waters that had sustained traditional subsistence economies. The result was a joyless anomie of family breakdown that often culminated in dysfunctional social relations, in which desperate rage and unfathomable frustration resulted in Grassy Narrows becoming, in the words of one elder, 'a diseased place to live.'[15] Second, confronted with what appeared to be a nationwide epidemic of this malaise, an insensitive state orchestrated a campaign to 'save' Aboriginal children from what was designated 'parental abuse or neglect.' Taken from their parents and placed in residential schools where there were, to put it mildly, neither the resources nor the expertise, let alone the political will, to grapple with the *historical* realities of Native people's dispossession, the children of this 'sixties scoop' became statistical fodder in the skyrocketing rates of Aboriginal incarceration, alcoholism, sexual abuse, and suicide. Their plight would soon be voiced in the fictions and life stories of Maria Campbell's *Halfbreed* (1973) and Beatrice Culleton's *In Search of April Raintree* (1983),[16] as well as in historical studies of the 1990s that exposed, decisively, the 'national crime' of the residential school system.[17]

This context of the sixties, as a period of efforts to address the legacies of material dispossession central to Aboriginal peoples, resulted in what might be called the dialectics of 'discovery.' A new urgency animated the growingly liberal Canadian state with respect to Native peoples. This liberalization of Aboriginal-state relations commenced as early as the years immediately after the Second World War. Reforms of the Indian Act in 1951 eased or eliminated a myriad of restrictions introduced in the years 1880–1930. The small print of these changes, however, tended to suppress Aboriginal culture and force status Indians to give up their identity as Native if they pursued involvement in Canadian society. These reforms were thus bricks in the assimilationist causeway.[18] When Harry B. Hawthorn, a traditionally trained anthropologist, conducted a mid-1950s study of social adjustment among British Columbia's Native peoples, with C.S. Belshaw and Stuart Marshall Jamieson, the academic trio reported widespread evidence of acculturation.

A decade later, Hawthorn would be saying different things. He was asked by the federal government in 1963 to canvass Native people's conditions of life and offer suggestions for policy initiatives. Hawthorn assembled a research team of fifty-two social scientists, and their two-volume compendium, *A Survey of the Contemporary*

Indians of Canada: A Report on Economic, Political, and Educational Needs and Policies, proved a landmark in the 'discovery' of the 'Indian.' This was not so much because of its recommendations, which remained very much framed within an ideology of liberal acculturation, but because of its reasonably objective presentation of Aboriginal destitution. As a copious and stark compilation of evidence confirming Native poverty, substandard housing, marginalization in the wage-labour economy, ill-health, and a poorly functioning residential schools educational system, the Hawthorn study opened eyes long sleepily shut. Given the sorry historical record chronicled by the report, the irksome issue of Aboriginal self-government could not entirely be skirted. Hawthorn and his team outlined a political culture of dependency, in which Indigenous initiative was stifled by the over-reliance of Native peoples on Ottawa and its Indian Affairs Bureau. Such a state of governance worked decisively against local autonomy and constrained any meaningful acculturation, highlighting the pitfalls of paternalism. This led to the report's most startling 'discovery.' 'In addition to the rights and duties of citizenship,' concluded Hawthorn and his research associates, 'Indians possess certain additional rights as charter members of the Canadian community.' The Indigenous subject was declared a 'citizen plus.'[19]

The 1966 Hawthorn study thus wrestled uneasily with the assimilationist current of state policy, confirming it, on the one hand, and, on the other, delivering against it a message of indigeneity's uniqueness. Talk of special status grated in federalist circles reluctant to concede sovereignty ground to Quebec. When, in 1969, Prime Minister Trudeau's Minister of Indian Affairs Jean Chrétien delivered his White Paper on Indian Policy to the House of Commons, it called for an end to anything approximating special status for Native peoples. Proposing the repeal of the Indian Act, shifting responsibility for Native peoples from the federal state on to the provinces, winding down the Department of Indian Affairs and Northern Development, and limiting treaty claims and obligations, Trudeau and Chrétien insisted that Native peoples in Canada would only achieve 'full, free, and non-discriminatory' lives if there was a complete 'break with the past.'

As Canada's increasingly militant Native movement recognized, this wholesale scrapping of the state's approach to Aboriginal-white relations was driven by liberal acquisitive individualism, and as such it was often at odds with the material realities within which Native collectivities lived. Red Power had, indeed, come into being before the tabling of the 1969 White Paper, but it was definitely given a particular boost by this threat of the state to turn the world of Aboriginal governance upside down.[20].

The Birth of Red Power

What shocked Aboriginal leaders in 1969 was that alongside the state's new-found and welcomed rhetoric of participatory democracy, consultation, and negotiation lay the same governmental arrogance and arbitrary top-down politics of rule by directive. Behind the facade of reform, some concluded, lay a fundamental continuity of state effort to deny Indigenous identity.

By this late date, the signs of a growing Aboriginal militancy were evident in central Canada and upstate New York as Iroquois militants figured prominently in the rise of the American Indian Movement (AIM) and in the revival of Native nationalism.[21] From Newfoundland to the Yukon, Aboriginal activists forged new organizations over the course of the 1960s. British Columbia was in the forefront of 1960s Aboriginal mobilization: eight organizations were established on the west coast. Ontario was not far behind, its long-established and relatively affluent reserves sustaining six new 1960s-founded Aboriginal bodies. Over the course of the years 1960–73, more Native political voluntary organizations were formed (86) than had been established in the entire period from the eighteenth century to 1959 (61).[22] By 1967–68 and the publication of the Hawthorn study, the National Indian Brotherhood had appeared to represent status Indians, and the Métis Council of Canada was founded as the voice of non-status Aboriginal peoples.[23]

This vibrant organizational and agitational context was further complicated by the growing belief that Canada's 'Indian problem' was the equivalent of the racial conflict and civil rights activism in the United States. Peter Gzowski, writing in *Maclean's,* found 'Our Alabama' in Saskatchewan, where 'Indian lover' was an epithet hurled with the same abusive vitriol as the Dixiecrat's snarled 'Nigger lover.' Gzowski detailed the racism of the prairie province, where the

11 May 1963 killing of Allan Thomas, a Saulteaux man, near North Battleford, a hundred miles northwest of Saskatoon, brought national attention to the impoverishment of the region's 7,500 status Indians and Métis. 'There *is* race prejudice in North Battleford,' concluded Gzowski, 'and it is ugly and in some ways frightening to behold.' Gzowski could, nevertheless, not refrain from qualifying this racism as peculiarly 'Canadian,' differentiating it, seemingly, from other (possibly 'American') racisms: 'it is, if this is possible, the race prejudice of a gentle, friendly people.'[24]

By 1969, however, few could close their eyes to the new reality of Native protests and the backlash against them. Northern Saskatchewan, site of killings and unexplained deaths of Métis families and Aboriginal activists, was being reported on by the Canadian Broadcasting Corporation as the 'Mississippi of Canada.'[25] A white social worker who supported Native peoples' struggles was brutalized by police, and communities like North Battleford looked to some to be little different from Selma, Alabama. Saskatchewan Premier Ross Thatcher, an ardent assimilationist chilled by talk of 'Indian' culture, treaty rights, and self-government, warned that Aboriginal grievance in Saskatchewan was a ticking time bomb. Progressive Conservative MP Don Mazankowski stood in the House of Commons to report on a supposed plot to train Canadian Indians in 'riot techniques.' In a branch of the Royal Canadian Mounted Police, documents were produced warning of a dangerous, AIM-inspired Aboriginal movement, part of an international conspiracy that, in its demands for social and economic equality for Native peoples, as well as insistence that their land claims be recognized, 'had become the principal threat to Canadian stability.' Red Power was giving the RCMP, whose role in other aspects of the 1960s is detailed in Steve Hewitt and Christabelle Sethna's contribution to this collection, a bad case of the security state jitters.[26]

An emerging layer of radical Aboriginal leadership took to heart African-American critiques of internal colonialism, such as those of Stokely Carmichael, which alluded to the subordination of Aboriginal nations. As James Walker's essay in this book on Rocky Jones and 1960s Halifax indicates, Carmichael's words had a profound impact on racialized Canadians. All of this prompted Native militants to take increasingly aggressive stands of opposition to white power that were theoretically informed by the growing anti-imperialism of the epoch. Anti-colonialist, pan-African movements led by figures such as Kwame Nkrumah and theorized by Frantz Fanon and others permeated the thought of young Canadian Aboriginal militants. Black Panther spokesmen received a warm welcome among Native activists in the Canadian west, where they were embraced as fellow revolutionaries. Saskatchewan Métis author Howard Adams later penned a powerful Aboriginal New Left assault on white colonialism and the subjugation of Native peoples, *Prison of Grass* (1975). He suggested that there was a parallel 'between Red Power in Canada and Black Power in the U.S.' Indeed, when Malcolm X was assassinated in 1968, Toronto's Native activists co-sponsored a memorial for the martyred black revolutionary with their African-Canadian counterparts.[27] More cautiously mainstream was Harold Cardinal, author of the highly influential *The Unjust Society* (1969), and a mere twenty-four years old at the time of the publication of his landmark book. Cardinal warned that if the Trudeau government insisted on following its path of coercive assimilation, 'then the future holds very little hope for the Indian unless he attempts to solve his problems by taking the dangerous and explosive path traveled by black militants of the United States.'[28]

Even as staid a publication as *Time* magazine appreciated that radical change was in the air, declaring in May 1967: 'For the first time, Canada's Indians have begun to think of themselves as a single ethnic group...an Indian civil rights movement is in the making.' In November 1969, Aboriginals on both sides of the Canada-U.S. border seized Alcatraz Island in San Francisco Bay and defiantly declared the former prison site Indian territory. 'We are a proud people. We are Indians! Our Mother Earth awaits our voices. We are Indians of All Tribes. *We hold the rock!*' Only months before the Alcatraz occupation, a Mohawk woman from the Kahnawake community south of Montreal, Kahn-Tineta Horn, addressed a Canadian student audience. Her rage at Trudeau's White Paper program exploded as she cried: 'Why don't you all go back where you came from? We were doing fine before you came. We own the land; we're your landlords. And the rent is due.'[29]

In a 1970 collection of essays by Aboriginal writers and activists in Canada, Andrew Nichols, a Malecite and executive director of the

Union of New Brunswick Indians, offered the following typical characterization of Red Power: '[Indian people are] going to wield the biggest goddam two-by-four on a stubborn "power structure" which has been screwing them for generation after generation. The destiny of Indian people will not be determined by the fickle finger of Fate; it's going to be determined by Indian people – and let no one forget it!'[30] Across the country like-minded young militants voiced the new radicalism of Red Power. The Okanagan Tony Antoine of Vancouver's NARP, the Manitoba Métis George Munroe, and the Saugeen-Métis Duke Redbird, for instance, all articulated and represented a new explosiveness in the politics of Aboriginal resistance.[31] 'I am the Redman/I look at you White Brother/And I ask you/Save not me from sin and evil/Save yourself,' declared Duke Redbird.[32]

The White Paper's arrogant and arbitrary expression of the starkness of the state's resurgent program of repressive acculturation galvanized further the increasingly militant Red Power movement of the later 1960s.[33] But it was centuries of subordination and generations of abuse, 'discovered' in the changed climate of radicalism that was 1967–68, which really ushered Red Power into being. As a *Star Weekly* journalist reported, in May 1968, 'The strong talk of the militants [was] far more common than the whispers of the conservatives.' In the new revolutionary tone of the sixties lay an inevitable clash that Trudeau's complacent liberal reification of individual rights and the marketplace of meritorious economic advance merely hastened. 'I don't think we should encourage the Indians to feel that their treaties should last forever so that they are able to receive their twine or their gun powder,' Trudeau declared contemptuously in a Vancouver speech in August 1969.[34]

This was no longer acceptable. As Cardinal's *The Unjust Society* made abundantly clear, Red Power militants had no love for the Indian Act that Trudeau proposed discarding. To those Indigenous youth and their elders who had 'discovered' a sense of Red Power in the 1960s, obliterating this newly proud Aboriginality 'from above' was no solution to centuries of dispossession, exclusion, and bigotry that whites had visited upon Native people. Cardinal coined the term 'buckskin curtain' to convey a sense of the racist indifference that had been lowered over Canadian society with respect to the accumulated wrongs done to the country's Indigenous population. Carefully chosen to mock Western 'democracies,' which prided themselves on their superiority over communist societies that needed 'iron curtains' to contain their populations, Cardinal's 'buckskin curtain' was an ironic reminder of the arrogance of countries like Canada. Playing on well-known metaphors of Canadian identity, contrasting seeming Canadian pluralism with the less tolerant United States, Cardinal demanded the right to remain 'a red tile in the Canadian mosaic.' He insisted that the buckskin curtain had to go up.[35]

Cardinal's book articulated as text what Native peoples across Canada were undertaking in practical protests and everyday undertakings that proclaimed a rebirth of Aboriginal identity. Akwesasne militants blockaded the International Bridge at Cornwall on 18 December 1968, protesting duties levied on articles valued in excess of five dollars. Hundreds of Natives, mostly women and youth, battled the RCMP. Forty-one of the Mohawk dissidents were arrested, including Kahn-Tineta Horn. Out of this struggle came the *Akwesasne Notes,* a militant Aboriginal newspaper that would prove of considerable importance in spreading the message of Native rights and Red Power throughout Canada and the United States. Mohawks rooted in the St Regis reserve led a spiritual revival that utilized a cross-continent caravan to rebuild Aboriginal appreciations of traditional religious values and spirituality. By 1969, they had reached California, where they met with students of the newly established San Francisco State College's Indian Studies program. They lectured on the Longhouse tradition, conducted Iroquois dances, and discussed the International Bridge protest. All of this linked loosely with the development of the American Indian Movement, whose pivotal leader, Russell Means, had been involved in a 1964 symbolic claiming of Alcatraz Island for all Aboriginal peoples.

AIM, established in Minneapolis in 1968, had-at first little connection to Canadian reserves or American reservations and was, in 1968–69, a nascent, but growing, pan-Indian movement. Aboriginal militants were, by this time, routinely crossing the Canada-U.S. border, often in defiance of immigration officials, on their way to various political meetings and strategy sessions. On 29 August 1969, for instance, a large intertribal motorcade crossed the Cornwall International Bridge en route to the Algonquin Maniwaki reserve, refusing to pay the bridge toll. The Maniwaki Labour Day weekend gathering, with hundreds in attendance representing seventy-five distinct Native nations, heard angry testimony of Aboriginal discontents: police brutality, residential school abuses, unemployment, and alcoholism topped the list. Rose Ojek, an Ojibway from Upper Slave Lake, Alberta, was adamant: 'The violence is here already! There are young Indians in Alberta who are going to burn the schools and the churches...I can't stand it when I hear of talking peace!'[36]

A west coast expression of the new Aboriginal radicalism was the non – reserve-based Native Alliance of Red Power, a decidedly youth-oriented New Left Vancouver body with connections to west coast Maoist and Trotskyist political organizations. Founded in 1967, NARP was led by a small committed cadre. It nevertheless managed to produce and distribute five thousand copies of its international newsletter; staff a 'Beothuck Patrol' that provided protection to the most vulnerable of urban Aboriginal street people, whose intoxication, poverty, or work in the lowest sectors of the sex trade subjected them to the abuse of police and others; hold educational forums and a variety of socials; and propagandize in the interests of various Aboriginal actions, including the Akwesasne International Bridge protest, a Fort Lawton, British Columbia land struggle, residential schools protests, and the occupation of Alcatraz. NARP intersected directly with various local Aboriginal initiatives in the late 1960s, including the Nisqually fish-in near Olympia, Washington. This action was supported by the Seattle Liberation Front, Jane Fonda, the Cree activist and celebrated folksinger Buffy Sainte-Marie, and the Black Panther Party, arguably the model for NARP's understanding of Red Power. A founding member of NARP, Henry Jack noted that this Vancouver voice of Red Power was composed primarily of 'ex-convicts, young Indian run-aways from the schools, young drop-outs from school, some academics (those who suck-holed their way through school) and unemployed as well as young workers who lived in the city.' NARP was firm in its belief that 'all the Indian peoples of North America are cousins, members of the same country, INDIAN; that we are not of Canada or the United States,' and that it was necessary for the 'scattered Indian groups' to consolidate and collectively oppose 'a fat, degenerate, ignorant enemy.'[37]

NARP also called for the abolition of the Indian Act and the colonialist Indian Affairs Branch. Ironically, with the June 1969

White Paper embracing exactly this course of action, the ramifications of such a legal and institutional dismantling of Aboriginal-state connections became anathema to most Native leaders and their constituencies on and off reserves. The White Paper managed to do, in the charged climate of the late 1960s, what centuries of past oppression could not: it brought Canada's Indigenous peoples together in a broad consensual opposition to the white state.[38]

From his base in Alberta, Harold Cardinal helped to orchestrate what would subsequently be heralded as the response of Canada's Métis and Indian population to the Trudeau-Chrétien mythology that such white heads of state could 'lead Indians to the promised land.' Under the authorship of the Assembly of Indian Chiefs of Alberta what came to be known as the Red Paper offered a point-by-point refutation of the federal government's proposed revision of Indian policy. Adopted by the National Indian Brotherhood, and presented to Trudeau by two hundred Indian leaders gathered in Ottawa to meet with state officials on 2–3 June 1970, the Red Paper stopped the implementation of the White Paper's policy shift. It proved an embarrassment for Indian Affairs Minister Jean Chrétien. Increasingly radical Native mobilization, nevertheless, did not lead to recognition of the Red Paper's essential demand, which harkened back to Hawthorn's view that 'Indians should be regarded as citizens plus.'[39]

The Legacy of Red Power

In the nearly forty years since the clash between the White and Red papers, Canada's 'Indian problem' remains as contentious as ever. Aboriginal peoples, however, have mounted a consistent and often quite successful set of campaigns to secure title to their lands, preserve their culture, and redress lives of poverty, ill-health, educational abuse, and neglect. At times they have even managed to win reparations of a sort, as in the admittedly inadequate material compensation finally secured for the suffering many generations of Native children endured in the residential school system. Slowly and always in the face of much resistance, Native people have pushed past Trudeau's 1969 speech on Aboriginal and treaty rights, in which he proclaimed that compensation for past injustices was an impossibility in a bourgeois democratic order. 'We will be just in our time,' he said. 'That is all we can do.'[40] Every victory, however, has been overshadowed by the continued oppression of Native peoples.

During the 1970s, the struggle for Native self-determination took on a new character.[41] Much of this was related to the brutal suppression of Red Power in the United States. The cross-border, transnational nature of the Native rights movement was evident in the reception accorded Dee Brown's *Bury My Heart at Wounded Knee* (1970) in both Canada and the United States. As AIM mythologized Wounded Knee further with its 1973 occupation and armed stand-off against the Federal Bureau of Investigation at Pine Ridge, Red Power activists in the United States such as Dennis Banks and Russell Means became well known in Canada. In the aftermath of a series of 1972–75 trials and aggressive repression that signalled an undeclared war on the part of the United States government against the most militant section of the Aboriginal movement, it was apparent that to the south no quarter was being allowed AIM radicals. They were now the targets of a virtual extermination order by the state. An AIM warrior, Leonard Peltier, a Sioux-Ojibwa brought up on the border of Canada and the United States, escaped north, seeking refuge in familiar territory. He was eventually arrested at a remote Cree encampment, 160 miles west of Edmonton and imprisoned at Oakalla, outside of Vancouver, awaiting extradition hearings that would see him returned to the United States and railroaded into prison. Vancouver's Indian Centre coordinated a Peltier defence campaign that utilized protest marches as well as traditional Aboriginal ceremonies involving sacred pipes, sweat lodges, and medicine bags, drawing support from Native peoples in both Canada and the United States.[42]

Given the brutal and relentless suppression of AIM in the 1970s, it is not surprising that Aboriginal activism in Canada combined protest and more moderate methods of opposition. Major land claims and sex discrimination (involving the 'out marriage' provisions of Aboriginal women losing their status entitlements through marriage to non-Natives) cases were fought through the Supreme Court of Canada in 1973. Native blockades at Kenora, Ontario, contested ownership of Anicinabe Park. The Quebec government's proposed hydro-electric development of James Bay culminated in a successful opposition movement of Cree and Inuit peoples, who wrestled the state to negotiate the first modern treaty involving hundreds of millions of dollars of compensation for Aboriginal cooperation. In the Northwest Territories, the Dene blocked the construction of the Mackenzie Valley gas pipeline and necessitated the calling into being of a state inquiry, headed by B.C. Supreme Court Justice Thomas Berger. By the 1980s, Aboriginal civil disobedience was commonplace.[43] The Lubicon Lake Cree fought for recognition of land claims in Alberta, the Innu in northern Quebec and Labrador battled to stop North Atlantic Treaty Organization flights over their homeland, and the Temme-Augaina Amishnabii in the Temagami region of northern Ontario struggled to restrict lumbering in a 40,000-hectare area of six townships. Major land claim victories were secured in the courts of British Columbia. The 1990s saw an eruption of militancy at Oka/ Kanestake in Quebec and at Stoney Point in Ontario. In both cases, Natives occupied lands and clashed with provincial police; the former conflict led to the death of a police officer and, at Stoney Point, provincial police shot and killed Dudley George, an unarmed Aboriginal militant. Nothing much had changed as the 1990s gave way to the opening decade of the twenty-first century.[44]

Of course, not all Aboriginal peoples were staunch opponents of capitalism and the state. As Métis radical Harold Adams, who led a cross-Canada caravan of Native protest that descended on Parliament Hill in 1974, only to be violently rebuked by the RCMP, has suggested, the success of post-1960s Aboriginal demands forced material concessions from the state that further divided Indigenous peoples. As the crumbs from the governing table of Indian appeasement grew, opportunities for red capitalism proliferated and with expanding possibilities for Native business came an increased class differentiation in the Aboriginal community. Conservatives and radicals clashed, as indeed they always had within Indigenous circles, but the stand-offs grew more and more embittered as the stakes rose and the opportunities for corruption and chances to garner cash proliferated. The result, according to Adams, was a leadership layer of conservative, pro-capitalist, and corrupt Native 'politicians' whose elitism separates them from the masses of Aboriginal people and whose lock on Indigenous organizations provide 'havens for multinational investment' and conduits for state aid.[45]

This shift also tended to drown the young and militant voices of Red Power in the deeper waters of Aboriginal negotiation with various levels of government. As Bobbi Lee suggested, the Red Power momentum of 1967–69 sank in the post – White Paper Aboriginal activism, which moved increasingly back into a state-funded series of chiefs' conferences and other more moderate developments. By 1972, she concludes, 'The tactics of the movement were usurped by the growing presence of government-funded organizations. Fewer people came out to the demonstrations organized by Red Power militants. They began to look like fringe fanatics.'[46]

Yet, it remains undeniable that the legacy of the militant 1960s survives in Canada's growing Aboriginal movements, more so perhaps than in any other section of society. This was symbolized dramatically in 1990, when attempts to implement federal constitutional reforms resting on recognition of Quebec as a distinct society, orchestrated by Conservative Prime Minister Brian Mulroney and agreed to by the provincial premiers in the Meech Lake Accord, were scuttled in the Manitoba Legislature by the sole Aboriginal MPP, Elijah Harper, an Oji-Cree from Red Sucker Lake. Elijah Harper's national prominence in 1990 signalled the irony of the dialectics of the 'discovery' of the 'Indian.' That process, so much of which took complicated and complex turns in the 1960s, left Canadian identity irrevocably tied, for better or for worse, to the conditions of Native peoples. It is surely not accidental that from the mid-1960s to the mid-1990s there have been some nine hundred royal commission and other government inquiries and/ or reports on Aboriginal matters, roughly thirty-five such studies and hearings a year.[47] If the colonial white state preferred a coerced assimilation that rocked few boats of conventional, capitalist authority, Native peoples rediscovered, revived, and reconfigured their history and their needs in the birth of sixties Red Power and the enhanced possibility of resistance and refusal. They would countenance no more the brazen denial of their past and subordination of their being.[48] This was a discovery of Aboriginal power that had a long history, one chapter of which surfaced meaningfully and with considerable political creativity in the 1960s, and that has proven impossible, in the years of change that followed, to stifle and suppress. [49]

FURTHER READING

Boldt, Menno. *Surviving as Indians: The Challenge of Self-Government*. Toronto: University of Toronto Press, 1993.

Chaat Smith, Paul, and Robert Allen Warrior. *Like a Hurricane: The Indian Movement from Alcatraz to Wounded Knee*. New York: New Press, 1996.

Francis, Daniel. *The Imaginary Indian: The Image of the Indian in Canadian Culture*. Vancouver: Arsenal Pulp Press, 1992.

Manuel, George, and Michael Posluns. *The Fourth World: An Indian Reality*. Toronto: Collier-Macmillan, 1974.

Miller, J.R. ed., *Sweet Promises: A Reader on Indian-White Relations in Canada*. Toronto: University of Toronto Press, 1991.

PART FIVE

Nationalism and the State

Students protest the American war in Vietnam outside the U.S. consulate in Toronto, 14 April 1966. The war did much to undermine faith in the United States and to foster nationalism in Canada.

Toronto Star, 14 April 1966. Permission of *Toronto Star*.

11

The Nationalist Moment in English Canada

Stephen Azzi[1]

For a moment in the late 1960s and early 1970s, Canadian nationalism found new strength and took on a new shape. This nationalist
impulse was widespread among anglophone Canadians. The nationalists thought of themselves as Canadian nationalists, not English-
Canadian nationalists; their imagined community was a political
entity (Canada), not a cultural one (English Canada), and it usually
included francophone Canadians as part of a pan-Canadian vision.
Nationalists defined their nation in relation to another: the United
States. In the 1960s, Canadian nationalism became more strident, as
nationalists reacted to the violence that the United States too often
seemed to embody. Critiques of racial conflict in the United States
and that country's war in Vietnam were the leitmotiv for the new
nationalists, particularly on university campuses.

Some nationalists wished Canada to resist U.S. economic, political,
and cultural influences. Others exhibited a visceral anti-Americanism,
lashing out at anything or anyone associated with the United States.
They all feared American domination of the Canadian economy and
the destructive power of U.S. political and military might, especially
in Vietnam. Nationalist ideas increasingly found a home in the political centre and on the left, although all nationalists drew on certain
elements from the conservative nationalist tradition. Members of the
New Left combined socialism and nationalism to argue that public
ownership of the means of production could ensure an independent
Canadian state. Still, the new nationalism was not only a reaction

to the United States; nationalists shared many ideas with American thinkers, drawing on critiques of U.S. society advanced by American writers.

The Conservative Nationalist Tradition

Canadian conservative nationalism was born at the time of the American Revolution. Quebec, Nova Scotia, and Prince Edward Island (then the Island of St John) did not join in the rebellion against British rule. After the revolution, about forty thousand American refugees settled in what would later become Canada. These Loyalists, their descendents, and many who later joined them came to emphasize Canada's ties to Britain and the British monarch. Subsequent generations of conservative nationalists sought to preserve the traditions, institutions, and values Canada had inherited from Britain. Order, stability, and community, together with the British connection, distinguished Canada from the United States, which conservative nationalists saw as violent, aggressive, individualistic, disorderly, and immoral. With the decline of British power in the years after the Second World War, Canadians saw less appeal in the idea of Canada as a British nation. Opposition to American values and influences thus became the foremost idea of conservative nationalists. By relying less on the British connection, conservative nationalists made their views more attractive to a broader range of Canadians. Until the 1950s, the Conservative Party had a virtual monopoly on conservative nationalism, but in subsequent years, many of their ideas also found a home in the Liberal and New Democratic parties.

Nationalist writings in the 1960s exhibited a clear connection to the traditional conservative nationalist view of the United States as a violent and immoral society. According to Farley Mowat, the United States 'engaged in almost every form of domestic and external brutality, aggrandizement, degradation of the individual, and destruction of freedom.' Margaret Atwood emphasized the violence in American society in a 1968 poem:

Star-spangled cowboy...
you are innocent as a bathtub
full of bullets.

Your righteous eyes, your laconic
trigger-fingers
people the streets with villains:
as you move, the air in front of you
blossoms with targets.

Poet and playwright Henry Beissel saw the U.S. political system, police forces, news media, business community, and labour movement as thoroughly corrupt: 'Justice is bought, professional integrity sold; trust is mortgaged, truth auctioned off...Bribery, extortion, price-fixing, embezzlement – anything from elementary cheating to murder goes.'[2]

Most nationalists believed that Canadians did not share these faults, or did not possess them to the same extent as Americans. For Peter C. Newman, English Canada's leading journalist in the 1960s, Canadians 'were more peaceable, more reasonable, more *civilized*' than Americans.[3] In the view of economist Kari Levitt, Canada was 'less of a jungle' than the United States, because 'there are more sanctions on people's antisocial behavior.' Unlike Americans, English Canadians had 'respect for law and order, regard for civil rights, abhorrence of mob rule and gangsterism (whether practiced at the bottom or the top of the social scale).'[4]

Conjunctural Nationalism

Several developments in the 1960s added force to traditional Canadian critiques of the United States. Conjunctural nationalism (the product of particular circumstances and events) was a reaction to conflicts within the United States and abroad, including violence against civil rights protestors, race riots in U.S. cities, the assassination of prominent American leaders, and the country's penchant for sending troops abroad – to places such as Vietnam and the Dominican Republic.[5] Canadians in the centre and on the left of the political spectrum had often identified with the liberal impulses of the United States. But in the 1960s, American liberalism self-destructed. 'Now it is plain to see that the American dream has become the American nightmare,' explained an editorial in the leftist magazine *Canadian Dimension:* 'Canadians wanted to be part of the American dream;

we have no wish to become part of the American nightmare.'[6] Philosopher George Grant, whose 1965 book *Lament for a Nation* helped inspire the nationalist movement, remembered that in the early 1960s, the Kennedy political family represented the United States in the Canadian mind. By the end of the decade, the Canadian view had changed. What stood out was America's 'perhaps unresolvable racial conflict, the expansion and decay of its cities, the increase of military influence in constitutional life, the effects of a century of environmental spoliation, etc. etc.'[7]

The most important factor in spurring nationalism in English Canada was the American war in Vietnam, which one activist described as 'the backdrop against which everything happened.'[8] It was, in the words of writer Michael J. Arlen, 'the Living-Room War,' the first armed conflict to be covered extensively on television.[9] Canadians as much as Americans could turn their television sets to the evening news and see graphic scenes from a war half a globe away. Canadian broadcasters, particularly the CBC, devoted considerable attention to Vietnam. The popular current events program *This Hour Has Seven Days* ran several critical stories on the war, including one in 1965, which, according to Member of Parliament Robert Temple, 'depicted the American in South Viet Nam as a stupid, sadistic moron who did not know anything except torture and war, and disregarded everything else.'[10] Even more damning was *The Mills of the Gods: Viet Nam,* a one-hour Canadian documentary that was broadcast on the CBC in 1965 as part of the monthly series *Document.* The most chilling scene, which the *New York Times* described as 'a sequence without parallel in the annals of television,' depicted a U.S. pilot, carrying out a napalm attack and then revelling in his success: 'Look at it burn! Look at it burn!...We can see the people running everywhere. It was fantastic...I've got four 20 mm cannons, you can see out here. And we really hosed them down, by Jove. That's great fun! I really like to do that!'[11] The film endeavoured to present both sides of the conflict, but it left the impression that the United States was embroiled in a brutal war that it could not win.

Although Vietnam was important, it was not the only factor undermining Canadian confidence in the United States. Televised images of whites attacking peaceful black civil rights protestors shocked Canadians. The assassinations of prominent American leaders – John

F. Kennedy, Martin Luther King, Jr, and Robert F. Kennedy – reinforced the idea that the United States was a country beset by violence. 'When [John] Kennedy was killed, I felt as though I had lost someone,' remembered poet and novelist David Helwig. He had a similarly emotional reaction to the struggle for black equality: 'Watching a freedom march, while Joan Baez and others sang "We Shall Overcome," I tried to explain to my young daughter what it was all about and found I couldn't talk right.'[12]

Largely in response to the increased violence and to the failure of American liberalism, many Canadian nationalists developed an increasingly harsh view of the United States. Unlike moderate nationalists who accepted that there was a struggle in the 1960s for the soul of the United States, radicals saw a monolithic America that was corrupt to the core and beyond redemption. The war in Vietnam was not a mistake, they thought, but the natural result of American values and priorities. The radicals condemned ideas or individuals coming from south of the border, including draft resisters and other political refugees who were seen, not as critics of American society, but as agents of American imperialism.

Nationalists expressed themselves in language that was meant to mirror America's cruelty. Writer Ray Smith suggested that Canadians celebrate their country's centennial in 1967 by sending a gift to U.S. President Lyndon Johnson: 'an American tourist's ear in a matchbox.'[13] Another author, Heather Robertson, revealed a similar sentiment in 1975: 'I confess to a desire to toss a hand grenade into every American camper I pass on the highway.' According to Robertson, her 'psychic rebellion' was 'encouraged by the crumbling of the Yankee colossus,' particularly the American failure in Vietnam, the Watergate scandal that brought down President Richard Nixon, and the problems of inflation and stagnation that beset the American economy.[14]

A North American Experience

Canadian denunciations of American politics and society were not only a reaction to these events in the United States, but also a reflection of a common North American intellectual and emotional experience. Canadian writers frequently shared the views of American liberals and radicals, asserting that the United States was not justified in intervening in other countries, that it was largely responsible for poverty in the developing world, and that its society and culture were shallow and materialistic. American and Canadian critics alike saw the United States as uniquely hypocritical; in no other country, they believed, was there a larger gap between a society's ideals and its reality.

One of the best-known nationalist tracts of the late 1960s, one that led the best-seller list, illustrates the impact of American ideas on Canadian nationalism. *The New Romans: Candid Canadian Opinions of the U.S.* was edited by the poet Al Purdy and published by the nationalist Mel Hurtig in 1968. The book consisted of contributions from almost fifty Canadian writers, including many of the most prominent ones, such as Margaret Atwood, Mordecai Richler, Farley Mowat, and Margaret Lawrence. Although some of the contributors defended the United States, most launched vigorous attacks, portraying the United States as a powerful empire with a global reach, but one that was decadent and on the decline. Many of the ideas in *The New Romans* came from American sources.[15] The authors summoned up historian William Appleman Williams when contending that the United States was involved in armed conflict abroad as a way of avoiding domestic social conflicts. They relied on economist Robert Heilbroner's argument that American anti-communism was motivated by a desire to defend the international position of the United States. They borrowed images from American poets, including Allen Ginsberg's description of the United States as a nightmare and Robinson Jeffers's view of a republic on the verge of collapse. American scholars – historian Charles A. Beard and sociologists C. Wright Mills and G. William Domhoff – were cited to prove that the United States did not live up to its self-image as an egalitarian and pluralistic society. Writer Mary McCarthy was mentioned twice, attesting to the powerlessness of the average American. Even the book's title, *The New Romans,* was drawn from an American source.[16]

Nationalists in the academic community showed a similar dependence on American ideas. Political scientist Gad Horowitz explained the differences in political culture between Canada and the United States by employing a model from American political scientist Louis Hartz.[17] Economists Mel Watkins and Abraham Rotstein also made use of Hartz, as well as historian Stanley Elkins, novelist James

Baldwin, and civil rights leader James Farmer.[18] Several of the contributors to *Close the 49th Parallel Etc.: The Americanization of Canada,* a 1970 collection of essays by Canadian scholars, relied on the work of Americans, too. In addition to Mills and Williams, the authors leaned on Herbert Marcuse, the philosopher and high priest of the American New Left. Political scientist Ian Lumsden's chapter on the impact of the United States on Canadian intellectuals was based almost entirely on the work of American Marxists. He cited Paul Baran and Paul Sweezy on American political economy, Harry Magdoff on American economic imperialism, and Andre Gunder Frank on the role of the hinterlands in the capitalist system. The chapter by Ellen and Neal Wood, which deplored 'the American way of doing things' in political science, rested heavily on arguments made a decade earlier by American scholars.[19]

Ideas and individuals have long moved easily across the Canadian-American border. Many of the prominent nationalists of the 1960s had strong ties to the United States. Cy Gonick was first exposed to radical thought while a student at the University of California at Berkeley. He later recalled that, when he returned to Canada in 1963, he 'knew no one in Canada and precious little about Canada.' All his reference points were American.[20] Margaret Atwood obtained an M.A. from Radcliffe College, before beginning doctoral studies at Harvard. James Minifie worked for the *New York Herald Tribune* from 1929 until 1943, when he became a correspondent for the CBC. The leading Canadian nationalist on the left, Mel Watkins, spent four years at the Massachusetts Institute of Technology, where he studied economics, supported Democratic presidential candidate Adlai Stevenson, and married a Boston-area woman. He returned to Canada in 1958 with a Boston accent, which stuck with him at least into the late 1960s.[21] In the Liberal Party, the most prominent nationalist advocate was Walter Gordon, who had extensive business dealings with Americans. His daughter graduated from Radcliffe, settled in the Boston area, and became the mother of Gordon's American grandchildren. The nationalism of Gordon and the others was not a product of ignorance about the United States, but was, rather, informed by an extensive knowledge of that country's politics and society.[22]

Canadians did not need to travel south to the United States to learn about that country. Many prominent American dissidents visited

Canada in the late 1960s and early 1970s. A mid-1960s speech by
Rennie Davis of the New Left organization Students for a Democratic
Society (SDS) had a powerful impact on Toronto students. According
to one witness, when he told his listeners to abandon their formal
education, 'a number of people proceeded to renounce school right
there on the spot.'[23] J.A. Wainwright, then a student at the University
of Toronto, remembered that the individual 'who stirred us up most
in those years' was Jerry Rubin, co-founder of the Yippies protest group.[24] Rubin so inspired a crowd at the University of British
Columbia in 1968 that they began an occupation of the faculty club
after his speech. Other visitors to Canadian campuses included
Marcuse, peace activist Staughton Lynd, civil rights leader Stokely
Carmichael, and William J. Lederer, co-author of the best-selling
novel, *The Ugly American.*

American ideas were even more widely distributed through
Canadian and U.S. media outlets. With the advent of cable television, an increasing number of Canadians were able to receive signals
from U.S. networks. Canadians could watch CBS reports on Vietnam,
brought to them by correspondent Morley Safer, who was a Canadian.
The two Canadian networks, CBC and CTV, depended on news material from their American counterparts and broadcast a substantial
amount of American entertainment programming. Critical comments
on Vietnam appeared with increasing frequency on American com-
edy and variety shows, including *Laugh-in* and the *Smothers Brothers*
show, both of which were broadcast on CTV. The story was the same
in print media. American magazines were available on Canadian
newsstands and by subscription. By 1969, Canadians were buying
three times more American than Canadian magazines.[25] American
ideas were also prevalent in Canadian periodicals, including newspapers, which often reprinted or commissioned work from American
commentators. The *Toronto Star* ran the syndicated column of Walter
Lippmann, the leading political analyst in the United States and a
prominent critic of American policy in Vietnam. Because Canadian
newspapers made extensive use of news stories from U.S. services, in
the words of one expert observer, 'Canadians learned about the U.S.
and about the world from a U.S. perspective.'[26]

At Canadian universities, students were exposed to American
liberal and radical views of the United States. The rapid growth of

student enrolment in the 1960s created the need for hundreds of new faculty members, a demand often filled by Americans. Many of them were draft resisters and other expatriates who had fled in disgust at the state of American politics and society. Gabriel Kolko, a member of the New Left and a prominent critic of U.S. foreign policy, taught at York University from 1970 until his retirement in 1986. John Warnock was a member of the U.S. Foreign Service, until he left in 1963 because he did not want to spend his life defending American foreign policy. He began a teaching career in Canada, first at the University of Saskatchewan and later at the University of Regina. Others made shorter stays in Canada. Andre Gunder Frank, a highly influential scholar who helped popularize dependency theory (the idea that the United States had become wealthy at the expense of the underdeveloped parts of the world), was a visiting professor at Sir George Williams University in Montreal from 1966 to 1968. Also making a temporary home at Sir George Williams was radical historian Eugene Genovese, who spent two years in Montreal after he was forced out of Rutgers University in New Jersey for saying that he would welcome a U.S. defeat in Vietnam.

The U.S. influence on Canadian nationalism was not merely intellectual. It was also reflected in protest techniques and slogans. Objecting to the treatment of civil rights protestors in Selma, Alabama, Canadian students gathered in March 1965 in front of the U.S. consulate in Toronto, singing 'We Shall Overcome,' the anthem of the civil rights movement in the United States.[27] As the war in Vietnam dragged on, American protestors frequently taunted U.S. President Lyndon Baines Johnson with the chant 'Hey, hey, LBJ, how many kids did you kill today?' These words reverberated on Canadian campuses and greeted Johnson when he attended Expo '67, the world's fair in Montreal.[28] To protest the war in Vietnam, Canadian activists borrowed from their American counterparts by organizing teach-ins, large public events that were part rally, part academic conference. In 1970, activists organized a teach-in at the University of Toronto to oppose the 'Americanization of Canada.'

Ideas did not only flow northward. The CBC documentary on the war in Vietnam, *The Mills of the Gods* (1965), was broadcast on public television stations in the United States. Some work by Canadian academics was read in the United States, including an article by historian

Kenneth McNaught on Canadian-American-Cuban relations, which was reprinted in *Monthly Review,* an American Marxist periodical. The Winnipeg rock group, the Guess Who, condemned American 'ghetto scenes' and 'war machines' in the song 'American Woman,' which was the number one single in the United States for three weeks in 1970. Gordon Lightfoot's 'Black Day in July,' about the 1967 Detroit race riots, got little play on mainstream AM radio stations in the United States, but was picked up by alternative FM stations. The Crosby, Stills, Nash, and Young song 'Ohio,' which was written by Canadian Neil Young in reaction to the 1970 shooting of four students at Kent State University by the Ohio National Guard, made its way to number fourteen on the *Billboard* charts, despite being banned by many U.S. radio stations. As historian Robert Wright has argued, Canadian musicians critical of the United States gained an audience south of the border, in part because their work fit within an American folk music protest tradition.[29]

The Migration of Nationalist Ideas

Beginning in the late 1950s, an increasing number of Liberals embraced nationalist concerns about American influence in Canada. Toronto accountant and management consultant Walter Gordon was the key figure in bringing conservative nationalism into the Liberal party. In the late 1950s, Gordon chaired the Royal Commission on Canada's Economic Prospects, which warned of the dangers of high levels of American investment in Canada. Gordon then gained a prominent position in the Liberal party because of his reputation as an efficiency expert, his close friendship with party leader Lester Pearson, and his ties to the *Toronto Star,* which was both the newspaper with the largest circulation in Canada and the most prominent liberal (and Liberal) voice in the Canadian media. When Pearson became prime minister in 1963, he appointed Gordon minister of finance. In his 1963 budget, Gordon tried to implement measures to limit foreign investment, but in the face of opposition from the business community he was forced to back down and withdraw his proposals. He had accomplished little on this issue by the time he resigned from the finance portfolio in 1965. He returned to Cabinet in 1967, and supervised a government report on foreign investment, selecting economist

Mel Watkins to chair the task force charged with preparing the report. Cabinet ignored the 1968 Watkins Report and Gordon again resigned. Although he had failed to restrict foreign investment and had never won a majority of his colleagues to his ideas, he had succeeded in introducing conservative nationalism to the Liberal Party and in raising public concerns about American investment.

In the late 1960s, the political left adopted and transformed conservative nationalist ideas. Initially, neither the Old Left nor the New Left were particularly interested in the nationalist cause. The Old Left in Canada, centred in trade unions, the Co-operative Commonwealth Federation (CCF), and later the New Democratic Party (NDP), was more inclined to use nationalism as a tool when pursuing other causes, such as preventing factory closings, rather than as an end in itself.[30] The New Left, composed largely of young university professors and their students, rejected the policies of the NDP and the labour movement as too moderate. In the early 1960s, the Canadian New Left showed little interest in the nationalist cause.[31]

The New Left's position on nationalism began to shift in the mid-1960s, as activists became increasingly disenchanted with the United States. In 1969, James Laxer, Mel Watkins, and others created the Waffle movement, fusing nationalism and the New Left. The Waffle's key objective was to push the NDP to embrace nationalism and radical socialism. The Waffle manifesto declared, 'the major threat to Canadian survival today is American control of the Canadian economy.' The solution was not to replace American capitalists with their Canadian counterparts, but rather 'public ownership of the means of production.' Socialism and nationalism had to work hand-in-hand, as 'economic independence without socialism is a sham.'[32]

For the Waffle and other nationalists on the left, the United States was the new Rome: a powerful, prosperous empire with a global reach, but one that was doomed to collapse because of internal corruption and external over-reach. The Vietnamese were victims of imperial exploitation, as were American blacks – and Canadians. Although these ideas had a strong socialist element, they were in part derived from the conservative nationalist tradition. Laxer later recalled the impact on his thought of George Grant's *Lament for a Nation,* the conservative nationalist bible, calling it 'the most important book I ever read in my life.' Members of the New Left were drawn to Grant's idea that Canada was and should be a more civilized country than the United States and to his critique of multinational corporations and consumer capitalism. Grant later reciprocated by contributing the foreword to *The Liberal Idea of Canada,* a book that Laxer co-wrote with his father Robert.[33]

The Waffle was significant for its role in linking nationalism and feminism in Canada. Although the nationalist movement had long included women, it had little to say about women's rights, with even the Waffle manifesto being silent on the issue. But shortly after the Waffle's founding, feminists such as Krista Maeots, Kelly Crichton, Jackie Larkin, Varda Kidd, and Pat Smart began working to ensure that the group's anti-imperialism included a concern for the rights of women. The Waffle pushed the NDP to include a minimum number of women in the party hierarchy and to adopt policies in favour of child care, equal pay, and abortion rights. The women of the Waffle had, thus, helped to establish socialist feminism in Canada.[34]

Although the Waffle had a tense relationship with the leaders of the labour movement, it was able to find common ground with unionists at the local level. In the early 1970s, the NDP-Waffle Labour Committee organized support for strikers, and Waffle members appeared on picket lines. Workers striking against American-owned firms increasingly accepted and promoted nationalist positions, as they became concerned that owners would close Canadian plants. Canadian sections began to push for more autonomy within (or even independence from) American-controlled international unions.[35] American headquarters, many Canadian union leaders argued, were siphoning resources and not investing in Canadian locals. Americans also had little understanding of the issues facing Canadian workers. In the early 1970s, fifty-two thousand Canadian members left the United Paperworkers International Union to form the Canadian Paperworkers Union, four thousand members of the Communications Workers of America broke away to create the Communications Workers of Canada, and nine thousand Canadians left an American union to establish the Canadian Union of United Brewery, Flour, Cereal, Soft Drinks, and Distillery Workers. The drive for independence also had success at the local level, particularly in British Columbia. Eighteen hundred workers at the Alcan plant in Kitimat, British Columbia, voted to leave the United Steelworkers of America and join the Canadian Aluminum Smelter and Allied Workers.

Largely because of the Waffle, nationalism became increasingly associated with the political left, a phenomenon that concerned nationalists who were not radical socialists. To wrest the nationalist agenda away from the Waffle, former Liberal Finance Minister Walter Gordon, *Toronto Star* editor Peter C. Newman, and economics professor Abraham Rotstein, supported by dozens of prominent Canadians, created the non-partisan Committee for an Independent Canada (CIC) in 1970. While the radicals in the Waffle pushed for an end to capitalism, the mainstream nationalists in the CIC preferred government regulation to protect Canada's economic and cultural independence.

Nationalist Policies

The strong sense of security explains the willingness of nationalists to reject U.S. investment. Most nationalists agreed that countering the influence of multinational corporations should be the government's first step in asserting Canada's independence from the United States. Responding to nationalist pressure, the often-reluctant government of Pierre Trudeau (1968–79, 1980–84) began creating public agencies to limit foreign control of the Canadian economy. Ottawa established the Canada Development Corporation in 1971 to purchase Canadian corporations that might otherwise fall into foreign hands. In 1974, the federal government launched the Foreign Investment Review Agency (FIRA), which would screen new foreign investment to ensure that it created a 'net benefit' for Canadians. The next year, the government established Petro-Canada to create a Canadian presence in all aspects of the petroleum industry, from oil exploration and extraction to retail sale at the pump.

Nationalists also pushed for an independent Canadian foreign policy. Canada had sold arms to the U.S. military and had provided the U.S. State Department with intelligence gained through Canada's membership on the International Control Commission, a body set up in the 1950s to supervise a truce in Vietnam. Canada should immediately put an end to this sorry record of complicity in the American war in Vietnam, nationalists insisted. Quiet diplomacy, Canada's practice of voicing concerns privately to U.S. officials, should be abandoned, replaced by a public denunciation of American policy. Canada should withdraw from the North American Air Defence Command

(NORAD) and the North Atlantic Treaty Organization (NATO), the two institutions that cemented Canada's military alliance with the United States. After a review of Canadian foreign policy, the Trudeau government made some changes, placing more emphasis on Canadian sovereignty and reducing Canada's military commitment to NATO. In January 1973, the House of Commons unanimously adopted a resolution critical of U.S. bombing raids on North Vietnam.

The sixties was also a period for developments in national cultural policy.[36] Innovations included Canadian content quotas for radio and the establishment of the Canadian Film Development Corporation to provide funding for Canadian feature films. Legislation helped Canadian magazines compete against the Canadian editions of American periodicals, editions with content from the American magazine but with advertising sold specifically for the Canadian market. Yet, these measures were, in the 1960s, often secondary to nationalists' concerns about the economy. The Waffle manifesto had little to say about culture, asserting that the major threat to Canada came from 'American control of the Canadian economy.' Similarly, the Committee for an Independent Canada 'was essentially an organization of economic nationalism,' to quote one of its presidents, Mel Hurtig. As cultural nationalist Susan Crean noted in 1976, 'The warnings of economic nationalists concerning American control of the Canadian economy are well known. But in the cultural sphere we are only beginning to make the connection between U.S. domination of the media and the suppression of Canadian culture and independence.'[37]

Because so many nationalists were professors or students, American influence in higher education became a prominent issue. Two English professors at Carleton University, Robin Mathews and James Steele, ignited a debate over the national origins of university faculty in 1968. The discussion quickly spread to campuses across the country. Mathews and Steele attempted to frame the issue as a crisis over the 'de-Canadianization' of universities, rather than opposition to American influence. Still, an abhorrence of the United States was sometimes apparent, as in 1969 when Mathews described the United States as a 'racist, imperialistic, militaristic, two-party, chauvinistic, culturally aggressive community.'[38] Mathews and Steele also targeted course content: universities offered few courses in Canadian politics, sociology, or literature. Canadian Studies advocates worked, with considerable success, to rectify this situation, creating Canadian Studies programs and courses with Canadian content at universities across the country.

The Passing of the Moment

The nationalist movement peaked in the mid-1970s. The government created FIRA and Petro-Canada, and public opinion polls showed economic nationalism at its apogee.[39] Afterward, the movement began a decline that only halted briefly in the mid-1980s, with the debate over free trade with the United States. Nationalists continued their fight for an independent Canada, but public opinion polls showed much less support for nationalist policies. Ultimately, the nationalists' success was their undoing. FIRA created the illusion that the government had met the nationalists' demands, even if the agency was largely ineffectual. The economic downturn that began in 1973 drew public attention to unemployment and inflation, and away from the question of American ownership. Equally important was the U.S. withdrawal from Vietnam in 1973. Criticism of the war had always been one of the pillars of the nationalist edifice, a unifying element for the disparate groups that constituted the nationalist movement in Canada. The departure from office of U.S. President Richard Nixon, which came shortly after the American withdrawal from Vietnam, helped to improve the image of the United States. The Watergate scandal had revealed Nixon as corrupt, but his forced resignation suggested that the American political system worked. Public opinion polls showed Canadian confidence in the United States growing in the mid-1970s.[40]

By 1975, the English-Canadian nationalist moment had declined in political influence. When the Americans pulled out of Vietnam, when the Canadian economy began to falter, the nationalist movement waned. Watkins, Hurtig, and other prominent nationalists continued to pursue the cause, but their movement could never achieve the same level of influence it enjoyed in the late 1960s and early 1970s.

FURTHER READING

Azzi, Stephen. *Walter Gordon and the Rise of Canadian Nationalism.* Montreal and Kingston: McGill-Queen's University Press, 1999.

Cormier, Jeffrey. *The Canadianization Movement: Emergence, Survival, and Success.* Toronto: University of Toronto Press, 2004.

Hillmer, Norman, and Adam Chapnick, eds. *Canadas of the Mind: The Making and Unmaking of Canadian Nationalisms in the Twentieth Century.* Montreal and Kingston: McGill-Queen's University Press, 2007.

Igartua, José E. *The Other Quiet Revolution: National Identities in English Canada, 1945–1971.* Vancouver: UBC Press, 2006.

Purdy, Al, ed. *The New Romans: Candid Canadian Opinions of the U.S.* Edmonton: Hurtig, 1968.

Seated with Mayor Jean Drapeau at a St-Jean-Baptiste Day celebration in Montreal, Prime Minister Pierre Trudeau refused to leave the stand despite rioting protestors.

Montreal Star/Library and Archives Canada/PA-136971.

Montreal Star, 24 June 1968. Permission of Woodbridge Co., Ltd.

12

Reconciling the Two Solitudes? Language Rights and the Constitutional Question from the Quiet Revolution to the Victoria Charter

Matthew Hayday

Language rights and political debates surrounding constitutional reform were intimately linked throughout the 1960s. The division of powers between the federal and provincial governments under Canadian federalism required both levels of government to cooperate and compromise on the development of language policies. Moreover, issues of English-French relations and Quebec's place in Canada were central to efforts to revamp and modernize the constitution. The debates which continue to surround these contentious policies today can be traced to the political conflicts of this period. But, as is the case with the other topics explored in this book, the political conflicts of this period were very much a product of the 'long sixties.' Debates surrounding language rights and constitutional reform were especially acute in the 1960s, but they emerged from long-standing grievance and profoundly shaped Canadian politics in succeeding years.

Few royal commissions in Canadian history have affected public policy as extensively as the Royal Commission on Bilingualism and Biculturalism. Established in 1963 by Prime Minister Lester Pearson, the commission consulted thousands of Canadians and initiated numerous studies on French-English relations during the 1960s. The first major legislative initiative to emerge from the B&B Commission's recommendations was the 1969 Official Languages Act, passed by the federal government of Pierre Elliott Trudeau. The act declared English and French as Canada's two official languages and obliged the federal government to offer services in both languages.

At the same time as the federal government was taking action on the language file, it was also engaged in an intensive constitutional renewal process with its provincial counterparts. Following on the heels of the provincially organized Confederation of Tomorrow Conference of 1967, four years of meetings between the prime minister and the premiers eventually produced the Victoria Charter in 1971. Much like the Gastown riot (see Boudreau, this volume) or the economic nationalist policies of the 1970s (see Azzi, this volume), the Victoria Charter was the culmination of historical developments that came to fore in the 1960s. Had it been adopted, the Victoria Charter would have entrenched the main provisions of the Official Languages Act into the Constitution and bound many of the provinces to uphold French and English language rights through a limited bill of rights. The Victoria Charter also included a new constitutional amending formula which would have granted a veto to the provinces of Quebec and Ontario. However, the Quebec government's refusal to endorse this constitutional reform package ultimately ensured its demise.

Rethinking English-French relations and the structure of the Constitution were both crucial to the overall redefinition of Canada which was taking place in the 1960s. In the years since Confederation, the average Canadian election has not featured riots; even more rare is the prime minister who has defiantly faced down a barrage of projectiles. And yet, this was the final scene of the 1968 federal election: newly selected Liberal leader Pierre Elliott Trudeau shrugged off his handlers and defiantly stood his ground in the reviewing stand at the St-Jean-Baptiste Day parade in Montreal, as Quebec separatists hurled rocks and bottles at him. The following day, Trudeau won a convincing majority government. This iconic image nicely captures a key element of Canadian politics in the late 1960s: the challenge of separatists being met head-on by a new, younger, bolder generation of political leadership. Of course, the political debates of the decade are more nuanced than this simple image. Although branded as the candidate of youth,[1] Trudeau was forty-eight when he became prime minister. Still, as Lexier notes in her chapter on the student movement, the perception of generational change had a powerful mobilizing effect in the 1960s, and in this context contributed to Trudeau's rise to power.

Moreover, for many English-speaking Canadians, the bilingual Trudeau held the potential to usher in 'safe,' manageable changes, rather than the often violent and radical upheavals that were rocking the world in the late 1960s.[2] Although he endorsed a bilingual Canada and as justice minister had proposed a host of changes to the law, especially the Criminal Code, that touched on controversial social issues such as divorce, abortion, contraception, and homosexuality, Trudeau was far less revolutionary than many other leaders of the decade. Similarly, most of the other 'new' Canadian political leaders of the 1960s were far from being members of the flower generation. Nevertheless, they did represent a sea change in Canadian politics, bringing new issues to the table and attempting to rework the structures of federalism and public policy to meet the demands of a rapidly transforming country.

New Directions in Canadian Federalism

The generational shift underway in the 1960s deeply affected North American politics. Most of the chapters in this collection explore grassroots mobilizing, whether regarding health foods (Carstairs), blacks (Walker), Aboriginals (Palmer), or labour (McInnis). But important changes were also underway within Canadian politics. A fresh new cohort of leaders including John F. Kennedy, in the United States, and Pierre Elliott Trudeau and Jean Lesage, in Canada, sought to transform their societies by working within established governmental structures. Indeed, the entire structure of Canadian political life was thrown into turmoil by Quebec's Quiet Revolution, which heralded an end to the *grand noirceur* (great darkness) of Maurice Duplessis and the Union Nationale (1936–39, 1944–60) and the rise of an assertive new generation of leaders who sought dramatic change both within their province and at the national level. The Quiet Revolution was the political culmination of a period of intellectual and cultural change which bore fruit in the 1960s with a rapid secularization of Quebec's society and tremendous growth of its state apparatus. The government of Liberal leader Jean Lesage was filled with a new generation of neo-nationalists who believed, like *Le Devoir* editor André Laurendeau, that for Quebec to be a dynamic, prosperous French-speaking society, its government would require additional powers beyond those granted by the British North America Act. For some, such as René Lévesque, a minister in Lesage's government who eventually left the Liberal

Party to found the Parti Québécois, even this rapid pace of change was too slow and timid; they sought a new political configuration with an independent Quebec. Within the Liberal and Union Nationale governments of the 1960s, Quebec's Cabinet ministers and senior civil servants sought opportunities to expand the powers and responsibilities of the provincial government, including the development of a provincial pension plan and an active foreign policy in sectors related to areas of provincial jurisdiction.

At times, this provoked conflict with the federal government. This was particularly the case after the federal Liberal Party underwent a process of renewal, welcoming new Quebec members Pierre Trudeau and Gérard Pelletier to its ranks. In the 1950s, Trudeau and Pelletier had written in the journal *Cité Libre* that although Quebec needed to modernize, it had sufficient powers within the existing Constitution to accomplish its objectives. Trudeau did accept, however, that additional steps were needed to make Ottawa a truly national government, including a policy of institutional bilingualism, language rights, and support for official language minorities throughout the country.

Meanwhile, the federal government was undergoing a period of expansion. After the Second World War, it assumed responsibility for new social programs and the development of the welfare state, including the creation of a national universal health care system and funding for university education and other social services. The federal spending power facilitated an unprecedented intervention into provincial jurisdictions, and the provinces accused the federal government of attempting to set priorities for the provinces. By the 1960s, a chorus of provincial governments, led by Quebec, but also including Alberta, British Columbia, and Ontario, were challenging the unrestricted use of the federal spending power.[3]

The expansion of the federal state and the emergence of the modern welfare state, as well as nationalist movements in English Canada and Quebec (see the chapters by Stephen Azzi and José Igartua in this volume), were central to constitutional talks in the 1960s. Fundamental, clashing conceptions of the Canadian federation were at stake. In Quebec, a *deux-nations* 'compact theory' of Confederation had taken hold. Initially promoted by Henri Bourassa and taken up by his intellectual heirs such as André Laurendeau, this vision of the country saw Canada as a partnership between two founding nations – the English and the French – and its adherents believed that any constitutional amending formula must recognize a special status for Quebec as the main voice of the French-speaking nation. Elsewhere in the country, a rival compact theory held that Confederation was a deal between ten equal provinces, and that none should have special status. Both versions clashed with those who believed that all provinces should be subordinate to a powerful central government, a model often supported by English-speaking Canadians abandoning a British-centred conception of the nation in favour of an aggressive pan-Canadian nationalism. These varied conceptions of Canada were vying for supremacy at the same time as the federal government was trying to patriate the British North America Act so that the Canadian Constitution could be amended without recourse to the British Parliament. To complicate matters further, the other provinces had their own constitutional issues which they hoped could be addressed at the same time as the Constitution was patriated.

These new constitutional pressures had a significant impact on the functioning of Canadian federalism in the 1960s. Garth Stevenson has identified a shift in these talks towards executive federalism, as federal-provincial first ministers' meetings assumed a central role, displacing the quieter administrative arrangements to work out the details of federal-provincial relations that had predominated in the 1950s.[4] Peter Russell views the 1960s as the first major period of mega-constitutional politics, when efforts to completely overhaul the Constitution replaced a more incremental approach.[5]

Federal leaders were concerned by the nationalistic dimensions of the Quiet Revolution. They noted that a key factor driving the Quiet Revolution was the desire of Quebec francophones, expressed in Jean Lesage's 1960 campaign, to become *maîtres chez nous* and to assert francophone political control in the one political jurisdiction in which they were a majority. To counter this, federal politicians and civil servants took steps to remedy the second-class status of French in federal government institutions, hoping to foster the image of a Canadian government fully responsive and open to both English- and French-speaking Canadians. But in their attempt to redress the inequality between the English and French languages, federal leaders faced widespread resistance.

The potential scope of action available for the federal government was limited by a number of factors. While remedial measures to improve the status of francophones in federal institutions were viewed as a positive step, they fell short of the demands for decentralized federalism being advanced by the politicians and bureaucrats in Quebec City. Nor would it be easy to promote a vision of a Canada with two official languages. Western Canadians, in particular, opposed the expansive use of the federal government's spending power and official bilingualism. These debates over constitutional renewal and competing visions of the nature of Canada would result in language policies that partially fulfilled Pierre Trudeau's vision and, yet, were clearly constrained by the limits of Canadian federalism.

The Provincial Language Policy Landscape

Prime Minister Lester Pearson appointed André Laurendeau and Davidson Dunton in 1963 to co-chair the Royal Commission on Bilingualism and Biculturalism. The commission's mandate was to 'inquire into and report upon the existing state of bilingualism and biculturalism in Canada and to recommend what steps should be taken to develop the Canadian Confederation on the basis of an equal partnership between the two founding races.'[6] A preliminary report, submitted two years later, concluded that 'Canada, without being fully conscious of the fact, is passing through the greatest crisis in its history.'[7]

The ten commissioners discovered a country that was deeply divided on questions of language. Quebec, the only province with a French-speaking majority, had the most expansive system of minority language education. English-speaking Quebeckers had complete access to education in their mother tongue, from kindergarten to university. Moreover, because anglophones dominated the economy, immigrant parents overwhelmingly opted to send their children to English-language schools.[8] Québécois nationalists sought to improve the status of French-speakers in the province's economy, and were concerned by demographic predictions that Montreal would lose its French-speaking majority by the turn of the century. One year before the 1969 Sir George Williams riot in Montreal (see chapter by Martel), massive demonstrations broke out in the Montreal suburb of St-Léonard over the right of immigrant parents to send their children to English-language or bilingual schools. The Union Nationale government of Jean-Jacques Bertrand responded by passing Bill 63, which affirmed the right of parents to choose the language of their children's education.[9] This did little to satisfy nationalists, and so the Quebec government appointed a royal commission to inquire into the status of the French language (the Gendron Commission).[10] Pressure to promote the French language and culture within the province's borders bore heavily on Premier Bertrand during federal-provincial constitutional negotiations. So, too, did rising support for separatism, which had spurred both a wave of terrorist attacks from the Front de Libération du Québec (FLQ),[11] and political support for a new separatist party, the Parti Québécois.

In the rest of Canada, French language rights had been extremely limited since the Conquest of 1760. Under the British North America Act, the right to use both French and English was only constitutionally guaranteed in the Parliaments and courts of the federal government and Quebec. In all other provinces, official and/or de facto recognition of the right to use French in provincial legislatures or education systems had either been explicitly stripped away (as in Manitoba and Ontario) or merely ignored in the decades prior to the 1960s.

Across Quebec's borders, the two provinces with the largest proportions of French speakers, New Brunswick and Ontario (which, together with Quebec form Canada's 'bilingual belt'[12]), were taking steps in the 1960s to reverse the past neglect of their francophone minorities. In New Brunswick, Liberal Premier Louis Robichaud devoted much of his decade in office (1960–70) to improving the status of the French-speaking Acadian population. He launched an extensive overhaul of the province's taxation policies, civil service, and education system to equalize regional disparities that disadvantaged Acadians. Meanwhile, Ontario's Progressive Conservative Premier John Robarts, who was extremely sensitive to the tumult in Quebec, organized a summit of the ten premiers in 1967 (the Confederation of Tomorrow Conference) to address Quebec's constitutional concerns. To demonstrate his own government's commitment to improving the status of French-speaking Canadians, Robarts took steps to permit the use of both English and French in the provincial legislature. One of his most notable legacies was ending, in 1967, a fifty-five year prohibition on government funding for French-language public secondary schools.

Beyond the bilingual belt, the B&B commissioners encountered fierce resistance to the idea of a bilingual and/or bicultural Canada.

Although governments in Nova Scotia, Newfoundland, and Prince Edward Island were not overtly hostile to bilingualism, they did not actively support francophone education. The situation was especially dire, however, in the west. British Columbia's government rejected the idea of two founding nations.[13] In the 1870s and 1880s, the prairies had been home to a sizeable French-speaking population; but successive waves of immigrants quickly overwhelmed them, and all three provinces took steps to eliminate any official status for the French language.[14] Western Canadians saw little reason why French should be granted equal status to English on a nationwide scale, arguing that other languages were more important in their local contexts. However, in the late 1960s, governments in Manitoba, Saskatchewan, and Alberta reduced the extent of their bans on French-language education and allowed school boards to authorize French instruction for a portion of the school day.

Federal Language Policy and Federalism

As the provinces debated the language question, the federal government struggled to reconcile federalism and official languages. Prior to the 1960s, the status of the French language in federal institutions was very weak. The language of work in the federal civil service was overwhelmingly English, and francophone civil servants were grossly underrepresented relative to their demographic weight in the general population.[15] Quebec nationalists pointed to this imbalance as evidence that Ottawa did not reflect francophone interests. While many neo-nationalists responded to this lack of representation by seeking additional powers for the Quebec government, Pierre Trudeau, along with Gérard Pelletier and Jean Marchand, opted instead to try to assert 'French power' within the federal government and change the system from within. Their influence is clear from the federal government's approach to language issues in the 1960s.

Pearson's Liberal government sought to reverse John Diefenbaker's Conservative government's poor record with respect to French Canada. In contrast to Diefenbaker, who had failed to appoint any senior French-speaking Cabinet ministers, Pearson, at the urging of senior civil servant Maurice Lamontagne, took pains to recruit high-profile francophone candidates such as Trudeau, Marchand, and

Pelletier, and to appoint them to his Cabinet. While Diefenbaker's 'One Canada' vision left little room for a distinctive French-Canadian identity, Pearson promoted a bilingual and bicultural Canada. Diefenbaker's constitutional reform efforts had likewise failed. Although his Justice Minister Davie Fulton had proposed entrenching linguistic and education rights in the Constitution as part of a broader patriation package, his efforts foundered under opposition from Saskatchewan's CCF government to the entrenchment of the division of legislative powers, which were also part of this proposal.[16]

The Liberal Party defeated Diefenbaker's Conservatives in 1963 and quickly moved forward on constitutional reform with what became known as the Fulton-Favreau formula. Drawing on the Fulton-era proposals, Liberal Minister of Justice Guy Favreau proposed a constitutional package in 1964 that would entrench the existing division of legislative powers between Ottawa and the provinces. Unanimous consent of the federal and provincial legislatures was required to change this division of powers and for any changes to the existing status of languages. The consent of seven provinces with 50 per cent of the population was required for other changes. There was little else in this constitutional package regarding official languages, or to provide new powers for the provinces. The general tenor of the agreement, which would patriate the Constitution but do nothing else to change the dynamics of Canadian federalism, proved unacceptable to the government of Quebec. Jean Lesage's government, which had sought additional powers for Quebec as part of this constitutional reform, refused to proceed with the agreement in January 1966.[17]

New developments in English-French relations further complicated constitutional negotiations. Quebeckers were increasingly adopting a provincial *Québécois* identity to replace the pan-Canadian *Canadien français,* and financial support from Quebec to French-Canadian and Acadian minorities outside the province was drying up.[18] Fearing the loss of financial and moral support for their continued survival, organizations representing these minority communities submitted briefs to the B&B Commission calling on the federal government to assume the role once played by the Quebec government, Catholic Church, and voluntary associations in promoting and protecting French-Canadian and Acadian communities and language rights.[19] Trudeau's appointment as justice minister, in April 1967, held much potential for francophone minorities. Trudeau had long called for the improvement of the status of the French language in federal institutions, and had spoken out in favour of constitutional reforms to guarantee absolute equality between English and French in federal government institutions and in provinces with a sizeable linguistic minority.[20] As justice minister he also called for entrenching language rights in the Constitution.[21]

The B&B Commission advocated sweeping changes to federal language policies. The commission recommended that the federal government, New Brunswick, and Ontario declare English and French as their official languages.[22] In addition, the commission supported the creation of bilingual districts across the country to provide government services to official language minorities in their mother tongue.[23] The commissioners further recommended that the federal government provide financial support to the provinces for minority-language education programs.[24]

Constitutional Talks: Starting Positions

The provinces approached the issue of constitutional reform from starkly different perspectives. In Quebec, Union Nationale Premier Daniel Johnson defeated Jean Lesage in the 1966 election. His campaign slogan of 'Égalité ou Indépendance' was a clear enunciation of the two-nations approach to federalism. Johnson laid out a program for decentralized federalism during the mega-constitutional talks of the late 1960s and early 1970s. He and his successor Jean-Jacques Bertrand sought a wide-ranging federal withdrawal from areas of provincial jurisdiction, a severe curtailment of the spending power, and the transfer of several areas of federal jurisdiction to provincial control. They insisted that this was necessary for Quebec's distinctive culture to flourish.[25]

Lester Pearson convened a first ministers' meeting in Ottawa to reopen constitutional talks in early 1968. The federal government's top priorities were repatriation of the Constitution with a bill of rights, and an approach to official languages rooted in constitutionally entrenched language rights. As the premiers made their opening statements before the television cameras – at what was the first televised constitutional conference – it was clear that deep cleavages separated them on a number of key issues. Ontario's John Robarts supported the federal government's national approach to official languages, and rejected Quebec's claims to special status as the heartland of French Canada. He boldly claimed that 'the Government of Ontario speaks for all people regardless of their origin.'[26] New Brunswick also endorsed a nationwide approach. Louis Robichaud decried the calls to strip powers away from the federal government as a development that would 'transform Canada from a nation into a cobweb.'[27] Quebec Premier Daniel Johnson, for his part, was not averse to a bill of rights or language rights, but his first priority was to address the division of powers.[28] He further noted that he had no desire to impose the French language on Canadians in other provinces where there was no need for it.

Premiers George Smith (Nova Scotia), Alex Campbell (Prince Edward Island), and Joey Smallwood (Newfoundland) were open to the bill of rights proposal, including some recognition of language rights. But all three men echoed Robichaud's comments regarding regional inequality and the need for federal financial support using its spending power. The Atlantic Provinces' position, however, did not find much support in the west. Alberta Premier Ernest Manning observed that his province 'does not accept the proposition that Confederation was a union of two races or two cultures.'[29] British Columbia Premier Bill Bennett opposed any constitutional recognition of duality, and further argued that the federal government needed to reel in its overspending. Saskatchewan's Ross Thatcher and Walter Weir of Manitoba shared their western colleagues' concerns about a bill of rights (including language rights), although they did not overtly share Bennett's concern about the federal government's use of its spending power.

These divisions over linguistic duality and the federal spending power did not bode well for the federal government. To complicate matters, not all of the pro-bilingualism provinces supported federal spending in provincial jurisdictions and vice versa. The policies that emerged from these talks reflect the new constraints of this period, while also demonstrating a certain vitality of the federal government's argument for its continued activism.

Bilingualism and Constitutional Talks:
Seeking a Compromise

While Prime Minister Pearson eagerly sought a new constitutional accord at the February 1968 first ministers' meeting, Trudeau was the federal government's main negotiator, and he was primarily concerned about language rights. Trudeau was worried that linking this issue too tightly to a broader deal on constitutional patriation could lead to several more years of delay on this pressing issue. He urged the first ministers to make language rights their top priority.[30] Shortly after he became prime minister in 1968, Trudeau's government introduced Bill C-120, the Official Languages Act, and began the process of implementing bilingualism throughout the federal government. Trudeau hoped that New Brunswick and Ontario would also follow the recommendations of the B&B Commission. Moreover, he was keen to convince the provinces to move beyond mere legislation, and to constitutionally entrench language rights.

There was a marked lack of consensus among the premiers. The four western premiers argued that the bilingualization of the judiciary invaded provincial jurisdiction and imposed a financial burden that they would be unable to meet.[31] Several premiers, notably Harry Strom of Alberta and Ross Thatcher of Saskatchewan, opposed a legalistic approach rooted in language 'rights' to the language dossier, preferring to respond to this issue through the education system. The four western provinces challenged the constitutionality of the Official Languages Act. The Supreme Court of Canada upheld the act in 1975.[32]

For his part, Quebec Premier Bertrand argued that the language bill was not sufficient to meet his province's main concerns. He noted that the current crisis existed 'not because our country is made up of individuals who speak different languages; it is because Canada is the home of two communities, two peoples, two nations between which relations need to be harmonized.' The central question, according to Bertrand, was how to take steps to ensure that there could be a strong Quebec within Canada.[33] Ontario, while supportive of the federal legislation, was unwilling to introduce comparable legislation at the provincial level. Only New Brunswick was wholeheartedly committed to the B&B Commission's vision. The province passed its own Official Languages Act in 1969, a few months before the federal legislation received unanimous support in the House of Commons.

The federal government also wanted to act on the B&B Commission's recommendation of federal financial support for minority official language education. Gérard Pelletier, secretary of state and minister responsible for official languages, indicated that the federal government was willing to consider financial support for second language instruction as well.[34] However, the federal government's intervention in pursuing education policies was a direct challenge to provincial jurisdiction over education. Several provincial governments, particularly Alberta, British Columbia, and Quebec, wanted to severely curtail the federal spending power. Conversely, not only did provinces that were less financially well-off call for a continuation of the federal spending power to counter-balance regional disparities, but they insisted on the need for federal funding to support official languages programs.[35] For Quebec, this was problematic. The province already offered extensive English-language education programs and English-as-a-second-language courses, and was thus unlikely to be able to use federal funds to expand its language programs. Moreover, the Quebec government did not accept the premise that Ottawa should be allowed to spend in this sector.

The question of how to provide federal funding for official languages programs in education in a way that would be acceptable to the provinces was assigned to two ongoing committees attached to the constitutional conference. A committee of officials dealt with administrative details while a ministerial committee handled the political dimensions of yet another federal spending program in a provincial jurisdiction. Lengthy negotiations ultimately resulted in the announcement, on 9 September 1970, of the Federal-Provincial Program of Cooperation for the Promotion of Bilingualism in Education.[36]

The structure of the new program reflected the ongoing dispute over the federal spending power. The provinces ultimately accepted the federal government's role in promoting official languages. They agreed to allow the federal government to provide financial support to cover the additional costs relating to minority and second language education in the official languages. The federal government could provide direct contributions for educational programs and projects designed to foster teacher training and student exchanges. The federal government would not, however, be permitted to conduct an independent evaluation of the effectiveness of the programs, and standards for provincial accountability were minimal. Nevertheless, the fact that this program was created at all, and before constitutional talks had been completed, reflected the federal government's commitment to official languages and the willingness of provinces to compromise on this issue.[37]

Although the Victoria Charter, reached in June 1971, was rejected in Quebec for its failure to grant the province additional jurisdiction over social policy, it is nevertheless worth examining how the charter was designed to deal with language rights. Several of its articles dealt explicitly with language rights, but these rights would have been unevenly applied across the country, representing the limits of what Prime Minister Trudeau could cajole the provinces into accepting. The Victoria Charter did establish English and French as Canada's official languages. The records, journals, and statutes of the Parliament of Canada would be printed and published in both official languages, and both versions of statutes would be authoritative. Canadians would have the right to use both official languages in Parliament, in any courts established by Parliament, in communications with the head or central office of any federal government department, and in regional offices that lay within proposed bilingual districts. However, only Quebec, New Brunswick, and Newfoundland were willing to agree to all of these provisions at the provincial level. Ontario and Prince Edward Island were willing to offer bilingual services from the central offices of government departments and agencies. British Columbia, Alberta, and Saskatchewan refused to support provisions for language rights in their respective legislatures.

The Victoria Charter was hardly a ringing endorsement of constitutionally entrenched language rights, but rather reflected the desire of most provinces to maintain flexibility in how (or if) they would deliver services to their French-language minorities. Harry Strom stated, 'Alberta cannot accept language provisions which apply to areas of provincial responsibility.' Bilingualism, Strom argued, would foster alienation in his multicultural province.[38] While the charter did include provisions that would allow provinces to opt into the language rights sections, on the whole, it demonstrated that there was no national consensus in favour of a constitutional solution on language rights, nor indeed any consensus on the nature of Confederation, and whether Canada was, or should be, a bilingual and bicultural country. Although the language proposals advanced by the Trudeau government represented moderate constitutional change when contrasted with those of the nationalist Quebec government, the separatist Parti Québécois, or the violent Front de Libération du Québec, they were still more than many provincial premiers were willing to countenance. Trudeau's pan-Canadian institutional bilingualism as the response to Quebec nationalism and the demands of francophone minorities was not fully acceptable to the current array of premiers. Pan-Canadian biculturalism and asymmetrical federalism with special treatment for Quebec were complete non-starters.

Conclusion

Constitutional debates and political conflicts surrounding language rights were a key feature of sixties politics in Canada. The failure of the Victoria Charter brought the 1960s round of constitutional talks to a close. Despite a number of concessions to the provinces, including more provincial control over social policy, a provincial role in the selection of Supreme Court justices, and a commitment to addressing regional disparities, the accord unravelled within two weeks. The weak provisions for language rights reflected the ongoing divisions surrounding the proper way to address linguistic duality in Canada. Indeed, most of the western provinces were unwilling to concede that Canada should be a bilingual or bicultural country.

Despite its failure to secure a constitutional agreement with the provinces, Trudeau's government could point to some significant advances. It managed to pass the Official Languages Act in 1969, and it introduced new funding mechanisms to sponsor official languages programs in the provinces' education systems. This, at least, demonstrated some provincial willingness to support Ottawa's official languages agenda, albeit as long as there were restraints on the federal spending power. Still, many obstacles remained before it would be possible to entrench language rights in the Constitution. Even Ontario, which generally favoured constitutional renewal, resisted the adoption of provincial .guarantees for French language rights.

Moreover, Quebec remained deeply dissatisfied with the constitutional proposals.

As other chapters in this collection document, new social issues mobilized Canadians in the 1960s, from concerns surrounding healthy foods, to the use of illegal narcotics among youths, to questions about university governance. Meanwhile, similar developments were occurring at the political level. A host of new issues was added to the already complicated constitutional debates, ranging from regional equalization to the use of the spending power to special status for Quebec. The nature of the constitutional debate also changed in the 1960s, and it would be an increasingly difficult challenge to patriate the Constitution. These challenges emerged within the context of a generational shift among the participants around the constitutional negotiating table. New models of identity and governance were being discussed, and consensus on how to address the political challenges of the 1960s remained elusive. Indeed, despite the intensive negotiations and major initiatives, such as the 1982 Constitution, that aimed to resolve these issues during the decades that followed, in many ways Canada's constitutional and language politics in the 1970s and early 1980s continued to reflect the unresolved concerns and divisions of the 'long sixties.'

FURTHER READING

Behiels, Michael D. *Prelude to Quebec's Quiet Revolution: Liberalism versus Neo-nationalism, 1945–1960.* Montreal and Kingston: McGill-Queen's University Press, 1985.

Bourgeois, Daniel. *Canadian Bilingual Districts: From Cornerstone to Tombstone.* Montreal and Kingston: McGill-Queen's University Press, 2006.

Hayday, Matthew. *Bilingual Today, United Tomorrow: Official Languages in Education and Canadian Federalism.* Montreal and Kingston: McGill-Queen's University Press, 2005.

Martel, Marcel. *Le Deuil d'un pays imagine: Rêves, luttes et déroute du Canada français.* Ottawa: Les Presses de l'Université d'Ottawa, 1997.

Russell, Peter. *Constitutional Odyssey: Can Canadians Become a Sovereign People?* 3rd ed. Toronto: University of Toronto Press, 2004.

Power was the issue of the Quebec 1962 provincial election, in which the Liberals obtained a mandate to nationalize Quebec's private hydro companies. Squeezing bolts of lightning that symbolize electric power under its grip, the closed fist on this Liberal Party campaign poster proclaims Quebec's political power. Taken from the Liberal Party manifesto, 'Maîtres chez nous' ('masters in our own house') affirmed the collective strength and unity of the Quebec people ('nous') against an unnamed 'them' (easily identified by the electorate as anglophone capitalists) while 'Maintenant ou jamais' ('now or never') gave the issue a sense of urgency graphically underlined by the stark white-on-black of the image. Hydro-Québec became the symbol of Quebec's new-found assertiveness and 'Maîtres chez nous' the slogan of the entire Quiet Revolution.

Parti libéral du Québec.

13

The Sixties in Quebec

José E. Igartua

There has been considerable scholarly debate as to the depth of the break with the past that the election of Quebec Liberal leader Jean Lesage's *équipe du tonnerre* (dream team) in June 1960 launched.[1] Was it a radical break from the *grande noirceur* (the 'great darkness' of the previous Duplessis regime), as voters in Quebec were led to believe at the time, or had it been in the works for some decades as a blooming of social and political forces seeded by industrialization and urbanization? The two views are not totally incompatible; they read the past from different perspectives. The longer view takes its cue from the French *Annales* reading of history as the product of economic and social forces, while the proponents of the radical break ground their interpretation, in part, from the transformations they witnessed in their own life from the 1950s to the 1960s. Certainly, in the late 1950s growing up in Montreal, with its diversity of cultures and the anonymity of crowds, was different from growing up in the homogeneous, sometimes oppressive society of small-town or rural Quebec, where the hold of traditional elites was still dominant. In either case, the Quiet Revolution may be read as a form of collective dissent against an established order which oppressed French Canadians economically and socially.

The End of the Duplessis Regime

During the postwar administration of Premier Maurice Duplessis, from 1944 to 1959, Quebec provincial politics resembled sporting contests between rival gangs, where patronage was both the aim of the game and the means to keep it going. For the vanguard of the baby boom generation attending the *cours classique* (classical studies) with its emphasis on the Christian values and the ideals of Western civilization, there was a marked cleavage between what politics was and what politics ought to be. For Quebeckers growing up in the 1950s, there was also a cultural cleavage between everyday life in Quebec and the attractions of modern, North American industrial and urban life. Quebec newsstands were filled with American consumption dream magazines, presenting the latest in photography equipment, in sound systems, or in automobiles. Like teenagers elsewhere in North America, Quebec youth consumed popular culture: transistor radios played the latest records from Elvis and other American pop artists whose lyrics were barely understood in francophone Quebec. Quebec singers imitated American pop idols with badly translated adaptations of the American hit parade. Yet, French-language Quebec television, dominated in the 1950s by Radio-Canada, mainly offered a mirror to Quebec society: its *téléromans* (soap operas) celebrated rural life, while news and public affairs shows such as René Lévesque's *Point de mire* (Crosshairs) offered a critical look at Quebec society and at significant events elsewhere in the world. But television also featured escapist entertainment: Sunday evenings were social occasions when families would gather around the set and watch the Radio-Canada variety shows or the CBS Ed Sullivan show carried by the CBC.

In late 1950s Quebec, the worlds of Europe and America perceived through print and electronic media were still imaginary, while Sunday Mass remained a social obligation. Quebeckers knew there was a different world out there, where priests did not dictate social behaviour, and where politics were more than patronage contracts, but there seemed few ways to move from the reality of local society to this other wonderful imagined reality.

It is in this sense that the death of Maurice Duplessis, leader of the Union Nationale Party, in September 1959, opened the floodgates. The Duplessis regime's corruption had been attacked with growing intensity in the pages of the daily *Le Devoir,* notably by two clerics, Fathers Dion and O'Neill, who denounced the Union Nationale's use of patronage and its manipulation of elections through intimidation and the buying of votes as violations of Christian ethics.[2] The strength of the Union Nationale had rested on Duplessis's personal charisma and informal network of small-town notables; the party had little formal organization and no mechanism to devise a political program. Duplessis's death represented the death of his regime, and it also symbolized the death of conservative, Church-dominated Quebec.

The death of Maurice Duplessis, at the age of sixty-nine, opened the door to a younger generation of political leaders. While Duplessis personified a jovial, rustic uncle, Liberal leader Jean Lesage played the urban, articulate patrician. Lesage was forty-eight when the Liberals won the 1960 provincial election; René Lévesque, who became his minister of mines and mineral resources, was only thirty-eight, while Paul Gérin-Lajoie, who would become minister of education, was forty. Pierre Laporte (forty-one) and Claire Kirkland-Casgrain (thirty-eight), Quebec's first woman deputy, joined the Lesage Cabinet in 1962.[3]

The Liberals' narrow victory in June 1960 (51.3 per cent of the popular vote and 51 deputies against 43 for the Union Nationale),[4] against a still-formidable Union Nationale machine strengthened the feeling that, as Lesage's election slogan had it, 'c'est le temps que ça change' (it's time for change). Change came mostly from Quebec's rural areas, as *Le Devoir* editor André Laurendeau noted on election night.[5] The Liberal win was aided by the timely publication, less than two months before the election, of Fathers O'Neill and Dion's *Le chrétien et les élections,* in which the priests argued that voting was a moral right violated by electoral fraud and that political critique was a democratic obligation.[6] Thus political change was cast within the continuity of Christian religious practice.

At the outset, the Liberals' victory produced an atmosphere where everything seemed possible and the younger generation could reshape Quebec society.[7] This sentiment became the cornerstone of the myth of the Quiet Revolution. Literary scholar François Ricard has debunked this myth in an essay on the first cohort of the Quebec baby boom generation, which he labelled *The Lyric Generation.* Ricard depicted this cohort as a Greek chorus admiring the dramatic actions taken by their elders and becoming, in the mid-1960s, the centre of attention of their society. According to Ricard, this lyric generation of adolescents was infused with the lightness of being, faith in their own power, identification with their peers, and a narcissistic affirmation of their difference, all traits of the adolescent personality.[8]

Ricard's cartoon-like portrayal needs to be nuanced. It is certainly true, as Ricard notes, that the architects of the Quiet Revolution were not the first wave of baby boomers, but the 'frustrated reformists,' in Ricard's phrase, of the 1950s. Ricard offers a stereoscopic image: on one side is the 'Pepsi generation' of consumers, and on the other are the spokespersons for the student movement, demanding control over their own education and student unionism. On one side the amorphous majority, on the other the militant minority. The stereoscopic image blends them together, yet they were hardly the same persons. Still, Ricard is right to underline the Quiet Revolution's ambience that everything was now possible: access to education, to health services, economic emancipation, cultural flowering, and a sense of control over one's destiny.

This was epitomized by Jean Lesage's televised message to the electorate on election night two years later, on 14 November 1962, when the provincial Liberals obtained the mandate to nationalize the province's power companies. Winning a larger majority than in 1960, Lesage thanked the voters for their support. The Liberals had asked for the 'key to our economic liberation' and undertook to 'open the doors to Quebec's economic future' with this key on the very morrow of the election. 'We have reached political maturity,' Lesage proclaimed; 'we are now ready for economic liberation. Now is the time to become masters in our own house.'[9]

The Quiet Revolution as National Emancipation

In a concise analysis of the Quiet Revolution, sociologist Guy Rocher, who was a key player in it, defines the Quiet Revolution as a series of reforms (changes within the system) aimed at turning Quebec into a 'modern' society, with the state playing the same kind of predominant role it played elsewhere in Canada.[10] In Quebec, rates of secondary school attendance, for instance, were much lower than in the rest of Canada. The Second World War had shown how the federal government could shape Canadian economic development. In Ontario, hydro-electric power had been a tool of state development since the beginning of the twentieth century. Quebec intellectuals argued that Quebec needed to effect a *rattrapage* with the rest of the country and Western society in general. The Quebec state could serve as an instrument of power for the majority French-speaking population. Indeed, the two most important reforms of the 1960s dealt with education and with the structure of economic power in Quebec.[11] Rocher also identifies two other major reforms: the revamping of the administrative structure of the government and the rise of separatist parties dedicated to making Quebec a sovereign nation. These four reforms make up the core of the political component of the Quiet Revolution in the sixties.

Education

The first actions of the Liberal government were to improve access to secondary education. Compulsory education was extended to the age of fifteen in 1961, and school boards had to make high school education available and free. As a result, high school enrolment nearly tripled from 1960–61 to 1970–71. The Lesage government created a royal commission on education in 1961, chaired by the chancellor of Laval University, Mgr Alphonse-Marie Parent. The creation of the commission followed the publication of a trenchant critique of Quebec secondary education by Marist Brother Jean-Paul Desbiens, whose best-selling *Les insolences du Frère Untel* decried, among other things, the poor quality of the French language spoken in Quebec.[12] The Parent Commission undertook a thorough examination of Quebec's education system and found it unsuited to a modern society.

A major recommendation of the Parent Commission was the creation of a level of schooling between high school and university. The Collèges d'enseignement général et professionnel (CEGEPs) were created in 1967 to prepare students either for university education through a 'general' stream or for the workplace through professional training. Students from both streams were to mix and enrich one another's learning experiences. At the end of the 1960s, nearly seventy-two thousand students were enrolled in CEGEPs.

The second major structural innovation in education accomplished during the Quiet Revolution was the creation of the Université du Québec system in 1968. The UQ network implemented a new conception of university governance called *autogestion* (self-administration). Programs were to be designed, administered, and assessed by *modules* (program committees) composed in equal numbers of students and faculty, to which were sometimes added representatives from the 'socioeconomic milieu.' Programs could draw upon the teaching resources of any department that offered relevant material; programs could thus easily be interdisciplinary. Departments, on the other hand, were mainly disciplinary; they were the locus of the research effort and regrouped full-time faculty and sessional lecturers. *Autogestion* did not always turn out to be a good idea, based as it was on the questionable assumption that students were as qualified as faculty to design courses and programs. Yet, the UQ network significantly increased university-level enrolment in Quebec, extending university education to Trois-Rivières, the Saguenay, the Lower St Lawrence, and the Outaouais regions. Existing universities in Montreal, Quebec City, and Sherbrooke also grew rapidly during the period.

Economic Emancipation

Along with the creation of these new educational institutions, the measures taken by the Lesage administration to give the provincial government more leverage in the province's economy were the fundamental innovations of the Quiet Revolution. Following the Liberal victory in the 1962 provincial election, the state-owned Hydro-Québec, created in 1944 to take over private power companies serving the Montreal market, purchased most of the province's remaining private utilities. The goal was to provide an economic lever for industrial development: increased production of electricity from hydro power would stimulate industrialization throughout the province, while uniform electricity rates gave rural areas access to cheaper power for industrial development.[13] Hydro-Québec also offered the rising francophone technical, scientific, and managerial classes a tool of economic and social advancement; it became the most visible symbol of francophone Quebec's economic emancipation.

Economic emancipation was a major issue. According to studies carried out by the Royal Commission on Bilingualism and Biculturalism, French Canadians were close to the bottom of the socioeconomic ladder in Quebec, while anglophones were on top.[14] Capitalism was a synonym for 'Anglo-Saxon.' Since the francophone private sector was too weak to give direction to the Quebec

economy, the government used public enterprises and public capital
as tools of economic development, particularly for natural resources,
most of which the state controlled. For instance, the Société Générale
de Financement (SGF) was created in 1962 to stimulate economic
development in Quebec through investments in natural resources and
in the creation of new enterprises. The SGF was also mandated to
nurture the growth of French-Canadian entrepreneurship. La Société
de sidérurgie (SIDBEC), a Crown company using electric power to
make steel, was created in 1964. Another Crown company, La Société
québécoise d'exploration minière (SOQUEM), was set up the following year for mining exploration. This form of state capitalism
produced uneven results, and SIDBEC, for example, was eventually
privatized in 1995.

Of more lasting effect was the creation of the Caisse de Dépôt et
Placement, which administers taxpayers' contributions to the Régie
des rentes, created in 1965 as the Quebec counterpart to the Canada
Pension Plan. The Caisse was to serve as a major economic instrument of economic development for Quebec. Its twin roles as both
pension fund and instrument of economic development and social
promotion for Quebec capitalists have at times been difficult to reconcile, as opponents of public sector capitalism often point out.

Administrative Reforms and the Unionization
of Public Employees

The Lesage government also reformed the provincial public administration with a Commission de la fonction publique modelled on
the federal public service commission. The provincial Liberals
lured francophone civil servants away from the federal administration, established formal bureaucratic rules, granted job security, and
raised salaries for civil servants, who unionized in 1964 and obtained
the right to strike the following year. Previously composed mainly
of untrained clerical workers hired as patronage appointments, the
Quebec civil service doubled in size during the 1960s and became
heavy with professionals in the social sciences and in administration.
The *longue marche des technocrates* (the long march of the tech-
nocrats), as sociologist Jean-Jacques Simard has described the rise
of the Quebec bureaucracy, soon met with resistance from the local

populations that the bureaucrats were trying to manage, particularly when the economists of the Bureau d'Aménagement de l'Est du Québec (BAEQ) sought to close down villages in the Lower St Lawrence region.[15]

The Rise of Separatist Groups

The creation of sovereignist political parties willing to play the electoral game is, according to Rocher, the fourth major 'reform' of the Quiet Revolution. Unlike the other three, it did not spring from government action, but it nonetheless profoundly altered the established political order. Independence was by and large a reformist, rather than a revolutionary, project, but it is not accurate to say, as Rocher does, that it was always promoted 'dans la légalité et sans violence' (legally and peacefully).[16]

The separatist idea has had a long history in Quebec, going back to the Patriotes in the 1830s, to the Ultramontanes of the late nineteenth century, to the equivocal dreams of Canon Groulx in the 1920s and 1930s, and to right-wing nationalists in the late 1950s. The work of political and economic emancipation undertaken with the Quiet Revolution created fertile ground for rejuvenated arguments in favour of Quebec independence. They came in August 1960, with the foundation of the Action socialiste pour l'indépendance du Québec, by Raoul Roy, the editor of the *Revue socialiste* (1959–65). Roy was competing with a right-wing separatist movement, the Alliance Laurentienne, and an anti-colonial movement, the Rassemblement pour l'indépendance nationale (RIN), created in the autumn of 1960, that drew some of its members from the Alliance Laurentienne. RIN wanted to rally separatists without regard to their views on religion, the economy, or social issues.[17] It was helped by the popular success of Marcel Chaput's book, *Pourquoi je suis séparatiste,* published in 1961 by Les Éditions du Jour, which specialized in cheap, popular, topical paperbacks. Chaput's book ran to six editions and an advertised thirty-five thousand copies by 1962; Ryerson Press published an English-language edition.[18] A chemist working in the Department of National Defence, Chaput was a rarity at the time, a separatist federal civil servant. At first only a political movement, RIN became a political party in 1963 and obtained 6 per cent of the votes in the 1966 provincial election. In 1968, most of its fourteen thousand members joined the newly created Parti Québécois.

During its existence, RIN was a movement as much as a political party. In May 1964, RIN chose as its leader a fiery young orator, Pierre Bourgault, who had a penchant for provocation. According to *Le Devoir,* RIN was the first Quebec movement to use sit-ins as a protest gesture, a tactic borrowed from the U.S. civil rights movement. In June 1964, it used the tactic in support of CN employees who were not being paid for observing what the CN deemed a 'regional holiday' on St-Jean-Baptiste Day.[19] The party also organized sit-ins at the Murray's restaurants in Montreal to get French-language menus.[20] It staged a protest against the Queen's visit to Quebec City in October 1964.[21] RIN had a flair for colours – posters and armbands – that could be uneasily reminiscent of Nazi symbols.[22] Perhaps its best-known protest occurred during the St-Jean-Baptiste Day parade in Montreal in June 1968, when RIN demonstrators clashed with police. The ensuing scuffles made Pierre Trudeau a hero on television, as he refused to leave the reviewing stand. RIN was disbanded in 1968, and its members were urged by Bougault to join the newly created Parti Québécois.

Two other separatist groups competed with RIN. Les Chevaliers de l'indépendance, led by boxer Reggie Chartrand and his band of toughies, also engaged in protest. Chartrand disrupted Victoria Day celebrations in May 1965 by chaining himself and his wife to the Patriotes monument at Pied-du-Courant in Montreal.[23] This was one of numerous incidents that marred the holiday in the city, including the bombing of the Prudential Insurance Company building, scuffles with police, and over a hundred arrests.[24] The Chevaliers also protested Dominion Day the following year.[25]

The Regroupement National (RN), a separatist right-wing group, was created by a small-town pediatrician, René Jutras, in 1964, in reaction to the perceived socialist bent of RIN. This had been preceded by the creation in 1962 of the Parti républicain du Québec by Marcel Chaput in a break from RIN. The founders of the Parti Républicain and of the Regroupement National were frightened by atheists and agnostics in RIN, whom they accused of wanting to reshape Quebec society after independence.[26] Merging with a Social Credit group in 1965, Jutras's party ran in the 1966 elections and joined Lévesque's Mouvement Solidarité-Association to form the PQ in 1968.

Political dissent also manifested itself through violence. In the autumn of 1962, the *réseau de résistance* (underground network), which believed democratic means would not lead to independence, began to spray-paint graffiti in favour of independence on symbols of 'Anglo-Saxon capitalism.' These youths (they were under 21) offered sophisticated arguments to a Radio-Canada reporter as reasons for their actions: they claimed to fight all forms of injustice and, in particular, the economic oppression of French Canadians.[27] The *réseau de résistance* turned into the Front de Libération du Québec (FLQ), and in 1963 nearly thirty bombs were planted by them, mainly in Montréal. The 1965 Victoria Day and Dominion Day holidays provided other occasions to target other symbols of 'Anglo-Saxon' oppression.[28]

This first wave of the FLQ displayed what historian Eric Bédard and others have labelled a millenarian concept of social change. Dissatisfied with the state of Quebec society, its members saw independence as heralding the dawn of a new society, a liberation that would allow Quebeckers to live rather than simply survive. And they saw themselves as the martyrs that would eventually make it happen.[29]

As the four types of political changes outlined by Rocher were taking place, Quebec society also experienced the rapid decline of the Catholic Church's influence. The state took over the Church's administration of hospitals and social services and ended clerical influence over most of education (school boards remained confessional until 1998). As other avenues of social promotion opened up for French Canadians, the Church suffered from dwindling enrolment in its seminaries and from large numbers of priests leaving it. Rigidly opposed to divorce, contraception, and abortion, the Church lost large numbers of adherents in urban areas. A visible symbol of the secularization of Quebec society was the conversion of church buildings into condominiums.

The Beginning of the End: The 1966 Election

Distrust of democratic change was deepened by the results of the Quebec provincial election of 1966. The Liberals got nearly 10 per cent fewer votes than in 1962, and the Union Nationale also lost a little over 3 per cent of its support, while RIN and the RN together obtained nearly 9 per cent of the votes. Yet, this translated into fifty-six seats for the Union Nationale and fifty for the Liberals. This lopsided result was caused in part by the Quebec electoral map, which overrepresented rural areas, and in part by an electorate scared by the swiftness of the Liberals' reforms.

The Union Nationale government of Daniel Johnson, who replaced Jean Lesage as premier, did not dismantle what the Liberals had created, and pushed ahead with several reforms, notably by creating educational institutions (1967–68) and health insurance (1969). But it focused on constitutional change, trying to give some substance to its electoral slogan of 'Equality or Independence.' With the death of Johnson, in September 1968, the Union Nationale government was set adrift and social protest grew louder.

The Bitterness of the End

The constitutional avenue to social change would soon close. Quebec premiers Lesage and Johnson demanded increased powers for the Quebec government as the government of one of the two 'founding peoples' of Canada. At a February 1968 constitutional conference, Premier Johnson was rebuffed by the new justice minister, Pierre Elliott Trudeau, under the glare of television cameras.[30] Trudeau and Johnson symbolized two divergent readings of the Quebec situation. Trudeau offered bilingual services from the federal government as the answer to the economic and social inferiority felt by French Canadians within their own province. Johnson argued that only a more powerful provincial government could achieve substantial socioeconomic improvements and give French Canadians real equality. The Trudeau solution held little appeal for those who, like Pierre Vallières, saw themselves as 'white niggers' in America. Michèle Lalonde's poem, 'Speak White,' conveyed the Québécois sense of oppression and quest for equality.

Reaction in the rest of Canada to Quebec's constitutional demands was less open than it had been when the Bilingualism and Biculturalism Commission proposed to implement true bilingual equality in the federal government. For English Canada, individual equality was one thing; asymmetrical federalism, to give it its scholarly label, or 'privileges for Quebec,' as it was more commonly viewed, went against the principle of 'equality of the provinces.' This principle extended to provinces the natural law concept of equality for all human beings. In reality, the 'principle' served more to throw the equality argument back in the face of Quebec than to buttress a genuine constitutional position; it conveniently ignored differences in provincial constitutions embedded in the British North America Act.

For some French-Canadian activists, joining the FLQ became the answer to the political impasse. The FLQ set nearly twenty bombs in 1968 and close to thirty in 1969, causing three deaths.[31] The results of the April 1970 provincial election seemed to darken prospects for substantial change even more: the Liberals were returned to power under the uninspired leadership of Robert Bourassa, a young economist promising jobs.[32] The PQ, which had received the second largest proportion of votes (23 per cent), won only seven seats, while the Union Nationale, with 10 per cent of votes, obtained seventeen seats, and the Ralliement Créditiste, a Quebec version of the Alberta Social Credit movement, with 11 per cent of votes, secured twelve seats. To youths in a hurry, democratic change seemed ever farther away.

The most famous acts of violent dissent, of course, were the FLQ kidnappings of British trade delegate James Cross and of Quebec Labour Minister Pierre Laporte, which led to the imposition of the War Measures Act, and the death of Laporte in October 1970. To anyone remotely familiar with radical protest in Quebec, it was obvious that the FLQ was a tiny organization that could hardly overthrow the established order. But the FLQ gave the federal government the occasion to reassert 'the rule of law' in Quebec and to tar peaceful movements of dissent with the violence of the FLQ.[33]

The illegal strike of the Common Front in May 1972 constituted the last major act of collective dissent of the Quiet Revolution. The Common Front was made up of the three major union federations in Quebec: the Confederation of National Trade Unions (CSN), half of whose members were public sector workers; the Quebec Federation of Labour (FTQ); and the Quebec Teachers Corporation (CEQ). The Common Front demanded job security and a symbolic $100 a week as a minimum wage. More than 210,000 workers took part in a ten-day general strike in April 1972. In response, the Quebec government introduced back-to-work legislation which imposed heavy fines on non-compliant unions and their leaders. At first, the leaders of the three union federations – Marcel Pepin of the CSN, Louis Laberge of the FTQ, and Yvon Charbonneau of the CEQ – urged their members to defy the legislation. The three were arrested and jailed. This act of repression provoked spontaneous work stoppages in the private as well as the public sector. For a time, it seemed as though an insur-rection was in the works. But there was no revolutionary leadership or any plans for an overthrow of the established order. The strike caused a rift within the CSN and the creation of a breakaway labour federation, the Confédération des Syndicats démocratiques (CSD). Still, in the autumn of 1972, the $100 a week was granted by the government.[34]

Quebec and the World

Dissent in Quebec in the 1960s was linked to dissent elsewhere in the world. The French weekly press was available in most newsstands, and the issue of decolonization figured prominently in French newspapers and magazines. So did the struggle for racial equality in the United States. For radical dissenters such as Raoul Roy, the founder of the *Revue socialiste,* for the impudent young writers of the socialist and separatist literary journal *Parti Pris,*[35] or for Pierre Vallières, the FLQ member whose autobiography, *White Niggers of America,*[36] equated the situation of francophone Quebeckers to that of U.S. blacks, the decolonization movement in Algeria as portrayed by Frantz Fanon, Albert Memmi, and Jacques Berque served as inspiration, as did French philosopher Jean-Paul Sartre's existentialism.[37] Reading and quoting Karl Marx, in a province where, a few years before, the only accept-able philosopher was Thomas Aquinas, was a gesture of provocation as much as an intellectual stance, a *pied de nez* to the social scientists established in the universities, few of whom were openly Marxist.

Quebec dissenters were inspired not only by the print media, but also by television. In the late 1950s, Radio-Canada public affairs shows such as *Point de mire* explained decolonization in terms that could suggest similarities with the situation in Quebec.[38] Coverage of international dissent movements increased in the 1960s, but the study of this coverage on Quebec French-language television remains largely unexplored.

The Radio-Canada archives offer a sample of international issues addressed by the network. The 22 February 1966 edition of the popular public affairs show *Le Sel de la semaine* reported on a demonstration in Montreal's Dominion Square and in front of the U.S. consulate. One thousand pacifist demonstrators demanded peace in Vietnam, chanting 'Le Vietnam aux Vietnamiens' to the tune of 'Le Québec aux Québécois.' Robert Cliche, head of the Quebec wing of the NDP, Daniel Latouche, of the Union Générale des Étudiants du Québec (UGEQ), and U.S. pacifist historian Staughton Lynd, the guest of honour, addressed the crowd.[39] Other groups taking part included the feminist group La voix des femmes, the community action group Mouvement de libération populaire, the Parti socialiste du Québec, as well as some unidentified anglophones.

'Non à la guerre au Vietnam,' *Caméra 67,* 7 November 1967, was a half-hour story featuring the demonstration of seventy-five thousand dissenters in Washington, DC, which included Dr Benjamin Spock, Castro supporters, students, and veterans of the Second World War.[40] Host Judith Jasmin interviewed French-speaking American students, who stressed the non-violent character of their protest, while in the background demonstrators chanted 'Hell no, we won't go!' How important is this youth movement? Jasmin asked sociologist Immanuel Wallerstein: Wallerstein answered that half of the U.S. student-age population was in college, implying that they all protested the war. Images of the Pentagon under siege and of soldiers with bayonets charging a group of protesters and dragging them into paddy wagons illustrated the story, which made reference to the Nuremburg trials and noted the ideological links of the demonstrators to the Black Power movement.

The black movement in the United States received more coverage on Radio-Canada with the death of Martin Luther King, Jr. Judith Jasmin's 'Martin Luther King assassiné: la fin d'un rêve,' *Caméra 68,* 10 April 1968, was a half-hour show on how the United States was 'on the edge of civil war' after three days of rioting.[41] The show contained images of King's funeral procession and excerpts from Coretta King's eulogy. It mentioned Black Power and the Student Non-Violent Coordinating Committee and showed the hundred thousand Atlanta marchers behind King's funeral procession. The black movement, Jasmin asserted, was intent on social revolution. Black students who occupied the Sir George Williams computer centre in early 1969 agitated in favour of civil rights movements in the United

States as well as locally. They saw themselves as suffering from the same kind of racism that oppressed blacks in the United States.[42]

Quebec and Canada

Let us now examine some Quebec dimensions of dissent in Canada discussed elsewhere in this volume. Most of the issues raised by English-Canadian dissent were also raised in Quebec, where they often took the added coloration of the national struggle. The interplay of English-Canadian and Quebec nationalisms, which provided the most obvious of the challenges to the established order, has, unfortunately, received very little scholarly attention. Editorial reaction in English Canada to the major political and constitutional issues raised by the Quiet Revolution has been examined,[43] but there is no equivalent study of Quebec perceptions of English-Canadian nationalism. The study of editorial opinion in English-language newspapers reveals a fundamental misunderstanding about the quest for French language rights. For Quebec nationalists, language rights were but an element of the affirmation of collective rights; for most English-Canadian editorial opinion, on the other hand, language rights largely remained a question of individual rights. The recognition of national rights as a form of collective rights remained elusive.

In Quebec as elsewhere in Canada, feminism had perhaps the most profound and the most lasting impact of the dissent movements. Feminism raised the issue of the class and ethnic identifications of feminists. By and large, Quebec feminists of the 1960s resembled their English-Canadian counterparts: they were educated, intelligent, witty, and dignified middle-class or upper-class women, as seen in the Radio-Canada archives news clip on the foundation of the Quebec Federation of Women in 1966.[44] Quebec women were still working for representation on the provincial scene. Their organizations were lobbying for studies and reports, and the creation of the Royal Commission on the Status of Women (Bird Commission) was viewed with some satisfaction, although sociologist Monique Bégin, the commission's secretary and research director, underlined the different preoccupations of French-Canadian women and of women elsewhere in Canada. Bégin claimed that French-Canadian women were more concerned with access to education and to the labour market and less preoccupied with legal issues than women from other parts of Canada.[45] According to the Radio-Canada program, *Femme d'aujourd'hui,* the Bird Report was received in different ways by male politicians[46] and by female militants, who were concerned by the narrow focus and the meliorist approach of the report.[47]

The Quebec student movement in the 1960s was more vigorous than its counterpart in English-speaking Canada. In Quebec universities, student associations broadened the scope of their demonstrations, not only for better education and free tuition, but also for broader causes such as Quebec nationalism or the strike of *La Presse* reporters. The student associations of Montreal universities created the Union générale des étudiants du Québec (UGEQ) in 1964. UGEQ defined itself as a non-confessional and democratic union. It sought to redefine the collective identity of students as 'young intellectual workers,' a phrase borrowed from the French student movement.[48] But soon tensions emerged within UGEQ: conflicts with the leaders of the student press, and a confrontational attitude towards the Canadian Union of Students (CUS) to which students at McGill and Loyola College belonged, weakened the movement.[49] In October 1968, CEGEP and university students went on strike demanding a second French-language university in Montreal, better student financial assistance, and improvement in the relations between students and staff. Strikers occupied some CEGEPs. Administrators at the CEGEPs resisted student demands and threatened them with expulsion if occupations did not cease. The student strike petered out at the end of October 1968. The outcome of the strike was mixed: the UQ network was created, but student unionism collapsed.[50]

The Sir George Willams University computer centre occupation, in February 1969, was not linked directly to the Quebec francophone student movement, but the atmosphere of *contestation* that prevailed in Montreal at the time probably made it seem an appropriate tactic.[51] Here, too, as in the CEGEPS, the capacity of university administrators to deal with delicate issues was called into question.

Student protest made education a nationalist cause. In March 1969, around fifteen thousand demonstrators massed in front of McGill University, demanding that the university be turned into a French-language institution. The movement resulted from cooperation between young anglophone Marxist students at McGill and UGEQ leaders. It created some panic among Radio-Canada reporters who covered the event.[52]

Driven by the winds of change blown by the Quiet Revolution, the student movement in Quebec was more militant than the student movement in the rest of Canada. It exhibited what has been labelled a millenarian view of its role in society: students, and the young generation more broadly, would overthrow the existing order and bring about a new millennium of peace, progress, and social justice.[53] The Radio-Canada clip of Claude Charron, UGEQ vice-president for international affairs, on 21 October 1968, gives the tone of the movement.[54] Charron excoriated the adult generation for its failures and repression and demanded power for youth. Student movements for social justice became more radicalized in the early 1970s, with the appearance of Maoist groups. Sociologist Jean-Philippe Warren argues that the failures of the October movements (the 1968 student strikes, the 1969 strikes by police and firemen, and the 1970 FLQ crisis) led to this radicalization; he sees the massive student strike in October 1968 as, in part, modelled after the Chinese 'cultural revolution.'[55]

As the occupation of the Sir George Williams computer centre in 1969 made clear, the American Black Power movement found echoes among Montreal's black community. This was a shock for white Montrealers, who usually viewed Quebec society as made up of English-speaking bosses and French-Canadian underdogs; other ethnic groups were seldom visible in public debate. This did not mean that relations between the many communities of Montreal were all to the good. In 'Le racisme ordinaire,' a Radio-Canada story by James Bamber broadcast on 26 February 1966, Montreal youngsters and adults openly voiced their racism on air.[56]

In contrast to the situation elsewhere in Canada, the leadership of the Quebec labour movement in the 1960s was militant enough for most of its members, who did not have to challenge the union establishment.[57] Indeed, with the 1972 Common Front, the Quebec labour movement became too militant for a large number of its members. Union membership in Quebec rose from 30.5 per cent of waged workers in 1961 to 39.3 per cent in 1970; this growth came, in part, but not exclusively, from the unionization of public sector workers. The ratio of days of work per worker lost due to strikes more than doubled from the first half of the 1960s to the second half. This was not quite as large an increase as in Ontario, where the rate tripled, but it was a substantial increase.[58] Some strikes, such as the nurses' strike of 1966 or that of *La Presse*'s typographers, from June to December 1964 and again in 1971, drew a lot of public attention. During the later strike at *La Presse,* in October 1971, fifteen thousand supporters were brutally attacked by police and the skirmish led to one death by asphyxiation.[59]

Even more disturbing of social order had been the Montreal police strike of October 1969.[60] Police and firemen held a one-day suspension of work as a pressure tactic in their collective bargaining with the City of Montreal. The city was left without police. Downtown Montreal was vandalized, storefronts broken, goods stolen, and one policeman died.

There is little space to mention other challenges to the established order, particularly from community action groups in Montreal and elsewhere. Some of these groups, such as those in the St-Henri and Pointe St Charles districts of Montreal, were inspired by American groups.[61] Their common feature was a mobilization of local residents under the leadership of local leaders and not, as was the case for community work in the preceding decades, under the leadership of clerics or well-meaning *bourgeoises.* In the early 1970s, these groups became the incubators of Maoist groups.[62]

Conclusion

In sixties Quebec, dissent took a multitude of forms, from the writing of petitions to the kidnapping of public figures. Dissent was seen as the first step in making over the world. This desire to remake the world was essentially a youth phenomenon, as François Ricard has argued; it was a way to go farther and well beyond what the polite reformers of the 1950s had attempted to do. Its legacy was three-fold.

First, some of the protest movements achieved their goals. Perhaps the most significant long-term gains were in the growth of postsecondary education, where institutions carried on the challenges to the established order that had led, in a way, to their creation.

Second, community action groups proliferated, not only in Montreal, but in smaller towns and in rural areas. Challenging the established order became part of the established order: groups petitioned local and provincial authorities, and fed the media's insatiable appetite for tension and drama.

Third, many of the leaders of the dissent groups gained prominence in politics and in the union movement, after the 1970 October Crisis made violent action disreputable. These young leaders repeated the pattern observable among their elders of the 1950s, such as federal Cabinet ministers Jean Marchand, Gérard Pelletier, and Pierre Elliott Trudeau, or, for that matter, PQ Premier Bernard Landry. Members of RIN such as Marcel Léger became ministers in PQ governments, as did community activists such as Louise Harel. So did student leaders, such as the vice-president of UGEQ, Claude Charron, who became a PQ minister and later a media personality.[63] Even former Maoists entered the electoral arena, as did Bloc Québécois leader Gilles Duceppe. In the 1960s FLQ ideologue Pierre Vallières would have considered such actions traitorous; but Vallières himself eventually abandoned violent action, if not the fight against injustice.[64]

Most struggles, of course, continue. Discrimination against blacks (and now Latinos, Muslims, Arabs, and Orientals) seems to have increased in proportion to the increase in their numbers.[65] Students have not obtained free university tuition and have continued to strike for better education and better financial help. Labour still fights for better wages and working conditions, even though the union movement has declined and has become more open to collaboration with employers; nowadays it even runs mutual funds. The feminist movement today is fighting the hypersexualization of pubescent girls as much as workplace equality. While the gay and lesbian movement, practically unknown in the 1960s, has made notable progress in Quebec, the situation of the Natives, hardly ever evoked in the 1960s, continues to be deplorable.[66] Independence has waned as a mobilizing ideology. For today's young generation, Quebec issues sometimes take a back seat to global problems such as the environment, famine in the Third World, ethnic cleansing, or the oppression of women and national minorities. But, like the rest of Canada, Quebec remains a small society, often prone to soul-searching, and the issues that provoked dissent in the sixties are never far removed from current political debate.

FURTHER READING

Dickinson, John, and Brian Young. *A Short History of Québec*. Montreal: McGill-Queen's University Press, 2000.

Igartua, José. *The Other Quiet Revolution: National Identities in English Canada, 1945–1971*. Vancouver: UBC Press, 2006.

Linteau, Paul-André, et al. *Quebec since 1930*. Toronto: Lorimer, 1991.

Ricard, François. *The Lyric Generation: The Life and Times of the Baby Boomers*. Toronto: Stoddard, 1994.

Rocher, Guy. *Le 'laboratoire' des réformes dans la Révolution tranquille: Conférence Desjardins, prononcée dans le cadre du Programme d'études sur le Québec de l'Université McGill, le 6 novembre 2001*. Montreal: Programme d'études sur le Québec, McGill University, 2001.

Notes

Introduction

1   For a survey of the American literature on the 1960s, see M.J. Heale, 'The Sixties as History: A Review of the Political Historiography,' *Review of American History* 31/1 (2005), 133–52; Andrew Hunt, 'When Did the Sixties Happen? Searching for New Directions,' *Journal of Social History* 3/1 (1999), 147–61.
2   Van Gosse, 'Postmodern America: A New Democratic Order in the Second Gilded Age,' in *The World the Sixties Made: Politics and Culture in Recent America* (Philadelphia: Temple University Press, 2003), 5. 'Americans know the era has ended and yet feel as though we are living in its aftermath, still debating its issues, and still trying to decide whether it had a positive or negative impact on contemporary American life.' Alexander Bloom, ed., *Long Time Gone: Sixties America Then and Now* (New York: Oxford University Press, 2001), 7.
3   Arthur Marwick, *The Sixties: Cultural Revolution in Britain, France, Italy and the United States, c.1958–c.1974* (Oxford: Oxford University Press, 1998).
4   See also Myrna Kostash, *Long Way from Home: The Story of the Sixties Generation in Canada* (Toronto: Lorimer, 1980); Denise Leclerc and Pierre Dessureault, *The 60s in Canada* (Ottawa: National Gallery of Canada, 2005). In contrast, some writers are exploring new themes relating to the 1960s: see Karen Dubinsky, '"We Adopted a Negro": Interracial Adoption and the Hybrid Baby in 1960s Canada,' in *Creating*

Postwar Canada: Community, Diversity and Dissent, 1945–75, ed. Magda Fahrni and Robert Rutherdale (Vancouver: UBC Press, 2007), 268–88; Elise Chenier, 'Rethinking Class in Lesbian Bar Culture: Living the "Gay Life" in Toronto, 1955–1965,' in *Rethinking Canada: The Promise of Women's History,* ed. Mona Gleason and Adele Perry (Toronto: Oxford University Press, 2006), 301–22.

5 Marcel Martel, 'Law versus Medicine: The Debate over Drug Use in the 1960s,' in Fahrni and Rutherdale, *Creating Postwar Canada,* 315–33; Jean-Philippe Warren, *Une douce anarchie: Les années 68 au Québec* (Montreal: Boréal, 2008).

6 Dimitry Anastakis, ed., *The Sixties: Passion, Politics and Style* (Montreal and Kingston: McGill-Queen's University Press, 2008).

7 M. Athena Palaeologue, ed., *The Sixties in Canada: A Turbulent and Creative Decade* (Montreal: Black Rose Books, 2009).

8 The essays in *New World Coming* share a belief that political and cultural movements of this period were motivated by a common transnational purpose. Karen Dubinsky et al., eds., *New World Coming: The Sixties and Global Consciousness* (Toronto: Between the Lines, 2009).

9 'The 1960s was a pivotal decade, then, not only because it was stamped with dissent, protest, and change. Canadians may have been forced to decisively shift their self-conception away from an age-old attachment to empire, in which much comfort could be taken in prideful understanding of keeping alive European traditions by sustaining a unique dominion of the north.' Bryan Palmer, *Canada's 1960s: The Ironies of Identity in a Rebellious Era* (Toronto: University of Toronto Press, 2009), 5.

10 A recently completed doctoral dissertation from Queen's University examines Montreal in the 1960s: see Sean Mills, *The Empire Within: Montreal, the Sixties, and the Forging of a Radical Imagination* (Montreal and Kingston: McGill-Queen's University Press, 2010).

11 Another recent book on this topic is *New World Dawning: The Sixties at Regina Campus,* by James M. Pitsula (Regina: University of Regina, Canadian Plains Research Centre, 2008).

12 The literature on second-wave feminism or the October Crisis (1970), for example, demonstrates the limited resources available to contemporary historians. Canadian historians still largely rely on Nancy Adamson et al.'s 1988 book *Feminists Organizing for Change* for a history of second-wave feminism. Most of the historiography on second-wave

feminism has been produced by individuals who were active in the movement. The literature on the October Crisis is even more slanted towards first-person accounts. Most historians still depend on Louis Fournier's 1984 unsourced book on the crisis and the FLQ. See Louis Fournier, *F.L.Q.: The Anatomy of an Underground Movement* (Toronto: NC Press, 1984); Nancy Adamson, Linda Briskin, and Margaret McPhail, *Feminist Organizing for Change: The Contemporary Women's Movement in Canada* (Toronto: University of Toronto Press, 1988). For a full list of secondary sources on the October Crisis, visit http://www. HistoryOfRights.com/reading_flq.html.

13 Hunt raises a similar issue (the generational divide among historians of the 1960s) in his review of the American literature: 'The current trend toward revisionism among younger scholars has been beneficial inasmuch as it has sought to examine the movement's neglected constituencies, but counterproductive to the degree that it has curbed further studies of protest and disparaged those who had the courage to apply their principles to action during this troubling time. The field would benefit enormously by producing more international comparative studies. Perhaps it is fitting that the Americanists have produced most of the literature, but we still await worthwhile contributions on Prague Spring, May '68 in Paris, and the emergence of New Left activism in Europe, Latin America, and Japan. Moreover, if sixties research has a future, it must begin to transcend the narrow confines of "movement" history by placing neglected constituencies and the different types of resistance into the broader context of social history. Such a trend would undermine the excessive periodization of the era, which means, sadly, we may have to put on our thinking caps and come up with a more descriptive term than "the sixties."' Hunt, 'When Did the Sixties Happen?' 160–1.

14 Warren, *Une douce anarchie,* 13.

15 Of course, numerous historians explore developments in the 1960s and engage with many issues and topics that are not detailed in this chapter. But despite competing interpretations on the impact or legacy of the 1960s, historians explicitly interested in the '1960s' as a phenomenon often draw on similar themes. In the Canadian context, see the following: Kenneth Westhues, 'Inter-Generational Conflict in the Sixties,' in *Prophecy and Protest: Social Movements in Twentieth-Century Canada,* ed. Samuel D. Clark, J. Paul Grayson, and Linda M. Grayson (Toronto: Gage, 1975), 387–408; Kostash, *Long Way from Home;* Cyril Levitt,

Children of Privilege: Student Revolt in the Sixties (Toronto: University of Toronto Press, 1984); Jaymie Heilman, 'Offspring as Enemy? How Canada's National Magazine Confronted Youth and Youth Culture in the 1960s,' *Past Imperfect* 6 (1997), 73–110; Robert Rutherdale, 'Fatherhood, Masculinity, and the Good Life during Canada's Baby Boom, 1945–1965,' *Journal of Family History* 24/3 (1999), 351–73; Mills, 'The Empire Within'; Margaret Hillyard Little, 'Militant Mothers Fight Poverty: The Just Society Movement, 1968–1971,' *Labour/Le Travail* 59 (2007), 179–98; Martel, 'Law versus Medicine'; Christabelle Sethna, '"Chastity Outmoded": *The Ubyssey,* Sex, and the Single Girl, 1960–1970,' in Fahrni and Rutherdale, *Creating Postwar Canada,* 289–314; Wendy Robbins et al., eds., *Minds of Our Own: Inventing Feminist Scholarship and Women's Studies in Canada and Quebec, 1966–76* (Waterloo: Wilfrid Laurier University Press, 2008); Stuart Henderson, 'Toronto's Hippie Disease: End Days in the Yorkville Scene, August 1968,' *Journal of the Canadian Historical Association* 17/1 (2006), 205–34; Michael Dawson, 'Leisure, Consumption, and the Public Sphere: Postwar Debates over Shopping Regulations in Vancouver and Victoria during the Cold War,' in Fahrni and Rutherdale, *Creating Postwar Canada,* 193–216; Greg Marquis, 'From Beverage to Drug: Alcohol and Other Drugs in 1960s and 1970s Canada,' *Journal of Canadian Studies* 39/2 (2005), 57–79.

16 *New World Coming* includes Canadian content, but does not place the Canadian experience in an international context. The Canadian experience is considered in isolation from other international developments explored in the collection.

17 'Periodizing the 1960s' was initially the project of literary scholar Fredric Jameson, who, with an eye on the Third World, began his analysis with the late 1950s and located an end 'in the general area of 1972–1974.' Arthur Marwick largely concurs. Focusing on four Western countries (including the United States), he proposed a 'long' 1960s, encompassing a cultural transformation between 1958 and 1974. Latina scholar Elizabeth Martínez stretches the decade from 1955 to 1975. 'Activists like to think that their movement is still ongoing. According to the sometime Weatherman Bernardine Dohrn in a recent essay, "The sixties began in 1954 and the real news is that they're not over yet." In this at least she concurs with Newt Gingrich, that sometime professor

of history, who speaks of the Sixties as "the long aberration." The Sixties, it has been said, was "the longest decade of the 20th century." Other scholars maintain that there is a case for a short 1960s. For example, Jon Margolis insists that the Sixties began in 1964, while Bruce Schulman claims the Sixties ended in 1968. Some authors have crystallized the Sixties into 1968, a sort of twentieth-century counterpoint to 1848, implying a turning point more important than the larger decade. (Marwick has fretted that undue emphasis on 1968 subverts his case for a "long" 1960s.) It has also sometimes been suggested that the decade has been seriously mislocated. David Frum perversely argues that the Sixties did not occur until the 1970s.' Heale, 'The Sixties as History,' 135–6. See also Bloom, ed., *Long Time Gone,* 7; Gosse, 'Postmodern America,' 2; Barbara L. Tischler, ed., *Sights on the Sixties* (New Brunswick: Rutgers University Press, 1992), 5–6; Frederic Jameson, 'Periodizing the 60s,' in *The Ideologies of Theory Essays,* vol. 2, ed. Frederic Jameson (Minneapolis: University of Minnesota Press, 1988).

18 Alice Echols, *Shaky Ground: The '60s and Its Aftershocks* (New York: Columbia University Press, 2002), 12.

19 It is our contention that, as for the United States and Europe, the 1960s are an appropriate and potentially insightful category for historical analysis in a Canadian context. We do not presume that this approach is necessarily appropriate outside this context, such as Africa or Asia.

20 Marwick offers a similar proposition in the context of Britain, France, Italy, and the United States, adopting a 'long-sixties' approach to his study. Marwick, *The Sixties,* 5.

21 Marwick attempts a more concise synopsis of the narrative *(The Sixties,* 17–20). For a sample of other international studies on the 1960s, see the following: Paul Berman, *A Tale of Two Utopias: The Political Journey of the Generation of 1968* (New York: Norton, 1996); Jérome Duwa, *1968, Année surréaliste: Cuba, Prague, Paris* (Paris: Institut Mémoires de l'édition contemporaine, 2008); Ronald Fraser, *1968: A Student Generation in Revolt* (New York: Pantheon, 1988); Sheila Rowbotham, *The Promise of a Dream: Remembering the Sixties* (London: Allen Lane, 2000); David Caute, *The Year of the Barricades: A Journey through 1968* (New York: Harper and Row, 1988); M.J. Heale, *The Sixties in America: History, Politics and Protest* (Edinburgh: Edinburgh University Press, 2001); Terry Anderson, *The Sixties* (New York: Pearson Longman, 2007).

22 On Canada's military during the Cold War, see Desmond Morton, *A Military History of Canada* (Toronto: McClelland and Stewart, 2007), chapter 6.

23 On the nuclear arms race and Pearson's decision to accept nuclear weapons, see Robert Bothwell, *Alliance and Illusion: Canada and the World, 1945–1984* (Vancouver: UBC Press, 2007), chapter 9; Robert Bothwell, *The Big Chill: Canada and the Cold War* (Toronto: Canadian Institute of International Affairs, 1998), 39–42.

24 On Canada and the Cuban Missile Crisis, see Bothwell, *Alliance and Illusion,* 166–78; Knowlton Nash, *Kennedy and Diefenbaker: Fear and Loathing across the Undefended Border* (Toronto: McClelland and Stewart, 1990).

25 On Canada's space industry and the Avro Arrow, see Bothwell, *Alliance and Illusion,* 141–2; Denis Smith, *Rogue Tory: The Life and Legend of John G. Diefenbaker* (Toronto: Macfarlane, Walter and Ross, 1995).

26 On Canada and the Vietnam War, see Victor Levant, *Quiet Complicity: Canadian Involvement in the Vietnam War* (Toronto: Between the Lines, 1986); Bothwell, *Alliance and Illusion*, chapters 11 and 12.

27 Levant, *Quiet Complicity,* 55.

28 New African governments emerged from the former British colonies of Kenya, Sierra Leone, Somalia, Nigeria, and Madagascar, and from the former French colonies of Dahomey, Niger, Upper Volta, Ivory Coast, Chad, Central Africa, Congo Brazzaville, and Mauritania.

29 On Canada's role in Africa, and the Commonwealth, see Bothwell, *Alliance and Illusion,* 300–3. On the Colombo Plan, see Levant, *Quiet Complicity,* 63–6.

30 The country's apartheid policies included the Extension of University Education Act (banning blacks from white universities in Cape Town and Witwatersrand, and establishing separate institutions for blacks) and the Immorality Act (forbidding sexual intercourse between white and non-whites).

31 Canada established embassies in China, Japan, and India in the 1940s. Smith, *Rogue Tory,* 353–66.

32 Levant, *Quiet Complicity,* 21–3. Canada did not join the American military alliances in the Pacific region, including ANSUZ (Australia, New Zealand, United States) created in 1952 or SEATO (Southeast Asia Treaty Organization) created in 1954. Levant, 27. 'Canadian policy

towards Indonesia, as with Canadian policy towards the decolonizing world in general, was an afterthought in postwar Canadian foreign policy.' David Webster, *Fire and the Full Moon: Canada and Indonesia in a Decolonizing World* (Vancouver: UBC Press, 2009), 4.

33 On Canadian foreign policy in Asia, see Bothwell, *Alliance and Illusion,* chapter 5; Webster, *Fire and the Full Moon.*

34 Fournier, *F.L.Q.,* 119.

35 On social movements in Canada in the 1960s, see Marie Hammond-Callaghan and Matthew Hayday, *Mobilizations, Protests and Engagements: Canadian Perspectives on Social Movements* (Halifax: Fernwood, 2008); Dominique Clément, 'Generations and the Transformation of Social Movements in Post-War Canada,' *Histoire Sociale/Social History* 42/84 (2009), 361–87; Dominique Clément, *Canada's Rights Revolution: Social Movements and Social Change, 1937–1982* (Vancouver: UBC Press, 2008); Suzanne Staggenborg, *Social Movements* (Toronto: Oxford University Press, 2007).

36 On the October Crisis, see Dominique Clément, 'The October Crisis of 1970: Human Rights Abuses under the War Measures Act,' *Journal of Canadian Studies/Revue d'etudes Canadiennes* 42/2 (2008), 160–86.

37 On Canadian music, there are several articles in the *American Review of Canadian Studies* 32/1 (2002). See also Robert A. Wright, '"Dream, Comfort, Memory, Despair": Canadian Popular Musicians and the Dilemma of Nationalism,' *Journal of Canadian Studies* 27/4 (1987/8), 27–43; Barry Grant, '"Across the Great Divide": Imitation and Inflection in Canadian Rock Music,' *Journal of Canadian Studies* 21/1 (1986/7), 116–27.

38 On Canada and drug history, see P.J. Giffen, Shirley Endicott, and Sylvia Lambert, *Panic and Indifference: The Politics of Canada's Drug Laws* (Ottawa: Canadian Centre on Substance Abuse, 1991).

39 Ontario, *Report of the Royal Commission on Metropolitan Toronto* (Toronto: The Commission, 1977).

40 On Canada and the birth control pill, see Christabelle Sethna, 'The Evolution of the Birth Control Handbook: From Student Peer Education Manual to Feminist Self-Empowerment Text, 1968–1975,' *Canadian Bulletin of Medical History/Bulletin canadien d'histoire de la médecine* 23/1 (2006), 89–118; Christabelle Sethna, 'A Bitter Pill: Second Wave Critiques of Oral Contraception,' in *Canada: Confederation to the Present,* ed. Bob Hesketh and Chris Hackett (Edmonton: Chinook Multimedia, 2001).

41 George Grant, *Lament for a Nation: The Defeat of Canadian Nationalism* (Ottawa: Carleton University Press, 1988).

42 On the Quiet Revolution, see José Igartua, *The Other Quiet Revolution: National Identities in English Canada, 1945–1971* (Vancouver: UBC Press, 2006); Yves Bélanger, Robert Comeau, and C. Métivier, *La Revolution Tranquille, 40 Ans Plus Tard: Un Bilan* (Montreal: VLB, 2000).

43 On the nationalist movement in Quebec, see Graham Fraser, *René Lévesque and the Parti Québécois in Power,* 2nd ed. (Montreal and Kingston: McGill-Queen's University Press, 2001); Alain-G. Gagnon, ed., *Quebec: State and Society*, 2nd ed. (Toronto: Nelson Canada, 1993); William D. Coleman, *The Independence Movement in Quebec, 1945–1980* (Toronto: University of Toronto Press, 1984).

44 The NDP formed a short-lived minority government with the federal Liberal Party in 1966, and Ed Schreyer led the NDP to victory in Manitoba in 1969.

45 On the NDP and the Waffle movement, see Pat Smart, 'Queen's University History Department and the Birth of the Waffle Movement,' in *The Sixties in Canada: A Turbulent and Creative Decade,* ed. M. Athena Palaeologue (Montreal: Black Rose Books, 2009), 310–18; John Bullen, 'The Ontario Waffle and the Struggle for an Independent Socialist Canada: Conflict within the NDP,' *Canadian Historical Review* 64/2 (1983), 188–215.

46 On the omnibus bill and other key public policy initiatives in the 1960s, see Canada, *Hansard* (*Debates of the House of Commons,* 1969), 4717–59; Alvin Finkel, *Social Policy and Practice in Canada: A History* (Waterloo: Wilfrid Laurier University Press, 2006).

47 For a detailed discussion on fads, consumerism, television, and youth culture in Canada in the 1960s, see Doug Owram, *Born at the Right Time: A History of the Baby Boom Generation* (Toronto: University of Toronto Press, 1996).

48 On Canada's economy, see Kenneth Norrie and Doug Owram, *History of the Canadian Economy,* 2nd ed. (Toronto: Harcourt Brace, 1996); Owram, *Born at the Right Time,* 71–3.

49 On the welfare state and consumer spending, see Finkel, *Social Policy and Practice;* Dominique Marshall, *The Social Origins of the Welfare State: Quebec Families, Compulsory Education, and Family Allowances, 1940–1955* (Waterloo: Wilfrid Laurier University Press,

2006); Raymond Blake, *From Rights to Needs: A History of Family Allowances in Canada, 1929–92* (Vancouver: UBC Press, 2008).

50 Some of the leading historians of the decade, many of whom are former 1960s activists, include Alice Echols, Todd Gitlin, Alexander Bloom, and David Farber in the United States; or, in Canada, Doug Owram, Cyril Levitt, and François Ricard. David Farber, *The Age of Great Dreams: America in the 1960s* (New York: Hill and Wang, 1994); Todd Gitlin, *The Sixties: Years of Hope, Days of Rage* (New York: Bantam Books, 1987); François Ricard, *La génération lyrique: Essai sur la vie et l'oeuvre des premiers-nés du baby-boom* (Montreal: Boréal, 1992); Palmer, *Canada's 1960s;* Owram, *Born at the Right Time;* Marwick, *The Sixties;* Kostash, *Long Way from Home;* Echols, *Shaky Ground;* Bloom, *Long Time Gone;* Levitt, *Children of Privilege;* Tischler, *Sights on the Sixties;* Rowbotham, *Promise of a Dream.* Hunt offers a more detailed list of the leading American literature produced by former activists ('When Did the Sixties Happen?' 148).

51 Clément, 'Generations and the Transformation.'

52 On RCMP illegal activities, see Jeff Sallot, *Nobody Said No: The Real Story about How the Mounties Always Get Their Man* (Toronto: Lorimer, 1979); Canada, *Certain RCMP Activities and the Question of Governmental Knowledge* (Ottawa: Queen's Printer, 1981). On Munsinger, see Palmer, *Canada's 1960s,* chapter 3; Reg Whitaker and Steve Hewitt, *Canada and the Cold War* (Toronto: Lorimer, 2003). On education, see Robin Mathews and James Steele, *The Struggle for Canadian Universities* (Toronto: New Press, 1969). On Toronto and Rochdale College, see Henderson, 'Toronto's Hippie Disease'; Kostash, *Long Way from Home,* part 3. On economic nationalism, see Stephen Azzi, *Walter Gordon and the Rise of Canadian Nationalism* (Montreal and Kingston: McGill-Queen's University Press, 1999). On Canadian literature, see Margaret Atwood, *The Edible Woman* (Toronto: McClelland and Stewart, 1969); Jacques Godbout, *Salut Galarneau! Le temps des Galarneau* (Saint Laurent: Fides, 2000). Northrop Frye, one of Canada's most internationally recognized writers in the 1960s, published one of his best known texts, *Anatomy of Criticism,* in 1957. On Quebec literature in the 1960s, see the following: André Gaulin, 'Une longue naissance: Abrégé historico-littéraire du Québec,' *French Review* 53/6 (1980), 787–93; Jacques Michon, 'Aspects du roman Québécois des années soixante,' *French Review* 53/6 (1980), 813–15. See also

Margaret Atwood, *Survival: A Thematic Guide to Canadian Literature* (Toronto: Anansi, 1972). On the labour movement, see Gary Teeple, ed., *Capitalism and the National Question in Canada* (Toronto: University of Toronto Press, 1972); Bryan Palmer, *Working-Class Experience: Rethinking the History of Canadian Labour, 1800–1991* (Toronto: McClelland and Stewart, 1992); Paul Knox and Philip Resnick, eds., *Essays in B.C. Political Economy* (Toronto: New Star Books, 1974); Gary Marcuse, 'Labour's Cold War: The Story of a Union that Was Not Purged,' *Labour/Le Travail* 22 (1988), 199–210. On the Bill of Rights, see Ross Lambertson, *Repression and Resistance: Canadian Human Rights Activists, 1930–1960* (Toronto: University of Toronto Press, 2005), chapter 8. On immigration, see Franca Iacovetta, *Gatekeepers: Reshaping Immigrant Lives in Canada* (Toronto: Between the Lines, 2006). On the administration of law reform, see Clément, *Canada's Rights Revolution,* chapter 2. On human rights, see Dominique Clément, '"Rights without the Sword Are but Mere Words": The Limits of Canada's Rights Revolution,' in *A History of Human Rights in Canada,* ed. Janet Miron (Toronto: Canadian Scholars' Press, 2009); Brian Howe and David Johnson, *Restraining Equality: Human Rights Commissions in Canada* (Toronto: University of Toronto Press, 2000), 43–60.

53 Dimitry Anastakis insists, in his own edited collection of essays on the 1960s, that 'the many totems of the period – the music, the protests, the clothes, the style – remain seared into the collective memories of the generations that have come after the baby boomers.' Anastakis, *The Sixties,* 4.

54 Jean-Philippe Warren suggests, in the context of the student movement in Quebec, that students lacked the radicalism we have often associated with this generation: 'Le spectacle offert par les années 1968, ce ne fut pas celui d'une génération qui, levant le poing dans un seul et même élan, voulut combattre l'ordre établi et jeter à bas toutes les formes d'asservissement du plus faible par le plus fort.' Warren, *Une douce anarchie,* 13.

55 See also Sheila Rowbotham, '1968: Springboard for Women's Liberation,' in *New World Coming: The Sixties and the Shaping of Global Consciousness,* ed. Karen Dubinsky et al. (Toronto: Between the Lines, 2009), 263–4; Wini Breines, 'Sixties Stories' Silences: White Feminism, Black Feminism, Black Power,' *NWSA Journal* 8/3 (1996), 101–21.

56 Bryan Palmer, however, suggests that while the 1960s might be categorized in a variety of ways, studying the period as a distinct decade
offers an opportunity to closely examine its legacy. On periodization and
history, see Catherine Gidney and Michael Dawson, 'Persistance and
Inheritance: Rethinking Periodisation and English Canada's Twentieth
Century,' in *Contesting Clio's Craft: New Directions and Debates
in Canadian History,* ed. Mike Dawson and Christopher Dummitt
(London: Institute for the Study of the Americas, 2009), 64–5; Palmer,
Canada's 1960s, 23; Van Gosse and Richard Moser, eds., *The World
the Sixties Made: Politics and Culture in Recent America* (Philidelphia:
Temple University Press, 2003), 284–5.

57 Anastakis, *The Sixties,* 4.

58 For a few examples of this debate, see Anastakis, *The Sixties*: Gretta
Chambers, 'The Sixties in Print: Remembering Quebec's Quiet
Revolution,' 18–24, where she argues that the 1960s in Quebec were a
'clean break with the past' (18); Nicholas Olsberg, 'California Casual:
"How the Slouch Sold the Modern,"' 167–82, where he claims that anti-
war activism 'began with the teach-in and ended with the Weathermen'
(168). Other Quebec historians have located the Quiet Revolution in
long-standing patterns prior to the 1960s. For a discussion of this, see
Ronald Rudin, *Making History in Twentieth-Century Quebec* (Toronto:
University of Toronto Press, 1997). For an analysis of how anti-war
activism existed outside of youth culture and university campuses, see
Frances Early, 'Canadian Women and the International Arena in the
Sixties: The Voice of Women/La voix des femmes and the Opposition
to the Vietnam War in Canada,' in Anastakis, *The Sixties,* 25–41; Amy
Swerdlow, *Women Strike for Peace: Traditional Motherhood and Radical
Politics in the 1960s* (Chicago: University of Chicago Press), 1993.

59 Magda Fahrni and Robert Rutherdale, 'Introduction,' in *Creating
Postwar Canada;* Owram, *Born at the Right Time,* 308–9.

60 Gosse and Moser, *The World the Sixties Made;* Gitlin, *The Sixties;* Wini
Breines, 'Whose New Left?' *Journal of American History* 75/2 (1988),
528–45.

61 Alice Echols, 'Across the Universe,' in Dubinsky et al., *New World
Coming,* 407.

62 On a critique of the concept of generation, see Clément, 'Generations
and the Transformation'; Gidney and Dawson, 'Persistance and
Inheritance,' 65; Anastakis, *The Sixties,* 4; Palmer, *Canada's 1960s,*

chapter 4. For a discussion of university students, dissent, and social change (an extended look at the idea of a 1960s generation), see Owram, *Born at the Right Time;* Kostash, *Long Way from Home;* Beth Bailey, *Sex in the Heartland* (Cambridge: Harvard University Press, 1999); Catherine Gidney, 'War and the Concept of Generation: The International Teach-Ins at the University of Toronto, 1965–1968,' in *Universities and War: Culture, Community and Conflict,* ed. Paul Stortz and E. Lisa Panayotidis (Toronto: University of Toronto Press, in press).

63 On alienation, see Palmer, *Canada's 1960s,* 251–3; Christopher Dummitt, 'A Crash Course in Manhood: Men, Cars, and Risk in Postwar Vancouver,' in Anastakis, *The Sixties,* 71–98; Doug Rossinow, *The Politics of Authenticity: Liberalism, Christianity, and the New Left in America* (New York: Cambridge University Press, 1998); Christopher Dummitt, *The Manly Modern: Masculinity in Postwar Canada* (Vancouver: UBC Press, 2007).

64 Palmer, *Canada's 1960s,* 430.

65 Ian McKay, 'Sarnia in the Sixties (or the Peculiarities of Canadians),' in Dubinsky et al., *New World Coming,* 24–35.

66 For an overview of the 'many 1960s' in the United States, see *The Columbia Guide to America in the 1960s,* ed. David Farber and Beth Bailey (New York: Columbia University Press, 2001).

1. Food, Fear, and the Environment in the Long Sixties

1 Thanks to Brianna Greaves and Michelle Dubois for research assistance.

2 Marjorie Harris, 'The Great Nutrition Game,' *Maclean's* 82 (April 1969), 76–80.

3 *Food Additives: What do you Think? Report on Opinion Survey Conducted Summer 1979* (Ottawa: Health and Welfare Canada, 1980), 6.

4 Wayne Clark, 'The Great Granola Gold Rush,' *Financial Post Magazine* (Oct. 1979), 28.

5 See, e.g., John C. Burnham, 'American Medicine's Golden Age: What Happened to It?' *Science* 21/5 (1982), 1474–9; Paul Starr, *The Social Transformation of American Medicine* (New York: Basic Books, 1982); Erika Dyck, 'The Psychedelic Sixties,' this volume.

6 Paul Boyer, *By the Bomb's Early Light: American Thought and Culture at the Dawn of the Atomic Age* (New York: Pantheon Books, 1985).

7 Ulrich Beck, *The Risk Society: Towards a New Modernity* (London: Sage, 1992); Ulrich Beck, *World Risk Society* (Malden: Polity, 1999).

8 Catherine Gidney, *The Long Eclipse: The Liberal Protestant Establishment and the Canadian University* (Montreal and Kingston: McGill-Queen's University Press, 2004); Valerie Korinek, *Roughing It in the Suburbs: Reading Chatelaine Magazine in the Fifties and Sixties* (Toronto: University of Toronto Press, 2000); Michael Egan, *Barry Commoner and the Science of Survival* (Cambridge: MIT Press, 2007). For literature on the civil rights movement and the sexual revolution, see the following: Charles Payne, *I've Got the Light of Freedom: The Organizing Tradition and the Mississippi Freedom Struggle* (Berkeley: University of California Press, 1995); Beth Bailey, 'From Panty Raids to Revolution Youth and Authority, 1950–1970,' in *Generations of Youth: Youth Cultures and History in Twentieth-Century America,* ed. Joe Austin and Michael Nevin Willard (New York and London: New York University Press, 1998), 187–205; and Alan Petigny, 'Illegitimacy, Postwar Psychology and the Reperiodization of the Sexual Revolution,' *Journal of Social History* (Fall 2004), 63–79.

9 Susanna Moodie, *Roughing It in the Bush* (Toronto: McClelland and Stewart, 1923); Douglas McCalla, 'A World without Chocolate: Grocery Purchases at Some Upper Canadian Country Stores 1808–1861,' *Agricultural History* 79/2 (2005), 147–72; Harvey Levenstein, *Revolution at the Table: The Transformation of the American Diet* (Berkeley: University of California Press, 2003); David Monod, *Store Wars: Shopkeepers and the Culture of Mass Marketing, 1890–1939* (Toronto: University of Toronto Press, 1996). Chain stores did not replace local stores as quickly in the Maritimes and in Quebec, where independent grocers could get a licence to sell beer, which enabled them to better compete with the big chains. F.M. Shore, 'Food Gets Better but Not Cheaper as Giants Battle,' *Financial Post,* 13 Oct. 1962, 59; 'Independent "Chains" Are Big Food Business,' *Financial Post,* 26 Sept. 1964, 66.

10 Stephen Nissenbaum, *Sex, Diet and Debility in Jacksonian America: Sylvester Graham and Health Reform* (Westport: Greenwood, 1980); Levenstein, *Revolution at the Table;* Robert G. Jackson, *How to Be Always Well* (Toronto: Print-Craft, 1927).

11 Harvey Levenstein refers to the period after the Second World War as the 'Golden Age of Food Processing,' in *Paradox of Plenty: A*

Social History of Eating in Modern America (Berkeley: University of California Press, 2003), 101–18.

12 'A Report on Eating,' *Maclean's* 68 (11 June 1955), 91.

13 Alice Munro, 'Family Furnishings,' in *Hateship, Friendship, Courtship, Loveship, Marriage* (Toronto: Penguin, 2001), 107.

14 Robert V. Tauxe and Emilio J. Esteban, 'Advances in Food Safety to Prevent Foodborne Diseases,' in *Silent Victories: The History and Practice of Public Health in Twentieth-Century America,* ed. John W. Ward and Christian Warren (Toronto: Oxford University Press, 2007), 18–43; J. Edgar Monagle, 'Adult Nutrition: From 21 to 101,' *Canadian Nutrition Notes* 17/2 (1961), 10; Donna Baxter, 'Putting Normal Nutrition Across,' *Canadian Nutrition Notes* 17/4 (1961) , 25; Sister Sainte-Jean-de-Jésus, 'Nutrition To-day and Tomorrow: Part Two,' *Canadian Nutrition Notes* 19/8 (1963) , 89.

15 Gayelord Hauser, *Look Younger, Live Longer* (New York: Farrar and Straus, 1950); Gaylord Hauser, *Be Happier, Be Healthier* (New York: Farrar, Straus and Young, 1952); Adelle Davis, *Let's Have Healthy Children* (New York: New American Library, 1972 [1951]); Adelle Davis, *Let's Eat Right to Keep Fit* (New York: Harcourt, Brace and World, 1954).

16 '"Death Ashes" Rained on Japanese Craft: Blame Atomic Test,' *Toronto Star,* 16 March 1954, 1; 'Schweitzer Urges World Opinion to Demand End of Nuclear Tests,' *New York Times,* 24 April 1957, 1; 'Excerpts from Message by Schweitzer,' *New York Times,* 24 April 1957, 4; 'Terrible Danger in Atomic Tests Says Schweitzer,' *Globe and Mail,* 24 April 1952, 2; 'What Is the Real Danger' Editorial, *Globe and Mail,* 25 April 1957, 6; House of Commons, *Debates,* 14 Jan. 1958, 3293. Quote from: 'A-Test Called for by 9,235,' *Globe and Mail,* 14 Jan. 1958, 1.

17 Michael Egan, *Barry Commoner and the Science of Survival: The Remaking of American Environmentalism* (Cambridge: MIT Press, 2007), 66–72.

18 House of Commons, *Debates,* 1959: 12 Feb., 944; 13 Feb., 998; 18 Feb., 1140; 25 Feb., 1375; 2 March, 1496; 12 March, 1910; 24 March, 2210; 25 March, 2246. Patricia McMahon, 'The Politics of Canada's Nuclear Policy,' doctoral dissertation, University of Toronto, 2000, 139–46. Quote from: Editorial, 'The Unseen Assassin,' *Toronto Star,* 6 April, 1960, 6; Candace Loewen, 'Making Ourselves Heard: "Voice of Women" and the Peace Movement in the Early Sixties,' in *Framing Our Past: Canadian Women's History in the Twentieth Century,* ed.

SharonAnne Cook, Lorna R. McLean, and Kate O'Rourke (Montreal
and Kingston: McGill-Queen's University Press, 2001), 248–51.

19 'Pill Endangers Unborn Babies, Doctors Warned,' *Globe and Mail,*
3 Feb. 1962, 2; 'Drug Believed to Malform Babies Banned from Market
after Case Reported,' *Globe and Mail,* 21 March 1962, 3; 'Deformed
Baby Is Placed in Home to Spare Mother Mental Anguish,' *Globe and
Mail,* 20 July 1962, 1; 'Mother "Wept All Day" for Armless, Legless
Baby,' *Toronto Daily Star,* 26 July 1962, 1; 'Les ravages de la thalido-
mide au Canada,' *Le Devoir,* 31 July 1962, 1; Arthur Daemmrick, 'A Tale
of Two Experts: Thalidomide and Political Engagement in the U.S. and
West Germany,' *Social History of Medicine* 15/1 (2002), 137–58. For a
look at the reasons why thalidomide was prescribed, see Barbara Clow,
'"An Illness of Nine Months' Duration": Pregnancy and Thalidomide
Use in Canada and the United States,' in *Women, Health and Nation:
Canada and the United States since 1945,* ed. Georgina Feldberg,
Molly Ladd-Taylor, Alison Li, and Kathryn McPherson (Montreal and
Kingston: McGill-Queen's University Press, 2003), 45–66.

20 Rachel Carson, *Silent Spring* (Boston: Houghton Mifflin, 1962), 2–3.

21 'Hundreds Die,' *Globe and Mail,* 23 Oct. 1965, 1; 'Ontario Tests for
Residue, but Maintains Policy of Finding DDT Substitute,' *Globe and
Mail,* 8 July 1969, 3.

22 'Pesticide Use Warning Is Urged after Inquiry,' *Globe and Mail,* 9 July
1969, 5; 'DDT Figures Not Alarming, Munro Says,' *Globe and Mail,*
10 July 1969, 1; 'Liberals Call for Ban on DDT in Ontario,' *Globe and
Mail,* 10 July 1969, 5. 'U.S. Agriculture Department Suspends Use
of DDT,' *Toronto Star,* 10 July 1969, 1. A Royal Commission on the
incident discovered that the ducks were probably killed by an employee
of the Ontario Waterfowl Research Foundation who used the pesticide
alphachloralose to render the ducks unconscious and collect them
for research purposes. *Report of the Royal Commission Appointed to
Inquire into the Use of Pesticides and the Death of Waterfowl on Toronto
Island* (Ontario: Queen's Printer, 1970). Thanks to Ryan O'Connor for
pointing me to this last source.

23 'U of T Zoology Chief Assails DDT, Threatens to Sue Ontario Board,'
Globe and Mail, 13 Sept. 1969, 13; 'Ontario Will Restrict almost All
DDT Use,' *Globe and Mail,* 25 Sept. 1969, 1; 'Munro Wants Talks
before DDT,' *Globe and Mail,* 25 Sept. 1969, 2; 'Response,' *Globe and
Mail,* 27 Sept. 1969, 6; 'DDT Could Wipe Out Humanity,' *Globe and*

Mail, 29 Sept. 1969, 11; 'Ottawa Will Cut Use of DDT 90%: Permit It on Only 12 Farm Crops,' *Globe and Mail,* 4 Nov. 1969, 10.

24 Norval Fimreite, 'Mercury Uses in Canada and Their Possible Hazards as Sources of Mercury Contamination,' *Environmental Pollution* 1/2 (1970), 119–31 (version used here was published as a manuscript by the Canadian Wildlife Service under the same title, 1); Sidney Katz, 'Mercury Poison Newest Threat in Land, Waters,' *Toronto Star,* 17 Nov. 1969, A1–A2; House of Commons, *Debates,* 25 March 1971, 5463; 'Mercury Poison Stops Lake St Clair Fishing,' *Toronto Star,* 25 March 1970, 1; 'No Ban on Sport Fishing in Manitoba,' *Winnipeg Free Press,* 12 May 1970, 8A; Michael Cobden, 'The Mercury Poison that Is Contaminating Fish Is a Growing Threat in Food and in the Air,' *Toronto Star,* 11 April 1970, 16; David A.E. Shephard, 'Methyl Mercury Poisoning in Canada,' *Canadian Medical Association Journal* 114 (6 March 1976), 463–72; Patricia A. D'Itri and Frank M. D'Itri, 'Mercury Contamination: A Human Tragedy,' *Environmental Management* 2/1 (1978), 3–16.

25 'Polluted Salmon Symptom of Neglect,' *Toronto Star,* 11 Oct. 1975, B4; 'We're Losing the Battle to Clean Up Great Lakes Gloomy Scientists Warn,' *Toronto Star,* 29 May 1976, A12; 'Toxic Chemical Widespread, Survey Indicates,' *Globe and Mail,* 2 Sept. 1972, W2; Arhie Hakala 'Chemicals Called PCBs Kill Birds, Taint Fish,' *Toronto Star,* 24 May 1975; 'Polychlorinated Biphenyls (PCBs),' Environment Canada http://www.ec.gc.ca/wmd-dgd/Default.asp?lang=En&n=75C647A7-1.

26 New labelling regulations, which forced a much greater array of products to list their ingredients on the box, were promulgated in March 1974. Manufacturers had until March 1976 to comply. Health and Welfare Canada, *Health Protection and Food Laws* (Ottawa: National Health and Welfare, 1979), 6–7; Health and Welfare Canada, *Health Protection and Food Laws* (Ottawa: National Health and Welfare, 1970), 5–6.

27 'Directorate Issues Ban on Two Food Colourings,' *Financial Post,* 10 Sept. 1960, 36; Rae Correlli, 'Look What They're Doing to Our Food,' *Toronto Star,* 28 May 1960, 7; Alan Phillips, 'Pollution: A Frightening Assessment of the Unfriendly World Man Has Created by His Systematic Poisoning of the FOOD We Eat, the WATER We Drink and the AIR We Breathe,' *Maclean's* (10 Sept. 1960), 14–15.

28 Yves Morin and Philippe Daniel, 'Quebec Beer-Drinkers' Cardiomyopathy: Etiological Considerations,' *Canadian Medical*

Association Journal 97 (7 Oct. 1967), 926–8; 'The Mystery of
the Quebec Beer-Drinkers' Cardiomyopathy,' *Canadian Medical
Association Journal* 97 (7 Oct. 1967), 930–1; Yves Morin, André Têtu,
and Gaston Mercier, 'Cobalt Cardiomyopathy: Clinical Aspects,' *British
Heart Journal* 33 (1971): Supplement, 175–8; 'Quebec Beer Scare Is
Called Whodunit without Last Page,' *Toronto Star,* 26 May 1966, 1.
'Food that Can Kill,' *Maclean's* 100 (27 April 1987), 26.

29 'Government Officially Announces Cyclamate Sweeteners Will
Be Taken Off Market,' *New York Times,* 19 Oct., 1969, 58; 'Ottawa
Studying Cyclamate Ban,' *Globe and Mail,* 20 Oct. 1969, 3; 'Canada to
Ban Cyclamates,' *Globe and Mail,* Oct. 22 1969, 1; R.L. Foster, 'Scare
Publicity,' *Vancouver Sun,* 3 Nov. 1969, 5; Douglas Ball, 'Cyclamates
and DDT,' *Toronto Star,* 29 Oct. 1969, 6.

30 James S. Turner, *The Chemical Feast: The Ralph Nader Study Group
Report on Food Protection and the Food and Drug Administration*
(New York: Grossman, 1970), 71; Justin Martin, *Nader: Crusader,
Spoiler, Icon* (Cambridge: Perseus, 2002).

31 Gene Marine and Judith Van Allen, *Food Pollution: The Violation of
Our Inner Ecology* (New York: Holt, Rinehart and Winston, 1972);
Jacqueline Verrett and Jean Carper, *Eating May Be Hazardous to Your
Health* (New York: Simon and Schuster, 1974), 42; Ross Hume Hall,
Food for Nought: The Decline in Nutrition (Hagersville: Harper and
Row, 1974); Linda Pim, *Additive Alert: A Guide to Food Additives for
the Canadian Consumer* (Toronto: Doubleday, 1979)

32 'Closer Study of Food Additives Described,' *Globe and Mail,* 15 April
1970, 11.

33 'Preservatives Restricted,' *Globe and Mail,* 11 July 1973, 10; Jeff
Carruthers, 'Citing Cancer Risks, Ottawa Bans Use of Some Meat
Preservatives,' *Globe and Mail,* 14 May 1975, 16; 'That Added Extra,'
Canadian Consumer (Aug. 1982), 10.

34 'Government to Suspend Use of DES as Growth Stimulant in Livestock
on Jan. 1, 1973,' *Globe and Mail,* 15 Aug. 1972, 4; Hall, *Food for
Nought,* 105–10; Julie Sze, 'Boundaries and Border Wars: DES,
Technology and Environmental Justice,' *American Quarterly* 58/3
(2006), 791–814.

35 H.H. Schaumberg, R. Byck, and R. Gertsl, 'Monosodium Glutamate:
Its Pharmacological Role in Chinese Restaurant Syndrome,' *Science*
163 (1969), 105–8; Verity H. Livingstone, 'Current Clinical Findings on

Monosodium Glutamate,' *Canadian Family Physician* 27 (July 1981), 1150–2; Ian Mosby, '"That Won-Ton Soup Headache": The Chinese Restaurant Syndrome, MSG and the Making of American Food, 1968–1980,' paper given at the Canadian Society for the History of Medicine, 31 May 2008; Editorial, 'Safety First on Additives,' *Globe and Mail,* 27 Oct. 1969, 6; '3 Manufacturers of Baby Food Drop Additive,' *Toronto Star,* 25 Oct. 1969, 8.

36 'Studied Link between Diet Hyperactivity; Group Says Findings Merit More Investigation,' *Globe and Mail,* 15 Jan. 1976, F5; Joan Hollobon, 'Speed-Type Drugs Should Not Be Denied to Active Children: MD,' *Globe and Mail,* 9 June 1975, 5; Ben Feingold, *Why Your Child Is Hyperactive* (New York: Random House, 1975); Howard Fluxgold, 'What Makes Paul Run,' *Globe and Mail,* 17 May 1979, T1; Matthew Smith, 'Into the Mouths of Babes: The Rise and Fall of the Feingold Diet for Hyperactivity, 1974–Present,' paper presented at the Canadian Society for the History of Medicine, 31 May 2008; Matthew Smith, 'The Hyperactive State: The History of Attention-Deficit/Hyperactivity Disorder (ADHD) and American Psychiatry, 1957–1980,' M.A. thesis, University of Alberta, 2004; House of Commons, *Debates,* 1975: 24 Oct., 8517; 21 Feb., 3441.

37 John Henkel, 'From Safety to Cereal: Seeing to the Safety of Color Additives,' *FDA Consumer* (Dec. 1993), at http://www.cfsan.fda.gov/~dms/col-221.html; 'Color Additives: Botched Experiment Leads to Banning of Red Dye No. 2,' *Science* 4226 (6 Feb. 1976), 450; 'Ottawa Decides Not to Ban Red Dye Linked to Cancer,' *Toronto Star,* 3 Feb. 1976, A16; Val Sears, 'U.S. Differs with Canada on Red Dye,' *Toronto Star,* 13 Feb. 1976, 1 and 6.

38 House of Commons, *Debates,* 20 April 1977, 4386.

39 Ellen Roseman, 'Labels Raise Questions about Chemicals in Food,' *Globe and Mail,* 6 Feb. 1978, 26.

40 Health and Welfare Canada, *Food Additives: What Do You Think? Report on Opinion Survey Conducted Summer 1979* (Ottawa: Author, 1980).

41 'People's Fear of Additives "Unscientific,"' *Globe and Mail,* 11 Aug. 1980, 11.

42 'The Safety of Food Additives,' *Canadian Home Economics Journal* 31/2 (1981), 82.

43 'Horror-Story Approach,' *Globe and Mail,* 27 July 1971, 9.

44 '"Hysterical" Fear of Food Additives Decried,' *Globe and Mail,* 13 June 1972, B7.

45 'Fabricated Foods: Quality Declines as Technology Takes Over,'
    Canadian Consumer, Oct. 1976, 2.
46 Davis, *Let's Eat Right to Keep Fit* and *Let's Have Healthy Children.*
47 Georges Ohsawa, *Zen Macrobiotics* (Los Angeles: Ohsawa
    Foundation, 1965).
48 Paavo Airola: *Are You Confused?* (Phoenix: Health Plus, 1971);
    Hypoglycemia: A Better Approach (Phoenix: Health Plus, 1977); *There
    Is a Cure for Arthritis* (New York: Parker, 1968)

2. The Psychedelic Sixties in North America

1 Marcel Martel, '"They Smell Bad, Have Diseases, and Are Lazy":
   RCMP Officers Reporting on Hippies in the Late Sixties,' *Canadian
   Historical Review* 90/2 (2009), 215–46.
2 Humphry Osmond, 'A Review of the Clinical Effects of Psychotomimetic
   Agents,' *Annals of the New York Academy of Sciences* 66 (1957), 418–34.
3 John Burnham, 'American Medicine's Golden Age: What Happened to
   It?' *Science* 19 (1982), 1474–9.
4 See, e.g., David Healy, *Let Them Eat Prozac: The Unhealthy
   Relationship between the Pharmaceutical Industry and Depression*
   (New York: New York University Press, 2004).
5 Andrea Tone, 'Tranquilizers on Trial: Psychopharmacology in the Age
   of Anxiety,' in *Medicating Modern America: Prescription Drugs in
   History,* ed. Andrea Tone and Elizabeth Siegel Watkins (New York: New
   York University Press, 2007), 156–82.
6 Osmond introduced Aldous Huxley to mescaline in 1953, which
   inspired Huxley to write *Doors of Perception.* They corresponded from
   this point forward (until Huxley's death on 22 Nov. 1963 – where he
   was injected with LSD on his deathbed by his wife Laura). Their correspondence contributed to the coining of the term 'psychedelic,' which
   Osmond wrote to Huxley in 1956.
7 The clinical studies conducted in Saskatchewan screened volunteers and
   patients for these trials. Anyone with a family history of schizophrenia
   was excluded, and 'normal' volunteers (as opposed to patient volunteers)
   were excluded if they exhibited liver problems. This was not necessarily the case with patients, esp. among the alcoholic patients. See Erika
   Dyck, *Psychedelic Psychiatry: LSD from Clinic to Campus* (Baltimore:
   Johns Hopkins University Press, 2008), 38.

8   Abram Hoffer and Humphry Osmond, *The Hallucinogens* (New York: Academic Press, 1967), 234–6.
9   Dyck, *Psychedelic Psychiatry,* chapter 4. These new subjects were largely drawn from positions in society that sociologists Ben-Yehuda and Goode claim disproportionately influence popular perceptions of moral authority. See Nachman Ben-Yehuda and Erich Goode, 'The Sociology of Moral Panics: Toward a New Synthesis,' *Sociological Quarterly* 27/4 (1986), 496.
10   Hoffer and Osmond, *Hallucinogens,* 106.
11   See esp. the theories of R.D. Laing, in e.g., Jonathan Andrews, 'R.D. Laing in Scotland: Facts and Fictions of the "Rumpus Room" and Interpersonal Psychiatry,' in *Cultures of Psychiatry and Mental Health Care in Postwar Britain and the Netherlands*, ed. Marijke Gijswijt-Hofstra and Roy Porter (Amsterdam: Rodopi, 1998), 121–50.
12   Barbara Clow, '"An Illness of Nine Months' Duration": Pregnancy and Thalidomide Use in Canada and the United States,' in *Women Health, and Nation: Canada and the United States since 1945,* ed. Georgina Feldberg, Molly Ladd-Taylor, Alison Li, and Kathryn McPherson (Montreal and Kingston: McGill-Queens University Press, 2003), 49.
13   Ibid., 47.
14   House of Commons, *Debates,* 1962: 26 Oct., 974–93; 12 Nov., 1522–7; 13 Nov., 1562–72 [Bill C-3].
15   Robert Greenfield, *Timothy Leary: A Biography* (Orlando: Harcourt, 2006), 177.
16   Ibid., 173.
17   A term that Cohen uses to describe individuals with an inordinate influence on moral authority. See Stanley Cohen, *Folk Devils and Moral Panics: The Creation of the Mods and Rockers* (Oxford: Martin Robertson, 1972), 196.
18   Saskatchewan Archives Board (SAB), A207 XVIII 25.b, Letter from Osmond to Leary, 10 Dec. 1966, 1; original emphasis.
19   'LSD Possession May Be Curbed by Government,' *Globe and Mail,* 2 Feb. 1967, 2.
20   'The Most Important –and Most Dangerous –Drugs of Our Time: The New Psychedelics,' *National Enquirer* 42 (1968), 1.
21   SAB, A207, Randall MacLean File, Vancouver School Board, 'An Open Letter to All Young People and Parents, Dangers of LSD (Lysergic Acid Diethylamide).'

22 See Erika Dyck, *Psychedelic Psychiatry: LSD from Clinic to Campus* (Baltimore: Johns Hopkins University Press, 2008), chapter 4.

23 Ibid., 115.

24 Duncan Blewett and Nick Chwelos, *Handbook for the Therapeutic Uses of LSD,* available at www.maps.org/ritesofpassage/lsdhandbook.html.

25 *National Enquirer* 42 (1968), 1.

26 The supplies were granted through medical personnel.

27 See Stuart Henderson, 'Making the Scene: Yorkville and Hip Toronto in the Sixties, 1960–1970,' doctoral dissertation, Queen's University, 2007.

28 *Lennon Remembers: The Rolling Stone Interviews* (New York: Straight Arrow Books, 1971), 76–7.

29 Tom Wolfe, *The Electric Kool-Aid Acid Test* (New York: Bantam Books, 1967), 10 (original emphasis).

30 Ken Kesey was the author of the book that became an award-winning film, *One Flew Over the Cuckoo's Nest,* and he became a well-known advocate of LSD use. He famously toured the United States in a painted bus distributing 'acid' at concerts and on university campuses.

31 See also Jill Jonnes, *Hep-Cats, Narcs, and Pipe Dreams: A History of America's Romance with Illegal Drugs* (Baltimore: Johns Hopkins University Press, 1996), 234, 298.

32 Martel, 'They Smell Bad, Have Diseases, and Are Lazy,' 223.

33 SAB, A207 Box 37 233-A-[73], LSD, newsclippings, 'Patients Said Helped by LSD,' *Saskatoon Star Phoenix,* 29 May 1964; 'LSD Said Safe as Salt, Sugar,' (no citation listed); 'Sask. Said Fortunate in LSD Use,' *Saskatoon Star Phoenix,* 5 Nov. 1963, 17.

34 See Stuart Henderson, 'Toronto's Hippie Disease: End Days in the Yorkville Scene, Augsut 1968,' *Journal of the Canadian Historical Association* 17/1 (2006), 206.

35 Henry Mietkiewicz and Bob Mackowycz, *Dream Tower: The Life and Legacy of Rochdale College* (Toronto: McGraw-Hill Ryerson, 1988), 76.

36 Dyck, *Psychedelic Psychiatry,* 109–17.

37 Marcel Martel, *Not This Time: Canadians, Public Policy, and the Marijuana Question 1961–1975* (Toronto: University of Toronto Press, 2006), 16; and Dyck, *Psychedelic Psychiatry,* chapter 5.

38 Canada, *Acts of Parliament of Canada, Statutes of Canada, 1968–9,* vols. 17–18, chapter 41, 'Food and Drugs, Narcotic Control, Criminal Code Amendments,' 991–5; United States of America, 89th Congress, Special Subcommittee on the Committee on Judiciary United States Senate, Amendendment to the Narcotic Rehabilitation Act of 1966,

'Statement of Timothy Leary, LSD Experimenter, Testifying on Behalf of the Castalia Foundation of Millbrook, N.Y,' 239–58.

39 U.S. National Archives and Records Administration, Document R-013 re Elvis-Nixon meeting, found in White House Central Files: Subject Files: EX HE 5-1; Nixon Presidential Materials Staff. Available at www.archives.gov.

40 Greenfield, *Timothy Leary,* 377.

41 This tour has since been commemorated in a film of the same name *Festival Express* (2003), and was reported in newspapers, e.g., 'A Mobile Rock Festival for 4 Cities,' *Globe and Mail,* 1 May 1970, 15.

42 'Leftist Groups Mounting Opposition to Rock Festival,' *Globe and Mail,* 25 June 1970, 10.

3. The Canadian Association of University Teachers

1 Catherine Gidney, *A Long Eclipse: The Liberal Protestant Establishment and the Canadian University, 1920–1970* (Montreal and Kingston: McGill-Queen's University Press, 2004), 84–91.

2 Frank Abbott, 'Founding the Canadian Association of University Teachers, 1945–1951,' *Queen's Quarterly* 93/3 (1986), 508. See also Frank William Charles Abbott, 'The Origin and Foundation of the Canadian Association of University Teachers,' doctoral dissertation, University of Toronto, 1985, 6, 10–11; Donald C. Savage, 'Professional Societies and Trade Unions: The Canadian Experience in Higher Education,' *CAUT Bulletin* [hereafter *Bulletin*] (March 1973), 4; Donald C. Savage and Christopher Holmes, 'The CAUT, the Crowe Case, and the Development of the Idea of Academic Freedom in Canada,' *Bulletin* (Dec. 1975), 22.

3 Michiel Horn, *Academic Freedom in Canada: A History* (Toronto: University of Toronto Press, 1999), 13, 220. For a similar view, see Savage and Holmes, 'The CAUT, the Crowe Case,' 22; David Cameron, *More Than an Academic Question: University, Government, and Public Policy in Canada* (Halifax: Institute for Research on Public Policy, 1991), 298. For the importance of the Crowe case, see also Frank Abbott, 'The Crowe Affair: The Academic Profession and Academic Freedom,' *Queen's Quarterly* 98/4 (1991), 818–39; Edward J. Monahan, 'Academic Freedom and Tenure and the C.A.U.T.–The First Twenty Years,' *Bulletin* 18/4 (1970), 80–91.

4 Cameron, *More Than an Academic Question,* 295.
5 Cyril Levitt, e.g., notes, 'The child-bearing and child-rearing generation of the fifties was cautious and conformist.' Doug Owram has stated, 'Ideological debate reasserted itself after the calm of the 1950s.' See Levitt, *Children of Privilege: Student Revolt in the Sixties. A Study of Student Movements in Canada, the United States, and West Germany* (Toronto: University of Toronto Press, 1984), 14; Owram, *Born at the Right Time: A History of the Baby Boom Generation* (Toronto: University of Toronto Press, 1996), 158.
6 For entry into this debate, see Van Gosse, *Rethinking the New Left: An Interpretative History* (New York: Palgrave, 2005); Alice Echols, 'The Ike Age: Rethinking the 1950s,' in *Shaky Ground: The '60s and Its Aftershocks,* ed. Alice Echols (New York: Columbia University Press, 2002), 51–60. See also Linda Eisenmann, *Higher Education for Women in Postwar America, 1945-1965* (Baltimore: Johns Hopkins University Press, 2006), 233. For an interpretation of the 1960s as a period of rupture, see Bryan D. Palmer, *Canada's 1960s: The Ironies of Identity in a Rebellious Era* (Toronto: University of Toronto Press, 2009).
7 Nicole Neatby, 'Student Leaders at the University of Montreal from 1950 to 1958: Beyond the "Carabin Persona,"' *Journal of Canadian Studies* 29/3 (1994), 27–8; Karine Hébert, 'Between the Future and the Present: Montreal University Student Youth and the Post-war Years, 1945–1960,' in *Cultures of Citizenship in Post-war Canada, 1940–1955,* ed. Nancy Christie and Michael Gauvreau (Montreal and Kingston: McGill-Queen's University Press, 2003), 163–200. Similarly, in the English-Canadian context, Valerie J. Korinek has argued that articles and editorials in *Chatelaine* magazine from the mid-1950s on pre-dated and anticipated the emphases of second-wave feminism. See *Roughing It in the Suburbs: Reading Chatelaine Magazine in the Fifties and Sixties* (Toronto: University of Toronto Press, 2000), 370.
8 Horn, *Academic Freedom in Canada,* 4.
9 'Message from the President,' *Bulletin* 1/1 (1953), 1.
10 Abbott, 'Origin and Foundation,' 13.
11 Editorial, 'F.S. Howes,' *Bulletin* 9/1 (1960), 5.
12 Abbott, 'Origin and Foundation,' 13, 15.
13 'Activities of Committees of the CAUT,' and 'Activities of Local Associations,' *Bulletin* 1/1 (1953), 3–4; 'State of the Profession,' *Bulletin* 2/2 (1954), 1. See also Abbott, 'Origin and Foundation,' 140.

This work continued through the 1960s. See, e.g., 'Reduction in Federal Government Research Grants,' *Bulletin* 15/1 (1966), 102; 'A Message from the President,' *Bulletin* 16/1 (1967), 3. Editorial, 'June Council Meeting and After,' *Bulletin* 13/1 (1964), 5.

14 'National Salary Scale,' *Bulletin* 5/1 (1956), 12–18; F.R. Scott, 'The Brief to the Gordon Commission,' *Bulletin* 5/1 (1956), 16–17; 'Report of the President,' *Bulletin* 7/1 (1958), 10–13; 'Autumn Meetings 1965,' *Bulletin* 14/3 (1966), 2.

15 Abbott, 'Crowe Affair,' 819.

16 The University of Montreal, e.g., had no Senate. Laval University had a unicameral system, with power concentrated in the hands of the directors of the Séminaire de Québec and the three heads of the university's original faculties. See Cameron, *More Than an Academic Question,* 310, 323.

17 Abbott, 'Crowe Affair,' 819.

18 At many universities, faculty were explicitly excluded from sitting on governing boards. See James Duff and Robert O. Berdahl, *University Government in Canada: Report of a Commission Sponsored by the Canadian Association of University Teachers and the Association of Universities and Colleges of Canada* (Toronto: University of Toronto Press, 1966), 5, 7. See also V.C. Fowke, 'Who Should Determine University Policy?' *Bulletin* 7/4 (1959), 4.

19 W.G. Fleming, *Ontario's Educative Society,* vol. 7, *Educational Contributions of Associations* (Toronto: University of Toronto Press, 1972), 4, 223.

20 Duff and Berhahl, *University Government in Canada,* 7; Cameron, *More Than an Academic Question,* 317.

21 Cameron, *More Than an Academic Question,* 344; Abbott, 'Origin and Foundation,' 140–1.

22 W.P. Thompson, 'The Faculty Association and the Administration,' *Bulletin* 7/1 (1958), 7.

23 William H. Nelson, *The Search for Faculty Power: The University of Toronto Faculty Association, 1942–1992* (Toronto: Canadian Scholars' Press, 1993), 10–13.

24 Thompson, 'Faculty Association and the Administration,' 8.

25 Abbott, 'Founding the Canadian Association of University Teachers,' 509.

26 'The Reform of University Government,' *Bulletin* 9/1 (1960), 12.

27 See 'A Note on the Constitution,' *Bulletin* 4/1 (1956), 4.

28 Editorial, 'University Self-Government,' *Bulletin* 5/2 (1957), 6–8.

29 H.B. Mayo, 'University Government: Trends and a New Model,' *Bulletin* 13/4 (1965), 16.

30 Abbott, 'Crowe Affair,' 835.

31 Quoted in Horn, *Academic Freedom in Canada,* 224.

32 Editorial, 'The Nature of the Crowe Report,' *Bulletin* 7/3 (1959), 2.

33 'Press Release,' *Bulletin* 14/2 (1965), 2. See also Horn, *Academic Freedom in Canada,* 270–4; Monahan, 'Academic Freedom and Tenure,' 83n2.

34 For these secularizing tendencies, see Horn, *Academic Freedom in Canada,* 264–5; Gidney, *A Long Eclipse.*

35 *Academic Freedom in Canada,* 225.

36 'Press Release,' *Bulletin* 14/2 (1965), 2.

37 Editorial, 'Academic Freedom and Tenure,' *Bulletin* 8/3 (1960), 2–3.

38 Cameron, *More Than an Academic Question,* 299.

39 George Whalley, ed., *A Place of Liberty: Essays on the Government of Canadian Universities* (Toronto: Clark, Irwin, 1964).

40 On the report and its effects, see Cameron, *More Than An Academic Question,* 305–34.

41 Ibid., 314.

42 Ibid., 311–19, 322–3.

43 Ibid., 310.

44 Murray G. Ross, 'The Dilution of Academic Power in Canada: The University of Toronto Act,' *Minerva* 10/2 (1972), 252, cited in Cameron, *More Than an Academic Question,* 329.

45 Cameron, *More Than an Academic Question,* 311, 313.

46 In the past five years, e.g., this type of activity has occurred at the University of Nipissing and at St Thomas University.

47 By 1951, seven Canadian universities had some form of faculty association: Alberta, Toronto, Queen's, McGill, Laval, Saskatchewan, and the University of British Columbia. See Abbott, 'Founding the Canadian Association of University Teachers,' 519. On the late 1960s, see 'Report on Simon Fraser University,' *Bulletin* 16/4 (1968), 5. See also Abbott, 'Origin and Foundation,' 12.

48 Fleming, *Ontario's Educative Society,* 7, 228–9.

49 Cameron, *More Than an Academic Question,* 310, 356.

50 Abbott, 'Founding the Canadian Association of University Teachers,' 517–18; N.A.M MacKenzie, 'Address,' *Bulletin* 6/2 (1958), 18–19; Thompson, 'Faculty Association and the Administration.'

51 N.A.M. MacKenzie, 'Faculty Participation in University Administration,' *Bulletin* 9/4 (1961), 8–14, and 'Address.'

52 W.P. Thompson, 'University Government,' *Bulletin* 9/2 (1960), 4–8.

53 Editorial, 'What the Federal Grants Are For,' *Bulletin* 5/2 (1957), 5–6; Gidney, *A Long Eclipse,* 86, 88. For the increasing perception in the postwar years of the importance of higher education to the growth of Canadian society, see Paul Axelrod, *Scholars and Dollars: Politics, Economics, and the Universities of Ontario, 1945–1980* (Toronto: University of Toronto Press, 1982), 23, 33.

54 Gidney, *A Long Eclipse,* xiii–xiv, 114–15; Roberta Lexier, 'The Community of Scholars: The English-Canadian Student Movement and University Governance,' in *Mobilizations, Protests and Engagements: Canadian Perspectives on Social Movements,* ed. Marie Hammond Callaghan and Matthew Hayday (Halifax: Fernwood, 2008), 125–44; Charles Levi, 'Sex, Drugs, Rock & Roll, and the University College Lit: The University of Toronto Festivals, 1965–69,' *Historical Studies in Education* 18/2 (2006), 163–90; Christabelle Sethna, 'The Evolution of the Birth Control Handbook: From Student Peer-Education Manual to Feminist Self-Empowerment Text, 1968–1975,' *Canadian Bulletin of Medical History* 23/1 (2006), 89–118; Patricia Jasen, '"In Pursuit of Human Values (or Laugh When You Say That)": The Student Critique of the Arts Curriculum in the 1960s,' in *Youth, University, and Canadian Society: Essays in the Social History of Higher Education,* ed. Paul Axelrod and John G. Reid (Montreal and Kingston: McGill-Queen's University Press, 1989), 247–71.

55 For these arguments, see Catherine Gidney, 'War and the Concept of Generation: The International Teach-Ins at the University of Toronto, 1965–68,' in *Canadian Universities and War: Histories of Academic Cultures and Conflict,* ed. Paul Stortz and Lisa Panayotidis (Toronto: University of Toronto Press, in press).

56 'A Message from the President,' *Bulletin* 16/1 (1967), 3.

57 The council consisted of sixteen lay members, eight alumni, twelve faculty, eight students, two presidential appointments, two administrative staff, and the president and chancellor with ex officio status. See Robin Ross, *The Short Road Down: A University Changes* (Toronto: University of Toronto Press, 1984), 55. For a student perspective on the change in

governance at the University of Toronto, see Lexier, 'Community of Scholars,' 125–44.

58 Horn, *Academic Freedom in Canada,* 220.

59 F.R. Scott, 'The Brief to the Gordon Commission,' *Bulletin* 5/1 (1956), 16–17.

60 'National Salary Scale,' *Bulletin* 5/1 (1956), 15.

61 Cameron, *More Than an Academic Question,* 307.

62 Arthur Marwick, *The Sixties: Cultural Revolution in Britain, France, Italy, and the United States, c. 1958–c.1974* (Oxford: Oxford University Press, 1998), 542. See also Gosse, *Rethinking the New Left,* 5.

63 'The North Hatley Conference on the Future of CAUT: Statement by the Executive-Secretary,' *Bulletin* 15/2 (1966), 4–28.

4. To Struggle Together or Fracture Apart

1 See *Report of the Royal Commission on National Development in the Arts, Letters and Sciences 1949–1951* (Ottawa: Edmond Cloutier, 1951); *Royal Commission on Canada's Economic Prospects: Final Report* (Ottawa: Queen's Printer,1957); and *Financing Higher Education in Canada: Being the Report of a Commission to the Association of Universities and Colleges of Canada, Successor to the National Conference of Canadian Universities and Colleges, and Its Executive Agency, the Canadian Universities Foundation* (Toronto: University of Toronto Press, 1965).

2 See Doug Owram, *Born at the Right Time: A History of the Baby Boom Generation* (Toronto: University of Toronto Press, 1996), 181; and Statistics Canada, *Historical Statistics of Canada,* W340–W438, for full-time university enrolment, by sex, Canada and provinces, selected years, 1920 to 1975.

3 See, e.g., Bryan D. Palmer, *Canada's 1960s: The Ironies of Identity in a Rebellious Era* (Toronto: University of Toronto Press, 2009); Jean-Philippe Warren, *Une douce anarchie: Les années 68 au Québec* (Montreal: Boréal, 2008); Karine Hébert, 'Between the Future and the Present: Montreal University Student Youth and the Post-war Years, 1945–1960,' in *Cultures of Citizenship in Post-war Canada, 1940–1955,* ed. Nancy Christie and Michael Gauvreau (Montreal and Kingston: McGill-Queen's University Press, 2003), 163–200; Nicole Neatby, *Carabins ou Activistes? L'idealisme et la radicalisation de la pensée étudiante à l'Université de Montréal au temps du duplessisme*

(Montreal and Kingston: McGill-Queen's University Press, 1997); Cyril Levitt, *Children of Privilege: Student Revolt in the Sixties, A Study of Student Movements in Canada, the United States, and West Germany* (Toronto: University of Toronto Press, 1984).

4 Several books have emerged in recent years on the history of the 1960s in Canada. Some of these, including Dimitry Anastakis's and Karen Dubinsky et al.'s collections of essays, do not address the Canadian student movement. Bryan Palmer, however, and several articles in M. Athena Palaeologu's recent collection address youth and the student movement. Karine Hébert and Jean-Phillipe Warren have also written about the 1960s student movement. See Dimitry Anastakis, ed. *The Sixties: Passion, Politics and Style* (Montreal and Kingston: McGill-Queen's University Press, 2008); Karen Dubinsky, Catherine Krull, Susan Lord, Sean Mills, and Scott Rutherford, eds., *New World Coming: The Sixties and Global Consciousness* (Toronto: Between the Lines, 2009); M. Athnea Palaeologue, ed., *The Sixties in Canada: A Turbulent and Creative Decade* (Montreal: Black Rose Books, 2009); Palmer, *Canada's 1960s;* Jean-Philippe Warren, *Les mouvements étudiants des années 1960* (Montreal: Lux, 2008); Warren, *Une douce anarchie.*

5 Owram, *Born at the Right Time,* 178. The age of majority was lowered to eighteen in 1971.

6 Paul Axelrod, *Making a Middle Class: Student Life in English Canada during the Thirties* (Montreal and Kingston: McGill-Queen's University Press, 1990), 128.

7 Paul Axelrod, 'The Student Movement of the 1930s,' in *Youth, University and Canadian Society: Essays in the Social History of Higher Education,* ed. Paul Axelrod and John G. Reid (Montreal and Kingston: McGill-Queen's University Press, 1989), 232.

8 David Allyn, *Make Love, Not War: The Sexual Revolution, an Unfettered History* (New York: Routledge, 2001), 94.

9 University of Toronto Archives (hereafter UTA), P78-0693. *Handbook '69,* 'discipline.'

10 Owram, *Born at the Right Time,* 178.

11 See, Catherine Gidney, *A Long Eclipse: The Liberal Protestant Establishment and the Canadian University, 1920–1970* (Montreal and Kingston: McGill-Queen's University Press, 2004), 114–16; and Owram, *Born at the Right Time,* 249.

12 Michiel Horn, *Academic Freedom in Canada: A History* (Toronto: University of Toronto Press, 1999), 29.

13 See, e.g., John Clarke, Stuart Hall, Tony Jefferson, and Brian Roberts, 'Subcultures, Cultures and Class,' in *Resistance through Rituals: Youth Subcultures in Post-war Britain,* ed. Stuart Hall and Tony Jefferson (London: Hutchinson, 1975), 18–20; and Bill Osgerby, *Youth in Britain Since 1945* (Oxford: Blackwell, 1998), 17.

14 See Philip Massolin, 'Modernization and Reaction: Postwar Evolutions and the Critique of Higher Learning in English-Speaking Canada, 1945–1970,' *Journal of Canadian Studies* 36/2 (2001), 138–9.

15 Gidney, *A Long Eclipse,* 120.

16 Beth Bailey, *Sex in the Heartland* (Cambridge: Harvard University Press, 1999),190–1.

17 Statistics Canada, *Historical Statistics of Canada,* W340–W438.

18 Bailey, *Sex in the Heartland,* 191. See also, Horn, *Academic Freedom in Canada,* 29.

19 Horn, *Academic Freedom in Canada,* 29.

20 See 'Whitney Hall Curfews Abolished,' *Varsity,* 26 Jan. 1966, 1; UTA, A1978-0028 Office of the President, File 010, 'Student Participation'; Committee of Presidents of Universities of Ontario, 'Student Participation in University Government,' Nov. 1967, 12; and Simon Fraser University Archives (hereafter SFUA), *Simon Fraser University Calendar,* 1966–67, 159.

21 See UTA, A1972-0023 Students' Administrative Council, Box 023, File 10, 'Brief,' [n.d.]; UTA, A1971-0011 Office of the President, Box 087, File 'Students' Administrative Council'; Douglas Ward, 'A Report to the Board of Governors from the President of the Students,' Administrative Council, Feb., 1964'; 'Editorial,' *The Sheet,* 16 Feb. 1962, 2. University of Regina Archives (hereafter URA), Students' Representative Council, *Survival seventy-one: Student Handbook, 1971–72,* 22; and 'The Proposed Constitution and Bylaws,' *Carillon,* 22 Jan. 1965, 4.

22 URA, 80-38 Principal's Papers, Box 17, File 404.10-1, 'Tripartite Committee 1973'; Students' Union, 'Proposal for Joint Student-Faculty Committees,' 1. See also, UTA, A1972-0023 Students' Administrative Council, Box 029, File 02, Douglas Hay, Victor Hori, and Jennifer Penney, 'Student Participation in the Government of the University of Toronto,' 26 Sept. 1966, 9.

23 Hay, Hori, and Penney, 'Student Participation,' 5.
24 See, e.g., Reg Whitaker and Gary Marcuse, *Cold War Canada: The Making of a National Insecurity State, 1945–1957* (Toronto: University of Toronto Press, 1994).
25 For some examples, see McMaster University Archives (MUA), Ontario Union of Students Fonds, Box 22, File 'Student Participation in University Government'; Ken Drushka, 'An Approach to University Reform,' Aug. 1965, 10. David Zirnhelt, 'A Student Manifesto: In Search of a Real and Human Educational Alternative,' in *Student Protest,* ed. Gerald F. McGuigan (Toronto: Methuen, 1968), 55. UTA, B1989-0031 Claude Bissell Collection, Box 003, File 'Student Movement in the 1960s,' 'Student Power –a Study in Dissent,' [1969], 11.
26 Zirnhelt, 'Student Manifesto,' 55.
27 'Let's Find Out –Now,' *Varsity,* 26 Jan. 1966, 4.
28 Levitt, *Children of Privilege,* 45.
29 UTA, B1989-0031, Claude Bissell Collection, File 012, '1966–67 President's Council,' Robin Ross, 'The Implementation of the Duff-Berdahl Report at the University of Toronto: Student Participation in University Government,' 23 Aug. 1966, 2.
30 Dr Glen H. Geen, Acting Head, Department of Biology, 'Letter to the Editor: SFU Clarification,' *Kelowna Daily Courier,* 28 Aug. 1968, 4.
31 Greg Kealey, interview with the author, 13 Jan. 2006.
32 See, e.g., 'Council Cools BoG Stand,' *Peak,* 21 Feb. 1968, 1; and Bill Engleson, interview with the author, 24 April 2006.
33 Patrick Johnston, *Native Children and the Child Welfare System* (Toronto: Lorimer, 1983), 120.
34 See UTA, A1977-0019 Office of the President, Box 016, File 'CAPUT,' 'Notes by R. Ross on steps that might be taken against possible trouble in the university in the Fall,' [1968], 3.
35 URA, Regina Council Minutes and Agendas 1970–May 1974. Memorandum to all members of faculty from Principal W.A. Riddell, 12 Sept. 1968.
36 URA, 80-38, Principal's Papers, Box 17, File 404.10-1 'Tripartite Committee, 1973,' W.A. Riddell, 'Student Participation in University Government University of Saskatchewan,' 28 Sept. 1970.
37 See, e.g., Ross, 'Implementation of the Duff-Berdahl Report,' 2; and Riddell, 'Participation in University Government.'
38 See ibid.

39 See UTA, *Torontonensis*. Mary Brewin, 'Report to the Students,' *'Nensis '66*, 74; Ken Mitchell, 'The Role of the Student,' *Carillon*, 20 Sept. 1965, 1; URA, 78–3 Principal's/Deans Office Files, Box 28, File 200.1-2 'Students' Representative Council 1967–69,' Memo 'To the People of Saskatchewan from Students at the University of Saskatchewan on Why We Are Protesting,' Oct. 1968, 2.

40 See Csaba Hadju, Letter to the Editor, *Peak*, 17 Nov. 1965, 2; Deanna Kamiel, 'UNAC yessed,' *Varsity*, 8 Oct. 1965, 1; James M. Pitsula, *As One Who Serves: The Making of the University of Regina* (Montreal and Kingston: McGill-Queen's University Press, 2006), 307–8; University of Saskatchewan Students' Union, 'Student Handbook, 1970–71,' 22; and 'Tuition Fees Up Again,' *Carillon*, 19 Sept. 1969, 1.

41 See 'Admin Student in Vanguard,' *Carillon*, 11 Oct. 1968, 5; and 'Demonstrators Attacked,' *Carillon*, 11 Oct. 1968, 10.

42 See Robin Harris, *A History of Higher Education in Canada, 1663–1960* (Toronto: University of Toronto Press, 1976); A.B. McKillop, *Matters of the Mind: The University in Ontario, 1791–1951* (Toronto: University of Toronto Press, 1994).

43 See Jasen, '"In Pursuit of Human Values (or Laugh When You Say That)": The Student Critique of the Arts Curriculum in the 1960s,' 247–71; Roberta Lexier '"The Backdrop against which Everything Happened": English-Canadian Student Movements and Off-Campus Movements for Change,' *History of Intellectual Culture* 7/1 (2007); Howard Adelman, *The Holiversity: A Perspective on the Wright Report* (Toronto: New Press, 1973).

44 Joel Lexchin, interview with the author, 21 March 2006.

45 'Dow Offers You More than Just Saran Wrap,' *Varsity*, 20 Nov. 1967, 4.

46 UTA, B1989-0031 Claude Bissell Collection, Box 3, Memo to J.F. Westhead from T.G.L. Lawson, 'Anti-Dow Chemicals Demonstration,' 2 Jan. 1968, 1.

47 Ibid., 3–4; Brian Cruchley, 'Petitioners Pursue Faulkner's Resignation,' *Varsity*, 24 Nov. 1967, 1.

48 Paul MacRae, 'Faulkner Returned to Office by 800-Vote Majority,' *Varsity*, 15 Dec. 1967, 1.

49 Peter Warrian, interview with the author, 9 March 2006.

50 Andy Wernick, 'A Guide to the Student Left,' *Varsity*, 24 Sept. 1969, 8–9.

51 On the Environmental Movement, see, e.g., Frank Zelko, 'Making Greenpeace: The Development of Direct Action Environmentalism

in British Columbia,' *BC Studies* 142–3 (Summer/Autumn 2004): 197–239. On the Gay and Lesbian Liberation Movements, see, e.g., Tom Warner, *Never Going Back: A History of Queer Activism in Canada* (Toronto: University of Toronto Press, 2002).

52 See Judy Rebick, *Ten Thousand Roses: The Making of a Feminist Revolution* (Toronto: Penguin, 2005); Roberta Lexier, 'How Did the Women's Liberation Movement Emerge from the Sixties Student Movements? The Case of Simon Fraser University,' *Women and Social Movements in the United States, 1600-2000* 13/2 (Sept. 2009).

53 See, e.g., Jeffrey Cormier, *The Canadianization Movement: Emergence, Survival and Success* (Toronto: University of Toronto Press, 2004); Stephen Azzi, *Walter Gordon and the Rise of Canadian Nationalism* (Montreal and Kingston: McGill-Queen's University Press, 1999).

54 See Roberta Lexier, 'The Community of Scholars: The English-Canadian Student Movement and University Governance,' in *Mobilizations, Protests and Engagements: Social Movements in Canada,* eds. Marie Hammond-Callaghan and Matthew Hayday (Halifax: Fernwood, 2008), 125–44.

5. 'Riot' at Sir George Williams

1 House of Commons, *Hansard,* 22 Oct. 1969, 11681–2. I would like to thank Matt Littlefair and Mathieu Lapointe who were hired as research assistants on this project. Also, I wish to thank the participants in the Workshop on the Sixties, held at the University of New Brunswick, 21–2 Aug. 2008, for their comments on a preliminary version of this chapter. This research project received financial support from the Avie Bennett Historica Chair in Canadian History.

2 'A Chronicle of Events,' *Georgian,* 28 Jan. 1969, 3.

3 'Security Meeting Minutes Reveal Administration's Real Fears,' *Georgian,* 28 Jan. 1969, 3.

4 Keith Pruden, 'The *Georgian* Spirit in Crisis: The Causes of the Computer Centre Riot,' essay submitted to the Department of History, Concordia University, 2004, 18–34; Library and Archives Canada (LAC), RG 146, Vol. 2730, Sir George Williams University (SGWU) – Occupation 29 Jan. to 11 Feb. 1969, Attachment 18-2-69, access A2008-00323, Vol. 2731, SGWU–Occupation 29 Jan. to 11 Feb. 1969, vol. 13, access A2008-00490, SGWU, 11 Feb. 1969, carding date, 21 May 1969.

5 Pruden, 'The *Georgian* Spirit,' 35–7.

6 H. Blair Neatby and Don McEown, *Creating Carleton: The Shaping of a University* (Montreal and Kingston, McGill-Queen's University Press, 2002).

7 Ibid. Doug Owram, *Born at the Right Time: A History of the Baby Boom Generation* (Toronto: University of Toronto Press, 1996).

8 On student movements, see Marie-Claire Lavabre and Henry Rey, *Les mouvements de 1968* (Paris: Casterman-Guinti, 1998); Arthur Marwick, *The Sixties: A Cultural Revolution in Britain, France, Italy, and the United States* (London: Oxford University Press, 1999).

9 'In the Data Centre: Occupation Continues,' *Georgian*, 31 Jan. 1969, 3; 'Open Meeting Friday: Students Demand New Committee,' *Georgian*, 3 Feb. 1969, 1.

10 'Students' Association Executive blasts Canadian University Press,' *Georgian*, 5 March 1969, 1.

11 'Council Withdraws from UGEQ, Fires Editor,' *Georgian*, 19 Feb. 1969, 2.

12 'College Professor Says He'll Sue over "Racism,"' *Toronto Star*, 15 Feb. 1969, 3.

13 *McGill Daily*, 17 Feb. 1969, 3; 25 Feb. 1969, 1.

14 'In the Data Centre. Occupation Continues,' 3.

15 'Students' Politics to Be Probed,' *Globe and Mail*, 14 Feb. 1969, 8; 'SAC Condemns SGWU Destruction,' *Varsity*, 14 Feb. 1969, 1; *Le Devoir*, 18 Feb. 1969, 4.

16 Jean Lamarre, '"Au service des étudiants et de la nation": L'internationalisation de l'Union générale des étudiants du Québec (1964–1969),' *Bulletin d'histoire politique* 16/2 (2008), 53–73. See James W. St G. Walker, 'Black Confrontation in Sixties Halifax,' in this volume.

17 House of Commons, *Debates,* 1969: 12 Feb., 5426–7; 13 Feb., 5461–4; 14 Feb., 5516; 17 Feb., 5586; 18 Feb., 5639–40.

18 'Le banditisme universitaire,' *La Presse,* 12 Feb. 1969, 4.

19 Steve Hewitt, *Spying 101: The RCMP's Secret Activities at Canadian Universities, 1917–1997* (Toronto: University of Toronto Press, 2002), 141, 151–6; LAC, RG 146, Box 66, vol. 11, access 96-A-00045 pt. 5, Memo: SGWU, RCMP-GRC, Division C, 9 March 1973.

20 LAC, RG 146, Box 66, vol. 4, access 96-A-00045 pt. 4, Memo: SGWU, 21 Feb. 1969.

21 LAC, RG 146, Box 66, vol. 4, access 96-A-00045 pt. 4, Memo: General
    Conditions and Subversive Activities amongst Negroes–Province of
    Quebec, RCMP-GRC, Division C, Detachment: Montreal S.I.B,
    29 Jan. 1969.

22 LAC, RG 146, Vol. 2730, SGWU–Occupation Jan. 29 to Feb. 11, 1969,
    Attachment 18-2-69, access A2008-00323. SGWU, 18 Feb. 1969.

23 LAC, RG 146, Vol. 2950, SGWU 26-2-69, vol. 1, access A2009-00048,
    SGWU Report 2, RCMP-GRC, Division C, Detachment: Montreal
    S.I.B., 3 Feb. 1969.

24 LAC, RG 146, Vol. 2950, SGWU 26-2-69, vol. 1, access A2009-00048,
    Memo: The Internationalists, Montreal, RCMP-GRC, Division C,
    31 Jan. 1969.

25 LAC, RG 146, Vol. 2730, SGWU–Occupation 29 Jan. to 11 Feb. 1969,
    attachment 18-2-69, access A2008-00323. SGWU, 18 Feb. 1969.

26 Ibid.

27 Hewitt, *Spying 101,* 152 and 154; *Georgian*, 10 March, 1978, 3;
    Dorothy Eber, *The Computer Centre Party: Canada Meets Black Power*
    (Montreal: Tundra Books, 1969).

28 David Austin, 'All Roads Led to Montreal: Black Power, the Caribbean,
    and the Black Radical Tradition in Canada.' *Journal of African
    American History* 92/4 (Fall 2007), 516–39.

29 Dennis Forsythe, 'The Black Writers Conference,' *Let the Niggers Burn!
    The Sir George Williams University Affair and Its Caribbean Aftermath*
    (Montreal: Our Generation Press, 1971), 66.

30 Sean Mills, *The Empire Within: Postcolonial Thought and Political
    Activism in Sixties Montreal* (Montreal and Kingston: McGill-Queen's
    University Press, 2010), 96.

31 Forsythe's *Let the Niggers Burn!,* Dorothy W. Williams's studies on
    Blacks in Montreal entitled *The Road to Now: A History of Blacks in
    Montreal* (Montreal: Véhicule, 1997) and *Les noirs à Montréal, 1628–
    1986: Essai de démographie urbaine* (Montreal: VLB, 1998) insist
    that the Sir George Williams events helped the development of a black
    conscientiousness.

32 Roosevelt Williams, 'Reactions: The Myth of White "Backlash,"' in *Let
    the Niggers Burn!* 141.

33 'Rioters at SGWU,' *Gazette,* 12 Feb. 1969, 2.

34 Martin O'Malley, 'A Tolerant People? Nice to Believe. We're Really
    Just Polite Racists,' *Globe and Mail,* 15 Feb. 1969, 7.

35 Clair Balfour, 'Students Destroy Computer, Start Blaze,' *Globe and Mail,* 12 Feb. 1969, 3.
36 Ibid.; 'Rioters at SGWU,' *Gazette,* 12 Feb. 1969, 2.
37 D.G. Cobb, Inspector, Memo 'Re: Sir George Williams University–Occupation, Montreal, Quebec, Jan. 29 to Feb. 11, 1969, 26 Feb. 1969,' 4 pages, LAC, RG 146, Vol. 2729, SGWU–Occupation 29 Jan. to 11 Feb. 1969, vol. 2, 12–15 Feb. 1969.
38 See the excellent historiographical review by Ibrahim Cerrah, *Crowds and Public Order Policing* (Aldershot: Dartmouth and Ashgate, 1998), 60.
39 Williams, *The Road to Now,* 123.

6. 'The Struggle for a Different World'

1 For more on the creation of Canada's drug laws and the moral panic associated with drugs, see Robert Solomon and Melvyn Green, 'The First Century: The History of Non-Medical Opiate Use and Control Policies in Canada, 1870–1970,' in *Illicit Drugs in Canada: A Risky Business,* ed. Judith C. Blackwell and Patricia G. Erickson (Scarborough: Nelson, 1988), 88–116; Greg Marquis, 'From Beverage to Drug: Alcohol and Other Drugs in 1960s and 1970s Canada,' *Journal of Canadian Studies* 39/2 (2005), 57–79; Catherine Carstairs, *Jailed for Possession: Illegal Drug Use, Regulation, and Power in Canada, 1920–1961* (Toronto: University of Toronto Press, 2005); and Marcel Martel, *Not This Time: Canadians, Public Policy, and the Marijuana Question, 1961–1975* (Toronto: University of Toronto Press, 2006).
2 Marquis, 'From Beverage to Drug,' 63.
3 Carstairs, *Jailed for Possession,* 11–12; and Marcel Martel, 'Law versus Medicine: The Debate over Drug Use in the 1960s,' in *Creating Postwar Canada: Community, Diversity, and Dissent, 1945–75,* ed. Magda Fahrni and Robert Rutherdale (Vancouver: UBC Press, 2008), 315.
4 In 1962–63, only twenty Canadians faced similar charges. Martel, 'Law versus Medicine,' 323.
5 Ibid., 326–8; and Martel, *Not This Time,* 195.
6 As quoted in Terry H. Anderson, *The Sixties,* 3rd ed. (New York: Pearson Longman, 2007), 126. *Time* named 'The Boomers' (baby boomers) as its 'Man of the Year' in 1967. This was the first time that the magazine had not bestowed this honour upon an actual person. *Time*

declared its 'Person of the year' for 2011 to be 'The Protester.' Kurt
Anderson, 'The Protester,' *Time*, 14 December 2011.

7 Jeremy Varon, Michael S. Foley, and John McMillian, 'Time Is an
Ocean: The Past and Future of the Sixties,' *The Sixties: A Journal of
History, Politics, and Culture* 1/1 (2008), 1.

8 Roberta Lexier, 'Dreaming of a Better World: Student Rebellion in
1960s Regina,' *Past Imperfect* 10 (2004), 79.

9 Doug Owram, *Born at the Right Time: A History of the Baby Boom
Generation* (Toronto: University of Toronto Press, 1996), 185–215.
Stuart Henderson has noted that long hair and beards were simple ways
for youth in Toronto's Yorkville district to express their difference. For
more on Toronto in the 1960s see Stuart Henderson, *Making the Scene:
Yorkville and Hip Toronto in the 1960s* (Toronto: University of Toronto
Press, 2011).

10 As quoted in James Pitsula, *New World Dawning: The Sixties at Regina
Campus* (Regina: Canadian Plains Research Centre, 2008), 200.

11 Ibid., 16.

12 Varon, Foley, and McMillian, 'Time Is an Ocean,' 3.

13 As quoted in Michael Barnholden, *Reading the Riot Act: A Brief History
of Riots in Vancouver* (Vancouver: Anvil Press, 2005), 89.

14 Myrna Kostash, *Long Way from Home: The Story of the Sixties
Generation in Canada* (Toronto: Lorimer, 1980), 123.

15 *Vancouver Sun*, 9 Aug. 1971.

16 In early 1971, British Columbia's unemployment rate was above 9%,
which was one of the highest rates in the country. Vancouver's population in 1971 was 426,256, an increase of 41,734 since 1961. Jean
Barman, *The West beyond the West: A History of British Columbia*, rev.
ed. (Toronto: University of Toronto Press, 1996), 295 and Table 17, 390.

17 *Georgia Straight*, 8–21 March 1968. 'Straight' or 'Straights,' were used
to describe anyone who was not a hippie. *Vancouver Sun*, 24 Sept. 1971.

18 *Vancouver Sun*, 8 May 1970.

19 The award read: 'To Lawrence Eckhardt, who, by closing his mind to
justice, his eyes to fairness, his ears to equality, has encouraged the
belief that the law is not only blind, but also deaf, dumb and stupid.'
L.A. Powe, 'The Georgia Straight and Freedom of Expression in
Canada,' *Canadian Bar Review* 48/3 (1970), 425–6.

20 Barnholden, *Reading the Riot Act*, 89–90.

21 George Lipsitz, '"Who'll Stop the Rain?" Youth Culture, Rock 'n' Roll,
and Social Crises,' in *The Sixties: From Memory to History*, ed. David

Farber (Chapel Hill: University of North Carolina Press, 1994), 225;
and Gary Bannerman, *Gastown: The 107 Years* (1974), 29, copy in the
City of Vancouver Archives (CVA). Abbie Hoffman, one of the founders of the Yippies in the United States, when asked, 'What's a Yippie?'
replied, 'A hippie who has been hit over the head by a cop.' As quoted in
Gerard J. DeGroot, *The Sixties Unplugged: A Kaleidoscopic History of
a Disorderly Decade* (Cambridge: Harvard University Press, 2008), 261.

22 *Georgia Straight,* 1–8 April and 2–9 Sept. 1970. According to Lawrence
Aronsen, between April 1970 and the Gastown riot in August of 1971,
there were twenty-five recorded incidents of youth protests in the
Vancouver/Victoria area. And the Yippies either initiated, or were central
to, all of these events. Lawrence Aronsen. *City of Love and Revolution:
Vancouver in the Sixties* (Vancouver: New Star Books, 2010) 108.

23 *The Non-Medical Use of Drugs: A Report to the Commission of Enquiry
into the Non-Medical Use of Drugs,* 5. Prepared by the Vancouver City
Police Department, Oct. 1969, copy in Library and Archives Canada
(LAC), RG 33, Vol. 15, File 1702.

24 Ibid., 10–11.

25 Ibid., 11; CAV, Series 616, PDS 25, *Vancouver Police Department,
Annual Report, 1972.*

26 *Vancouver Sun,* 2 Aug. 1971.

27 Ibid., 7 Aug. 1971.

28 Ibid., 2 Aug. 1971. For the year Aug. 1970 to Aug. 1971, there were
1,314 arrests for Opium and Narcotics Act violations in Vancouver.
CVA, Series 616, PDS 25, *Vancouver Police Department, Annual
Report, 1971.*

29 *It's Your Turn: A Report to the Secretary of State by the Committee on
Youth* (Ottawa: Information Canada, 1971), 57 and 71.

30 *Georgia Straight,* 6 Aug. 1971.

31 Ibid., 6–10 Aug. 1971.

32 Lipsitz, 'Who'll Stop the Rain?' 214.

33 CVA, Series 20, Affidavits, 142-A-5, File 4, City Council and Office of
the City Clerk.

34 Ibid. RCMP Constable Ronald Paul, who worked uncover at the
Jamboree, later testified that he saw at least ten members of the Yippies
in attendance. *Globe and Mail,* 23 Sept. 1971.

35 Emphasis in original. The Committee on Youth argued that this 'protest *culture*... shows no signs of abating. Neither wishful thinking nor
tokenism will eradicate it. Only the most serious attempts on the part

of the older generation to understand the cultural experience of young people will reinstate any measure of harmony between generations.' The Committee on Youth was appointed by the federal government in 1969 to study the 'aspirations, attitudes and needs of youth' in Canada. *It's Your Turn,* 77.

36 *Vancouver Sun,* 24 Sept. 1971.

37 *Report on Gastown Inquiry,* 4.

38 *Vancouver Sun,* 25 Sept. 1971. *Report by Chief Constable J.R. Fisk, to the Vancouver Police Commission, re: Gastown Disturbance, Saturday, Aug. 7, 1971,* 51. A redacted copy of this report, received from the Vancouver Police Board, 25 July 2006, is in the author's possession.

39 In an attempt to prevent more people from going to Gastown and taking part in the riot, radio stations imposed a black-out on reporting about the incident until it had ended. *Vancouver Sun,* 9 Aug. 1971.

40 *Report on Gastown Inquiry,* 4; and *Vancouver Sun,* 29 Sept. 1971.

41 *Vancouver Police Department, Annual Report, 1971.*

42 Approximately 100 affidavits were sworn out by people who had witnessed the riot. CVA, Affidavits.

43 CVA, Series 483, Mayor's Office Fonds, File 25, 45-E-4, Mayor's Correspondence.

44 Dominique Clément, *Canada's Rights Revolution: Social Movements and Social Change, 1937–82* (Vancouver: UBC Press, 2008), 77–8; CVA, Affidavits; *Report by Chief Constable J.R. Fisk,* 53–4. This report also stated that henceforth, 'under no circumstances will plain-clothes members equipped with riot gear be involved in ... the policing of crowds.'

45 *Globe and Mail,* 9 Aug. 1971; CVA, Affidavits.

46 *Halifax Chronicle-Herald,* 10 Aug. 1971.

47 *Vancouver Sun,* 7 Aug. 2001.

48 Ibid., 9 Aug. 1971.

49 CVA, Mayor's Correspondence.

50 Ibid.

51 *The Non-Medical Use of Drugs,* 17–18.

52 CVA, Mayor's Correspondence. The idea that hippies' call for the legalization of marijuana constituted a threat to Canadian society was crafted, according to Marcel Martel, by the RCMP to undermine the credibility of hippies, and young people generally, and to strengthen the Mounties' argument to the federal government not to change Canada's drug laws.

Marcel Martel, "'They Smell Bad, Have Diseases, and Are Lazy'": RCMP Officers Reporting on Hippies in the Late Sixties,' *Canadian Historical Review* 90/2 (2009), 244–5.

53 CVA, Mayor's Correspondence. As Bryan Palmer has noted, the explosion over drug use in Canada is best revealed in the Gastown riot. Bryan D. Palmer, *Canada's 1960s: The Ironies of Identity in a Rebellious Era* (Toronto: University of Toronto Press, 2009), 498–9n65.

54 CVA, Mayor's Correspondence; *Globe and Mail,* 11 Aug. 1971.

55 *Vancouver Sun,* 20 Aug. 1971.

56 *Report by Chief Constable J.R. Fisk,* 42–7.

57 *Vancouver Sun,* 2 and 7 Sept. 1971. Thomas Dohm was appointed to the B.C. Supreme Court in 1966 and served until 1972. Constance Backhouse, *Carnal Crimes: Sexual Assault Law in Canada, 1900–1975* (Toronto: Irwin Law, 2008), 416n56.

58 *Report on Gastown Inquiry,* 4–12 and 15–16. Dohm also recommended that plain-clothes police not be used for crowd control and that uniformed police officers, including the riot squad, should wear numbers on their helmets so that they would be easily identifiable. Moreover, Dohm believed that the police should film all protests because filming may have the 'salutary effect' of making protesters more conscious of their actions, and thus conduct themselves in a more lawful manner.

59 Ibid., 7–8.

60 *Georgia Straight,* 8–12 Oct. 1971.

61 *Report on Gastown Inquiry,* 13.

62 *Georgia Straight,* 8–12 Oct. 1971.

63 The B.C. Civil Liberties Association, *The Police and the Community: Implications of the Report of the Commission of Enquiry by Mr Justice Dohm* (Vancouver, 1971), 4–5, copy in LAC.

64 *Vancouver Police Department, Annual Report, 1972.*

65 *Vancouver Sun,* 23 Dec. 1971. The Police Commission demoted one officer, Constable John Whitelaw. The Chief of Police found that Whitelaw had committed four breaches of the department's disciplinary code as a result of his actions during the riot. *The Province,* 22 Aug. 1972.

66 *The Province,* Oct.–Dec. 1971. In Sham Williams's case, he had allegedly yelled obscenities, including 'pig,' and was handed a fine of $100. The charge against Frank Barbeau of performing an indecent act was laid because he had allegedly climbed to the top of a hotel and

'mooned' the police. Barbeau was fined $200 and placed on six months' probation.

7. Sex Spying

1 The authors wish to thank the British Academy and the Association for Commonwealth Universities for their financial assistance that made this research possible.

2 Judy Bernstein, Peggy Morton, Linda Seese, and Myrna Wood, 'Sisters, Brothers, Lovers...Listen...Fall 1967,' in *Women Unite! An Anthology of the Canadian Women's Movement* (Toronto: Canadian Women's Educational Press, 1972), 31–9.

3 'Introduction,' in ibid., 9–13; Alison Prentice et al., *Canadian Women: A History* (Toronto : Harcourt Brace, 1996), 352–64.

4 Constance Backhouse and David Flaherty, eds. *Challenging Times: The Women's Movement in Canada and the United States* (Montreal and Kingston: McGill-Queen's University Press, 1992); Ruth Pierson et al., *Canadian Women's Issues: Twenty-Five Years of Women's Activism in English Canada* (Toronto: Lorimer, 1993); Nancy Adamson, Linda Briskin, and Margaret McPhail, *Feminist Organizing for Change: The Contemporary Women's Movement in Canada* (Don Mills: Oxford University Press, 1988); Judy Rebick, *Ten Thousand Roses: The Making of a Feminist Revolution* (Toronto: Penguin, 2005).

5 Colin Leys and Elizabeth Grace, 'The Concept of Subversion and Its Implications,' in *Dissent and the State,* ed. C.E.S. Franks (Don Mills: Oxford University Press 1989), 62.

6 Frank Donner, *Protectors of Privilege: Red Squads and Police Repression in Urban America* (Los Angeles: University of California Press, 2002), 76.

7 Doug Owram, *Born at the Right Time: A History of the Baby Boom Generation* (Toronto: University of Toronto Press, 1996), 166–7, 219. For more on the New Left in Canada, see *The New Left in Canada,* ed. Dimitrios J. Roussopoulos (Montreal: Black Rose Books, 1970). For more on the targeted groups, see the essays in this collection by José Igartua, Bryan D. Palmer, James St G. Walker, and Roberta Lexier.

8 Royal Commission of Inquiry Concerning Certain Activities of the Royal Canadian Mounted Police (hereafter McDonald Commission), *Second Report: Freedom and Security Under the Law,* vol. 1

(Ottawa: Supply and Services Canada 1981), 518; Canadian Security
Intelligence Service (CSIS), Royal Canadian Mounted Police Security
Records (RCMP), Contacts-Police-Canada, access request 117-98-1,
Insp. J.G. Long, in charge of sources, to William Kelly, Director of
Security Intelligence, 28 July 1967; CSIS, access request 117-98-71,
Contacts-'Key Sectors'-Canada, Data Processing in Security Service 'D'
Operations-Situation report, 14 Oct. 1976.

9 CSIS, access request 88-A-18, Key Sectors-Canada, Memo: Supt.
Draper for D.S.I., 7 Nov. 1967; Library and Archives Canada (LAC),
RG 146, vol. 2772, file 98-A-00130, pt. 1, (deleted: Mountie name) for
Director, Security and Intelligence, to Divisional C.O.s and l Officers i/c
S.I.B. 'C,' 'E,' and 'O,' 'Re: Instructions re: Subversive Investigations
and Correspondence,' 1 Sept. 1970; file: Memo to divisions and officers,
17 March 1969.

10 Mercedes Steedman, 'The Red Petticoat Brigade: Mine Mill Women's
Auxiliaries and the Threat from Within, 1940s–1970s,' in *Whose
National Security? Canadian State Surveillance and the Creation
of Enemies,* ed. Gary Kinsman, Mercedes Steedman, and Dieter K.
Buse (Toronto: Between the Lines Press, 2000), 55–72; Julie Guard,
'Women Worth Watching: Radical Housewives in Cold War Canada,'
in *Whose National Security?* 73–90; Franca Iacovetta, 'Making Model
Citizens: Gender, Corrupted Democracy, and Immigrant and Refugee
Reception Work in Cold War Canada,' in *Whose National Security?*
154–70.

11 Steve Hewitt, 'The Masculine Mountie: The Mounted Police as a
Male Institution,' *Journal of the Canadian Historical Association* 6
(1996), 153–74.

12 R.W. Connell, *Masculinities* (Cambridge: Polity, 1995), 196.

13 Steve Hewitt, *Riding to the Rescue: The Transformation of the RCMP
in Alberta and Saskatchewan* (Toronto: University of Toronto Press,
2006), 28–44.

14 For more on government beauty pageants, see Patrizia Gentile,
'"Government Girls" and "Ottawa Men": Cold War Management
of Gender Relations in the Civil Service,' in Kinsman et al., *Whose
National Security?* 131–41.

15 For more on the nature of the Canadian security state, see Gary Kinsman
and Patrizia Gentile, *The Canadian War on Queers: National Security as
Sexual Regulation* (Vancouver: UBC Press, 2009).

16 LAC, RG 146, access request A2005-00441, RCMP report, 11 April 1972. Rita MacNeil is a well-known Canadian folk singer, an activist for a number of social justice causes, and recipient of the Order of Canada.

17 For more on this concept, see Eve Sedgwick, *Between Men: English Literature and Male Homosocial Desire* (New York: Columbia University Press, 1985).

18 Ruth Rosen, *The World Split Open: How the Modern Women's Movement Changed America* (New York: Penguin, 2001), 260.

19 Kathryn S. Olmsted, 'Blond Queens, Red Spiders and Neurotic Old Maids: Gender and Espionage in the Early Cold War,' *Intelligence and National Security* 19/1 (2004), 80–1. For more on the concept of 'framing' in a security sense, see David Cunningham and Barb Browning, 'The Emergence of Worthy Targets: Official Frames and Deviance Narratives within the FBI,' *Sociological Forum* 19/3 (2004), 347–69.

20 Steve Hewitt, *Spying 101: The RCMP's Secret Activities at Canadian Universities, 1917–1997* (Toronto: University of Toronto Press, 2002), 130. For more on 'entryism' in various forms, see David Robertson, *The Routledge Dictionary of Politics* (London: Routledge, 2003), 166; Jan Willem Stutje, 'Trotskyism Emerges from Obscurity: New Chapters in Its Historiography,' *International Review of Social History* 49/2 (2004), 279–92; Nick Thomas-Symonds, 'A Reinterpretation of Michael Foot's Handling of the Militant Tendency,' *Contemporary British History* 19/1 (2005), 27–51.

21 FBI, as quoted in Rosen, *The World Split Open,* 241–3.

22 Rebick, *Ten Thousand Roses,* 18.

23 Simon Fraser University Archives (SFUA) F-126-2-0-22 YS/LA Split, Young Socialists and the League for Socialist Action 1970, Isolde Belfont et al., 'The Way Forward: How to Build A Mass Movement for Women's Liberation.'

24 Adamson, Briskin, and McPhail, *Feminist Organizing for Change,* 43.

25 LAC, RG 146, vol. 2974, Women's Liberation Group-Canada, pt. 1, RCMP report, 29 Oct. 1969.

26 Ibid., vol. 2787, access request A-96-A-00045, pt. 24, 'Women's International Terrorist Conspiracy from Hell,' 3 March 1971.

27 Suzanne Staggenborg, *Social Movements* (Toronto: Oxford University Press, 2007), 20–2.

28 A similar pattern was evident with the FBI in the United States. Rosen, *The World Split Open,* 247, 260.

29 LAC, RG 146, vol. 2974, access request A-2004-00173, Women's
    Liberation Groups-Canada General pt. 1, 13 May 1969.
30 Ibid., vol. 2783, access request A-96-A-00045, pt. 19, Vancouver
    Women's Caucus, 29 Aug. 1969.
31 Ibid., vol. 2974, access request A-2004-00175, Women's Liberation
    Groups Canada, pt. 9, RCMP report, 1 Sept. 1971.
32 Ibid., access request A-2004-00176, Women's Liberation Group
    Canada, pt. 1, RCMP report, 12 Nov. 1969.
33. Ibid., vol. 2987, Toronto Women's Caucus, pt. 5, RCMP report,
    27 Feb. 1973.
34 Christabelle Sethna and Steve Hewitt, 'Performing Protest: The
    Vancouver Women's Caucus, the Abortion Caravan, and the RCMP,'
    paper presented at the European Social Science History Conference,
    Lisbon, Feb. 2008.
35 LAC, RG 146, vol. 2974, access request A2005-00441, Assistant
    Commissioner L.R. Parent to Robin Bourne, 25 April 1972.
36 CSIS, access request 117-99-14, Memo from Superintendent Chisholm,
    20 March 1972.
37 LAC, RG 146, vol. 69, access request 96-A-00045, University of Toronto,
    pt. 22, Composite report on the University of Toronto, 7 Aug. 1973.
38 LAC, RG 146, vol. 2974, access request A2005-00441, RCMP
    report, 2 July 1977.
39 Hewitt, *Spying 101*, 32.
40 For more on the history of the use of informers by domestic security
    agencies, see Steve Hewitt, *Snitch: A History of the Modern Intelligence
    Informer* (New York and London: Continuum, 2010).
41 LAC, RG 146, vol. 2972, access request A-2006-00164, Vancouver
    Women's Caucus, pt. 1, RCMP report, Nov. 3, 1969, 000019.
42 For American examples of this genre, see Rosen, *The World Split Open*,
    246–8.
43 LAC, RG 146, vol. 2974, Women's Liberation Groups Canada, pt. 2,
    RCMP report, 3 Nov. 1969.
44 LAC, RG 146, vol. 2974, access request A2005-00441, RCMP Files
    Related to Women's Liberation, pt. 6, 19 May 1970.
45 'Angry U.S. Women Use Canada as Forum for Their Militant Anti-war
    Views,' *Globe and Mail*, 4 April 1971,
46 LAC, RG 146, vol. 2974, access A-2004-00175, Women's Liberation
    Group Canada, pt. 9, RCMP report, 22 April 1971.

47 Rosen, *The World Split Open,* 253.

48 Ibid., 259–60.

49 For some examples of the impact, see Ellen Schrecker, *No Ivory Tower: McCarthyism and the Universities* (New York: Oxford University Press, 1986); Ward Churchill and Jim Vander Wall, *Agents of Repression: The FBI's Secret Wars against the Black Panther Party and the American Indian Movement* (Cambridge: South End Press, 1988); Reg Whitaker and Gary Marcuse, *Cold War Canada: The Making of a National Insecurity State, 1945–1957* (Toronto: University of Toronto Press, 1996); Len Scher, *The UnCanadians: True Stories of the Blacklist Era* (Toronto: Key Porter Books, 1992).

50 Letty Pogrebin, as quoted in Rosen, *When the World Split Open,* 259.

51 LAC, RG 146, vol. 2973, Vancouver Women's Caucus, pt. 4, Barrette to Beavis, 30 April 1970.

52 See a description of the FBI's 'Responsibilities Program' in the early Cold War. Schrecker, *No Ivory Tower,* 258, 291–3.

53 LAC, RG 146, vol. 2987, Toronto Women's Caucus, pt. 3, Starnes to Goyer, 11 June 1971.

54 Ibid., vol. 2973, pt 8, access request A2006-00162, Assistant Commissioner L.R. Parent to Art Butroid, Special Asst., Office of the Assistant Deputy Minister, Immigration Division, Dept. of Manpower and Immigration, 24 Dec. 1971.

55 LAC, RG 146, vol. 2987, Toronto Women's Caucus, pt. 4, Parent to Butroid, 10 Jan. 1972.

56 Ibid. , pt. 5, 25 April 1972, 17 March 1972.

57 LAC, RG 146, vol. 3124, National Action Committee on the Status of Women, pt. 1, RCMP report, 30 Nov. 1982. See also ibid., RCMP report, 20 July 1983.

58 Reg Whitaker, 'The Politics of Security Intelligence Policy-making in Canada, Part 2: 1984–91,' *Intelligence and National Security* 7/2 (1992), 53–76; Richard Cleroux, *Official Secrets: The Story Behind the Canadian Security Intelligence Service* (Toronto: McGraw-Hill Ryerson 1990), 194–5.

59 Rosen, *The World Split Open,* 260.

8. 'Hothead Troubles'

1 C.W. Gonick, 'The Trusteeship and the Decline of Canadian Trade-Unionism,' *Canadian Dimension* (Dec. 1963–Jan. 1964), 7–8. Aggregate

membership figures from 1958 to 1963 were stagnant and membership in unions in key industrial sectors declined between 1952 and 1962.

2 A standard interpretations of wildcat strikes is Martin Glaberman and Seymour Farber, *Working for Wages: The Roots of Insurgency* (Lanham, MD: Rowman and Littlefield, 1998).

3 See, e.g., 'Angry State of the Unions,' *Maclean's* 79 (2 April 1966), 2–3. Wilfred List, 'Labour 1966: A Most Demanding Year,' *Globe and Mail,* 2 June 1966, 7; Arthur Kruger, 'Strike Wave – 1966,' *Canadian Forum* (July 1966), 73–5; Mungo James, 'Labour Lays It on the Line,' *Saturday Night* (Dec. 1966), 25–8.

4 Details of the wartime legislation are discussed in Peter S. McInnis, *Harnessing Labour Confrontation: Shaping the Postwar Settlement in Canada, 1943–1950* (Toronto: University of Toronto Press, 2002).

5 On the activities of the RCMP, see Steve Hewitt and Christabelle Sethna, 'Sex Spying,' in this volume; Reg Whitaker and Gary Marcuse, *Cold War Canada: The Making of a National Insecurity State, 1945–1957* (Toronto: University of Toronto Press, 1994), 310–41.

6 For analysis of the 1947 Taft-Hartley Act in the United States, see Christopher L. Tomlins, *The State and the Unions: Labor Law and the Organized Labor Movement in America, 1880–1960* (New York: Cambridge University Press, 1985).

7 Stuart Marshall Jamieson, *Times of Trouble: Labour Unrest and Industrial Conflict, 1900–1966* (Ottawa: Task Force on Labour Relations, 1968), 395–451.

8 'Work Time Lost to Strikes May Pass 25-Year Record,' *Financial Post,* 10 Dec. 1966, 15.

9 Library and Archives Canada (LAC), RG 27, Department of Labour, D2 Economics and Research Branch, Strikes & Lockouts (hereafter S&L) Files, nos. 286 23–27 (June 1966).

10 LAC, S&L File no. 112 (31 March 1966). A three-hour wildcat at GM-Oshawa resulted in one- to four-week suspensions for twenty-eight UAW members. The union did not protest the disciplinary measures. A separate wildcat at Chrysler-Windsor led to UAW Local 444's 'promise to discipline their members if they caused any more trouble.' S&L File no. 254 (23 June 1966).

11 An explanation of the moral economy is presented in E.P. Thompson, 'The Moral Economy of the English Crowd,' *Past and Present* 50 (Feb. 1971), 76–136.

12 'International' in this context refers to the uniquely North American arrangement whereby many of the largest trade unions functioning in Canada had their headquarters in the United States and pursued policies generally reflecting the American economic and political situation.

13 *Windsor Star,* 8 Aug. 1966, 7.

14 'Four Labour Leaders Discuss Problems and Prospects,' *Globe and Mail,* 4 Jan. 1967, B4–B6.

15 LAC, MG 32 B34, Jack Pickersgill Fonds, vol. 114, file 10-2. CLC presentation to the Government of Canada, 8 Feb. 1967. Pickersgill was then minister of transport in the Pearson Cabinet.

16 'Diagnosing Industrial Unrest,' *Labour Gazette* (Oct. 1967), 624–5, 656; 'How Lethargy Breeds Union Militancy,' *Executive* 8 (Summer 1966), 49–50.

17 'The Impatient Generation: Younger Workers Want Cash Now, Not Security,' *Montreal Star,* 5 Sept 1966, 8. LAC, Canadian Brotherhood of Railway, Transport and General Workers (CBRT-GW) Fonds, vol. 54 (1966–67), R.A. Gingerich, *Commission of Inquiry into the Organization, Policies and Structure of the Brotherhood,* 3.

18 'Labour Unrest Is Epidemic,' *Toronto Star,* 26 Aug. 1966, 2.

19 Typical headlines include, 'Gangs on Docks Rampage, 50 RCMP with Dogs Sent In,' *Globe and Mail,* 1 June 1966, 1. 'Mob Rule around Stelco Plant,' *Globe and Mail,* 5 Aug. 1966, 1; 'Hard-Core Wildcatters try to Sabotage Inco Agreement,' *Toronto Star,* 15 Sept. 1966, 3.

20 Stuart Jamieson, 'Some Reflections on Violence and Law in Industrial Relations,' in *Law and Society in Canada in Historical Perspective,* eds. David J. Bercuson and L.A. Knafla (Calgary: University of Calgary Press, 1979), 141–55.

21 William Marr and Donald G. Paterson, *Canada: An Economic History* (Toronto: Macmillan, 1980), 188–221.

22 On masculinity and postwar strike activity, see Stephen H. Norwood, *Strike-Breaking and Intimidation: Mercenaries and Masculinity in Twentieth-Century America* (Chapel Hill: University of North Carolina Press, 2002), 228–47.

23 For details on labour-related violence, see Mr Justice T.G. Norris, *Royal Commission Concerning Matters Relating to the Disruption of Shipping on the Great Lakes and St Lawrence River System and Connecting Waters* (Ottawa: Queen's Printer and Controller of Stationery, 1963);

Ian Radforth, *Bush Workers and Bosses: Logging in Northern Ontario, 1900–1980* (Toronto: University of Toronto Press, 1987), 157–8.

24 LAC, S&L File, no. 183 (May 1966).

25 *Vancouver Sun,* 10–13 May 1966.

26 John H. Goldthorpe et al., *The Affluent Worker in the Class Structure* (London: CUP Archive, 1969).

27 'Militant Labour Now Demands Good Living,' *Montreal Star,* 7 Dec. 1966.

28 See, e.g., LAC, S&L Vol. 3108-126, Hiram Walker Distillery and the Distillery Workers' Union, June 1965.

29 *Globe and Mail,* 5 Aug. 1966.

30 A.W.R. Carrothers, *Report on the Study on the Labour Injunction in Ontario,* vol. 1 (Toronto: Ontario Dept. of Labour, 1966); Jamieson, *Times of Trouble,* 426–41.

31 LAC, MG 31, D-169, H.D. Woods Fonds, vol. 2; *Canadian Industrial Relations: The Report of the Task Force on Labour Relations* (Ottawa: Information Canada, 1969). 'Progress Report: Task Force on Labour Relations,' *Labour Gazette* (May 1968), 268, 270.

32 'Are Twelve Wise Men the Answer?' *Labour Gazette* (Dec. 1968), 686, 688; 'Is There a Place for a Labour Court in Canada?' *Labour Gazette* (Aug. 1968), 464–5; *Royal Commission of Inquiry into Labour Disputes* (Rand Report) (Toronto: Queen's Printer, 1968); *Ontario Federation of Labour, What Do You Think of the Rand Report?* (Don Mills: Ontario Federation of Labour, 1968).

33 Bill C-230, 'The Maintenance of Railway Operation Act,' ordered the non-operating unions back with an 18% increase pending the final report of mediator Carl H. Goldenberg. See 'The Rail Strike,' *Labour Gazette* (Nov. 1966), 630–2; 'Rail Unrest Spreads,' *Globe and Mail,* 3 Sept. 1966, 1.

34 Leo Panitch and Donald Swartz, *From Consent to Coercion: The Assault on Trade Union Freedoms,* 3rd ed. (Aurora: Garamond, 2003), 1–23, 223–42.

35 LAC, CBRT-GW Fonds, vol. 51.

36 Ibid. Letter from Local 150 (Kamloops, B.C.) to William J. Smith, 13 Sept. 1966. See also Local 96 (London, ON) to Smith, 17 Sept. 1966; Local 108 (Brantford, ON) to Smith, 18 Nov. 1966; Local 9 (Truro, NS) to Smith, 16 Jan 1967.

37 LAC, S&L File, no. 152 (June 1965); 2,000 freight handlers at Montreal and Toronto spearheaded the wildcat.

38 LAC, CBRT-GW Fonds, vol. 51. William Apps to William J. Smith, 'Special Report on the Railway Strike,' 14 Sept. 1966. Apps blamed possible CNTU infiltrators in the CNR-Sleeping and Dining Car Department. Some CBRT officials had received threatening telephone calls at their homes.

39 LAC, CBRT-GW Fonds, vol. 51, Sept. 1966.

40 This phrase is drawn from, Alvin Finkel, *Our Lives: Canada after 1945* (Toronto: Lorimer, 1997), 260–77.

9. Black Confrontation in Sixties Halifax

1 The official Census of Canada listed 32,127 'Negroes' in 1961, but community sources placed their numbers at around 40,000 including about 20,000 in Nova Scotia. For a reasonably concise outline of African-Canadian history in all parts of the country, see James W. St G. Walker, 'African Canadians,' in *An Encyclopedia of Canada's Peoples,* ed. P.R. Magosci (Toronto: University of Toronto Press, 1999), 139–76. For more information, consult Robin W. Winks, *The Blacks in Canada: A History,* 2nd ed. (Montreal and Kingston: McGill-Queen's University Press, 1997).

2 In the interest of full disclosure, the reader should know that I have been a friend of Burnley A. 'Rocky' Jones since we first met during a civil rights demonstration in 1965, and I was close to him throughout the events described in this chapter. Furthermore Dr Jones and I, with Dr George Elliott Clarke, are collaborating on a book about the 'Black Movement' in Nova Scotia and Dr Jones's pre-eminent role in it from the 1960s to the present. It is important to note, however, that the narrative offered here is not intended to represent Dr Jones's perspective or to reveal his own private thoughts and personal experiences. The chapter is my interpretation of the events, based on an analysis of the documentary record, my own lived experience in 1960s Halifax, and my previous research into African-Nova Scotia history. A full description of Dr Jones's involvement will appear in our forthcoming book.

3 *Montreal Star,* 15 Oct. 1968.

4 Ibid., 12 Oct. 1968.

5 *Halifax Chronicle-Herald,* 18 Oct. 1968.

6 Ibid.

7 Ibid., 26 Nov., 5 Dec. 1968; Barbara Hinds, 'Black Power: Has Halifax
Found the Answer?' *Atlantic Advocate* 59/5 (1969), 11–13. Jones was
indeed under surveillance. He has in his possession numerous RCMP
documents, obtained under Access to Information and Privacy regulations, detailing his every move during this period. The documents
merely confirm what he and his friends had been aware of at the time.
For further examples, see Steve Hewitt and Christabelle Sethna, 'Sex
Spying,' in this volume.

8 Library and Archives Canada (LAC), MG 31, H191, Paul Winn Papers,
vol. 1, 'What Is Happening to the Black Man in Nova Scotia?' typescript by W.P. Oliver.

9 Ibid., vol. 1, 'An Evaluation Report of the Black United Front,' by Peter
J. Paris, Oct. 1972, 15; vol. 2, 'History on the Formation of the Black
United Front,' unsigned typescript; *Chronicle-Herald,* 3 Dec. 1968;
Frank Boyd, 'The Politics of the Minority Game: The Decline and Fall
of the Black United Front,' *New Maritimes,* March 1985, 10–12.

10 W.P. Oliver, 'Cultural Progress of the Negro in Nova Scotia,' *Dalhousie
Review,* 29 (1949), 293–300; Colin A. Thomson, *Born with a Call:
A Biography of Dr William Pearly Oliver, CM* (Dartmouth: Black
Cultural Centre for Nova Scotia, 1986); Jules R. Oliver, 'Nova Scotia
Association for the Advancement of Colored People: An Historical
Evaluation of the NSAACP and the Role It Has Played in the Area of
Employment,' Master of Social Work thesis, Maritime School of Social
Work, Acadia University, 1969; Eugene E. Williams, 'Nova Scotia
Association for the Advancement of Colored People: An Historical
Review of the Organization and Its Role in the Area of Education,'
Diploma in Social Work, Maritime School of Social Work, Acadia
University, 1969.

11 LAC, MG 28, vol. 75, Jewish Labour Committee (JLC) Papers, vol. 40,
file 10, 'Alan Borovoy's Trip to Halifax, Aug. 1962,' Borovoy to
Committee nd (Sept. 1962); file 13, Orlikow to Wedderburn, 14 Feb.
1964, reply, 24 Feb., Wedderburn to Orlikow, 2 March, reply, 10 March.
David Lewis Stein, 'The Counterattack on Diehard Racism,' *Maclean's*
(20 Oct. 1962). Stein accompanied Borovoy on his Halifax trip. Three
sets of minutes for the Halifax Advisory Committee on Human Rights,
which overlap but not completely, are in the JLC Papers, the Dalhousie
University Archives (DUA); Nova Scotia Archives and Records
Management (NSARM), MG 20, no. 421, 'Human Rights Association.'

Before its destruction in the late 1960s, Africville was a black community of about 400 people on the northern fringes of Halifax. Its story is told in Donald Clairmont and Dennis Magill, *Africville: The Life and Death of a Canadian Black Community,* 3rd ed. (Toronto: Canadian Scholars' Press, 1999), and Africville Genealogical Society, *The Spirit of Africville* (Halifax: Formac, 1992).

12   Halifax Advisory Committee, minutes of meeting, 21 Sept. 1962; JLC Papers, vol. 40, file 13, Orlikow to Wedderburn, 10 March 1964, reply, 21 April; file 14, Wedderburn to Orlikow, 7 April 1965, enclosing L.H. Jones to Charles Coleman, 24 Nov. 1964, Orlikow to Wedderburn, 9 and 22 April 1965, Wedderburn to Orlikow, 27 Sept. 1965.

13   *Halifax Mail Star,* 16 Nov. 1964; *Time* (Canada ed.), 27 Nov. 1964.

14   Records documenting the Nova Scotia Project, including the newsletter *Nova Scotian Scene,* are in the Mills Library, McMaster University, Combined Universities Campaign for Nuclear Disarmament-Student Union for Peace Action-New Left Committee Fonds. For background on student activism, see Roberta Lexier, 'To Struggle Together or Fracture Apart,' in this volume.

15   National Film Board of Canada, 'Encounter at Kwacha House,' directed by Rex Tasker, 1967.

16   JLC Papers, vol. 40, file 15, Wedderburn to Orlikow, 3 Oct. 1966; file 16, Wedderburn to Borovoy, 12 Jan. 1967; Submission to Mayor Allan O'Brien, 30 Jan.; *Chronicle-Herald,* 22 Feb. 1966; *Mail Star,* 8 March 1967; 'Final Report on the Problem of Unemployment for the Negro,' appended to Jules Oliver's MSW thesis, 'NSAACP.'

17   W.P. Oliver, 'What Is Happening to the Black Man in Nova Scotia?'

18   *Chronicle-Herald,* 26 Oct. 1968.

19   *Mail Star,* 11 Oct.; *Chronicle-Herald,* 12 Oct. 1968.

20   Nova Scotia Human Rights Federation, letter dated 26 Nov. 1968, Conference Program, 6–7 Dec. 1968.

21   *Chronicle-Herald,* 6 Dec. 1968.

22   Ibid., 9 Dec. 1968, and personal observation.

23   Quoted in Joy Mannette, '"Making Something Happen": Nova Scotia's Black Renaissance, 1968–1986,' doctoral dissertation, Carleton University, 1987, 173–4.

24   NSARM, Black United Front (BUF) Fonds, 2002-066/008, File 1, 'The Black United Front,' by W.P. Oliver; JLC Papers, vol. 41, file 1, 'A Pilot

Project in Self-Determination on the Part of Nova Scotia's Negroes,'
16 Jan. 1969.
25 Ibid., vol. 40, file 19, Wedderburn to Orlikow, 31 Jan. 1969; vol. 41, file
1, Wedderburn to Orlikow, 24 Feb. 1969; W.P. Oliver, answering a question in St Francis Xavier University, 'The Black Man in Nova Scotia
Teach-In Report,' Jan. 1969, 8.
26 'The ACLM,' vol. 1, no. 1, March 1969.
27 'Teach-In Report,' 20.
28 Dorothy Eber, *The Computer Centre Party: Canada Meets Black
Power* (Montreal: Tundra, 1969); *Let the Niggers Burn! The Sir George
Williams University Affair and Its Carribean Aftermath,* eds. Dennis
Forsythe et al. (Montreal: Black Rose Books, 1971); P. Kiven Tunteng,
'Racism and the Montreal Computer Incident of 1969,' *Race* 14 (1973),
229–40; David Austin, 'All Roads Led to Montreal: Black Power, the
Caribbean, and the Black Radical Tradition in Canada,' *Journal of
African American History* 92/4 (2007), 516–39. See also Marcel Martel,
'"Riot" at Sir George Williams,' in this volume.
29 *Globe and Mail,* Weekend Magazine, 15 Feb. 1969.
30 JLC Papers, vol. 41, file 1, 'Submission for Developmental Phase
Demonstration Project,' 17 March 1969.
31 LAC, RG 29, vol. 1513, file 201-6-7, vol. 3, Joseph Willard to
John Munro, 12 March 1969, and Munro's handwritten notation;
vol. 4, Munro to R.G. Hattie, 21 Aug. 1969, Ian Howard (Munro's
executive assistant) to James Lorimer, 12 Sept., 'Reference Manual –
Demonstration Projects,' n.d.
32 LAC, RG 2, vol. 6349, file 636/69, Memo: John Munro and Gerard
Pelletier, 16 June 1969, and Memo: Norbert Prefontaine, secretary, 17
June.
33 Ibid., vol. 6340, Cabinet Minutes, 26 June 1969. The White Paper on
Indian Policy had just been released.
34 Ibid., vol. 6351, file 811/69, Memo: Munro and Pelletier, 28 July;
vol. 6352, file 839/69, Memo: Pre fontaine, 30 July; vol. 6340, Cabinet
Minutes, 31 July 1969.
35 *Toronto Telegram* and *Canadian Press,* 11 June 1969. This announcement came before the formal Cabinet approval.
36 There are dozens of letters in RG 29, vol. 1513, file 201-6-7, vol. 4,
and more in RG29, accession 1981–82/184, box 33, file 45-6-3. Since
these files had to be acquired under Access to Information and Privacy

regulations, the citizens' names were blacked out before I saw them. The city of origin was left, however, and it was possible to note that protests came from all over Canada.

37 LAC, RG 29, vol. 1513, file 201-6-7, vol. 4, B.J. Iverson to F.R. MacKinnon, 16 July, in reply to MacKinnon to Iverson, 10 July 1969; RG 29, accession 1981–82/184, box 33, file 45-6-3, Iverson to Deputy Minister, 14 Aug.; NSARM, RG72, Department of Public Welfare Fonds, vol. 59, file 11, 'Black United Front, 1969.'

38 *Mail Star,* 15 Aug. 1969.

39 *Chronicle-Herald,* 4 Dec. 1968; *Mail Star,* 25 June 1969; LAC, Paul Winn Papers, vol. 1, 'An Evaluation Report of the Black United Front,' by Peter J. Paris, Oct. 1972, 1, 15–17.

40 'Evaluation Report,' 33, 49; Boyd, 'The Decline and Fall of the Black United Front,' 11; *Grasp,* Sept. 1972.

41 NSARM, BUF Fonds, 2002-066/003, 'Annual Progress Report,' April 1970–March 1971; 2002-066/007, files 2–7, 'Executive Director's Progress Reports,' 1969–1977; 2002-066/008, file 10, 'An Evaluation Report' by L.F. Heinemann, 1975; LAC, Winn Papers, vol. 1, 'Mid-Course Study, Evaluation and Recommendations –Nov. 1970'; Memo to Staff, 27 Sept. 1971; 'Evaluation Report,' 23–31, 42–5.

42 'Evaluation Report,' 20, 30. Paris was originally from Nova Scotia, but in 1972 was assistant professor in the Vanderbilt University Divinity School.

43 *Chronicle-Herald,* 31 Oct. 1970.

44 The foremost practitioner and analyst of the Black Renaissance is poet George Elliott Clarke. See, in particular, his introductions to *Fire on the Water: An Anthology of Black Nova Scotian Writing,* 2 vols. (Lawrencetown Beach: Pottersfield Press, 1991, 1992), and *Eyeing the North Star: Directions in African-Canadian Literature* (Toronto: McClelland and Stewart, 1997), and the essays in his collection *Odysseys Home: Mapping African-Canadian Literature* (Toronto: University of Toronto Press, 2002).

45 Dorothy E. Moore, 'Multiculturalism –Ideology or Social Reality?'doctoral dissertation, Boston University, 1980, 408–9. See also Daiva K. Stasiulis, 'The Political Structuring of Ethnic Community Action: A Reformulation,' *Canadian Ethnic Studies* 12/3 (1980), 35–6.

46 NSARM, BUF Fonds, 2002-066/021, File 6, 'Case Files: Oland Issue,' 1970.

47 In 2004, the University of Guelph conferred an honorary Doctor of Laws degree on Burnley Jones, in recognition of his many contributions

to the advancement of racial equality in Canada including his landmark Supreme Court victory in the case of *R v S. (R.D.)* [1997] S.C.R. 484. Jones graduated from the Dalhousie Law School in 1991.

10. 'Indians of All Tribes': The Birth of Red Power

1 In this essay I use the terms Aboriginal, Native, and Indigenous interchangeably, referring to all peoples who have, for various reasons and at various times, been constructed as categories in the colonization project. 'Indian' is a term of classification that designates people living under the terms of the Indian Act. But it is also a term of self-identification among Native peoples themselves, who have a broader understanding of indigeneity. State categorizations do not correspond to the lived experience of a variety of Aboriginal peoples, let alone the co-mingling of colonizers and Indigenous peoples that resulted in yet another category: Métis. At this point, state-defined classifications of Native peoples have created difference and confusion. It is thus not accidental that Red Power, as a 1960s-originating mobilization, accented pan-Indian protest, in which 'Indians of All Tribes' were called upon to unite. On labelling, see Michael Kew, 'Making Indians,' in *Workers, Capital, and the State in British Columbia,* eds. Rennie Warburton and David Coburn (Vancouver: UBC Press, 1988), 24–34; Bonita Lawrence, *'Real' Indians and Others: Mixed-Blood Urban Native Peoples and Indigenous Nationhood* (Vancouver: UBC Press, 2004).

2 Vine Deloria Jr maintains that the protests of the 1960s were a continuation of older traditions and that in accenting the newness of Red Power the mainstream media of the late 1960s missed 'the entire meaning of the protest.' Vine Deloria Jr, *Behind the Trail of Broken Treaties: An Indian Declaration of Independence* (New York: Dell, 1974), 4. While not wanting to understate continuity in Native protest, I would suggest that Red Power, like the New Left, needs to be considered both in its historical context and as something of a break from past protest traditions. For a fuller elaboration of evidence and argument in this essay, see Bryan D. Palmer, *Canada's 1960s: The Ironies of Identity in a Rebellious Era* (Toronto: University of Toronto Press, 2009), 367–414.

3 Kiera L. Ladner, 'Rethinking the Past, Present, and Future of Aboriginal Governance,' in *Reinventing Canada,* eds. J. Brodie and L. Trimble (Toronto: Canadian Scholars' Press, 2003), 47; Peter Kulchyski, '"A Considerable Unrest": F.O. Loft and the League of Indians,' *Native*

Studies Review 4 (1988), 95–117; E. Brian Titley, *A Narrow Vision: Duncan Campbell Scott and the Administration of Indian Affairs in Canada* (Vancouver: UBC Press, 1968), esp. 102–9; Paul Tennant, *Aboriginal Peoples and Politics: The Indian Land Question in British Columbia, 1849–1989* (Vancouver: UBC Press, 1990), esp. 84–113; Murray Dobbin, *The One-and-a-Half Men: The Story of Jim Brady and Malcolm Norris, Métis Patriots of the Twentieth Century* (Vancouver: New Star, 1981).

4 See Peter McFarlane, *Brotherhood to Nationhood: George Manuel and the Making of the Modern Indian Movement* (Toronto: Between the Lines, 1993). Note as well Hugh Shewell, 'Jules Sioui and Indian Political Radicalism in Canada, 1943–1944,' *Journal of Canadian Studies* 34 (Autumn 1999), 211–42.

5 McFarlane, *Brotherhood to Nationhood*, 45–72; Tennant, *Aboriginal Peoples and Politics*, 125–8; George Manuel and Michael Posluns, 'The Fourth World,' in *Out of the Background: Readings on Native History*, eds. Robin Fisher and Kenneth Coates, (Toronto: Copp Clark, 1988), 285–91.

6 Dobbin, *One-and-a-Half Men*, 183–200; Gerald R. [Taiaiake] Alfred, *Heeding the Voices of Our Ancestors: Kahnawake Mohawk Politics and the Rise of Native Nationalism* (Toronto: Oxford University Press, 1995), esp. 67, 131, 158–61. In a later study, Alfred accents what he considers the factional fractures, dysfunctional debate, and violently self-destructive politics of the 1960s, which he attributes to colonization and control by whites. Yet the period was also in his view 'a revolutionary time,' and one that laid the basis for future developments. See Taiaiake Alfred, *Peace, Power, Righteousness: An Indigenous Manifesto* (Toronto: Oxford University Press, 1999), 6.

7 Howard Ramos has provided evidence that the 1960s witnessed the first of three waves of vigorous Aboriginal protest in Canada. See Ramos, 'What Causes Aboriginal Protest? Examining Resources, Opportunities and Identity, 1951–2000,' *Canadian Journal of Sociology* 31 (Spring 2006), 211–34; Ramos, 'Aboriginal Protest,' in *Social Movements*, ed. Suzanne Staggenborg (Don Mills: Oxford University Press, 2007), 55–70.

8 Fred Gudmundson, 'Managing Our Own Lives: An Interview with George Erasmus,' *Canadian Dimension* 18 (Oct.–Nov. 1984), 27. Note also the succinct introduction in Howard Adams, *A Tortured People: The Politics of Colonization* (Penticton: Theytus Books, 1995), 75–92.

9 See Peter Kulchyski, 'Forty Years in Indian Country,' *Canadian Dimension* 37 (Nov.–Dec. 2003), 33–4; J.W. Warnock, 'Red Power: An Interview with Howard Adams,' *Canadian Dimension* 5 (April–May 1968), 21–3. See also Tennant, *Aboriginal Peoples,* 141; Ramos, 'Aboriginal Protest,' 62.

10 See Jeannette C. Armstrong, *Slash* (Pentiction: Theytus Books, 1990); Lee Maracle, *Bobbi Lee: Indian Rebel* (Toronto: Women's Press, 1990); Eden Robinson, *Monkey Beach* (Toronto: Knopf, 2000).

11 Maracle, *Bobbi Lee,* esp. 158–9, 208–9. Maracle's account presents a sustained discussion of the contacts between Red Power advocates and the ultraleft in the 1960s.

12 *Poverty in Canada: Report of the Special Senate Committee on Poverty* (Ottawa: Information Canada, 1971), 34–5; Ian Adams, William Cameron, Brian Hill, and Peter Penz, *The Real Poverty Report* (Edmonton: Hurtig, 1971), 68–74; Jim Harding, 'Canada's Indians: A Powerless Minority,' in *Poverty in Canada,* eds. John Harp and John R. Hofley (Toronto: Prentice-Hall, 1971), esp. 240–3. For a broad historical appreciation, see Hugh Shewell, *'Enough to Keep them Alive': Indian Welfare in Canada, 1873–1965* (Toronto: University of Toronto Press, 2004).

13 Heather Robertson, *Reservations Are for Indians* (Toronto: James, Lewis, and Samuel, 1970).

14 On the attractions of the reserve, see Wilfred Pelletier, 'Childhood in an Indian Village,' in *This Book Is about Schools,* ed. Satu Repo (New York: Pantheon, 1970), 18–32; Peter Gzowski, 'Racism on the Prairies,' in Gzowski, *A Peter Gzowski Reader* (Toronto: McClelland and Stewart, 2001), 14. On the exodus from the reserves and Skid Row, see Hugh Brody, *Indians on Skid Row* (Ottawa: Northern Science Research Group, Department of Indian Affairs, 1971).

15 Reserve relocation has a long history, but some particularly egregious relocation projects, such as that of Grassy Narrows, were undertaken in the decade. See Anastasia M. Shkilnyk, *A Poison Stronger than Love: The Destruction of an Ojibwa Community* (New Haven and London: Yale University Press, 1985).

16 Maria Campbell, *Halfbreed* (Toronto: Seal, 1973); Beatrice Culleton, *In Search of April Raintree* (Winnipeg: Pemmican, 1983). Note, as well, Patrick Johnston, *Native Children and the Child Welfare System* (Toronto: Lorimer, 1983).

17 J.R. Miller, *Shingwauk's Vision: A History of Native Residential Schools* (Toronto: University of Toronto Press, 1996); John S. Milloy, *A National Crime: The Canadian Government and the Residential School System, 1879–1986* (Winnipeg: University of Manitoba Press, 1999).

18 For the record of liberalization, see *Contemporary Indian Legislation, 1951–1978* (Ottawa: Treaties and Historical Research Centre, Corporate Policy, Department of Indian and Northern Affairs, 1981); Canada, *Report of the Royal Commission on Aboriginal Peoples,* vol. 1, *Looking Forward, Looking Back* (Ottawa: Minister of Supply and Services, 1996), 307–19.

19 H.B. Hawthorn, ed., *A Survey of the Contemporary Indians of Canada: A Report on Economic, Political, and Educational Needs and Policies,* vol. 1 (Ottawa: Indian Affairs Branch, 1966), esp. 13. For discussion of Hawthorn, see Alan C. Cairns, *Citizens Plus: Aboriginal Peoples and the Canadian State* (Vancouver: UBC Press, 2000), and for a subsequent radical Indigenous response to Cairns, see Dale Turner, *This Is Not a Peace Pipe: Towards a Critical Indigenous Philosophy* (Toronto: University of Toronto Press, 2006), esp. 38–56.

20 The above paragraphs draw on and quote from *Statement of the Government of Canada on Indian Policy* (Ottawa: Queen's Printer, Indian Affairs and Northern Development, 1969). For a thorough treatment of this period and its subsequent evolution, see Sally M. Weaver, *Making Canadian Indian Policy: The Hidden Agenda, 1968–1970* (Toronto: University of Toronto Press, 1971).

21 Alfred, *Heeding the Voices of Our Ancestors,* 160–1; Laurence M. Hauptman, *The Iroquois Struggle for Survival: World War II to Red Power* (Syracuse: Syracuse University Press, 1986), esp. 136–9, 150, 208, 225.

22 Vic Satzewich and Terry Wotherspoon, *First Nations: Race, Class, and Gender Relations* (Scarborough: Nelson, 1993), 229; J.S. Frideres, *Native Peoples in Canada: Contemporary Conflicts* (Toronto: Prentice-Hall, 1988), 268.

23 McFarlane, *Brotherhood to Nationhood,* 98; Satzewich and Wotherspoon, *First Nations,* 231.

24 McFarlane, *Brotherhood to Nationhood,* 70; Peter Gzowski, 'This Is Our Alabama,' in *Gzowski Reader,* 103–15.

25 Adams, *Tortured People,* 82–4; Dobbin, *One-and-a-Half Men,* 224–54.

26 McFarlane, *Brotherhood to Nationhood,* 97; Peter Matthiessen, *In the Spirit of Crazy Horse* (New York: Viking, 1983), 279; Steve Hewitt,

*Spying 101: The RCMP's Secret Activities at Canadian Universities,
1917–1997* (Toronto: University of Toronto Press, 2002), 146, 156–8.

27 Howard Adams, *Prison of Grass: Canada from the Native Point of
View* (Toronto: General Publishing, 1975); Adams, *Tortured People,* 75;
and Hartmut Lutz, ed., *Howard Adams: Otapawy! The Life of a Métis
Leader in His Own Words and Those of His Contemporaries* (Saskatoon:
Gabriel Dumont Institute, 2005); Dick Fidler, *Red Power in Canada*
(Toronto: Vanguard, 1970), 15.

28 Harold Cardinal, *The Unjust Society* (Vancouver: Douglas and McIntyre,
1999 [1969]), 40.

29 Myrna Kostash, *Long Way from Home: The Story of the Sixties
Generation in Canada* (Toronto: Lorimer, 1980), 147–65; Hauptman,
Iroquois Struggle for Survival, 224–7; Richard Oakes, 'Alcatraz Is Not
an Island,' *Ramparts* 11 (Dec. 1969), esp. 35.

30 Andrew Nichols is quoted in 'New Brunswick Indians –Conservative
Militants,' in Waubageshig, ed., *The Only Good Indian* (Don Mills: New
Press, 1974), 50.

31 Redbird began writing poetry in his radical period of the late 1960s,
much of it a condemnation of what white colonization had done to
Native peoples. By 1977 he had mellowed somewhat and his best-
known poem, 'I Am a Canadian,' was presented to Queen Elizabeth
II during the Silver Jubilee celebrations. See Duke Redbird, 'I Am a
Canadian,' in *An Anthology of Canadian Native Literature in English,*
eds. Daniel David Moses and Terry Goldie (Don Mills: Oxford
University Press, 2005),114–15; and for Redbird's 1980 statement of
Métis nationalism, Duke Redbird, *We Are Metis: A Metis View of the
Development of a Native Canadian People* (Toronto: Ontario Metis and
Non-Status Indian Association, 1980).

32 Duke Redbird, 'I Am the Redman,' in Waubageshig, *Only Good Indian,* 61.

33 See among many possible general statements, James Burke, *Paper
Tomahawks: From Red Tape to Red Power* (Winnipeg: Queenston
House, 1976); Tennant, *Aboriginal Peoples and Politics,*139–64.

34 See Trudeau's full speech in *Native Rights in Canada,* eds. Peter A.
Cumming and Neil H. Mickenberg (Toronto: Indian-Eskimo Association
of Canada, 1980), 331–2.

35 Cardinal, *The Unjust Society.*

36 The above paragraphs draw on Hauptman, *Iroquois Struggle for
Survival,* 149–50, 208, 222–7; Ernest Benedict, 'Indians and a Treaty,'

in Waubageshig, *Only Good Indian*, 157–60; Oakes, 'Alcatraz Is Not an Island,' 35–40; Troy Johnson, 'The Occupation of Alcatraz: Roots of American Indian Activism,' *Wicazo Sa Review* 10 (Autumn 1994), 63–79.

37 For a useful discussion of NARP, see Maracle, *Bobbi Lee*. Also insightful is Armstrong, *Slash*, esp. 68–72, which suggests the emerging late 1960s connection of Red Power bodies like NARP and AIM. For a succinct and illuminating statement of NARP's history and politics, see Henry Jack, 'Native Alliance for Red Power,' in Waubageshig, *Only Good Indian*, 162–78, which is followed by a statement made by NARP activist Gerry Gambill at a Conference on Human Rights at the Tobique Reserve in New Brunswick in Aug. 1968 (179–80). The quote at the end of the paragraph comes from the same book, Lloyd Roland Caibaiosai, 'The Politics of Patience,' 149.

38 See Ramos, 'Aboriginal Protest.'

39 Cairns, *Citizens Plus*, 20. The Indian Chiefs of Alberta Red Paper, under the title 'Citizens Plus,' was reprinted in Waubageshig, *Only Good Indian*, 5–42. See, as well, Harold Cardinal, *The Rebirth of Canada's Indians* (Edmonton: Hurtig, 1977).

40 Cumming and Mickenberg, *Native Rights in Canada*, 332.

41 Consider the discussion in Wayne Warry, *Unfinished Dreams: Community Healing and the Reality of Aboriginal Self-Government* (Toronto: University of Toronto Press, 1998).

42 Dee Brown, *Bury My Heart at Wounded Knee: An Indian History of the American West* (New York: Holt, Rinehart, and Winston, 1970); Dennis Banks with Richard Erdoes, *Ojibwa Warrior: Dennis Banks and the Rise of the American Indian Movement* (Norman: University of Oklahoma Press, 2004); and for the best discussion of repression and the case of Peltier, see Matthiessen, *In The Spirit of Crazy Horse*.

43 For a regional study, see Nicolas Blomley, '"Shut the Province Down": First Nations Blockades in British Columbia, 1984–1995,' *BC Studies* 111 (1996), 5–35.

44 For a succinct overview, see Kulchyski, 'Forty Years in Indian Country.' Specific struggles are discussed in Burke, *Paper Tomahawks;* John Gallagher and Cy Gonic, 'The Occupation of Anicinabe Park,' *Canadian Dimension* 10 (Nov. 1974), 21–40; Vern Harper, *Following the Red Path: The Native People's Caravan* (Toronto: NC Press, 1979); Richard F. Salisbury, *A Homeland for the Cree: Regional Development in James Bay, 1971–1981* (Kingston and Montreal: McGill-Queen's

University Press, 1986); Mel Watkins, ed., *Dene Nation: The Colony Within* (Toronto: University of Toronto Press, 1977). For different perspectives voiced at the time of a 2007 National Day of Action, see Floyd Favel, 'Buckskin Revolution: A Cree Cultural Leader Speaks Out,' *Globe and Mail,* 12 June 2007; Collin Freeze, 'Mohawk Activist Resigned to Time Behind Bars,' *Globe and Mail,* 2 July 2007.

45 For a scathing indictment of Aboriginal leaders' corruption and integration into the state and capitalism, one that draws very much on his experience in the Saskatchewan Métis politics of mobilization, see Adams, *Tortured People,* 177–95. Adams had alluded to this problem as early as 1968, in Warnock, 'Red Power: An Interview with Howard Adams,' 23. A Manitoba critique appears in Burke, *Paper Tomahawks.*

46 Maracle, *Bobbi Lee,* 218–19. On state funding of Aboriginal organizations at this time, see the brief comments in Tennant, *Aboriginal People and Politics,* 165–80; Leslie A. Pal, *Interests of State: The Politics of Language, Multiculturalism, and Feminism in Canada* (Kingston and Montreal: McGill-Queen's University Press, 1993), 5, 48; and Sally M. Weaver, 'The Joint Cabinet/National Indian Brotherhood Committee: A Unique Experiment in Pressure Group Politics,' *Canadian Public Administration* 25 (Summer 1982), 211–39.

47 Adams, *Tortured People,* 83.

48 See Taiaiake Alfred, *Wasáse: Indigenous Pathways of Action and Freedom* (Peterborough: Broadview, 2005).

49 On Harper see, among many possible commentaries, Cairns, *Citizens Plus,* 146; Noel Dyck, *What Is the Indian 'Problem'? Tutledge and Resistance in Canadian Indian Administration* (St John's: Institute for Social and Economic Research, 1993),160–1. Lee Maracle, *Sundogs* (Penticton: Theytus Books, 1992) is a fictional account of Native peoples' positive reaction to Harper, as well as their support for the Mohawk struggle to preserve their land in the armed stand-off pitting Aboriginals against developers and the Quebec state in Oka over the period July– Sept. 1990. For more on the complexity of Oka, see Gerald R. [Taiaiake] Alfred, 'From Bad to Worse: Internal Politics in the 1990 Oka Crisis at Kahnawake,' *Northeast Indian Quarterly* 8 (Spring 1991), 23–32.

11. The Nationalist Moment in English Canada

1 Tim Greenough provided indispensible assistance with the research for this chapter. The editors of this volume, the other contributors, and Van

Gosse offered perceptive advice. Brian McKillop suggested the title. Norman Hillmer and Sara Burke provided valuable commentary on the manuscript. I am grateful to them all.

2　See the following selections from *The New Romans: Candid Canadian Opinions of the U.S.,* ed. Al Purdy (Edmonton: Hurtig, 1968): Farley Mowat, 'Letter to My Son,' 4; Margaret Atwood, 'Backdrop Addresses Cowboy,' 10; Henry Beissel, 'A New Nest of Eagles,' 129.

3　Peter C. Newman, *Here Be Dragons: Telling Tales of People, Passion and Power* (Toronto: McClelland and Stewart, 2004), 254; original emphasis.

4　Quoted in Edward Cowan, 'Canada: Economic Nationalism,' *New York Times,* 7 Feb. 1971, section 3, 1, 14; Kari Levitt, *Silent Surrender: The Multinational Corporation in Canada* (Toronto: Macmillan, 1970), 144.

5　In his study of anti-Americanism in France, Ezra Suleiman contrasts 'conjunctural' anti-Americanism with 'ideological anti-Americanism.' To avoid the term 'anti-Americanism,' I have employed the phrase 'conjunctural nationalism.' I agree with Max Paul Friedman that the label 'anti-American' 'is not an analytic category; it is a distorting lens…and it is an obstacle to understanding what is going on in the world.' As I demonstrate later in this chapter, the ideas of Canadian nationalists were often as much American as anti-American. Ezra N. Suleiman, 'Les Atermoiements des élites,' in *L'Amérique dans les têtes: Un siècle de fascinations et d'aversions,* eds. Denis Lacorne, Jacques Rupnik, and Marie-France Toinet ([Paris]: Hachette, 1986), 142; Max Paul Friedman, 'Anti-Americanism and U.S. Foreign Relations,' *Diplomatic History* 32/4 (2008), 505.

6　'A Dimension Editorial Statement,' *Canadian Dimension* (Aug.–Sept. 1969), 8.

7　George Grant, 'Introduction to the Carleton Library Edition,' in *Lament for a Nation: The Defeat of Canadian Nationalism* (Ottawa: Carleton University Press, 1997), 9–10.

8　Martin Loney, president of the Canadian Union of Students, as quoted in Roberta Lexier, '"The Backdrop against which Everything Happened": English-Canadian Student Movements and Off-Campus Movements for Change,' *History of Intellectual Culture* 7/1 (2007), 10.

9　M.J. Arlen, 'Living-Room War,' *New Yorker* (15 Oct. 1966), 200–2.

10　House of Commons, *Debates,* 12 Apr. 1965, 238.

11 Jack Gould, 'Canada Brings Style to News,' *New York Times,* 30 Jan. 1966, X17; *Mills of the Gods: Viet Nam,* produced by Beryl Fox, 55 min., CBC, 1965.

12 David Helwig, 'A Borderline Case,' in Purdy, *The New Romans,* 155.

13 Ray Smith, 'Cape Breton Is the Thought Control Centre of Canada,' in Purdy, *The New Romans,* 30.

14 Heather Robertson, 'Confessions of a Canadian Chauvinist Pig,' *Maclean's* (April 1975), 96.

15 The examples that follow are from these chapters in Purdy, *The New Romans:* C.W. Gonick, 'Enlightened (?) Self-Interest of the U.S,' 163, 164; Raymond Souster, 'Death Chant for Mr Johnson's America,' 66; John W. Warnock, 'The Great Liberal Myth,' 43; Stephen Vizinczey, 'If Throughout His Reign Napoleon...,' 83.

16 John Keats, *The New Romans: An American Experience* (Philadelphia: Lippincott, 1967).

17 G. Horowitz, 'Conservatism, Liberalism, and Socialism in Canada: An Interpretation,' *Canadian Journal of Economics and Political Science* 32/2 (1966), 143–71.

18 Abraham Rotstein and Melville H. Watkins, 'An American Dilemma,' *Canadian Forum* (Sept. 1965), 126–8.

19 See the following in *Close the 49th Parallel Etc.: The Americanization of Canada,* ed. Ian Lumsden (Toronto: University of Toronto Press, 1970): C.W. Gonick, 'Foreign Ownership and Political Decay,' 55; John W. Warnock, 'All the News It Pays to Print,' 117; Ellen and Neal Wood, 'Canada and the American Science of Politics,' 180; George Martell, 'What Can I Do Right Now? Notes from Point Blank School on the Canadian Dilemma,' 297–300; and Ian Lumsden, 'American Imperialism and Canadian Intellectuals,' 334. On the Woods' reliance on American anti-behaviouralists, I am indebted to Carl Smith, 'Review of *Close the 49th Parallel Etc.: The Americanization of Canada,* ed. Ian Lumsden,' *Canadian Journal of Political Science* 4/1 (1971), 146.

20 Cy Gonick, 'The CD Story (So Far),' *Canadian Dimension* (Sept.–Oct. 2003), 13.

21 Walter Stewart, 'On the Left, Mel Watkins; in the Middle, Joe Greene: The Heavyweight Contest to Choose Captain Canada of 1971,' *Maclean's* (Nov. 1970), 33; Christina Newman, 'The True Compromise, Good and Sane: How Mel Watkins Brought Socialism

to the NDP,' *Saturday Night* (Sept. 1970), 24; Mel Watkins, 'Getting to Democratic Socialism: Points of Departure,' in *Gordon to Watkins to You, A Documentary: The Battle for Control of Our Economy,* eds. Dave Godfrey and Mel Watkins (Don Mills: New Press, 1970), 3–4. Anthony Westell commented on Watkins's 'New England twang' in 1969. Anthony Westell, 'New Nationalists May Push Trudeau to the Left,' *Toronto Star,* 29 Nov. 1969, 1, 5. I heard no trace of it when I first met Watkins in March 1994.

22 Other nationalists with American connections were Gad Horowitz (Ph.D., Harvard), Robin Mathews (M.A., Ohio State), and Stephen Hymer (Ph.D., Massachusetts Institute of Technology).

23 Myrna Kostash, *Long Way from Home: The Story of the Sixties Generation in Canada* (Toronto: Lorimer, 1980), 11.

24 J.A. Wainwright, '"New Skin for the Old Ceremony": Canadian Identity Revisited,' Essays on Canadian Writing 63 (Spring 1998), 64.

25 Canada, Special Senate Committee on Mass Media, *Report,* vol. 1, *The Uncertain Mirror* (Ottawa: Queen's Printer, 1970), 156.

26 Joseph Scanlon, 'Canada Sees the World through U.S. Eyes: One Case Study in Cultural Domination,' paper presented to 'New Approaches in the Study of Canadian-American Relations: A Transnational Perspective,' Carleton University, 10 Nov. 1973, 7.

27 Kostash, *Long Way from Home,* 10.

28 John Herd Thompson and Stephen J. Randall, *Canada and the United States: Ambivalent Allies,* 4th ed. (Montreal and Kingston: McGill-Queen's University Press, 2008), 222; J.L. Granatstein, *Yankee Go Home? Canadians and Anti-Americanism* (Toronto: HarperCollins, 1996), 180.

29. Robert A. Wright, '"Dream, Comfort, Memory, Despair": Canadian Popular Musicians and the Dilemma of Nationalism, 1968–1972,' *Journal of Canadian Studies* 22/4 (1987–88), 39. See also Robert Wright, *Virtual Sovereignty: Nationalism, Culture and the Canadian Question* (Toronto: Canadian Scholars' Press, 2004), 57–78; Ryan Edwardson, *Canuck Rock: A History of Canadian Popular Music* (Toronto: University of Toronto Press, 2009), 95, 135.

30 See, e.g., Steven High's work on how the labour movement wrapped itself in the flag to protest plant closings, or Philip Resnick's judgment that CUPE came 'to use Canadian nationalism in its bid for greater power within the CLC,' or Irving Abella's argument that national identity was secondary to material benefits for Canadian organized labour.

Steven High, '"I'll Wrap the F*#@ Flag around Me": A Nationalist Response to Plant Shutdowns, 1969–1984,' *Journal of the Canadian Historical Association* 12 (2001), 203; Steven High, *Industrial Sunset: The Making of North America's Rust Belt, 1969–1984* (Toronto: University of Toronto Press, 2003), 169–70; Philip Resnick, *The Land of Cain: Class and Nationalism in English Canada, 1945–1975* (Vancouver: New Star Books, 1977), 186; Irving Martin Abella, *Nationalism, Communism, and Canadian Labour: The CIO, the Communist Party, and the Canadian Congress of Labour, 1935–1956* (Toronto: University of Toronto Press, 1973). For a different point of view, see Joan Sangster, 'Remembering Texpack: Nationalism, Internationalism, and Militancy in Canadian Unions in the 1970s,' *Studies in Political Economy* 78 (Autumn 2006), 41–66.

31 James Laxer, 'The Student Movement and Canadian Independence,' *Canadian Dimension* (Aug.–Sept. 1969), 29.

32 'For an Independent Socialist Canada,' *Canadian Dimension* (Aug.–Sept. 1969), 8–10.

33 Laxer quotation is from Charles Taylor, *Radical Tories: The Conservative Tradition in Canada* (Toronto: Anansi, 1982), 148. See also George Grant, foreword to James Laxer and Robert Laxer, *The Liberal Idea of Canada: Pierre Trudeau and the Question of Canada's Survival* (Toronto: Lorimer, 1977), 9–12.

34 Varda Burstyn, 'The Waffle and the Women's Movement,' *Studies in Political Economy* 33 (Autumn 1990), 177. According to Nancy Adamson, Linda Briskin, and Margaret McPhail, 'women were social-ists and feminists but had little, if any, sense of socialist feminism' before the late 1960s. Nancy Adamson, Linda Briskin, and Margaret McPhail, *Feminist Organizing for Change: The Contemporary Women's Movement in Canada* (Toronto: Oxford University Press, 1988), 50.

35 Sangster, 'Remembering Texpack'; John Bullen, 'The Ontario Waffle and the Struggle for an Independent Socialist Canada: Conflict within the NDP,' *Canadian Historical Review* 64/2 (1983), 188–215; Bryan D. Palmer, *Canada's 1960s: The Ironies of Identity in a Rebellious Era* (Toronto: University of Toronto Press, 2009), 237–40; Gilbert Levine, 'The Waffle and the Labour Movement,' *Studies in Political Economy* 33 (Autumn 1990), 185–92.

36 For an examination of cultural nationalism and cultural policy, see Ryan Edwardson, *Canadian Content: Culture and the Quest for Nationhood* (Toronto: University of Toronto Press, 2008).

37 Interview with Mel Hurtig, 10 May 1994; S.M. Crean, *Who's Afraid of Canadian Culture?* (Toronto: General Publishing, 1976), 5.
38 Quoted in Granatstein, *Yankee Go Home?* 206–7.
39 In 1974, only 45% of those polled believed that U.S. investment in Canada was a 'good thing.' The percentage was never again so low. J. Alex Murray and Lawrence LeDuc, *Public Attitudes and Foreign Investment Screens: The Canadian Case* (Waterloo: Wilfrid Laurier University, 1985), 16. The Gallup poll showed that, in June 1975, 71% believed that Canada now had 'enough' U.S. capital, the highest figure since Gallup started asking the question in 1956 (*Toronto Star,* 19 July 1975, A2; see also Canadian Institute of Public Opinion, *Gallup Report,* 1956–1984).
40 Gallup asked Canadians about their confidence 'in the ability of the United States to deal wisely with present world problems.' The low point for Canadian confidence in the United States was reached in Sept. 1973, when only 28% of Canadians reported 'very great' or 'considerable' confidence, while 60% had 'little,' 'very little,' or no confidence in Canada's neighbour (*Toronto Star,* 7 Nov. 1973, D5).

12. Reconciling the Two Solitudes? Language Rights

 1 Paul Litt, 'Trudeaumania: Participatory Democracy in the Mass-Mediated Nation,' *Canadian Historical Review* 89/1 (2008), 40.
 2 Consider the student protests in Paris, the 1968 assassinations in the United States, and the Prague Spring, to name but a few examples.
 3 P.E. Bryden, *Planners and Politicians: Liberal Politics and Social Policy, 1957–1968* (Montreal and Kingston: McGill-Queen's University Press, 1997). Dennis Guest, *The Emergence of Social Security in Canada,* 3rd ed. (Vancouver: UBC Press, 1997).
 4 Garth Stevenson, *Unfulfilled Union: Canadian Federalism and National Unity,* 4th ed. (Montreal and Kingston: McGill-Queen's University Press, 2004), 221–9.
 5 Peter Russell, *Constitutional Odyssey: Can Canadians Become a Sovereign People?* 3rd ed. (Toronto: University of Toronto Press, 2004), 72–91.
 6 Canada, Royal Commission on Bilingualism and Biculturalism (RCBB), *Report of the Royal Commission on Bilingualism and Biculturalism,* vol. 1, *The Official Languages* (Ottawa: Queen's Printer, 1967), 173.

7 Canada, RCBB, *Report of the Royal Commission on Bilingualism and Biculturalism, Preliminary Report* (Ottawa: Queen's Printer, 1965), 13.

8 Michael D. Behiels, *Quebec and the Question of Immigration: From Ethnocentrism to Ethnic Pluralism, 1900–1985* (Ottawa: Canadian Historical Association, 1991).

9 Kenneth McRoberts, *Quebec: Social Change and Political Crisis,* 3rd ed. with a Postscript (Toronto: McClelland and Stewart, 1993), 216–17.

10 Government of Quebec, Commission of Inquiry on the Position of the French Language and on Language Rights in Québec, *The Position of the French Language in Québec,* 3 vols. (Montreal, 1972).

11 Louis Fournier, *FLQ: Anatomy of an Underground Movement* (Toronto: NC Press, 1983).

12 Richard J. Joy, *Languages in Conflict* (Toronto: McClelland and Stewart, 1972).

13 Canada, *Constitutional Conference Proceedings, Second Meeting, 10–12 Feb. 1969* (Ottawa: Queen's Printer, 1969), 77.

14 Manitoba passed its Official Language Act in 1890, abrogating the official status for French contained in the Manitoba Act, 1870. The North-West Territories eliminated official status for French in 1892 and then limited access to French-language education. Alberta and Saskatchewan strongly resisted any official status for French when they attained provincial status in 1905.

15 For more detail on the historical status of the French language in the federal civil service, see RCBB, *Report of the Royal Commission on Bilingualism and Biculturalism,* vol. 3, *The Work World* (Ottawa: Queen's Printer, 1969).

16 Stevenson, *Unfulfilled Union,* 240–1.

17 Russell, *Constitutional Odyssey,* 72–4.

18 Marcel Martel, *Le deuil d'un pays imagine: Rêves, luttes et déroute du Canada français* (Ottawa: Les Presses de l'Université d'Ottawa, 1997), 147–8.

19 Library and Archives Canada (LAC), RG 33, Series 80, RCBB. This theme occurs repeatedly. See, e.g., vol. 41, file 730-153, Mémoires, Nouveau-Brunswick, Société nationale des acadiens (1964), 26–9.

20 Pierre Elliott Trudeau, 'Quebec and the Constitutional Problem,' in *Federalism and the French Canadians* (Toronto: McClelland and Stewart, 1968), 48–50.

21 Trudeau, 'A Constitutional Declaration of Rights,' in ibid., 55–6.

22 In the 1960s, Quebec was Canada's only effectively bilingual province, obligated by the BNA Act to permit the use of both English and French in its courts and legislature, a status which was de facto extended to most other sectors of government activity.

23 RCBB, *Report,* vol. 1, *The Official Languages,* 147–8.

24 RCBB, *Report of the Royal Commission on Bilingualism and Biculturalism,* vol. 2, *Education* (Ottawa: Queen's Printer, 1968), 299–304.

25 Canada, *Constitutional Conference Proceedings, First Meeting, 5–7 Feb. 1968* (Ottawa: Queen's Printer, 1968), 53–69.

26 Ibid., 25.

27 Ibid., 105.

28 Ibid., 53–9.

29 Ibid., 161.

30 Ibid., 491.

31 Ibid., *Second Meeting,* 68, 79–80, 115–16.

32 David Bourgeois, *Canadian Bilingual Districts: From Cornerstone to Tombstone* (Montreal and Kingston: McGill-Queen's University Press, 2007), 62. *Jones v. Attorney General of New Brunswick* [1975], 2 R.C.S., 182, at 199.

33 Canada, *Constitutional Conference Proceedings, Second Meeting,* 28–30.

34 Provincial Archives of New Brunswick, RS 416 Louis Robichaud, 1969, file 131, 'Committee of Officials on the Constitution,' Letter from G. Pelletier to L. Robichaud, 17 Dec. 1969.

35 Canada, *Constitutional Conference Proceedings, Third Meeting, 8–10 Dec. 1969* (Ottawa: Queen's Printer, 1970), 243–4.

36 Archives of Ontario, RG 2-200, Council on French-Language Schools, Acc. 17121, box 2, file 'Fed/Prov –Bilinguisme 1972,' Secretary of State News Release, 'Federal-Provincial Program on Bilingualism in Education Agreement Reached with Provinces Concerning Financial Assistance,' 9 Sept. 1970. The program was unofficially known as the Bilingualism in Education Program, throughout the 1970s, before being renamed the Official Languages in Education Program.

37 Matthew Hayday, *Bilingual Today, United Tomorrow: Official Languages in Education and Canadian Federalism* (Montreal and Kingston: McGill-Queen's University Press, 2005), 57–9.

38 Canada, *Constitutional Conference Proceedings, Victoria, B.C., 14–16 June 1971* (Ottawa: Queen's Printer, 1971), 42.

13. The Sixties in Quebec

1 For a recent overview, see Yves Bélanger et al., *La Révolution tranquille 40 ans plus tard: Un bilan* (Montreal: VLB, 2000).
2 Gérard Dion and Louis O'Neill, *Deux prêtres dénoncent l'immoralité politique dans la province de Québec* (Montreal: Comité de moralité publique, 1956).
3 Biographical sketches of Quebec provincial politicians are available at http://www.assnat.qc.ca/fra/membres/notices/index-g.html.
4 Paul-André Linteau et al., *Quebec since 1930* (Toronto: Lorimer, 1991), 530. This work provides an exhaustive account of Quebec history from 1930 to 1980. Unless otherwise referenced, the factual information in this chapter is taken from this work.
5 'Élections 1960: Révolution tranquille,' *Les Archives de Radio-Canada,* at http://archives.radio-canada.ca/politique/elections/clips/14281/.
6 Gérard Dion and Louis O'Neill, *Le chrétien et les élections: Textes pontificaux et épiscopaux, documents historiques, textes divers sur la moralité politique* (Montreal: Éditions de l'Homme, 1960).
7 See Matthew Hayday, 'Reconciling the Two Solitudes?' in this volume.
8 Ricard, *The Lyric Generation: The Life and Times of the Baby Boomers* (Toronto: Stoddart, 1994), 91–6, 141, 82, 94, 115–16.
9 'Jean Lesage: Maîtres chez-nous,' at http://archives.radio-canada.ca/politique/partis_chefs_politiques/clips/14280/.
10 Guy Rocher, *Le 'laboratoire' des réformes dans la Révolution tranquille: Conférence Desjardins, prononcée dans le cadre du Programme d'études sur le Québec de l'Université McGill, le 6 novembre 2001* (Montreal: Programme d'études sur le Québec, McGill University, 2001).
11 Léon Dion, *La révolution déroutée: 1960–1976* (Montreal: Boréal, 1998), 232–52, offers a summary of the 'achievements' of the Quiet Revolution.
12 Jean-Paul Desbiens, *Les insolences du frère Untel* (Montreal: Éditions de l'Homme, 1960).
13 Carol Jobin, *Les enjeux économiques de la nationalisation de l'électricité (1962–1963)* (Montreal: Saint-Martin, 1978), 169–71.

14 Royal Commission on Bilingualism and Biculturalism, *Report of the Royal Commission on Bilingualism and Biculturalism* (Ottawa: Queen's Printer, 1969), vol. IIIa, Tables 3 and 5.

15 Jean-Jacques Simard, *La longue marche des technocrates* (Montreal: Editions Saint-Martin, 1979).

16 Rocher, *Le 'laboratoire,'* 15.

17 Jean-François Nadeau, *Bourgault* (Montreal: Lux, 2007), 93.

18 Marcel Chaput, *Why I Am a Separatist* (Toronto: Ryerson Press, 1962).

19 'Manifestation du RIN,' *Le Devoir,* 25 June 1964, 1.

20 Nadeau, *Bourgault,* 196–7.

21 '1964 Quebec Riots,' CBC Digital Archives, at http://archives.cbc.ca/ society/monarchy/clips/235/; 'La vieille capitale accueille la reine,' and Les Archives de Radio-Canada, at http://archives.radio-canada.ca/ societe/celebrations/clips/12629/.

22 'Le RIN, le rêve de l'indépendance,' at http://archives.radio-canada.ca/ politique/partis_chefs_politiques/clips/11909/, shows some of the RIN staging.

23 'Résistance passive à deux pas du monument des Patriotes,' *La Presse,* 25 May 1965, 7.

24 '24 mai: Bagarres et vandalisme; une explosion, 114 arrestations,' *La Presse,* 25 May 1965, 1. The editorial 'Le gouffre de l'hystérie,' *La Presse,* 25 May 1965, 4, condemned the violence.

25 '1 juillet 1966–Manifestation des Chevaliers de l'indépendance au parc Lafontaine,' *Bilan du siècle* at http://bilan.usherbrooke.ca/bilan/pages/ evenements/21018.html.

26 According to Bourgault's biographer, RIN was 'un parti très réformiste qui se donne des airs révolutionnaires.' Nadeau, *Bourgault,* 178.

27 'Les barbouilleurs sévissent,' at http://archives.radio-canada.ca/societe/ jeunesse/clips/13142/.

28 '24 mai: Bagarres et vandalisme.' 'L'explosion d'une bombe à Westmount et l'arrestation de quatre manifestants marquent la fête de la Confédération au Québec,' *Le Devoir,* 2 July 1965, 1.

29 Éric Bédard, 'The Intellectual Origins of the October Crisis,' in *Creating Postwar Canada: Community, Diversity and Dissent, 1945–75,* eds. Magda Fahrni and Robert Rutherdale (Vancouver: UBC Press, 2008), 45–60.

30 'L'entrée en scène de Pierre Elliott Trudeau,' at http://archives.radio-canada.ca/politique/national/clips/5724/. See also Hayday, 'Reconciling the Two Solitudes?'

31 Marc Laurendeau, *Les Québécois violents* (Montreal: Boréal, 1990), 213–20.

32 Jean-Guy Vaillancourt, Guy Lord, and Daniel Latouche, *Le processus électoral au Québec* (LaSalle: Hurtubise, 1976), 98.

33 See Dominique Clément, 'The October Crisis of 1970: Human Rights Abuses under the War Measures Act,' *Journal of Canadian Studies / Revue d'études canadiennes* 42/2 (2008), 160–86.

34 On the Common Front, see Magnus Isacsson, Marcel Simard, and Claude Cartier, *Le grand tumulte,* VHS (Montreal: National Film Board, 1996).

35 See Robert Major, *Parti pris: Idéologies et littérature* (LaSalle: Hurtubise, 1979).

36 Pierre Vallières, *White Niggers of America* (Toronto: McClelland and Stewart, 1971).

37 Sean Mills, *The Empire Within: Montreal, the Sixties, and the Forging of a Radical Imagination* (Montreal and Kingston: McGill-Queen's University Press, 2010).

38 'La plus ancienne émission de Point de mire,' at http://archives. radio-canada.ca/politique/partis_chefs_politiques/clips/12343/; 'La guerre d'Algérie,' at http://archives.radio-canada.ca/guerres_conflits/ desordres_civils/clips/13776/.

39 'Le Vietnam aux Vietnamiens,' at http://archives.radio-canada.ca/ guerres_conflits/guerre_vietnam/clips/1755/.

40 'Non à la guerre du Vietnam,' at http://archives.radio-canada.ca/ guerres_conflits/guerre_vietnam/clips/1748/.

41 'Martin Luther King assassiné: La fin d'un rêve,' at http://archives.radio-canada.ca/politique/droits_libertes/clips/11382/.

42 Dorothy Eber, *The Computer Centre Party* (Montreal: Tundra Books, 1969). See Marcel Martel, '"Riot" at Sir George Williams,' and James W. St G. Walker, 'Black Confrontation in Sixties Halifax,' in this volume.

43 José E. Igartua, *The Other Quiet Revolution: National Identities in English Canada, 1945–1971* (Vancouver: UBC Press, 2006).

44 'Une fédération pour les femmes du Québec,' at http://archives.radio-canada.ca/politique/droits_libertes/clips/7280/. For an introduction to Quebec women's movements in the 1960s, see Diane Lamoureux, *Entre le féminin et le féminisme* (Quebec: Université Laval, Laboratoire d'études politiques et administratives, 1991).

45 'Création de la Commission royale d'enquête,' at http://archives.radio-canada.ca/politique/droits_libertes/clips/91/.

46 'Statut de la femme: parole aux politiciens,' at http://archives.radio-canada.ca/politique/droits_libertes/clips/120/.

47 'Quel accueil au rapport Bird?' at http://archives.radio-canada.ca/politique/droits_libertes/clips/121/. Besides what the women panelists said, it is fascinating to observe their appearance and demeanour, which had the requisite Radio-Canada propriety.

48 Pierre Bélanger and Association nationale des étudiants et étudiantes du Québec, *Le mouvement étudiant québécois: Son passé, ses revendications et ses luttes (1960–1983)* (Montreal: Association nationale des étudiants et étudiantes du Québec, 1984), 5, 7.

49 See Roberta Lexier, 'To Struggle Together or Fracture Apart,' in this volume.

50 Jean-Philippe Warren, *Une douce anarchie:Les années 68 au Québec* (Montreal: Boréal, 2008).

51 See Martel, '"Riot" at Sir George Williams,' in this volume.

52 'McGill français!' at http://archives.radio-canada.ca/politique/langue_culture/clips/6929/.

53 Bédard, 'The Intellectual Origins of the October Crisis'; Yves Couture, *La terre promise: L'absolu politique dans le nationalisme québécois* (Montreal: Liber, 1994).

54 'Qui est ce leader du mouvement étudiant?' at http://archives.radio-canada.ca/politique/partis_chefs_politiques/clips/15255/.

55 Jean-Philippe Warren, *Ils voulaient changer le monde: Le militantisme marxiste-léniniste au Québec* (Montreal: VLB, 2007), 34.

56 'Cent millions de jeunes,' at http://archives.radio-canada.ca/emissions/1477-13144/.

57 See Peter S. McInnis, 'Hothead Troubles,' in this volume.

58 Jacques Rouillard, 'Le militantisme des travailleurs au Québec et en Ontario: Niveau de syndicalisation et mouvement de grèves (1900–1980),' *Revue d'histoire de l'Amérique française* 37/2 (1983), 208, 217, 220. See http://www.erudit.org/revue/haf/1983/v37/n2/304154ar.pdf.

59 Warren, *Ils voulaient changer le monde,* 62.

60 'L'anarchie frappe Montréal,' at http://archives.radio-canada.ca/societe/syndicalisme/clips/1800/.

61 Denise Boucher et al., *Pointe Saint-Charles: Un quartier, des femmes, une histoire communautaire* (Montreal: Éditions du remue-ménage, 2006). My thanks to Magda Fahrni for this reference.

62 Warren, *Ils voulaient changer le monde,* 40–57.

63 See his biographical notice on the Quebec National Assembly website.
64 See the following obituaries: Brian Myles, 'Pierre Vallières (1938–
    1998),' *Le Devoir,* 24 Dec. 1998, A6; Pierre Vennat, 'Malgré ses virages
    et ses contradictions, Pierre Vallières a toujours haï l'injustice,' *La
    Presse,* 24 Dec. 1998, A8.
65 Micheline Labelle, Ann-Marie Field, and Jean-Claude Icart, *Les dimen-
    sions d'intégration des immigrants, des minorités ethnoculturelles et des
    groupes racisés au Québec,* Report to the Commission de consultation
    sur les pratiques d'accommodement reliées aux différences culturelles
    (Montreal: Université du Québec à Montréal, 2007). See http://www.
    accommodements.qc.ca/documentation/rapports/rapport-9-labelle-
    micheline.pdf.
66 See Bryan D. Palmer, 'The Birth of Red Power,' in this volume.

Contributors

Stephen Azzi is an associate professor of political management in the Arthur Kroger College of Public Affairs, Carleton University. He is the author of *Walter Gordon and the Rise of Canadian Nationalism.*

Michael Boudreau is an associate professor in the Department of Criminology and Criminal Justice at St Thomas University, and a member of the editorial board of the *Journal of New Brunswick Studies.* He is currently researching the history of capital punishment in the Maritimes.

Lara Campbell is an associate professor in the Department of Gender, Sexuality, and Women's Studies at Simon Fraser University. She is the author of *Respectable Citizens: Women, Gender, and the Family in Ontario's Great Depression.*

Catherine Carstairs is an associate professor at the University of Guelph. Her work focuses on the social and cultural history of health and the body. She is the author of *Jailed for Possession: Illegal Drug Use, Regulation and Power, 1920–1961,* which examines the impact of harsh drug laws on the lives of drug users.

Dominique Clément is an assistant professor in the Department of Sociology at the University of Alberta. He specializes in the study of social movements and human rights, and is the author of *Canada's Rights Revolution: Social Movements and Social Change, 1937–82.*

Erika Dyck is an associate professor and Canada Research Chair in the History of Medicine in the Department of History at the University of Saskatchewan. She is the author of *Psychedelic Psychiatry: LSD from Clinic to Campus.*

Catherine Gidney is the author of *A Long Eclipse: The Liberal Protestant Establishment and the Canadian University, 1920–70* (winner of the Founders' Prize for best book in the history of education in Canada, 2004–06). She has published articles on the social history of youth and education which have appeared in the *Canadian Historical Review,* the *Journal of the Canadian Historical Association,* and the *Journal of Canadian Studies.*

Matthew Hayday is an associate professor of Canadian history at the University of Guelph. He is the author of *Bilingual Today, United Tomorrow: Official Languages in Education and Canadian Federalism,* as well as of articles dealing with issues of cultural and language policy in Canada.

Steve Hewitt is a senior lecturer in the Department of American and Canadian Studies at the University of Birmingham in the United Kingdom. He is the author of *Spying 101: The RCMP's Secret Activities at Canadian Universities, 1917–1997* and *Riding to the Rescue: The Transformation of the Mounted Police in Alberta and Saskatchewan, 1914–1939.*

José E. Igartua is professor emeritus at l'Université du Québec à Montréal. He is the author of numerous articles as well as monographs on the history of French and English Canada, including a recent book titled *The Other Quiet Revolution: National Identities in English Canada, 1945–1971.*

Gregory S. Kealey is the vice-president (research) and provost of the University of New Brunswick and a professor in the Department of History. He is the former editor of *Labour/Le Travail* and the author of numerous works on working-class history, including *Toronto Workers Respond to Industrial Capitalism, 1867–1892, Workers and Canadian History, Dreaming of What Might Be: The Knights of*

Labour in Ontario, 1880–1900, and *Secret Service: Political Policing in Canada from the Fenians to Fortress America.*

Roberta Lexier is a post-doctoral fellow in the Centre for Canadian Studies at Mount Allison University. Her work focuses primarily on Canadian social movements, and she has published extensively on the student movement and the women's liberation movement. Her current research examines the history of the Waffle movement and explores the interactions between formal political structures and institutions and social movements.

Marcel Martel is an associate professor in the Department of History at York University, where he holds the Avie Bennett Historica Chair in Canadian History. He is the author of *Not This Time: Canadians, Public Policy, and the Marijuana Question, 1961–1975.*

Peter S. McInnis teaches in the Department of History at St Francis Xavier University. He is the author of *Harnessing Labour Confrontation: Shaping the Postwar Confrontation in Canada, 1943–1950.*

Bryan D. Palmer is the Canada Research Chair in Canadian Studies at Trent University and editor of the journal *Labour/Le Travail.* He is the author of numerous books, including a recent monograph titled *Canada's 1960s? The Ironies of Identity in a Rebellious Era.*

Christabelle Sethna is an associate professor in the Institute of Women's Studies and in the Faculty of Health Sciences at the University of Ottawa. She has published on sex education, contraception, and abortion. Her three major projects include a study on the impact of the birth control pill on single, Canadian, university-aged women between 1960 and 1980; research on the travel Canadian women undertake to access abortion services; and an investigation of RCMP surveillance of women's liberation groups during the 1960s and 1970s.

James St G. Walker is a professor in the Department of History at the University of Waterloo. He is the author of *The Blacks in Canada* and *'Race,' Rights and the Law in the Supreme Court of Canada.*

Index

THE CANADIAN SOCIAL HISTORY SERIES

Mariana Valverde,
'The Age of Light, Soap and Water':
Moral Reform in English Canada,
1885–1925, 1991.
ISBN 978-0-8020-9595-4

Bettina Bradbury,
Working Families: Age, Gender, and
Daily Survival in Industrializing
Montreal, 1993.
ISBN 978-0-8020-8689-1

Andrée Lévesque,
Making and Breaking the Rules:
Women in Quebec, 1919–1939, 1994.
ISBN 0-7710-5283-9

Cecilia Danysk,
Hired Hands: Labour and
the Development of Prairie
Agriculture, 1880–
1930, 1995.
ISBN 0-7710-2552-1

Kathryn McPherson,
Bedside Matters: The Transformation
of Canadian Nursing, 1900–1990,
1996.
ISBN 978-0-8020-8679-2

Edith Burley,
Servants of the Honourable Company:
Work, Discipline, and Conflict in the
Hudson's Bay Company, 1770–1870,
1997.
ISBN 0-19-541296-6

Mercedes Steedman,
Angels of the Workplace: Women and
the Construction of Gender Relations
in the Canadian Clothing Industry,
1890–1940, 1997.
ISBN 0-19-54308-3

**Angus McLaren and Arlene Tigar
McLaren,** The Bedroom and the State:
The Changing Practices and Politics
of Contraception and Abortion in
Canada, 1880–1997, 1997.
ISBN 0-19-541318-0

**Kathryn McPherson, Cecilia
Morgan, and Nancy M. Forestell,
Editors,** Gendered Pasts: Historical
Essays in Feminity and Masculinity in
Canada, 1999.
ISBN 978-0-8020-8690-7

Gillian Creese,
Contracting Masculinity: Gender,
Class, and Race in a White-Collar
Union, 1944–1994, 1999.
ISBN 0-19-541454-3

Geoffrey Reaume,
Remembrance of Patients Past: Patient
Life at the Toronto Hospital for the
Insane, 1870–1940, 2000.
ISBN 0-19-541538-8

Miriam Wright,
A Fishery for Modern Times: The State
and the Industrialization of
the Newfoundland Fishery,
1934–1968, 2001.
ISBN 0-19-541620-1

Judy Fudge and Eric Tucker, Labour
before the Law: The Regulation of
Workers' Collective Action in Canada,
1900–1948, 2001.
ISBN 978-0-8020-3793-0

Mark Moss,
Manliness and Militarism: Educating
Young Boys in Ontario for War, 2001.
ISBN 0-19-541594-9

Joan Sangster,
Regulating Girls and Women:
Sexuality, Family, and the Law in
Ontario, 1920–1960, 2001.
ISBN 0-19-541663-5

Reinhold Kramer
and Tom Mitchell,
Walk Towards the Gallows: The
Tragedy of Hilda Blake, Hanged 1899,
2002.
ISBN 978-0-8020-9542-8

Mark Kristmanson,
Plateaus of Freedom: Nationality,
Culture, and State Security in Canada,
1940–1960, 2002.
ISBN 0-19-541866-2

Robin Jarvis Brownlie
A Fatherly Eye: Indian Agents,
Government Power, and Aboriginal
Resistance in Ontario, 1918–1939,
2003
ISBN 0-19-541891-3 (cloth)
ISBN 0-19-541784-4 (paper)

Steve Hewitt,
Riding to the Rescue: The
Transformation of the RCMP
in Alberta and Saskatchewan,
1914–1939, 2006.
ISBN 978-0-8020-9021-8 (cloth)
ISBN 978-0-8020-4895-0 (paper)

Robert K. Kristofferson,
Craft Capitalism: Craftsworkers and
Early Industrialization in Hamilton,

Ontario, 1840–1872, 2007.
ISBN 978-0-8020-9127-7 (cloth)
ISBN 978-0-8020-9408-7 (paper)

Andrew Parnaby,
Citizen Docker: Making a New Deal
on the Vancouver Waterfront, 1919–
1939, 2007
ISBN 978-0-8020-9056-0 (cloth)
ISBN 978-0-8020-9384-4 (paper)

J.I. Little
Loyalties in Conflict: A Canadian
Borderland in War and Rebellion,
1812–1840, 2008
ISBN 978-0-8020-9773-6 (cloth)
ISBN 978-0-8020-9825-1 (paper)

Pauline Greenhill
Make the Night Hideous:
Four English Canadian Charivaris,
1881–1940, 2010
ISBN 978-1-4426-4077-1 (cloth)
ISBN 978-1-4426-1015-6 (paper)

Rhonda L. Hinther and
Jim Mochoruk
Re-imagining Ukrainian Canadians:
History, Politics, and Identity, 2010
ISBN 978-1-4426-4134-1 (cloth)
ISBN 978-1-4426-1062-0 (paper)

Lara Campbell, Dominique Clément,
and Gregory S. Kealey
Debating Dissent: Canada and the
Sixties
ISBN 978-1-4426-4164-8 (cloth)
ISBN 978-1-4426-1078-1 (paper)

STEELMAN LIBRARY

3 9844 00158 8488